Maria Ward

Female Life Among the Mormons

A narrative of many years' personal experience by the wife of a Mormon elder,

recently from Utah

Maria Ward

Female Life Among the Mormons
A narrative of many years' personal experience by the wife of a Mormon elder, recently from Utah

ISBN/EAN: 9783337295677

Printed in Europe, USA, Canada, Australia, Japan

Cover: Foto ©ninafisch / pixelio.de

More available books at **www.hansebooks.com**

FEMALE LIFE

AMONG THE MORMONS;

A NARRATIVE

OF MANY YEARS' PERSONAL EXPERIENCE.

BY THE WIFE OF A MORMON ELDER,

RECENTLY FROM UTAH.

NEW YORK:
J. C. DERBY, 119 NASSAU STREET.
CINCINNATI: H. W. DERBY. BUFFALO: WANZER, M^cKIM & CO.
CHICAGO: D. B. COOKE & CO. DETROIT: KERR, MORLEY & CO.
ST. LOUIS: EDWARDS & BUSHNELL.

1855.

ENTERED according to Act of Congress, in the year 1855, by
J. C. DERBY,
In the Clerk's Office of the District Court for the Southern District of New York.

W. H. TINSON, STEREOTYPER.
PUDNEY & RUSSELL, PRINTERS.

INTRODUCTORY.

That "one half of the world cannot imagine how the other half live," is no less true than trite; and the lesson the adage affords, our experience and observation daily tend to verify. Then, too, when we consider the ever-varying phases of human passion, and the discordant elements from which all novel and fanatical sects are moulded, it can scarcely seem surprising that a faithful record of actual events should exceed in singularity the wildest dream of romance; or that crimes, both strange and unnatural, should be perpetrated in a far-off country, on the outskirts of civilization, which people in another state of society would never imagine possible. Knowing, as I do know, the evils and horrors and abominations of the Mormon system, the degradation it imposes on females, and the consequent vices which extend through all the ramifications of the society, a sense of duty to the world has induced me to prepare the following narrative, for the public eye. The romantic incidents connected with my experience, many may think bordering on the marvellous. To them I would say, that this narrative of my life only proves, what has so often been proved before, that "TRUTH IS STRANGER THAN FICTION."

THE AUTHOR.

CONTENTS.

CHAPTER I.
INTRODUCTORY.

A False Angel—Magnetic Influence—Curiosity Awakened 9

CHAPTER II.
THE MORMON MEETING.

The Midnight Assemblage—Arrival of Joe Smith—The Frantic Mother—The Dead Quickened—Interruption of the Meeting—The Mob and is Victim—Female Heroism 15

CHAPTER III.
MORMON VEXATIONS.

Grievous Annoyances—Ridiculous Catastrophe—Preparation to move West—A Startling Proposition 30

CHAPTER IV.
SUNDRY MORMON MATTERS.

Mr. Ward offers his Hand and Heart—The Young Wife has Strange Fears—Domestic Happiness Destroyed—A Wife's Duties Defined—Deplorable Results—The Doctrine of Spiritual Wives 38

CHAPTER V.
MORMON REMOVALS.

A Mormon Heroine—Difficulties Encountered—A Mormon Ruse—The Stratagem Successful—The First Halt—The Abduction of Hannah—Ellen's Narrative—A Mother's Instinct—The Pursuit—Discomfiture of Mrs. Bradish . . . 50

CHAPTER VI.
THE RECAPTURE.
Death of Bounding Bet—Speculations concerning the Prophet—Alarming Intelligence—Hapless Fate of Poor Ellen—Arrival at the Promised Land . . 71

CHAPTER VII.
THE MORMON SETTLEMENT.
Mormon Merchandise—The Ambitious Mormon—Startling Revelations—Mrs. Murray discloses Secrets 81

CHAPTER VIII.
MORMON FAITH AND WORSHIP.
The Mormon Millenium—Interior Economy of Heaven 91

CHAPTER IX.
MORMON PROPHETS AND ELDERS.
Quaint Portraits of Mormon Elders—A Missionary's Experience—Absurd Visions and Sore Temptations 95

CHAPTER X.
MORMON CHURCH GOVERNMENT.
Fools and Knaves—Mormon Tools—Mormon Estimate of Women—Sufferings of a Spiritual Wife—The Marriage Contract Annulled 99

CHAPTER XI.
MORMON OUTRAGES.
Systematic Robberies—The "Regulators"—Tidings of Mrs. Clark . . . 108

CHAPTER XII.
REGULATORS.
Unwelcome Visitors—Midnight Murder—Escape of Mr. Ward 114

CHAPTER XIII.
THE FOREST.
Mr. Ward's Account of his Escape—The Regulators take Vengeance—The Dilemma—Agonizing Suspense—Character of Mrs. Bradish 120

CHAPTER XIV.
RETURN OF THE MESSENGER.
Mrs. Bradish in a Dungeon—An Attack Contemplated . . . 130

CONTENTS.

CHAPTER XV.
THE LIBERATION, AND SOMETHING ELSE.

Death of the Prophet—The Oath and Its Penalty 135

CHAPTER XVI.
THE NEW LEADER.

Description of the New Leader—Heartless Conduct of the Prophet . . . 140

CHAPTER XVII.
GOING OFF.

Preparations for Departing—Return of Mrs. Bradish—Mrs. Bradish relates her Adventures—Mode of making New Converts—Family Jars 144

CHAPTER XVIII.
EMILY'S NARRATIVE.

The Prophet's Favorite—Incipient Vanity—Scenes in a Poor-House—The Poor-House in an Uproar 157

CHAPTER XIX.
SUNDRY MATTERS.

Polygamy encouraged by the Prophet—A Stampede—A Rain-storm in the Prairies—A Solemn Sight—The Closing Scene 166

CHAPTER XX.
FORDING A RIVER AND ITS CONSEQUENCES.

The First Great Difficulty—Perilous Passage—The Catastrophe—Alarmed by Indians 174

CHAPTER XXI.
WOMEN LOST OR CAPTURED.

Foolhardiness of Mrs. Bradish—Fears for the Missing Women—The Fearless Scout—The Re-Capture 182

CHAPTER XXII.
EMILY'S NARRATIVE CONTINUED.

The Buffaloes—The Bitter Taunt—Emily learns who She is—The Lost Will . . 191

CHAPTER XXIII.
FURTHER DEVELOPMENTS.

Strange Advice for a Woman to give—Trouble in Store for Louisa—The Painful Discovery—The Mischief Maker—Two of a Trade can't agree—The Listeners—The Voice of Nature will be heard—Fond Hearts re-united—The Disappointed Match-Maker 198

CHAPTER XXIV.

LOVE IN THE WILDERNESS.

Courting by the Camp-Fire—A True Woman—She Would and She Wouldn't . 215

CHAPTER XXV.

A WIFE'S TROUBLE.

The Power of the Will—Blissful Ignorance—Snake Indians and their Captive—Attempts at Ransom 223

CHAPTER XXVI.

AN UNEXPECTED ENCOUNTER.

The Intercepted Letter—Fan Catches a Tartar 230

CHAPTER XXVII.

A NEW CHARACTER.

The Beau Ideal—Fraternal Love—A Childish Vision—Santa Fé Traders . . 235

CHAPTER XXVIII.

THE FUGITIVES.

Anxiety for the Absent—A New Flora's Interpreter—Young Blood *vs.* An Old Head—The Sacrificial Dance—Hide and Seek 243

CHAPTER XXIX.

WATER! WATER! WATER!

Murmurings in the Camp—Horrible Sufferings—More of Fan's Coquetries—Hostile Indians 252

CHAPTER XXX.

OTHER DIFFICULTIES.

A New Difficulty—Ethleen the Indian Girl—Picturesque Scenery—An Indian Altar The Last Trial 261

CHAPTER XXXI.

BEAR RIVER VALLEY.

The Secret Enemy—Dissatisfaction Broods in Secret—The Sacred Garments—Mrs. Bradish Declines the Honor—The Promised Land—The Startling Missive . . 270

CHAPTER XXXII.

OTHER EMIGRANTS.

Discourses on Polygamy—A Scene at " Meal-Time "—Sport and Scandal—The Rejected Lover—The Prophet Braved by a Woman—Destiny will Decide . . 281

CHAPTER XXXIII.
A HOME IN THE DESERT.

The Source of Mormon Stability—The New City—An Old Fool and a Young Flirt—Evil Results of Polygamy—Mrs. Haley in Trouble—The Bitter Sorrow—Ancient Practices Revived 294

CHAPTER XXXIV.
EMILY'S NARRATIVE CONTINUED.

The Prophet and his Victim—The Bravado—Family Secrets—The Conspirators . 309

CHAPTER XXXV.
CHURCH AND STATE.

Primitive way of Choosing Preachers—Little Spirits in want of Bodies—Debasing tendency of Polygamy—A Father sells his Daughters—Brother Weldy's Chief Blessing—The Sale Consummated 315

CHAPTER XXXVI.
THE SELF-ACCUSER AND THE DYING HUSBAND.

The Forsaken Wife—The Perfection of Meekness—Bitter Reflections—Mother and Daughter—The Poison Root 323

CHAPTER XXXVII.
A SCENE.

The Ill-boding Wife—Meeting Troubles half way—She put it in his Head—A Domestic Scene—Difficulties Thicken—Mutual Recriminations 339

CHAPTER XXXVIII.
EMILY AGAIN.

The Missing Maiden—The Alarm Increases—An Expedition starts in Search of Emily 350

CHAPTER XXXIX.
MARRIAGES.

She Mourns as for the Dead—A Hard-hearted Old Man—The Hoary Lover and Youthful Victims—A Model Father—Matrimonial Speculations . . . 356

CHAPTER XL.
A CONSULTATION.

The Unsuccessful Search—The Prophet's Mandate—The Prophet Suspected—Mrs. Bradish Utters Treason—Ambition Thwarted 366

CHAPTER XLI.

DIFFERENCES.

A Gigantic Scheme—Mormonism Antagonistic to Republicanism—Mormon Hunters kill Strange Game—Peculiarities of Utah Indians 376

CHAPTER XLII.

THE NEW WIFE.

A Discontented Mind—A Mormon Dinner-table—The Solution of the Riddle—A House divided again Itself—The Non-Intercourse System—The Tables Turned—The Quarrel . . . , ... 384

CHAPTER XLIII.

ETHLEEN'S ADVENTURE.

Grief of the Indian Wife—Harmer relates his Adventures—Sagacity of Ethleen . 399

CHAPTER XLIV.

THE GOLD FEVER AND ITS EFFECTS.

The Gold Fever—Portrait of a Mormon Lady—Indian Vengeance—Awful Effects of the Poison—Return of the Gold Hunter 407

CHAPTER XLV.

REVELATIONS.

Mesmerism in aid to Mormonism—Mrs. Bradish Reveals Secrets—Re-appearance of Emily—Harmer finds his Betrothed 416

CHAPTER XLVI.

MYSTERIES.

Mysterious Disappearances—Gross Deception—Mormon Barbarities—Having Eyes they See Not—Interesting Dialogue 424

CHAPTER XLVII.

LIGHT.

Important Discovery—Murder of Gunison's Party—Dangerous Knowledge—Horrid Treachery—She is Doomed 435

CHAPTER XLVIII.

UNCERTAINTY—CONCLUSION.

Doubts and Fears—Escape of the Author—The Warning—Conclusion . . 445

FEMALE LIFE AMONG THE MORMONS.

CHAPTER I.

INTRODUCTORY.

MY early life was passed in that beautiful and picturesque region, which borders the Skaneateles Lake, in the State of New York. The season of my childhood passed in comparative peace and happiness, but circumstances, over which I had no control, brought me into contact with enemies, who sought, by the most malicious and slanderous reports, to injure my reputation—in which they succeeded; and smarting under the neglect of former friends, I determined to abandon my home, and privately visit some relatives of my mother, who were living near Albany. For this purpose I left the house of A—— J——, in Spafford, Ouondaga County, New York, and took the stage for Utica in the same State. I had not previously apprised my friends of this intended visit, because I feared that my enemies might thus be informed of my destination, and I could not feel safe from their malice, however great the distance, if they knew where I was.

The only passenger in the stage except myself, was a gentleman, apparently middle-aged, of rather handsome features and prepossessing appearance. The Mormon Bible and opinions were at that time the general topic of discussion, in all society through this vicinity, and after a few general remarks on the state of the roads, weather, and kindred subjects, he inquired with a piercing look, what I thought of the Mormons.

"I think it is all delusion," I replied.

"And why do you think so?" he inquired.

"Many reasons conspire to strengthen this opinion," I answered.

"Please state them."

"In the first place, then, I have seen this Joseph Smith, the author of the Mormon Bible, and I could discover nothing in his appearance at all corresponding with a divine character."

"Yet, if I have been rightly informed, many persons in your part of the country think otherwise."

"It is true," I answered, "that many people of my acquaintance, in Scott and Spafford, have embraced Mormonism, but every delusion, however absurd, will have its believers."

"There was a family in Coldbrook by the name of Cheeny, I think," suggested the man.

"Yes," I answered, "Mr. Cheeny's family were considered very fine people, were members of the Free-will Baptist Church, and the Pulsifers too; Pulsifer, the Swamp Angel," and I burst into a laugh.

"The Swamp Angel?" said my fellow traveller, inquiringly, "who was that?"

"There were two families by the name of Pulsifer, both believers in Mormon," I answered. "A child died in one of these families, and the Mormons gave out that, on a certain night, an angel would come and carry the body to heaven. The time appointed arrived, the relatives of the dead were assembled, when a figure in white, and with small bells attached to its garments, appeared. A party of the unbelievers, lying in ambush, immediately gave chase. The figure ran for a neighboring swamp, but was pursued, taken, stripped of its angel robes, and proved to be Pulsifer, the uncle of the deceased."

"False," said my companion.

"I assure you it was the truth," I continued ; "and poor old Mr. Humphrey was deceived by them, too. The old man was determined to be right, if possible. He was first a member of the Free-will Baptists ; then he joined the Seventh-day Baptists —left them, and was baptized to the faith and order of Mormon ; subsequently deserted the Mormons, and united with the Baptists again, and then finally returned to the Mormons, by whom he was dipped seven times in succession, on account of his apostasy. He remained faithful to them after that, but always observed the seventh day."

"Well," observed the gentleman, "the Mormons were not chargeable with the absurdities of their devotee."

"Oh, no !" I answered, "but they have enough of their own."

"Were you ever acquainted with Elder Gould ?" he inquired.

"I have seen him ; he used to preach in Spafford."

"He did, and with great acceptability, yet he joined the Mormons."

"And poor Mrs. Maxson was induced to leave her husband and children and go with them ; and Maria Ripley, a young woman, left her aged and infirm parent, and went off, too."

"For which they were wholly justifiable," said the man. "For he that loveth father, or mother, or husband, or wife, more than me, is not worthy of me."

"Are you then a believer in Mormon ?" I inquired.

"I am, or I am not," he answered.

"Hardly a fair way of answering a question," I said ; and the conversation came to a pause.

At this time I was wholly unacquainted with the doctrine of magnetic influence; but I soon became aware of some unaccountable power exercised over me by my fellow traveller. His presence seemed an irresistible fascination. His glittering eyes were fixed on mine; his breath fanned my cheek; I felt bewildered and intoxicated, and partially at least lost the sense of consciousness, and the power of motion.

The stage stopped to change horses. The weather was excessively cold, and my companion proposed that we should go into the inn to warm. I made no objection; indeed, I felt incapable of resistance to his wishes. We were ushered into a warm and comfortable parlor, the floor of which was covered by a cheap carpet, yet looking very neat and tidy; and the papered walls, hung with several pictures, in oaken frames. My companion requested me to be seated, and called for refreshments. I obeyed mechanically, and when the wine and cakes were furnished partook sparingly. My companion became communicative; informed me that his name was Ward, that he was a man of property, and a widower, with two children, that he was well acquainted with many people in Scott, my native place, and had frequently heard the name of my father mentioned as a citizen of exalted reputation.

Here I made some allusion to the length of time which the stage seemed stopping. He said it was nothing unusual in cold weather, and that, for his own part, he would prefer not to go farther that day. "I suppose, that you can stay if you wish," I said. "Not without you," he answered, and again fixing on my face one of his piercing looks. I became immediately sensible of some unaccountable influence drawing my sympathies towards him. In vain I struggled to break the spell. I was like a fluttering bird before the gaze of the serpent-charmer.

At length, by a powerful effort of will, I succeeded in releasing myself from the captivation, and, rising, went towards the door, to ascertain when the stage would be ready. There I met a boy, and inquired of him :

"Laws, ma'am, the stage has been gone this hour," he said, wonderingly. "'T won't be back neither 'fore day after next," he continued.

Mr. Ward was just behind me.

"'Tis strange," he said. "I wonder what the rascal of a driver was thinking of to leave us in this manner." I recollect at the moment that a faint perception that Ward was at the bottom of the matter, crossed my mind. I turned to accuse him of it, but the landlady just then came into the room, to inquire of what I stood in need.

"The stage has left us," said Ward, "but I consider it fortunate rather than otherwise. The weather is too cold to travel."

"The weather is certainly cold," said the landlady, "and we shall be happy to entertain you both till the stage comes round again. Shall I have a fire made for Madam in a separate apartment?"

"Certainly," I said, and the landlady departed.

"On more accounts than one," resumed Ward, "I regard this circumstance as fortunate. The Mormons are to have a great meeting here this very evening."

"And what is that to me?" I said, interrupting him.

"It may, it must be something to you," he answered; "I desire you to go and see, and hear for yourself."

"Go," I answered, astonished at the audacity of the proposal; "go into such a company of entire strangers?"

"And what if they be strangers; you have seen too much of the world, I imagine, to be afraid of strangers."

"I am not afraid of strangers," I began.

"Then what is there to hinder your going?" he interrupted. "It will be much more interesting than staying in this stupid place."

"Very likely."

"To be sure it will; you can go with me."

Here Mr. Ward left the room for a short time, and I began to examine the books which lay on the table. The first one I took up was the Book of Mormon, and during my examination of it Mr. Ward returned. He commended my employment, and said that my room would soon be ready, which was a great mistake, as I heard no further mention of it. I have since had reason to believe that he countermanded my orders, through fear of losing his influence over me. Be that as it may, the hours passed on, and the night came, while I yet remained the occupant of the parlor. Mr. Ward, in the meantime, had spared no pains to win my confidence, and ingratiate himself in my esteem. He bore letters of recommendation and introduction to some of the first men in the country. These, I have since learned, were forgeries from beginning to end, being a species of Mormon imposture.

"The landlady seems very dilatory in getting your room ready," he said, at length. "She certainly cannot expect that you are going to stay all night in the parlor."

"I will go and inquire."

"It is unnecessary, I will inquire for you."

Before I could reply, he disappeared, but soon returned with the disagreeable information that the rooms were already occupied, and that it would be impossible for them to entertain me. This was in direct contradiction to what I had previously heard, and my astonishment was depicted on my countenance, when Mr. Ward, to reconcile the discrepancy, told me that a large wedding party, relatives of the landlord, had just arrived, and that the apartment designed for me, had been appropriated to the bride. "But," he continued, "it will be some consolation for you to know, that I discovered the trunk containing your wardrobe standing in the hall. The rascally stage-driver must have misunderstood your orders, and thought that you were at the end of your journey."

"But the fare?" I suggested.

"If he has gone off without his pay, it will injure no one but himself. He was half-drunk, I suppose."

"Is there no other inn in the village?" I inquired.

"None that I know of; however, if you will go with me I can introduce you to a worthy lady of my acquaintance, who will be happy to receive you."

And I went with him; what else could I do?

CHAPTER II.

THE MORMON MEETING.

"THE lady to whom I am about to introduce you," said Mr. Ward, as we walked, in the pale, misty moonlight, along the slippery streets, "is a Mormon; and the meeting to-night is to be held at her house."

"Why did you not tell me of this before?" I inquired.

"What difference would that have made?" he answered. you are constrained to depart from the inn; you have no acquaintance here; I could not introduce you to a more hospitable person; and you must excuse me, but I considered it a fine opportunity to make you acquainted with some of our leading tenets."

That word "*our!*" he was, then, a Mormon, and I was morally in the power of that fanatical sect. Yet it was too late to retreat: my sympathies were with Mr. Ward; and then a strange and unaccountable feeling of curiosity took possession of my mind. I had heard much said about Mormon Meetings—the miracles and supernatural appearances said to attend them—and now was to have the chance of judging for myself. I felt half-pleased with the idea, but hesitated about telling my companion so. As we passed along, two or three persons came up to Mr. Ward, at different times, and exchanged with him rapid signs, and some inarticulate words, of which I could only distinguish "ready," on one side, and "soon" on the other.

The house of Mrs. Bradish stood at some distance from the main road, in the midst of a large yard that was bounded on the north by a deep, dense wood. The building itself was a very large antique structure, built long before the Revolution, and serving, under the seigniorial tenures then in vogue, as the mansion-house of the hereditary lords of the soil. Some parts of it had fallen into decay, but enough remained in a good state of preservation to furnish a very handsome residence to a wealthy family.

Mrs. Bradish received us with a stately and dignified hospitality, yet with such a conciliating manner as made me feel myself welcome, although she did not say so. She was a fine-looking woman, with a head and face decidedly intellectual. She conducted me to an elegant, yet old-fashioned, apartment in the eastern wing of the building, where a substantial supper was spread by one of the domestics; her family having already partook of the evening meal. She sat, however, and served at the table. Her conversation was deeply interesting, and contained a long and full description of Mormon tenets.

"And you will meet with us to-night, Miss B——, will you not?" she said, in conclusion.

"I hardly know, Mrs. Bradish," I answered; "something tells me that I had better not."

"It is the evil spirit, my child," she answered, fervently; "depend upon it, the tempter seeks your destruction."

I could scarcely forbear a smile.

"Do not smile," she said, solemnly; "do not tamper with your eternal interests. And then we are to have a miracle to-night."

"A miracle?"

"Yes: the dead restored to life."

"Impossible! Mrs. Bradish, you jest."

"I do not," she answered, solemnly. "Was not Lazarus raised from the dead, and the son of the widow of Nain. Do you think that the arm of the Lord is shortened, that he cannot save, or that the miracles which attended his first revelation would be withheld from the second? We are in expectation of even greater things than these."

"What could be greater?" I inquired.

"The resurrection of the living."

"Explain yourself."

"By the resurrection of the living, I mean the adoption of the faith of Mormon. You understand me?"

I could not say that I did; but when she again invited me to be present at the meeting, I signified my assent. She then retired to make preparations, informing me that, when the assembling-hour, which was that of midnight, arrived, she would call for me.

Left alone with my thoughts, I was forcibly impressed with the singularity, not to say danger, of my situation, and more than once regretted my precipitate abandonment of home. But it never was my habit to indulge in unpleasant reflections; so I looked around for some book of amusement. A volume of Swedenborg was all that the room contained in the shape of literature. The subject of this was new, and consequently interesting. Buried in the dreams and reveries it rehearsed, I took no note of the flight of time, until the clock chimed eleven. It yet wanted one hour of the time appointed for the meeting.

I felt somewhat drowsy, and rose to examine my room. It contained a bed, with snow-white counterpane and curtains; a large massive table, in antique style, with feet and legs carved to resemble the corresponding limbs of a bear or some other uncouth animal; washstand of the same pattern, with furniture of more modern appearance; two or three chairs, carved and stuffed; a case of drawers, and a small mirror. There was also a wide, old-fashioned open fireplace, in which a roaring fire was blazing and crackling. Near the fireplace was a window hung with thick, heavy curtains; at the further end of the apartment, and directly opposite the window, was a door. It was locked; but immediately over it hung the key. Perhaps it was a breach of hospitality, but my curiosity overcame my discretion. I applied the key: the bolt flew back, and the door swung open I now perceived that this was the entrance to a long hall or passage, with doors on either side, communicating with other rooms. I advanced to one of them, and plainly perceived the glimmering of light through the crevices, and heard the indistinct murmur of voices. At length, one louder than the others, in which I instantly recognized that of Mr. Ward, exclaimed: "How wonderful!" "'Tis more than wonderful," said another; "'tis miraculous. Praise the Lord!"

The clock struck twelve, there was a movement as of rising in the room, and I retreated to my apartment, locking the door to prevent intrusion.

Fifteen minutes elapsed before Mrs. Bradish arrived; her countenance wore an expression of unusual solemnity, and taking me by the hand, she said in a low voice, that slightly trembled.

"The power of the Most High God will be exhibited to-night, but do not be alarmed; indeed, there is no cause for fear."

"I am not afraid," I answered; neither was I so far as personal violence was concerned, though the remarkable character of what I had heard, had certainly affected my nerves with a slight tremor. Having sufficiently adjusted my hair and apparel, we descended together. The room in which the Mormons were assembled, was a large oblong hall, with curtained windows. The furniture consisted of a few rude benches, and a table resembling a huge desk, stood at the upper end, on which a small candle was feebly burning. It was impossible to form anything like a correct calculation of the numbers assembled, on account of the obscurity. I could only perceive an indiscriminate mixture of men and women, many of whom were fantastically disguised. Some were seated, others standing; but the High Priest of the ceremonies had not yet arrived.

"And who," said I to Mrs. Bradish, "conducts the meeting to-night?"

"Brother Smith," she answered.

"What; Joe Smith!"

"Brother Joseph Smith, and since the advent of Jesus Christ, the world has never seen a greater. I am ready to exclaim with Simeon of old 'Now, Lord, lettest thou thy servant depart in peace, for mine eyes have seen thy salvation.'"

"Was it possible," thought I, "that a woman of such a dignified and intellectual countenance could be the dupe of a vile man. I remembered Joe Smith, as an ignorant, stupid dolt of a fellow, who presence was never tolerated in good society. Mrs. Bradish disturbed my revery by whispering that Brother Smith had arrived. There was a slight stir, a murmur of applause in the apartment; I raised my eyes; side by side with Mr. Ward, at the further end of the room, stood a tall, elegant-looking man, with dark piercing eyes, and features, which if not handsome, were imposing. His manners, too, were wonderfully improved. The centre of all eyes, he seemed neither shy, embarrassed, nor reserved, neither was there anything bold or forward in his appearance. How unlike the lazy, impudent Joe Smith, of my memory. I whispered to Mrs. Bradish, "whence came this Mr. Smith ?"

"He has been out West," she answered, "in company with a party of the saints, who have settled in the Promised Land, the Canaan, on the other side of Jordan."

This struck me as exceedingly laughable and ludicrous.

Smith now commenced speaking, and the utmost silence prevailed. His discourse was on the nature of miracles, and the promise of Christ to his followers, that miraculous powers should attend them, even to the end of the world. I observed that he quoted much more from the Hebrew Scriptures, than the Book of Mormon, and remarked the same to Mrs. Bradish.

"That is perfectly consistent," she answered, "since much that is contained in one Bible, is to be found in the other. They harmonize perfectly; that is, we make them."

The sermon was very short, in order that more time might be employed in the performance of miracles. At its close the light was removed from the desk, and placed in a socket directly over it. Smith then knelt, the others followed his example, and the whole company remained some time in silent prayer. At length he rose, the others still knelt. After a moment's silence he uttered the solemn and impressive words :

"It is my word, saith the Lord, ye shall be delivered from death, which is the power of the devil, from sorrow and sighing. Therefore, in the might of the Spirit, I command you, bring forth your dead !"

The deep stillness which succeeded these words was awfully impressive. The door slowly opened, and two men entered bearing a corpse. It was the body of a young and beautiful female, clad in the white habiliments of death, and locking, Oh! how ghastly and ghostly in the dim obscurity of the uncertain light. The limbs were stiff and rigid, the eyes and mouth partially open, and the whole aspect of the countenance that of death. The bearers stretched her on the desk. Smith turned to them with an expression of feature I could not fathom ; Ward stood beside him, and I detected him glancing more than once at myself.

" Whose child is this ?" said Smith.

" Mine," answered one of the men, solemnly.

" Did she die suddenly ?"

" She did."

" When ?"

" This afternoon."

" Believest thou ?"

" I believe," said the man, impressively, " help thou my unbelief."

" Did this child believe ?"

" She was a believer."

" 'Tis well ; thy child shall be restored."

There was a faint shriek from the group of spectators, and a woman, whom I subsequently ascertained to be the mother of the dead, rushed forward and threw herself at the feet of Smith.

" Restore my child," she cried, passionately ; " she was too young, too good, and too beautiful to die. Restore her, and I will worship you for ever."

" Woman, I said it," he replied ; then turning to the company he said, " let some one of the sisters look after this woman, she must not be permitted to interfere."

Mrs. Bradish went forward, and raising the woman, led her to a seat.

" Let the believers rise," resumed Smith, " and sing the Hallelujah Chant."

A moment after the strain begun, low at first, but swelling out wild and tumultuous as the enthusiasm increased, and the passions of the assembly were brought into exercise.

When Nephi came out of Palestine,
And Tebi from among the heathen,
The great and mighty ocean was driven back before them;
The mountains fled away;
The hills sunk in the lakes,
And the rivers were dried up.
Then was life brought back from death,
And souls restored from the grave,
By the mighty power of faith.
    Hallelujah!
And it shall be so again,
    Hallelujah!
Even now our eyes behold it,
    Hallelujah!
The pale, cold corpse is waking,
    Hallelujah!
Strength is returning to its limbs,
    Hallelujah!
We shall see her again as we have seen her,
    Hallelujah!
In the pride and beauty of life,
    Hallelujah!
With no cerements clinging to her bosom,
    Hallelujah!
It comes, the power of the Most High God for ever,
    Hallelujah!
He has listened to the voice of His servant and Apostle,
    Hallelujah!
He has arrested the might of death at His bidding,
    Hallelujah!
As He did at the bidding of Moses and Elijah,
    Hallelujah!
As he did at the bidding of Christ and Saul of Tarsus,
    Hallelujah!

The intense interest of the scene, however, became too deeply absorbing for singing. Voice after voice ceased until the whole company relapsed into the most profound silence. Smith meanwhile stood beside the apparently dead body. He pressed and stroked the head, breathed into the mouth, and rubbed the frigid limbs, saying in a deep, low tone, "Live thou again, young woman. Let sight return to these eyes, now sightless, and strength to these limbs, now nerveless. Let life, and vigor, and animation, inspire this wasted frame."

Presently there was a slight movement of the muscles, the eyes opened and shut, the arms were flung out and then brought together again; and at last the body sat up. The effect on the assembly was electrical. The mother fell into violent hysterics; many of the females shrieked, others sobbed, Mrs. Bradish trembled violently; and what shall I say of myself? I stood gazing, absorbed, almost incapable of sense or motion; my reasoning faculties altogether at fault on such a subject. A voice breathed in my ear, "Dost thou now believe?"

I turned; Mr. Ward was at my side.

"I am astonished, if not convinced," I answered.

"You have seen the dead restored to life. Look; she speaks and walks."

I looked, it was indeed, as he said. She had descended from the table, and with her grave clothes on, was making the circuit of the room, leaning on the arm of Smith. Oh! for language to express my feelings as she approached me. Oh! the awe, the reverence attending the presence of one who had tasted the mystery of death, and been plucked from the hand of the king of terrors; who had known by awful experience the fearful combat with the last great enemy; yet there was nothing pertaining to death about her now. Her cheeks were flushed with life and health, her eyes sparkled with animation, and her rounded and voluptuous form contrasted strangely with her ghastly habiliments. She retired in company with a sister to change her dress, while Smith again took his station at the further end of the room.

"If any believer is lame, or rheumatic, or deaf, or blind, let him have faith, and come forth to be cured. The power exercised on earth by Jesus of Nazareth is delegated to me," he said, in a loud voice.

A moment after an old man hobbled along; he was lame with rheumatism.

"Believest thou?" said Smith.

"Lord; I believe!" and he laid his hand on his breast impressively.

"How long have you been lame?"

"For a long time, I was a Revolutioner ———."

"Never mind that," said Smith, stooping to rub and manipulate the part affected. "Have faith in God, and thou shalt be made whole."

Could I believe my eyes; in a few minutes he walked around the room without crutch or staff. A deaf person next advanced. The same questions were propounded to him, and answered in the same manner. Smith breathed upon him, made a few strokes and passes, put his fingers in the ears of the patient, and then addressed him in a low voice. He heard perfectly well; the deafness had departed. In the same manner a woman partially blind, was restored to sight, and others who were, or believed themselves to be sick, were restored to health. At that time I was ignorant of the power of mesmeric influence, and the strange proceedings enacted there and then, were consequently the more astounding and unaccountable.* I found it impossible to reconcile what I had seen with any known laws of physical agencies; my mind was in a tumult of doubt and perplexity. It was by the exercise of such power, and the performance of such deeds as these, that Smith acquired his wonderful influence. It is not strange that those who felt their diseases removed, who found their senses restored, and who even believed themselves to have been recovered from death, should attribute divine power and inspiration to the man, who so far exceeded ordinary mortals in that particular at least; that they should fear to offend him, and obey his bidding with an alacrity that bordered on servility; nor did the exhibition of his power cease with the recovery of diseases.

"Brother Babcock," he said, "will you take this chair?" a chair had been brought in for the purpose.

"You have nothing to fear, you are my friend; but I wish to

* Joseph Smith was one of the earliest practitioners in ANIMAL MAGNETISM; and it was the use of this power at that time, that convinced his disciples of his supposed miraculous gifts.

manifest to all, the power which the Almighty has vouchsafed to me, and how, when I please, I can deal with my enemies."

Babcock advanced timidly; he feared to refuse, yet hesitated to obey. Seated in the chair, Smith took a station opposite, looked him directly in the face, motioned his arms towards him, passed his hands along the body and extremities of the subject, when the eyes of the latter closed, his limbs became palsied, without feeling or motion, and every sense and perception seemed closed to external objects.

"You see now," said Smith, pointing towards Babcock, "you see the power which God has delegated to me, you cannot doubt how immediately with a motion of my hands and a glance of my eyes, I could transform my enemies to lifeless, senseless, lumps of clay; how I could deprive them of their senses, or compel them to do my bidding, even to take their own lives."

"But we are friends," called out several, who were evidently afraid that he would exercise his power over them.

"Certainly, you be," he answered; "I heal my friends, but smite my enemies, even as Paul smote Elymus, the sorcerer." With a motion or two of his hands, Smith restored Babcock to his strength and senses; others were then invited to come forth to be operated on. But all declined on the ground that they were perfectly satisfied, and needed no further proof to convince them of the greatness of his power.

Two or three times, during the last half hour, I had fancied something unusual was going on outside the house, such as the trampling of feet, and the drawing of a heavy body along the ground. Suddenly, at this juncture, a noise, loud as the loudest clap of thunder, or the discharge of artillery, resounded through the house, the windows rattled, the door flew open, and a party of half drunken men and boys rushed into the room. One single friendly voice, which I knew to be that of Ward, called out to the Mormons, "disperse for your lives." I heard the opening and shutting of doors, the screams of women, and the vociferations of men. The light had been immediately extinguished, and all involved in utter darkness. I felt a strong arm thrown around my waist, and myself forcibly drawn along a passage into another apartment. Then a voice whispered, "be not alarmed, you are safe." It was Mrs. Bradish.

"What does it all mean?" I inquired.

"We have long been obliged to hold our meetings in the latter part of the night, and to employ as much secresy as possible, on account of the mobs, who seek every occasion to raise a disturbance. But the Saints must be content to endure persecution. It has been their lot in all ages of the world."

"My dear madam," I replied, "you view the matter in a very consolatory light."

"Troubles, and trials, and tribulations in this world, or until we reach the Promised Land; peace and happiness in the next."

"But why does not Mr. Smith exercise his wondrous power for the destruction of his enemies?"

"Oh! he is too merciful, too lamb-like for that; but hark, the ruffians are returning in full force."

We could plainly hear the trampling of many feet, a confused mixture of voices blending in curses and execrations; next, a volley of stones were fired at the house, smash went the windows, the doors slammed and banged.

"They are now in the house," said Mrs. Bradish, "but if we are perfectly still I scarcely think that they will discover us."

I trembled from head to foot with apprehension. "Is it possible," I said, "that they are looking for us?"

"Not exactly for us," she answered. "When the mob broke into the house, the brethren fled; the mob pursued, and probably not finding those they wished to abuse, have come back here to make further search."

"Are any concealed in the house?"

"I suppose so," she answered; "heaven preserve them."

"Amen!" was my hearty response, for the noise and confusion was becoming truly frightful.

"They are destroying your furniture—hark!"

"Yes, I hear."

Another moment, and the piercing shrieks of a woman rose wild and shrill above the other voices,

"Oh, mercy! mercy! Indeed I cannot tell you, for I know not where he is."

"Fool! liar; you shall tell. I'll pull every lock of your hair out by the roots. Where is Joe Smith? say: won't tell—then here goes," cried a sharp, stern voice.

"Don't kill me; don't kill me," shrieked the woman again. There was a wild burst of laughter, and the screams became shriller.

"I cannot, and will not bear this," said Mrs. Bradish. "Stay here while I go to her assistance."

"If you go, I go too."

"Well take this, then," and she thrust a loaded pistol into my hand, and whispered: "Be perfectly silent."

I took her arm, and we glided along to the room where the noise told us that the mob had assembled.

We paused in the shadow of the door to reconnoitre. A bright fire was burning within, for the villains had broken the chairs and other furniture, and taken them for wood. In the centre of the apartment, surrounded by her tormentors, stood the helpless victim of lawless rage, and in her I instantly recognized the female who, in my presence that night, had been recovered from the power of death. They were crowding around her, pulling her hair, pinching, striking and abusing her in every conceivable manner. The form of Mrs. Bradish seemed to dilate, her eye to burn, and every feature to glow with intense passion, as she advanced towards them, stood a moment like a Pythoness, and cried "Stop!"

Every eye turned towards her.

"What do you mean," she continued, "breaking into my house at this time of night, and conducting in this manner? Begone, every one of you!"

"We are after Joe Smith. Where is he?" they answered.

"I don't know where he is, and if I did, I wouldn't tell you."

"You do know, and you shall tell us," said one, who appeared to be the leader.

"Roast her in the fire, yonder, that will fetch her to her speech," said another.

"Yes! yes! roast her; pretty woman she is, concealing that vagabond. I dare say he is in her bedroom."

Here the ruffians set up a loud laugh, and advanced towards her.

"The first one who lays the weight of his finger on me is a dead man," said Mrs. Bradish.

"Show fight, eh! but we ain't afraid of petticoats. On to her, boys."

They rushed upon her; two pistols exploded the same instant. Two of the villains reeled and fell groaning; two more received the weapons themselves hurled by her hand with deadly effect; the others drew back, for she stood calm, yet terrible with suppressed passion, and brandishing a long, glittering knife.

"Come on," she cried, with the voice of a lioness, "come on, every mother's son of you. Oh! there'll be two or three villains on this earth of knaves and fools the less. Thieves! murderers! house-breakers! you ain't prepared to fight. Cowards! wretches! how I hate and despise you! Now, sneak off home, poor, pitiful dogs, and tell your confederates that you were beaten by a woman."

The poor girl, the moment she beheld Mrs. Bradish, rushed towards her, and now knelt clinging to her garments, and weeping like an infant.

"Don't weep so, poor child," said the former, soothingly. "They shall torture you no more. Oh! they can amuse themselves with the cries and agonies of the helpless; cowardly knaves and midnight assassins as they be."

One of the more resolute advanced towards her, and received a desperate wound in the shoulder. The whole party seemed satisfied with this, and gathering up their wounded companions beat a hasty retreat.

"We are clear of them at last," said Mrs. Bradish. "Did they hurt you much, Ellen, dear; that is, injure you seriously?" she continued.

"I don't know that they did; they just wished to tease and torture me, and I was so frightened," said Ellen.

"Well, dear, compose yourself; and you, too, Miss B———," said Mrs. Bradish, turning to me, "I fear that this night's agitation will injure your health."

I assured her that she need have no anxiety on that account, and that probably the excitement would do me good.

"Well, at any rate, you require rest and slumber," she said, and lighting a small lamp, she accompanied me to my room. Ellen, I learned, would share her chamber, and both bade me "good-night" affectionately. The day was just breaking, but overcome by fatigue and excitement, I retired to bed, and after some time spent in thought, fell asleep.

CHAPTER III.

MORMON VEXATIONS.

THE morning was far advanced, when a slight tap at the door awakened me. I instantly rose, finished my toilet hastily, and opened it. Mrs. Bradish extended her hand with a sweet smile, and "How do you find yourself this morning, dear?"

"Quite well, I thank you."

She then informed me that Ward had called, and inquired for me, and invited me to walk down and meet him at breakfast. Is it necessary to say, that I felt gratified by the attention, or that I bestowed more than usual care on my toilet that morning?

We found Mr. Ward in the parlor with Ellen. He looked exceedingly well, and led me to a seat.

"I am very much concerned," he said, "that you should have been exposed to the reckless fury of the mob; when the villains pursued us, I had no idea that they would return to attack the house."

"For my part," said Mrs. Bradish, jocosely, "I think it will have a salutary effect on Miss B——. She has learned something of the violence and lawless character of our enemies, and I tell you we have done things up for them."

"Mrs. Bradish is brave as a lion," I said.

"As to that," she answered, "I'll own to having some blood in my veins, and then the manner in which us, free citizens, have been treated, just for presuming to exercise the right of opinion, is really outrageous. Miss B—— knows nothing about it yet. We were prevented from baptizing our converts in the day-time, by the multitudes of men and boys, who would gather with drums, horns, and frying-pans, and shout, yell, and dance, with all manner of hideous noises and antics. Then we concluded to have our baptisms privately in the night; but the wretches found it out, and went and collected all the carrion in the country, which was no small quantity, and taking it to the water, threw it in, precisely in the place where the administrators were accustomed to enter, with the expectation that the holy man would thereby be defiled with filth. On another occasion, when the night was very dark, and we had only one small lantern, in order to avoid observation as much as possible, the trees along the bank of the stream were suddenly illuminated by the most hideous and awful-looking faces that mortal eyes ever beheld; many were so frightened that they ran shrieking from the place."

"What were they?" I inquired.

"We subsequently ascertained that a party of boys had ascended the trees, with a parcel of gourd-shells cut in a frightful manner, with candles in the cavities, which, being lit on a preconcerted signal, gave them the terrifying appearance we witnessed."

"Did you run, Mrs. Bradish?" inquired Ward.

"Now, Mr. Ward, you know better than to ask that; you know very well that I did not; you are perfectly aware, that if Anna Bradish ever runs from boys or gourd-shells, the time has yet to come."

"I believe so," said Ward.

"Was any one of your people injured in the fracas of last night?" I inquired.

"None mortally, that I have heard of, but Hannah Donnelly

was nearly frozen by being thrown down, tied neck and foot, and rolled in the snow for a foot-ball," said that gentleman.

"The wretches," said Mrs. Bradish, "how I wish that I had been there."

"No, Mrs. Bradish," I answered, "we could not possibly have done without you last night."

"Then my presence was required in two places at one time."

"In half a dozen places, you might have said," cried Ward; "for they tied Betsy Basset to a stump, and then heaped snow on her, till she was buried five or six feet beneath the surface."

"And what else."

"Stripped Hetty Camel entirely nude, and left her to make the best of her way home."

"I shouldn't suppose she tarried long on the route," said Ellen, composedly.

"Oh! the wretches," said Mrs. Bradish, "but I done for two of them; what next?"

"The last that I have seen of Brother Bradley, he was going off on a rail, borne by four stout fellows, who were singing lustily:

"'Mormon came across the ocean,
All through storm, and wind, and hail,
And if we had him here this evening,
We would ride him on a rail.'"

"Oh! the blasphemous infidels!" said Mrs. Bradish, "I wonder that fire don't come down out of heaven and devour them."

Breakfast was now served, but the conversation continued.

"I subsequently heard," resumed Ward, "that they carried that good brother to the Creek, cut a hole in the ice, and ducked him three or four times."

"Horrible!"

"He arrived at home, however; but more dead than alive, with his clothes frozen to his body."

"Did you ever hear the beat, Miss B——?" said Mrs. Bradish, indignantly. "And those people had done nothing at all to excite the malice of their tormentors, except, indeed, to differ from them in opinion."

"It was certainly too bad."

"You know how exceedingly timorous old Mr. Wood is," resumed Ward.

"I know that he is."

"Well, the ruffians surrounded him, it seems through clear deviltry; talked, hooted, halloed, and made him think that something dreadful was to pay. However, he succeeded in breaking from them, at last, and his thoughts naturally reverted to his son Neddy; he tore down the street like a locomotive broke loose, for he is exceedingly fat, screaming at the top of his voice: 'Neddy! Neddy! Neddy!' Arrived at his home, he was too badly frightened to wait and open the gate, so he burst through it; and, instead of going into the house, could not find the door, and ran around it three times, when, seeing the henhouse open, he rushed into it, and carefully ensconced himself in one corner. The outraged poultry flew out, shrieking and squaling, just as Neddy, who had discovered that something unusual was going on, came out of the house."

"That was rather ludicrous than otherwise, as it seems no one was injured," I observed.

Mrs. Bradish thought otherwise; she could not see anything laughable in the affair: did not believe in frightening people out of their senses; and, finally, ended with assuming there would be neither peace nor rest for the saints on earth.

"Their inquiries here were for Smith, and I suppose that if they could have found him, they would have let the others alone," I observed.

2*

"That may be ; but he is altogether beyond their power."

"Think so ?"

"I know it. Christ was annoyed by the presence of the devil, but the enemy had no power over him. I have seen Brother Smith in situations of peril that would have alarmed an ordinary man, yet it never moved him a hair."

"I believe," said Mr. Ward, "that we had better take Brother Smith's advice—dispose of our property as we best can, and remove West. We shall always be exposed to persecutions here, among these heathen ; there we can raise a pure and acceptable vineyard to the Lord, and sit under our own vines and fig-trees, with no one to make us afraid."

"As to that," replied Mrs. Bradish, "I am not afraid here. The law allows me the privilege of self-defence, and that is about all I ask."

"But all are not so courageous as yourself," said Mr. Ward. "I remember very well when the crackers and blue-lights came dancing through the school-house, you were the only one who retained anything like presence of mind. You must pity the weaker brethren."

Mrs. Bradish was never displeased with compliments on her superior courage ; and, beginning to be interested in the recital of these incidents, which, though vexatious to the Mormons, partook largely of a ludicrous character, I inquired in what way blue-lights and school-houses were connected.

"It surpasses the bounds of belief," said Mrs. Bradish. "What infinite pains our enemies have taken to torment and perplex us. You see it was in the first days of Mormonism, the devil had not become so rampant and roaring as he has since, and we were accustomed to hold meetings in the school-house. Brother Smith generally presided ; at other times, we had the services of Brother Harris. Both were present on the occasion of which I am speaking : the exercises were highly interesting, and Brother Smith was relating a vision with which he had been favored, when a large ball, apparently of fire, descended from a hole in the ceiling overhead. It was immediately followed by a discharge of innumerable small crackers and snap-dragons, which flew hopping, hissing, and fizzing in every direction. I believe every one in the house got out the best way they could, except myself. I stuck to the ship; and, when the shower slackened, piled the benches one above the other, mounted them, and thrust my head through the aperture. About half-a-dozen youngsters were up in the loft, and the alarm had been occasioned for their amusement."

"Many of the Mormons have gone West," said Mr. Ward, "and others are preparing to follow. The plan is, doubtless, a good one; and believers cannot do better than fall in with it."

"I have thought much of it lately myself," said Mrs. Bradish, "and have come to the conclusion to go with the rest; and, as I have neither child nor chick in the world, to leave my property to the church when I have done with it—thereby building up the temporal prosperity of Zion."

"The plan is excellent," said Ward.

"Your father will go, Ellen, will he not?" said Mrs. Bradish.

"I suppose so," said Ellen, thoughtfully.

"But, my love, why are you so sad and moody this morning?" said Mrs. Bradish; "you have scarcely spoken a word, and we can all testify that you have eaten nothing."

Ellen smiled sadly, and, after a short time, rose from the table and said she felt very ill.

"The effects of your recent fright," said Mrs. Bradish. "Go to my chamber; rest and compose yourself."

Ellen left the room.

"Poor girl! I pity her," said Mrs. Bradish.

"And I almost envy her."

"Why so?" said Mrs. Bradish, with a look of astonishment.

"How can you ask, after what I witnessed last night? How I longed to inquire of her what were the sensations of dying—what her knowledge of the Dread Unknown—and whether she did not regret her restoration to earth; but fearing to agitate or distress her, I had not the heart to allude to the subject in her presence."

A peculiar expression, which I found it impossible to interpret, flitted over the countenance of Ward.

"It is well you did not," said Mrs. Bradish; "she has more trouble than some of us."

"She seems young."

"She is young; but youth is rather favorable to love. Her afflictions are of that nature. In short, Ellen was betrothed to Henry Manners, about one year since. The young man appeared good-tempered and amiable, and there was every prospect of a happy match, till Ellen, with her family, embraced the truth of Mormon. This made him outrageous. He sought an interview with her, to ascertain the fact, and then sternly and at once revoked his promise—told her to go with the scoundrels, and never let him see her face again. But he softened a little, after that; obtained another interview, and sought by threats, entreaties, and even tears, to change her purpose, but she remained inflexible; and since that time, he has treated her with studied neglect. An effort was made to induce him to join with us, but he threatened to horsewhip the elder who visited him, accused Brother Smith of all manner of deceptions, and raved awfully."

"Could not Ellen become his wife, and retain her creed?" I inquired.

"Oh, no," said Mrs. Bradish. "The saints are not permitted to intermarry with the heathen."

"And you regard all as heathens who are not Mormons?"

"So the Scriptures regard them," said Mrs. Bradish.

"Not exactly," said Mr. Ward, seeing that I rather winced under the appellation. A rapid glance was exchanged between the two, and the lady said :

"Oh, well, maybe I was rather too fast in making that assertion. However, Miss B——, we should be extremely happy to reckon you a sister. In short, why cannot you give up this idea of visiting your relatives, and become one of us?"

"I should not make a good devotee," was my reply. "I have little faith in dreams or visions; and I understand that these are the chief bases of Mormonism."

"But, my dear, you must not believe mere rumors without proof," said Mrs. Bradish. "You are the very person I desire for a companion on my journey. Your relatives cannot do better by you than I will. How long since you have seen them?"

"It has been some years," I replied.

"Were they aware of your intended visit?"

"They were not."

"Allow me, then, Miss B——, as a person of more experience than yourself, to suggest that you write them a letter with the information, desiring an immediate answer, and remain with me till you receive one."

"Where is the necessity of that?" I inquired.

"If you receive an answer, with an invitation, you will be certain of an hospitable reception; if no answer arrives, you will be spared the mortification of being treated with neglect or indifference. I speak plain; but a friend of mine was actually turned from the door of some relatives, who even refused to recognize her, though they had passed the previous season at her residence."

Similar incidents had fallen beneath my knowledge; and, thinking it probable that the vile breath of slander had reached even there, the plan appeared a feasible one; so, thanking Mrs.

Bradish for the interest she felt in my welfare, I informed her of my accedence to her proposal.

"And while you are waiting for the answer, you must consent to be my guest," said the lady.

This I readily concurred in.

"The stage comes along to-morrow; you can write the letter to-day, and I will bear it to the Post-office," said Mr. Ward.

The letter was accordingly written and dispatched.

CHAPTER IV.

SUNDRY MORMON MATTERS.

WHILE waiting for the invitation to visit my relatives, I had frequent opportunities of seeing the Mormon leaders. They professed great piety and great faith—talked much of their persecutions and troubles—and were loud in their praises and confident in their expectations of happiness in the Promised Land. Mrs. Bradish, as a person of large property, seemed to be held by them in great consideration. She delighted to be considered a sort of priestess among them, and they were willing to indulge her pardonable vanity. Smith came once or twice, but said little to me, or any one. He was not calculated by nature or education to shine in general conversation, and so he wisely forbore remark.

Mr. Ward was a constant visitor; and, before a week had elapsed, made me a formal offer of his hand, and introduced me to his children. I had expected as much, and was prepared with an answer.

"I cannot embrace Mormonism."

"I shall not require you to," he answered. "Be my wife and the mother of these orphans, and I shall be too happy to attempt your conversion to that faith."

"But I thought marriage was interdicted between members of the church and unbelievers."

"It is, if the husband, or he who aspires to that situation, is an unbeliever; but unbelieving females are gladly welcomed to the marriage rite with believing husbands."

"And wherefore the difference?"

"Circumstances alter cases, you know."

He then drew a glowing picture of the western country; said we need not live in the midst of the Mormon settlement, but only on the suburbs, and held out the various inducements of wealth, position, and respectability.

"Mr. Ward," I answered, candidly, "there is no use in denying that you have made an impression on my mind, and yet I cannot find it in my heart to consent to marry you on so short an acquaintance, especially when I recollect that you are a Mormon."

"But you would not repudiate an honest man for his opinions?"

I made no answer.

"You cannot, Miss B——, you are too much of a republican, for that belief is not governed by will, but proof. You have seen with your own eyes the miraculous exhibitions of divine power that attends our doctrines. In your presence, the dead have been restored to life, the deaf made to hear, the blind to see, and the lame to walk. If I regard these evidences sufficient to substantiate my faith, and you look upon them as insufficient, wherefore is my credulity more to blame than your unbelief?"

"There is nothing to blame in either case," I answered; "but how can two walk together except they be agreed?"

"By agreeing to disagree; you are to have perfect liberty to believe as you see fit; to attend the Mormon meetings only when you see proper. I require the same liberty; if granted all will go well."

These, and similar arguments, silenced my objections; but, requiring a week to consider of it, I determined to be governed by the circumstances connected with the proposed visit. However, as no letter had arrived at the expiration of the week, I consented to be his wife.

Mrs. Bradish was profuse in her congratulations, and insisted that we should abide with her till our removal West. The children of Mr. Ward were likewise domiciled in the same dwelling. The marriage took place privately. The ceremony being first performed by a gentleman who was introduced to me as a Justice of the Peace. It was then performed after the Mormon ritual, which, however, differs but little from the other, to satisfy the conscience of my husband. Mrs. Bradish was present as a witness. She shook my hand warmly, pressed my cheek, called me her spiritual sister, and said she was now certain of meeting me in heaven, as the unbelieving wife would be sanctified by the husband.

You ask if I was happy, and satisfied with the lot I had chosen. At times I was not; for it seemed that some undue influence had been exercised over me, though of its character I had no definite idea. I seemed to have been cajoled and brought into the measure, rather as a third person than chief actor; but there was no retreat, and nothing remained but to make the best of it.

My step-children were docile, amiable and affectionate; both girls, Mary and Martha; both beautiful and well educated for their ages, which were seven and nine. Their mother died when the youngest was born; but they had experienced a mother's care and attention from their aunt. The good lady wept bitterly when bidding them adieu; conjured me to be a mother to them. I answered, "to the best of my ability, I will."

"Your countenance is good," she said, observing me with tearful eyes ; "I am something of a physiognomist, and I fear that you have been deceived."

"By whom?"

"The Mormons."

"I am not one of them."

"Yet you are amongst them, and exposed to all their arts, wiles and deceptions."

"I hope to be able to take care of myself."

"Probably you may, yet it is my greatest grief that these dear children must be brought up among them ;" then affectionately kissing her darlings, she bade me farewell.

Mrs. Bradish soon found a purchaser for her property. Mr. Ward also disposed of his possessions ; but, to my great astonishment, I was not required to be present at the consummation of the bargain. Mr. Ward said it was no matter ; that the purchaser felt no apprehension of trouble from my claims.

"You are my wife spiritually ; my wife for this world and the next ; but you must cling to me, believe in me, and accept me as your spiritual head."

"Excuse me, my husband," I replied, "but I fail to apprehend your meaning. Am I not your temporal wife, as well as spiritual?"

Probably fearing to initiate me further into the mysteries of Mormon marriage at this early period of our union, he came towards me with his arms extended, "you are my beloved," he said, "and no power on earth, but our voluntary wills, can separate us."

"And can our voluntary wills do it?"

"Certainly, we need not cohabit unless we choose."

"But cohabitation is not marriage."

"In one sense it is—"

"In a legal sense it is not ; because married people, through life, are bound to each other, and neither absence nor distance can break the tie."

"Oh well ; we will not dispute about trifles."

"But marriage is no trifle."

"If marriage in itself is not, the peculiar form in which it is celebrated is. However, make yourself easy ; consult Mrs. Bradish on matters of religion or domestic economy, and you, will do well."

Saying this, he arose and left the house. I pondered long on this conversation, but without coming to a definite conclusion as to his exact meaning, or the tenor of his remarks. I could not divest myself of the impression that more was implied than spoken. Then I knew nothing of Mormon views of marriage. I have since learned them to my cost.

Though the Mormons held no more meetings, they had continual accessions of new converts, chiefly the disaffected members of other churches, and several females. Among these latter was a Mrs. Clarke, who had become accidentally acquainted with Smith and his tenets. Her husband was a very fine man, in good circumstances; and herself the mother of three beautiful children. She came, in company with Smith, to the residence of Mrs. Bradish, and he introduced her to that lady as a well-beloved daughter of the church, who was ready to forsake all for the love of truth. They conversed together for some time, and it was finally decided that Mrs. Clarke should reside with her spiritual sister. I learned from Mrs. Bradish that her husband was ignorant of her destination or her attachment to the Mormons. He succeeded in discovering it, however ; for, in about a week, he came for her. At first she refused to see him ; but as he threatened to call in the officers of the law, Mrs. Bradish advised her to comply.

"You know, dear," she said, "that he cannot compel you to return with him, unless you wish to."

"I must not, I cannot go back," she anwered; "I have taken a fearful oath that I will not, I."——

"You regard your professions in a very serious light," said Mrs. Bradish, interrupting her.

"I think any one would. My oaths"——

"Oh well, dear, you are agitated now, and your husband is coming in."

Mr. Clarke came in. He looked pale, sad, and disconsolate; and it even seemed that his eyes bore traces of recent tears. He advanced towards his wife, who averted her face.

"Look at me, Laura," he said; "in what have I offended?"

"You are the serpent that would tempt me from my duty," she replied.

"Say rather to your duty. You have a family, it is your duty to care for it."

"It is not."

"Woman, are you crazy? is it not a mother's duty to care for her babes?"

"That depends on circumstances."

"To what fiend's teaching have you been listening?" Then changing his tones to those of entreaty, he said, extending his hand, "Oh! come, Laura, come, go home with me. Poor little Willie cries every day for mamma, while Caddy and Sarah were nearly frantic with joy when I told them that I had heard where you were, and was going to bring you home. Oh! Laura, Laura, I cannot go back without you, to witness the sorrow and disappointment of the poor children; indeed, I cannot;" and the strong man, overcome by his emotions, sunk on his knees. Mrs. Bradish looked stern and solemn; Mrs. Clarke covered her face and trembled; for myself, I sobbed aloud. "You will go, won't you?" he said, at length, rising and advancing towards her.

"Urge me no further; for I cannot go with you."

"Is this your last resolve?" he said, somewhat sternly.

"It is."

"Then you have no regard for me, no pity for your children, no respect for the solemn ties of marriage. For a heartless, wandering vagabond, who is beneath the dogs of the kennel, you abandon your family, your home, and your friends. Have I not always treated you well, provided for you in health, watched over you in sickness; have I not kept and preserved you as the apple of my eye?"

"You have, you have," she almost shrieked; "but why torture me now?"

"It is your conscience that tortures you," he said, solemnly. "Heaven grant that it be not the foretaste of the quenchless flame and the deathless worm; and mark my words"—

"Don't curse me, don't curse me," she cried, imploringly; "you must not curse me."

"I curse you? you have cursed yourself; as you have forsaken me, you shall be forsaken; as you have deserted your children, you shall be deserted; as you have abandoned your friends, you shall be abandoned. You will not pity our distress, neither shall any eye pity you. And, now, weak, sinful, erring creature, stay with your vagabond companion till he loathes and hates your presence; stay with him till he thrusts you out in the tempest at midnight, and takes to his bosom a younger and fairer bride; but let it strike like the knell of death to your soul, 'that whatsoever measure ye mete shall be measured to you again,'" and turning, he strode from the room. Mrs. Clarke gave one long agonizing shriek, and fell senseless to the floor.

We hastened to her assistance.

"Poor child!" said Mrs. Bradish, "she has had a hard struggle with her duty, but the truth triumphed."

A Wife's Duties Defined. 45

We lifted her to the sofa, and Mrs. Bradish busied herself in procuring and applying restoratives, meanwhile remarking that she loved to see great sacrifices made for duty; that those only were worthy of the Crown, who had borne the Cross, and that she had faith to believe a glorious reward would attend her in this world, and a richer one in the next.

"Mrs. Bradish, this is all nonsense and humbug," I said, at length, rather impetuously. "It was this woman's duty to go with her husband: 'What God hath joined together let no man put asunder.' 'Let not the woman forsake her husband.' You cannot pretend to believe that a woman's duty ever calls her to abandon her helpless, innocent offspring, or her loving husband; you cannot believe that duty ever compels her to plunge her friends and relatives in deep distress. Here is something palpable and real; there is mere shadow, opinion. If she wishes to believe in the faith of Mormon, let her do so; but, at the same time, let her perform the relative and conjugal duties, which she assumed voluntarily. Let her comfort and cherish her husband, and bring up her children to virtue; and in that path only can a wife and mother discharge her duty."

Mrs. Clarke soon exhibited signs of returning consciousness. She opened her eyes wildly. "Where am I?" she said, "I thought my husband was here, and that he cursed me."

"Oh! no," said Mrs. Bradish, soothingly; "you have been dreaming, darling."

"Is no one here?"

"Mrs. Ward and myself only."

"But there has been; my husband has been; my husband no longer. Oh, heaven! that I should live to say it."

"Compose yourself, love," said Mrs. Bradish. "Go to sleep, and you will feel better soon."

Mrs. Clarke endeavored to obey, but it was clearly evident that she was suffering a violent mental conflict. When Mr.

Ward was informed of the circumstances, he called her a heroine and martyr, and joined with Mrs. Bradish in trying to establish her wavering conviction, that she had chosen wisely. Oh ! how I longed to persuade her to go back to the friends she had abandoned ; but I feared to displease my husband, and so remained silent.

Subsequently Mrs. Clarke informed me how she first became acquainted with Smith. He visited her neighborhood, and held meetings, to which she was induced to go through curiosity, but without the knowledge of her husband. And here, methought, was the first wrong step. He should have been her confidant and her companion. Half the evils of married life would be averted if wives would confide in their husbands more, and their strength less. Doubtless, she would have smiled, or considered herself insulted, had any one at that time given her this friendly warning. Under the pretence of visiting a sick relative, she left her home and her babes, and night after night listened to the teachings of Smith, witnessed his miraculous powers, and finally became a convert to his doctrines. He narrowly observed her, read in her countenance the operations of her mind, sought and obtained an interview. What then and there passed, heaven only knows, but she declared herself to be bound to him for time and eternity. And thus an error led directly to a heinous crime.

One day, a gentleman, Brother Norris, came to the house of Mrs. Bradish. He did not look happy, and I mentioned it.

"He can scarcely be sorrowing for his wife," said the lady.

"Sorrowing for his wife ?" I repeated, "Is he then a widower ?"

"Not exactly, his wife is only dead to him."

"I hardly understand you."

"In plain terms, he left his wife to become one of us."

"And that family is broken up."

"She went back to her father. They say that she is in a decline, and cannot live long; if, indeed, she is not already dead."

"How cruel in him to leave her, whom he had sworn to cherish and protect."

"Such things must be. She would not yield to his wishes, and embrace our doctrines. He could not sacrifice his soul, and so they parted. They say that she was governed in her decision by the advice of her pastor."

"And are such things common?" I said to Mrs. Bradish.

"Not very common, yet there have been several such instances," she answered. "Brother Weatherby left his wife and ten children. Of course, some of them were able to take care of themselves. Others, however, were not, and one was an idiot."

"What became of them?"

"They were put out, I believe, some to one place and some to another. The idiot went to the poor-house, and the youngest, Mrs. Weatherby supports, washing by the week."

"Have they no property?"

"Some—principally in money; but that belonged to him. Indeed it must have been a judgment upon her for refusing to receive the truth."

"And a judgment will fall upon him, I fear for deserting her."

"But he was commanded to do it."

"By whom?"

"God."

"And how by God?"

"Through Brother Smith."

"Oh, Mrs. Bradish! Can"——

"I see, Mrs. Ward," said the lady, interrupting me, "I see that you are yet ignorant of the most essential doctrines of

Mormonism. Brother Smith stands in precisely the same relation to us that Moses did to the children of Israel. In both cases God speaks through the mouth of his servants. Moses was empowered to work wonders, and do miracles, and lead the chosen people to the promised inheritance. Were not the Israelites commanded to spoil the Egyptians? Suppose that some of the Jews had heathen wives, or that some of the Jewish women were united to Egyptian men. What would have been the command of God in this case? Why, that the believers should abandon their heathen companions, and go forth with the children of God."

"But we are not Jews, neither are the others Egyptians."

"That makes no difference, as the circumstances are exactly parallel.

"I do not see them so."

"Then you are one of those, who, having eyes, see not. The same as Moses and Elijah, Brother Smith is gifted with the faculty and power of Revelation. Is any one doubtful what course to pursue, he can always explain to them the will of God in the matter."

"Does he then profess to have interviews with the Divine Being?"

"He sees Him as Moses saw Him in the bush; understands His will by dreams and visions, and then interprets them in the language of men."

Mr. Ward now came in.

"I am trying to instruct Mrs. Ward in the principles and beauties of Mormonism, and she does not prove a very apt learner," said Mrs. Bradish, half reproachfully.

Mr. Ward looked as if he considered it a matter of perfect indifference, and other company coming in, the conversation became general, but all relating to Mormon matters of local import; what diseased persons had been healed, what heathen converted, and what happiness would result to the faithful from their establishment in the Promised Land.

I had recently seen but little of Ellen, yet the poor girl seemed suffering acutely, and no one pitied her.

"How it is possible for Ellen to be so in love with that outcast, is incomprehensible to me!" said Mrs. Bradish.

"An outcast! I thought he was a very respectable man."

"Oh, he is respectable in the eyes of the world, but an outcast from the Saints. If her heart was where it should be, on spiritual things, she would cease grieving for him."

"But all, my good friend, have not your mental stamina, and strength of purpose."

"Neither do they try to have, but sit down and grieve over the first affliction. That is no way of doing."

"I cannot help pitying her," I said; "she seems so artless, gentle, and innocent; so bowed down by sorrow. Could not your elders relax for once the stern discipline of their creed in her favor? Indeed it would make me happy to see her united to her lover."

"I am astonished, Mrs. Ward, at your dullness of comprehension; if, indeed, it is not, as I half suspect, assumed; our elders are not the originators of our creed, neither can they change the expressed purposes of heaven. Women can only be saved through their husbands. The husband is saved by faith—the wife is saved by the husband; therefore, you see that she could not be saved if united to an unbelieving husband."

"And if they have no husbands?"

"They must be the spiritual wives of some brother."

"Will you please to enlighten me on the subject of this spiritual wifery?"

"I scarcely think you sufficiently initiated in the mysteries of the faith to understand it fully. At some future time it will be expedient to inform you."

Thus I was left in the dark.

CHAPTER V.

MORMON REMOVALS.

SPRING came, soft, warm and balmy ; came as it will come when we have returned to dust. The Mormons had made every preparation for removal. They numbered fourteen families, besides several others who had been separated from their families, or who had none. Smith was the life and soul of the party. He directed everything, and governed every one. In all cases of difference he urged a special revelation, and that settled the question. He was king, prophet, and High Priest ; consulted like an oracle, and obeyed like a god. A certain proportion of the property had been placed in the hands of Smith, for his disposal, while the remainder was retained in possession of the original proprietors. In order to avoid all contact with the heathen, it was decided to remove in wagons; to take a large store of all necessary provisions ; and only to purchase such articles as were absolutely indispensable, and could not be otherwise obtained. Mrs. Bradish seemed in her element. It is impossible to form an adequate idea of that woman's activity, or how she flew from thing to thing, and party to party, advising one, consoling another, and playfully chiding a third. One sister wished to take her carpet, and this Mrs. Bradish considered preposterous.

"Take her carpet, indeed, why I sold all mine, Brussels,

Ingrain and Turkey. Hers is nothing but rags, nohow great in bulk and weight, and nothing in value. I wonder what she is thinking of—but that's the way with some people; they are so afraid of sacrificing something! they ought to known what I sacrificed; my fine set of Sèvres China, elegant paintings, and antique furniture." However, the carpet was interdicted. Indeed, it seemed that almost every one had set his or her mind on some article, and designed to remove it; and it was equally certain that the other members of the party would prohibit its removal; for each family was subject to the supervision of all the rest. This occasioned numberless little delays and bickerings, in which either Mrs. Bradish or Smith would be called in to decide the matter. They wished to go off secretly in the night, and unknown to their enemies, especially as it was currently reported that a mob had been organized, and that the principal bridges in the neighborhood were closely watched. Mrs. Bradish armed herself with knives and pistols, and looked a very heroine of romance. She had a pet palfrey that she determined to take along, in order to alternate the long journey between riding in the wagon, and on horseback, no one presumed to interfere with her arrangements. Mr. Ward said the plan was a good one, and thus it was settled.

"By the by, Mrs. Bradish," said I, one day, "have you heard anything from those fellows you saluted so handsomely at the time of the riot?"

"Not a word," she answered, "they knew better than to make it known, and I hardly suppose they were desperately wounded."

"If they were, they deserved it, and should we be attacked again, I suppose that you will be equally heroic."

"I certainly shall; I have made preparations for such emergencies. Be ye courageous, and faint not; neither spare your enemies, when ye go in to possess the good land."

Mrs. Bradish was to go in our wagon, which contained Mr. Ward, myself, and the two children beside. Another wagon was particularly appropriated to Mrs. Clarke, Ellen, and two other women, whom I had not seen before; other wagons were entirely laden with goods, and the teams driven by men without families; those having such incumbrances rode with them in other wagons. The order of march being decided upon, the cavalcade started about midnight. The heavens were perfectly dark with clouds, not a star, not a moonbeam, not a sound, but the heavy tramp of the horses, the roll of the wagon wheels, the snorting and running of the cows and oxen that were driven loose to furnish food by the way; now and then a word of command, as it passed in whispers along the line. There were several men on horseback, and the whole party was completely armed. We had gone some distance, and I began to hope that no danger was to be apprehended, when one of the horsemen rode up to our wagon, drew the curtains, and whispered something to Mr. Ward. He instantly resigned the reins to the custody of Mrs. Bradish, who was accustomed to drive, dismounted without saying a word, and disappeared.

"I wonder what can be the matter," said I.

"We shall know soon enough, probably," she answered.

We moved on slowly; then a long low cry, like that of some night-bird echoed through the air. It was a preconcerted signal, and every wagon came to a halt. Five minutes probably elapsed; five minutes of breathless suspense, when the curtains of our wagon were suddenly lifted, and a woman thrust in; I could not see her face, but heard the rustle of her dress, and the sound of her weeping. The curtains were pulled down again; she found a seat somehow in the obscurity, and Mrs. Bradish addressed her by inquiring why she was weeping, but in a whisper so low and suppressed, that it scarcely seemed articulate.

"My husband is coming after me," said the woman, "and I

am afraid of him. They brought me to this wagon as a place of greater safety. They have taken Irene to another. Oh, dear!"

"And who is Irene?" I was a very Eve in curiosity.

"Irene is a young woman from our neighborhood. Her father was exceedingly angry when he found out that she had joined you, and actually threatened to shoot her, if he ever laid eyes on her again."

Excited by conversation, the stranger had forgotten to weep.

"I wonder what they are doing anyhow," said Mrs. Bradish, impatiently. "I've a great mind to go and see. Who wants to stand here all night? Pshaw! I'd go on, and when an enemy appeared, I'd fight him. How absurd to be waiting here."

Presently there was a movement among the wagons beyond ours, and the next minute the horses were taken by the head, softly spoken to, and turned off in another direction.

"It's really too bad, that Mr. Ward don't come to tell us what it all means," said the lady. "Positively I'll never forgive him, as long as I live."

"I can tell you what it means," said the woman.

"What is it then?" said Mrs. Bradish, angrily.

"Why the bridge down yonder, has been taken possession of by the mob, and they are turning off to go through the woods, and ford the creek higher up. I heard them say that they should have to do so."

"Heard who say so?"

"The brethren," said the woman.

I thought Mrs. Bradish was dissatisfied, because something had been undertaken without her advice and concurrence. We moved on through the woods, but silence was impossible. The wagons would creak, the cattle run and snort, the brushwood crackle, and the boys halloo. Yet we passed on without being attacked, and finally came to the ford. This was got over without difficulty, but when we had journeyed two or three hundred yards farther, Mr. Ward came to the side of the wagon, and informed us that our enemies were collected, apparently in considerable numbers, at the Cross Roads, about half a mile distant ; "Mr. Gable," he continued, "and Harley Cook, appear to be the leaders. We have had a parley, and they demand that Irene Gable and Mrs. Cook, shall be immediately restored to their husband and father. If we accept these conditions, they will leave us to pursue our journey unmolested ; if not they will take the women by force."

"That is, if they can get them," said Mrs. Bradish, "but what answer did you return?"

"That we knew nothing of such women ; and of course we shall not give up the ladies, if they decide to stay with us."

"I should prefer to stay. I am afraid of my husband, he threatened to shoot me ; and yet, to avoid involving you in difficulties, and prevent violence and bloodshed, perhaps I had better go back."

"Not on that account ; you shall not, Mrs. Cook. We can muster twenty men, well armed."

"Count me two," said Mrs. Bradish.

"Well, twenty-two, then," resumed Mr. Ward. "But the greatest fear is, that the country will rise, and that we shall be pursued and harassed a great distance."

Mrs. Cook was sobbing again.

"Dry your tears, woman," said Mrs. Bradish sternly. "This is the time for action. Mr. Ward, I have thought of a plan that will, I think, work well."

"Let's have it, quick."

"I will take Mrs. Cook behind me on Bounding Bet (this was the name of the palfrey); let some other courageous woman take Irene on another horse. We can strike out in an easterly direction along that dark, unfrequented road through the Maple

Woods, and which intersects the turnpike two or three miles beyond the Corner, where the heathen are gathered."

"Well, what then?"

"Go forward and tell the men that the women they are in pursuit of are not in the company."

"We have told them so already, but they would not believe us."

"Invite them to come and search for themselves."

"They swear that they will tar and feather Smith if they find him."

"They had better say if they knew him."

"I think so, too. He is so well disguised that his mother wouldn't know him."

"He looks like a man a hundred and eighty years old," said Mrs. Bradish. "But come, I am in a hurry to be off."

"Well, I must communicate your scheme, and see how the others like it. To me it looks feasible. But have you no fears?"

"Anna Bradish afraid?" she said, contemptuously.

"I know you are made of sterner stuff than any other woman I ever beheld."

"Yes! yes! I know all that too, but be off now, and let me know how about it soon."

Mr. Ward obeyed. He returned in a few minutes, with the information that the plan was approved of, and that Mrs. Stone volunteered to go with Irene.

"She is an excellent horsewoman," said Mrs. Bradish, "and Roan is almost equal to Bounding Bet."

The palfrey had been fastened behind the wagon. She was now brought round, and the two women quickly mounted. Another moment, and they were joined by Mrs. Stone and her charge.

"Now give me a long rope," said Mrs. Bradish."

"What can you want with that?" I inquired.

"Here, fasten this end to the pommel of my saddle. Now, give the other end to Mrs. Stone. We cannot possibly see each other in the dark woods, yet we must keep in company. I will put Bet in a steady easy canter. She goes like a cat. You do the same by Roan. And now, Mr. Ward, you know where the road that we are to follow intersects the other. Whichever party arrives there first must wait for the other. This shall be the signal," and she set up a cry exactly like some bird of night.

"It shall be as you say," he answered, "and may Providence protect you."

"Amen!" they all responded fervently.

There was the sound of a low word, the easy shuffling of ambling feet, and the women were off.

"I declare," said Mr. Ward, "the heroism of that woman makes me ashamed of myself. But now for the remainder of the drama." He then left the wagon.

It is scarcely necessary for me to say that I felt not a particle of that heroic spirit which animated Mrs. Bradish, or that I would have implored him to stay with me, had not shame restrained such an expression of fear. But he soon came back, saying that a delegation had been sent to the enemy, with an invitation for them to search the wagons for themselves.

"But is there no danger of violence from them?" I inquired.

"I think not," he answered. "They are not the class that mobs are usually composed of, but several respectable and influential men are among them. Brother Smith's female converts occasion us a good deal of trouble. These men care nothing about our faith as Mormons, but they say that we are carrying off their wives and daughters, and that they will not endure it. When they ascertain that the women are not here, they will probably disperse quietly."

The wagons moved on slowly, and we were soon met by the Committee of Search, who were headed by Cook and Gable. Lights were speedily produced, every curtain raised, and every wagon thoroughly searched, but neither wife nor daughter could be found. The searchers could not be satisfied. Again and again they looked, examined, hunted, retracing the same places over and over. At last Mr. Gable spoke.

"Gentlemen," he said, addressing his comrades, "we are altogether at fault. It is certain that the persons we are looking for are not here. We have been led on a false scent, and now I think that we owe these gentlemen our apologies, for the unnecessary delay and trouble we have put them to."

Mr. Ward expressed great gratification that they were satisfied, and after the exchange of mutual good wishes, we were permitted to move on peacefully, and the others dispersed to their homes.

"And now," said I, "where are we to meet Mrs. Bradish ?"

"About three miles ahead."

"It was hardly right to deceive them so."

"Perfectly," he answered. "As the Israelites deceived and spoiled the Egyptians, we, as saints, may deceive and spoil the heathen."

I was silenced, but not convinced, by this kind of argument. Mr. Ward indulged himself in laughing heartily at the expense of those who had been cheated, and deceived, as he quoted it, by a woman's wit.

The clouds had partially broken, and now and then a little twinkling star peeped timidly through the firmament. Indeed, the darkness, to my great relief, was much less intense. My apprehensions, however, had been less for myself than Mrs. Bradish and her companions. My thoughts constantly referred to the long dark woods, and the lonely midnight ride.

"Are there no wild animals in the Maple Woods ?" I inquired.

3*

"There are," he answered, " or at least I suppose so."

"Is Mrs. Bradish in no danger, then?"

"She is in danger, doubtless. It is only a short time since a man was pursued by a pack of wolves. Nothing but the fleetness of his horse saved him; but Providence will protect her."

"Providence protects those who take care of themselves," I answered : "but is there no danger of her taking the wrong road."

"Not much, I guess," he replied. "To be sure there are many different paths, but she knows the direction."

"However, it seems to me that we shall never see her again.".

"Weak and silly," he replied, "you judge of her by yourself."

We travelled on in silence. At length the wagons came to a full stop. We had arrived at the intersection of the roads.— The signal agreed upon was given. All listened breathlessly. It was not answered, but after a few minutes a dull sound was heard. It came nearer and nearer, settling at last in the long steady gallop of horses. Again the signal was given; and this time answered. They soon came up. Mrs. Bradish and Mrs. Cook took places in our wagon; Mrs. Stone and Irene in theirs.

"Thank heaven," I said, grasping the hand of the first lady, "thank heaven you are safe."

"Safe, child ; did you dream that there was danger?"

"Certainly; was not a man pursued through these very woods by a pack of wolves?"

"To be sure there was, but the wolves didn't pursue me. I had no fears of them."

"And you got through perfectly safe and easy?" said Mr. Ward ; "I had some misgivings myself."

"I had none; but how did you get along with the enemy?"

"First rate; when they found that those they sought for were not among us, they even offered to apologize."

"Trust a woman's wit," said Mrs. Bradish, bursting into a laugh. "Oh, it is too good."

"I don't know what we should do without you," said Mr. Ward; "I am very confident no one else would have thought of such a scheme."

Mrs. Bradish received the congratulations of the whole company, and it seemed to me on this, and on many occasions afterwards, that her shrewdness was more than a match for Smith's inspiration.

We travelled the remainder of the night, and halted in a pleasant valley the next morning about sunrise. As it had been decided to have no dealings with the heathen, we prepared to take breakfast on the green sward. The wagons were drawn up in a line, the teams unharnessed, turned loose, and fed; the men, women, and children gathered into groups, preparing or partaking of their food. Smith still retained his disguise, and I observed that his attentions were divided between Mrs. Clarke and Mrs. Cook. Ellen seemed neglected by every one. She sat apart from the rest, and looked so sad and disconsolate, that one's heart ached to behold her. Even her own mother rarely looked towards her, or spoke to her. I observed the same to Mrs. Bradish. She smiled, and said it was nothing.

We rested for two hours, and then the teams were again harnessed, the passengers mounted in the wagons, and we set off.

Mrs. Cook was no longer in our company, but had returned to the wagon in which she had first ridden, and in which Smith also rode.

There is very little romance in a journey out West. The dull monotony of the route; the long interminable winding roads, through valleys, over hills, and beside water courses; the straggling villages, looking so near like each other that you are almost tempted to believe yourself to be in the condition of persons, who, becoming bewildered in some forest, describe a circle instead of progressing onwards, and continually, though without consciousness of it, review the same scenes. Doubtless we were a godsend to many a villager half dying with ennui, who had retailed her last piece of scandal, reported the last short-coming of the pastor, and the last frailty of an erring sister. In many places the inhabitants turned out en masse to behold us. Groups would be stationed on the hills, the women holding aloft their infants as if to show them a glimpse of some great natural curiosity, troops of children, staring and gaping at first, and then running and whooping like young savages when they had settled the question that we looked exactly like other people. But Smith was certainly the greatest curiosity, particularly with the women. The moment our encampment was made at night, if in a habitable neighborhood, we were thronged with visitors. Fat ladies came, sometimes bringing small presents, oftener with their pipes and snuff-boxes. Beautiful girls, with and without protectors, swarmed around us. Dirty men from their work, saturated with the fumes of tobacco and whisky, with now and then a gent, would insist on knowing all about Mormonism, or on being present at our morning and evening devotions.

I believe that we should have got along very well, had not Smith, as usual, been possessed with the mania of making converts ; and on this occasion, as well as others, the subjects of his exertions were young and beautiful girls. One warm, beautiful evening, two sisters came to visit us in company with their parents. The place of our encampment was on the border of a wood, near the banks of a limpid stream. I had wandered off by myself, and sat down on a fallen log behind a clump of elders and laurels, yet in plain view of the encampment, and where I could see all that was going on without being seen. The parents were in deep conversation with some Mormon elders, when Irene laughingly approached the sisters, and asked them how they would like to be Mormons.

"I think I should like it," said Hannah, a gay, sprightly creature; and she glanced inadvertently towards a group of young men, who had come in from the village, and in which I suppose she had a lover.

"Well, then," said Irene, "you had better go with us."

"Wonder if I hadn't though?" she returned; and thus the two girls kept up a sort of playful badinage.

Smith was in disguise; but I knew him, and determined to watch his motions. He soon approached Hannah.

"My daughter," he said, in a voice modulated exactly like that of an aged man, "sit down here, and converse with an aged grandfather, who is a Mormon, but who once had a beautiful daughter, exactly like yourself."

"Had you?" she said, archly.

"Indeed, I had."

"What became of her?"

"She died."

"Died, dreadful!"

"Dying is not dreadful to the good; but sit here beside me, and I will tell you about it."

She sat down beside him. Irene drew the sister's arm within hers, and they took a short stroll together. What he said to her no other ear heard, what arts he employed upon her it is impossible to tell. It was something, however, of no ordinary character, as the result will show.

Meanwhile a light gust of clouds swept over the sky; it became quite dark, and the parents wished to go home, but Hannah was not to be found. Inquiries being made, Irene said that Hannah had gone with another young lady, her cousin, and would not return till the next day.

"That is strange, anyhow," said the old lady; "why did she not speak to me about it?"

"I know nothing about that," returned Irene, coldly.

"Well, we shall have to let her go, I s'pose;" and they walked off.

And where was Smith during this conversation?

He stood by like some quaint, antiquated grandfather.

That night a special revelation directed that he should have a wagon especially appropriated to his own use; and consequently the ladies who had occupied it formerly, were distributed here and there. Ellen came to us, and I was glad of it, as it would give me an opportunity to have some conversation with her. Mrs. Bradish had gone to nurse and prescribe for a sick child belonging to the company. Mr. Ward took up his lodgings in a wagon exclusively occupied by men, and no one remained with us capable of appreciating or reporting our conversation.

"The old lady didn't seem to relish her daughter's going off so unceremoniously," I said, at length.

"Her daughter didn't go anywhere," answered Ellen, quietly.

"Where is she then?"

"In yonder wagon."

"What one?"

"Ours."

"Ellen, Miss Bradly, are you sure of what you say?"

"Sure, certainly, didn't I see him lift her in; didn't I hear him tell Irene to forge that lie. Oh! Mrs. Ward, I could tell you things of that man which would make you shudder."

"Tell me, Ellen, do," I said, soothingly. "I have long known that some dreadful burden was on your mind. I am your friend, confide in me as in a sister."

"Oh, I dare not; he would kill me."

"Who would kill you, my poor child?"

"I am afraid to speak it; it seems to me that he can read my thoughts, and I fear to look at him. My mother is angry with me, because she says I have no faith in him; how can I have faith in a man whom I know to be so desperately wicked?

"I believe, she said, after a time, "I believe that I can confide in you. You are not one of them. You have not experienced the power of that dreadful man as I have."

"No; I am not a Mormon in belief, and yet I know that Smith at least possesses power, with which men generally are not endowed."

"Yes," said Ellen; "and it is that which frightens me."

"I have longed wished to ascertain what were your sensations on that eventful night of the Mormon meeting. Excuse me, Ellen, but were you really dead?"

"I know not."

"Had you been sick?"

"Be patient, and I will relate the whole. Smith had frequently given out that under peculiar circumstances, he could raise the dead. Two or three times some mother, agonizing over the loss of her offspring, had implored him to try, but a special revelation would always come in to forbid it. At length some of the brothers gave him to understand that they must see an exhibition of his work, or hear no more about it. He engaged to resurrectionize the first believer who fell beneath the power of the enemy, and there the matter rested. Smith came to our house on the day in question. I was entirely alone, and sat sewing by the window. His deportment was very grave, and something unusual seemed to weigh on his mind. I had a presentiment that it related to me, and whenever was a presentiment at fault? At length he spoke, and his voice sent a thrill of horror through my heart.

"'Ellen,' he said, 'you are about to die.'

"'How—when?' I answered, commanding my voice as well as I was able.

"'Now, immediately. I had a special revelation of it; and, knowing that you were alone, came in to aid and comfort you. But fear not, child; the presence of God is with you—look at me.'

"His words struck me with inexpressible dread. To die—to leave the beautiful earth, and all I loved; the thought was horrible! yet I doubted not of its fulfillment, and looked towards him, as he bade me. I was fascinated by his gaze, so deep, earnest and steady. A strange sensation of drowsiness overpowered my senses. I wished, but could not struggle against it. The consciousness that I was dying came over me; and yet how different from all that I had imagined of death. No pain, no torture, no agonizing convulsions, but all calm, sedate, and tranquil. A gradual suspension of feeling and perception, a blending of indistinct images, like objects in a dream, that mingle and then melt to nothingness. Yet I knew that a warm hand closed my eyes; that the same hand moved gently down my extremities; and that was the last."

"And did Smith call your parents?"

"He did. He told them that Providence sent him to me to soothe my dying moments; and that it had been revealed likewise that I should rise from the dead."

"'Tis strange, 'tis passing strange," I said involuntarily.

"I once read," said Ellen, slowly, and with awful emphasis, "I once read of a man who had made a bargain with the Evil One: power was given on one side—on the other, the immortal soul was sold. It sometimes seems to me that he has employed the same fearful means to effect his purposes. That it comes from heaven, as he professes, I cannot believe."

"But you are not a believer in him?"

"Once I was; but now"——

"But now, what?"

"He must be a wicked man. It cannot be otherwise. I could unfold a tale. I have been among the initiated."

This was said incoherently, and more as a soliloquy than as if addressed to me.

"What is it, Ellen?"

"When I first saw Joseph Smith, I was pure and happy—betrothed to an amiable young man, whom I loved, and who loved me. Smith, by his hellish arts, succeeded in making my parents believe that, to ensure my salvation, the marriage must be broken off, unless my lover could be converted to Mormonism. That, they well knew, was impossible; and so we were forbidden to see or speak to each other. It is true that, hearing continually the praises of Smith, and witnessing the exhibitions of his power, astonished and filled me with awe and veneration. His presence was that of the basilisk. He exerted a mystical magical influence over me—a sort of sorcery that deprived me of the unrestricted exercise of free will. It never entered into my brain that he could cherish impure motives; that one professing such sainted holiness could seek the gratification of lawless passions. No friendly voice was near to warn me, and I fell"——

"Oh! Ellen, you frighten me; yet I suspected as much."

"And it frightened me; but hear me out. I became a mother!"

"Worse and worse."

"Indeed, you may well say that; for the worst is yet to come."

"What became of your child?"

"I know not. Into my mother's ear, I poured the tale of my wrongs and woes. Where else could I go with it? yet, so deep was her reverence for that man, that she refused to believe me. My father mentioned it to Smith; but he utterly and totally denied the whole. At length, however, it became necessary that something should be done, and a meeting was called. At that meeting only four persons were present."

"And who were they?"

"The knowledge will probably embitter your whole life—do you wish to know?"

"Certainly."

"Your husband, Mrs. Ward, my father, Smith, and Mrs. Bradish."

"Is it possible! But what was decided upon?"

"That I only know by the results. I was taken to the house of Mrs. Bradish. There my sickness occurred. I well knew my condition—well knew the meaning of the fierce pangs that seized me; then I sunk into a state of partial unconsciousness, not totally oblivious to passing events, and yet incapable of speech or motion. I woke from this state to ask for my child, and they made strange of it—laughed, and said I was beside myself—wanted to know what made me imagine such an absurdity—and, finally, threatened to send me to the lunatic asylum, if ever I mentioned such a thing again. Imagine my anguish; for description is powerless. I said no more, for I feared them; but set myself to remember and connect the events of the few past hours. I had distinctly heard the feeble wail of an infant; then it seemed that I heard or saw (for everything was confused) Mrs. Bradish go stealthily to the closet-door, open it, and remark: 'It can lay here a short time.' That the closet-door was then closed, when there was a slight whispering, and some one said: 'All for the best. It would have disgraced us in the eyes of the heathen.' My child was in that closet, dead! I knew, I felt that it must be so. Dead! yet it was not stillborn; for I heard its feeble wail. Dead now, nevertheless; and how? The thought was horrifying! and then I lay still—oh! how still!—but my thoughts were busy, and they all revolved round that dead child; and the intense burning desire to behold it grew stronger every moment, and seemed to give me a supernatural strength and energy as well as insight into their dark designs. Then it came to me that they would take and bury it while I slept. 'But I will sleep no more,' I said to the inward monitor, and resolutely refrained from slumber. Mrs. Bradish soothed and counselled me to rest, even recommended a narcotic; but this time I had a purpose unfulfilled, and was not to be cajoled. Faint, sick, and weary, as I was, I overmatched these resolute and strong women. Oh, what is there that an unconquerable will cannot effect! Mrs. Bradish seemed really exasperated, and chid me smartly for my wakefulness. She then went out and called the attendant. They whispered in suppressed tones; but, on parting, one said to the other: 'Some time near morning, when she falls asleep;' the other assented, and the attendant came back to watch with me."

"And who was this attendant?"

"I never saw her before or since; she was probably one of those miserable women, who, for gold, will commit almost any crime. How I loathed her hateful presence; but knowing that the success of my wishes depended on lulling her suspicions, I said nothing. At length she grew drowsy, for the muscles of her neck began to relax, and her head to nod. 'You had better compose yourself into a comfortable position, and sleep,' I said, addressing her; 'I can call you if necessary.' With a yawn or two she complied with the suggestion, and her heavy breathing soon made it apparent that she had fallen asleep.

"And then I rose in the bed. Sickness and faintness overpowered me for a moment, but mastering these sensations by a strong effort of resolute will, I slipped from my couch. But my tottering limbs refused to support me, and I sunk to the floor. Then dragging myself heavily along, I made my way to the closet, opened the door silently, and drew thence a small bundle, which my heart too plainly told me, was bone of my bone and flesh of my flesh. Unwinding it carefully, an infant was disclosed, with a thick piece of brown paper drawn tightly over its mouth. I knew the purpose of this, and no longer able to contain myself, I shrieked aloud, my brain swam, there was a noise like the rush of waters in my ears ; then all was darkness.

"When I recovered, Mrs. Bradish was sitting beside me. I feared to look at her, and covered my face with the bed-clothes.

"'Are you better, dear?' she said, soothingly. 'You have been very ill.'

"I dared not trust my voice to speak, and remained silent, while she continued : 'Will you not have an anodyne, or some little nourishment? Oh ! I perceive you are too weak to answer,' and without ceremony she went to a small cupboard, poured out a glass of wine, and bringing it to me, raised my head slightly, and compelled me to swallow it."

"And all this happened, and I an inmate of the same house ?"

"All this, and much more," continued Ellen. "When I recovered, Smith consented to receive me as his spiritual wife, for a time. The same as he has received Irene and those foolish women, who have abandoned their homes for him. Now Hannah will be added to the number. When he tires of her, she will be cast off, or given to some one else."

"Perhaps her relatives will reclaim her ?"

"No hopes of it. Once in his hands, there is no rescue or remedy. Oh ! it is horrible !"

And what a revelation was this to me—me, so closely connected with the principal aiders and abettors in such deeds of crime. But after a violent struggle with my feelings, I concluded that silence and apparent ignorance would be the best policy, since the confidence of Ellen could not be betrayed, and I had no other proof.

The next morning the encampment was broken up, and the cavalcade under way two hours earlier than usual. I had a shrewd suspicion of the reason. Mrs. Bradish, however, said, that they wished to travel in the cool of the morning, in order to have a longer time for rest in the heat of the day. The words of Ellen had awakened my suspicions, and I determined to watch that woman. I soon discovered that something unusual was going on, and was not long in conjecturing the cause. Bounding Bet was brought forward, saddled and bridled for a ride.

"I think a gallop this morning will be decidedly pleasant and exhilarating," said Mrs. Bradish.

"Do you ride alone?" I inquired.

"I have hardly decided," she answered. "some of the girls can ride with me if they choose."

Then she mounted, and rode around in the direction of the leading wagons. I could not see at the time whether she took off any of the girls or not, but soon perceived her galloping off in a circular direction, with a woman, in whom I recognized Hannah, mounted behind her.

We journeyed on probably four or five miles, when we heard the sound of an approaching company, and presently eight or ten young men, armed and mounted, came up. One, a little ahead of the others, ordered the wagons to halt, and demanded his sister.

"Your sister? what have we to do with your sister?" said Smith, affecting utter indifference to the subject.

"You know very well who I mean," said the young man, unable to restrain his rising passion. "And if you don't tell me where she is, by G—d, I'll blow your brains out! that I will."

Mr. Ward advanced to the young fellow, and said, in a conciliating manner, "Indeed, sir, how can we tell you where your sister is, when we don't know ourselves?"

"But you do know. She came last night; that's certain. When mother wanted to go home, some of you told her that Hannah had gone off with her cousin. It was a lie, the whole of it. Jacob Ware told me that he saw her get into one of your wagons."

"Well, you can search the wagons."

"And we will search them."

A thought struck me. I had been considered good at sketching; could I not communicate to him a knowledge of his sister in that way? Pencil and paper were handy, no one was with me but the children, and I began. In a few minutes I had formed a tolerable picture of a horse, with two women on his back, flying over the hills. When it came the turn of our wagon to be searched, I contrived to slip it unperceived into his hand, and by a gesture enjoined silence. He thrust the paper into his pocket, and a moment after retired beyond observation. Rejoining the others, he gazed earnestly and steadfastly at me, when I pointed the direction they had taken. He nodded assentingly.

"Are you now satisfied?" inquired Mr. Ward, when the wagons were all searched.

"I am not," answered the young man; "your company are not all here."

"Are not? and who is missing, pray?"

"That tall, elegant woman, with such a dignified aspect and carriage, and that ambling pony, for which I offered two hundred dollars last night. That pony would carry double finely;" and giving a significant whistle, his party mounted almost in a second, and set off at full speed.

The Mormons appeared actually paralyzed.

"Some one must have given him a hint," he said, soliloquizing.

"A hint of what?"

"Nothing," he answered, suddenly recalled to consideration.
"Nothing, at least that concerns you."

The cavalcade now moved on, but it was very evident that unusual apprehensions were entertained by the saints. Every countenance wore a look of anxiety, and every eye was occasionally strained far off in the distance, as if to discover if possible some traces of the fugitives. At least two hours elapsed, when we caught the sound of firearms, discharged apparently in a neighboring wood. Then loud voices, two or three screams, and all became silent.

CHAPTER VI.

THE RECAPTURE.

"I THINK," said Mr. Ward, "that we must send some of our men off to see what is going on."

Three of the horsemen were accordingly directed to ride off into the woods, and reconnoitre. They soon returned, bringing Mrs. Bradish severely wounded, and almost suffocated with rage.

I was seriously alarmed, as the blood was flowing freshly from a deep wound in her arm. Her hair was dishevelled, her bonnet gone, her clothes torn, and in the wildest disorder. The whole party crowded round her, asking a thousand questions in a breath. "How had it all happened?" "Where was Hannah?" "Where was Bounding Bet?"

Mr. Ward thrust them aside, and kindly interrogated her as to the cause and extent of her misfortunes.

"Oh, the wretches!" she shrieked, "that I should live to tell it—that Anna Bradish should be beaten by a parcel of boys."

"Never mind that," he said, "but tell us how it happened."

"We rode pretty smart at first," she commenced, "but—oh, Mrs. Ward, you hurt my arm dreadfully. What are you doing?"

"I am trying to dress the wound, but I fear the bone is broken, or the joint injured, or both," I answered.

"Well, like enough; the ball went right through it."

"Let me see," said Mr. Ward.

He examined the wound, and having some general knowledge of surgical affairs, soon decided that the bone was severely shattered. One of the party was instantly dispatched to a neighboring village for a surgeon, and an encampment made on the border of the wood to wait his arrival. Mrs. Bradish refused to lie down, but sat in an arm-chair to rehearse her adventure.

"Where is Smith?" she said; "I don't see him."

The lady was irritated, and left off the cognomen of brother.

"Round yonder, behind the wagons," said some one.

"Oh! I see," she said sarcastically. "He is ashamed of himself. I don't wonder—these new converts of his are always getting us into trouble."

"Mrs. Bradish, you forget yourself," said Mr. Ward.

"At any rate I want him to hear just how I have been outraged and insulted on his account."

"On account of the truth," suggested Mr. Ward.

Smith soon came up to the lady, and condoled with her misfortunes, said that he had been detained by a vision which assured him that she would speedily recover, and that great honors and rewards would recompense her in the next world for all she suffered in this. Some of the more zealous wished him to exert his miraculous powers, and restore her arm at once.

He said that it was forbidden on account of their want of faith, that he believed there was an Achan in the camp, and that the accursed thing must be found out and expunged.

The countenance of Mrs. Bradish expressed anything but satisfaction at this harangue. At length she said :

"Brother Smith, my advice is that you attempt no more conversions among these heathen women. Trouble always comes of it. Now Bounding Bet is killed, and I am wounded, for that silly thing, Hannah."

"Bounding Bet killed?" cried Irene, who had come up, and stood listening to the conversation.

"To be sure she is. The wretches shot her as they would a hill sheep-dog."

Smith, who probably feared that his sacredness in her eyes might suffer by the remarks of Mrs. Bradish, commanded her to retire. She obeyed with evident reluctance, as her curiosity was unsatisfied.

According to the account of Mrs. Bradish, she had been pursued, and suddenly overtaken, while pausing to rest in the wood. Depending on the speed of her palfrey, she started off on a sharp gallop. The boys seeing the game so near, gave a loud halloo, and took after her. Bounding Bet, however, was distancing them finely, when some one fired a ball at her with deadly effect. It was followed by another and another. The palfrey fell. Hannah screamed, and Mrs. Bradish with great difficulty extricated herself from the fallen horse, only to be seized and maltreated by her enemies.

"And Hannah?"

"The wretches took her with them; her brother positively swearing that he would give her a horsewhipping when he got home."

"Well, she deserves it; that I know, miserable, silly dupe," I remarked.

4

The countenance of Ellen glowed with an expression I could not fathom. It seemed a mixture of joy, sorrow, astonishment, and gratification. She stood near me when the surgeon came. He examined the wound, expressed his opinion of its severity, and his fears that an amputation would be necessary.

This she steadfastly refused. Her body, she said, came into the world without any deficiency, it should go to the grave in the same condition. In vain we reasoned and argued. She would trust in Providence, and we were constrained to yield. He declared, however, that travelling was out of the question, and so it was decided to remain in the encampment two or three days.

"This seems a very remarkable wound to have been made in the manner you describe," said the surgeon, when he came the next day. "I thought so, yesterday; it is still more apparent to-day. If I understood you aright, you were thrown from your horse?"

"I was thrown from my horse," said the lady briefly.

"And yet here is every evidence of a pistol-shot wound."

"Mr. Surgeon," said Mrs. Bradish, "I understand your curiosity. Your village, the same as all others, has its gossip without any doubt. We, as Mormons, are despised and persecuted. Falsehoods are circulated, vile rumors raised and reported purposely to draw on us the contempt of the community. What you may have heard I cannot tell. The facts are these: I had a beautiful palfrey that I rode when weary and tired of jostling in the wagon. Yesterday morning I fancied it would be exceedingly pleasant to gallop through the woods. There I was waylaid, my horse shot under me, and myself wounded as you see."

The surgeon, on hearing this, wondered what the country was coming to; said it was hardly safe for a man to ride alone, much less a woman; supposed that the rascals might be apprehended, as they certainly deserved to be; and even offered to bring a lawyer to consult with them on the subject. Mrs. Bradish did not consider it desirable. For her part, she looked for justice to a Higher Power. The saints could not expect peace and happiness in this world, but their reward in the next was certain.

"Great consolation in that," said the surgeon.

I caught his eye that moment, when he turned away to conceal his laughter. He evidently understood the game.

He subsequently informed me that the adventure of Mrs. Bradish had created a great sensation through the country. Indeed, how could it be otherwise?

"You were very popular," said the little man—"very popular before this happened; everybody wanted to make you a visit. Your Prophet here was the principal talk of the women."

"And yet very few of them knew anything about him, or, if they had visited us, ascertained his identity," said I.

"Likely enough. I think, however, I have heard at least a dozen descriptions of him," returned the surgeon. "Some said he was a handsome man, tall and elegant in demeanor, that his hair and eyes were black, and that he wore magnificent whiskers. Another asserted quite as positively that he was a small man, with light hair, blue eyes and red whiskers; and yet another asserted that he wore no whiskers at all."

"They were all deceived," I answered. "The fact is, he wishes to travel without being known. When people have visited the encampment, and requested to see him, some one of the Mormons has been pointed out to them, and they have gone away in the belief that they had seen and spoken to the great Mormon Prophet. This accounts for the discrepancies."

"It does, indeed," he said laughing; "but since that unfortunate adventure all the old women in the neighborhood regard you as a band of kidnappers, and not a few are confident in their assertions that Smith is in league with the Old One himself. Old Mrs. Pettigrew said she couldn't sleep at night for thinking of it ; all the girls are kept closely housed after dark, and very few men venture abroad. Some of them are even concerned about me, but I tell them that a physician can defy the devil !"

"At any rate, such as belong to our company. Smith is possessed with a mania to make converts," said I.

"And his greatest success is among the women. Excuse me, madam, but that is always the case. Fanatics of every class and character find their devotees in that class of the community. It matters not how great the absurdity, how ridiculous and contrary to common sense the doctrine, women will be smitten with it, and many are weak enough to abandon comfortable homes and situations, in order to follow some mad fanatic, or be the dupe of some knavish impostor."

The third morning after the disaster, the surgeon called again, examined his patient, expressed his gratification that the symptoms were so favorable, and concluded by giving us a friendly warning to move.

"And that we will readily do," said Mr. Ward, "if this lady can be removed with safety."

"The danger will be greater, perhaps, if she stays, than if she goes. The fact is, the country is getting too hot to hold you."

"What's the matter?" said Mrs. Bradish, who, from her litter could only catch a word or two of the conversation.

"I'm telling these people that the country is getting too hot to hold you," said the surgeon.

"I wish to the Lord we were out of it," she answered.

"And the best thing you can do will be to get out this day."

"What new mine has been sprung ?" asked Mr. Ward.

"Well, that Hannah of your acquaintance."

"Not mine," said Mr. Ward.

"Your Prophet's, then, has made certain disclosures to her mother that set them all on fire—touched 'em off just like a powder magazine. There was a meeting about it last night, and it was settled that if you stayed another night in this locality, something should be done."

"And what might the something be?"

"Various ugly and dirty tricks which it would be a disgrace to any community to have perpetrated in its midst, and by its members. But you know it's quite as difficult to disgrace some kinds of people as it is to spoil some kinds of meat," and the little surgeon laughed at his own wit.

Thanking the surgeon for his friendly information, Mr. Ward at once proceeded to make immediate preparations for our departure. Mrs. Bradish was placed in a bed, on one of the wagons, the goods packed away, the cattle collected, and before an hour had passed, the company had taken up its line of march.

The surgeon, whose course lay for a short distance in the same direction, rode by the side of our wagon. When the place came to separate, we again thanked him, and Mrs. Bradish did not forget to remunerate him amply.

"And now," he said, "as you confess that I have done you some little kindness, I have a favor to ask."

"Name it, and if it is anything within the bounds of reason, you shall be gratified."

"I wish to know which one of these men is the Prophet—not a spurious article, but the veritable man, himself."

"You will betray his disguise while we are in the country?" said Mr. Ward, inquiringly.

"Indeed I would not."

"He is that man, yonder, in the wagon with those women."

"What, that very old-looking man?"

"Yes; that's the one."

"Why, I suspected that he was young, not over middle-aged, certainly."

"Have I not told you that he is in disguise?"

"Oh, I forgot; yes, yes."

The little surgeon, having looked and gazed at Smith till entirely satisfied, bade us farewell, and went on his way.

There was a man in the company named Peter Short, who, to excessive boorishness of manner united a most repulsive countenance and forbidding disposition. He was extremely ignorant, having not even mastered the first rudiments of education. But, as might be expected, he was a great devotee, a firm believer in all the visions and miracles of the Prophet, and the firm adherent of all his doctrines. Peter, though already possessing a wife and ten children, seemed to have been struck with the pensive grace and beauty of Ellen. He seemed never to weary of gazing at her, or talking to her, though it was equally perceptible that she loathed and hated him. She rarely looked towards him, answered his questions only by monosyllables, and otherwise manifested every symptom of dislike to him and his society. I had frequent opportunities for observing this, and it seemed to me, from the first, that some difficulty would grow out of it. I was walking a little apart from the others, when Ellen came to me, pale as death, and trembling with agitation.

"Oh, Mrs. Ward!" she said, "I have come to you as the only person on earth in whom I can confide. What shall I do? Can't you save me from this dreadful fate?"

"What is it, Ellen?" I said, soothingly; "what new trouble has happened to you?"

"Oh, that horrible Peter Short! They certainly wish to kill me, or they would save me from him."

"My dear," said I, "compose yourself, and let me know the whole affair."

"And the whole affair can be summed up in a few words.

Peter Short has asked me of Smith for his spiritual wife. Smith has consented, and now commands me to accept him as my husband in the faith—him I loathe, and hate, and despise, as I never hated man before."

"But your mother—cannot she save you from this fate?"

"My mother is blinded and bigoted. She says that I must obey the commands of the Prophet, and that nothing he orders can be wrong. But it cannot be so. Has he not connived at murder, and deception, and all kinds of vice? Has he not ruined me already, soul and body? Has he not made me a thing to be pitied and abhorred by the pure? But this has overflowed the cup. I might have borne the rest; I might have hidden my shame and sorrow, and obtained peace and content at last. But to be transferred from one villain to another, is awful—horrible."

"What do they mean by spiritual wife?"

"You know Smith teaches that women can only be saved through their husbands; and that unmarried females must be ever debarred from the pleasures of the blest. Consequently every woman must be provided with a spiritual husband. In that capacity, myself, Mrs. Cook, Mrs. Clarke, and Irene, have been the wives of Smith. Now he has tired of me. He will soon tire of them. Oh, misery!"

Greatly as I pitied the poor girl, it was impossible, under the circumstances, to give her advice; and so assuring her of my sympathy and friendship, and recommending her to put off the evil day as long as possible; and that probably something might happen to prevent it altogether, I left her.

The next morning, Ellen was missing; and when search was made, her body was found in the cool depths of a pool that lay a short distance from the encampment. They laid her out on the smooth, green sward, and one after another came to look on the pale, sweet face, and to touch the pallid hand. Smith came among the rest, and so did Peter Short. Yet the wan lips uttered no cry of vengeance against them; the dim eyes no longer turned from their presence. She slept to wake no more.

"This is really death," I thought; "beyond dispute or question, it is death; and will Smith endeavor to restore her to life —she, his spiritual wife—the daughter of his church, and the companion of his journey to the Promised Land?"

Mrs. Bradley was strong in the faith.

My daughter," she said, in the utmost confidence, "my daughter shall live again."

"Not till the resurrection at the Last Day," said Smith, who heard the remark. "The suicide is accursed."

The poor mother gave a faint shriek.

"Yes," he continued, with the most brutal indifference to her feelings, "an angel could not restore the life of a person who had thus voluntarily surrendered it."

"But you don't know as she did—you don't know as she did; she might have fallen in there," said the mother.

"No one could be drowned where she was, unless the act was voluntary," said Smith.

"And why should such an act be voluntary?" I said, approaching where they were standing, and eyeing him sternly; "to whose cruelty and depravity is it to be attributed, that one so young and beautiful became thus early tired of life? Whose fanaticism blighted the hopes of that pure spirit, degraded her aspirations for love and truth, and turned the sweetness of her life to gall and wormwood? 'The suicide accursed!' Say, rather, that those men are cursed, whose vileness makes death a last resource to the weak, against crime and oppression."

"And who shall say that this was the case with Ellen?" inquired Smith.

"I say so. With her own lips she told me of her sorrows and persecutions, and your vileness. Yes, Joseph Smith, Prophet and priest, as you pretend to be, of your vileness, your hateful arts and impostures; but she is dead, now—you can torment her no more."

Smith walked away muttering imprecations.

Mrs. Bradley seemed actually frightened at my boldness. I could only regard her with pity and contempt.

Ellen was buried in a green shady place beside the wood. Smith would not attend the ceremony, and no prayer was uttered, not a passage of Scripture read. Was the wretch angry that his victim had escaped him? Was he angry at me for questioning his authority and inspiration? Probably both.

CHAPTER VII.

THE MORMON SETTLEMENT.

WHEN we reached the Mormon settlement, in Illinois, Mrs. Bradish had recovered from her injuries. A naturally strong constitution, and remarkably firm will, had accomplished the cure independent of spiritual or miraculous agencies. She was active as ever again, going hither and thither, counselling one, commanding another, and reproving a third, yet all seemingly in the same breath.

"And how do you like the Promised Land?" said Mr. Ward to her one day, after she had been unusually busy for a long time, trying to overcome the stubbornness of some friends, who persisted in doing as they thought proper, contrary to her advice.

"I should like it first rate, if these children would do as I bid them, but they're just like the heathen. Every one must have his own way."

To me, however, the situation of affairs looked anything but promising. The Mormon village contained about fifty houses, and every house could number two or three families. They were of every imaginable size, shape, and description ; that is, to begin at ordinary log dwellings, and descend in regular gradation to the meanest and most contemptible of hovels. Many of them had neither floors nor chimneys, quite a proportion were without either doors or windows. When these accommodations were possessed, the rudest materials had been employed in their construction. The people were generally poor, and the multitudes of children exceeded all belief. Very few of these seemed at all acquainted with the appurtenances belonging to civilization. They certainly resembled young savages much more than the offspring of the Faithful. With faces unwashed, hair uncombed, and feet so long ignorant of shoes or covering that they appeared of the color and consistence of huge toads. The females did not appear much better ; indeed, what could be expected of them ? All intercourse with the heathen having been precluded, thorns were used instead of pins ; there was but one needle in the village, and that was rarely called into exercise, it was so seldom that thread could be obtained. The most ordinary and indispensable toilet appendages were unknown. Great girls of ten or twelve had nearly forgotten the use of a mirror. The cheapest and coarsest calico was esteemed a real luxury. Wooden bowls served for cups, and plates of the same material were used instead of Queensware. To be sure, we enjoyed more comforts than the others, as having recently arrived, our stock was not exhausted. But we were plagued and worried incessantly by borrowers. One wanted the pot, another the kettle, a third the pail. Many household articles took a regular round through the village, and only arrived at home to commence a new start. Our house was superior to most of the others in many respects. It had a plank floor, a **chimney of unhewn, unmortared stones, a covering of bark, a** door that had been transferred from a neighboring barn, a window containing four panes of glass, and other things in conformity. The staircase was a ladder, the cupboard a couple of rude shelves, the wardrobe a corner, and the chamber a lumber-room. There were no conveniences. An oven was a thing unknown, but there were two churns, three washing-tubs, and one tin baker.

Subsequently, however, matters changed. It was decided that the church should open a store. By the church we are to understand the elders and prophets, with Smith at their head. The goods were a joint concern. A young man, son of one of the proprietors, was shopman ; and we congratulated ourselves on the prospect of once more possessing the necessaries of housekeeping. We soon found ourselves mistaken. The goods were of the poorest quality, and the prices most enormous. Three-fourths of the articles were damaged. The dishes were cracked, the calico streaked, the clothing soiled. The ginger was a combination of red pepper and corn meal, the spice had been adulterated, the black pepper mixed with something, it was impossible to tell what ; and, to cap the climax, the tea, by some mischance or other, had become so deeply imbued with the taste of spirits of turpentine, that it was impossible for any mortal man, or woman either, to drink it. Mrs. Bradish finally became outrageous. She had been accustomed to comforts and luxuries, and consequently felt the present restriction in a greater degree. For her part, she considered it too bad that the heathen should be permitted to appropriate all the good things ; she could see no reason why the saints were not entitled to a reasonable share, or, so far as that was concerned, to the whole. Smith, however, and the elders were inexorable, and the faithful were forbidden, under the penalties of excommunication and anathema, to have any dealings with the heathen. In fact, the store was nothing but a great swindling speculation on the part of the

Mormon leaders. They bought up worthless articles for almost nothing, and then, exacting a great price, sought to compel the believers to purchase them. In this way they doubled and trebled their outlay.

Soon after our arrival, a school was established, and Irene installed by Smith as teacher. This institution partook of the ludicrous in no small degree, and was certainly a great relief to the matrons of the place. But it is rarely the lot of man to witness such a combination of dirt, rags, filth and ugliness, as was there exhibited. All were sadly ignorant, and very few manifested any desire to learn. The exercises were chiefly oral, as books could not be obtained, neither would they have been admitted if obtainable. Smith formed a small volume in manuscript, which he gave to Irene, and from which she instructed the children in the duties and principles of Mormonism. In style and manner, it was a direct imitation of the Catechism. This, with instructions in reading from the Mormon Bible, and a little writing on thin greasy paper, completed the course of instruction.

To secure their further independence, they determined to have a bank, of which the circulating medium was to be confined to themselves. But, although professing to despise the heathen, they were anxious to be considered by them in good circumstances. Accordingly, when the building designed for the bank was ready, an unbeliever was employed to assist them to remove the specie into the vaults. This was contained in a great many kegs, all very heavy, and the coverings of some being removed, displayed the gold beneath. However, it was subsequently ascertained that the kegs were filled with lead, a very small quantity of gold being placed on the top.

Mrs. Bradish took an active part in all the public business. She was a directress of the bank, and a visitor at the school. I even thought that her antipathy to the store was owing, in one sense, to the fact that her name was not included in the list of proprietors. But my domestic affairs were quite sufficient for me, and I meddled very little with them or their doings.

I had one friend in the village—a good, kind woman, who had removed from her home in New York, the season previous. She had been accustomed to all the elegances and appliances of wealth ; but she bore the great change in her fortunes with singular fortitude. Her dwelling, though rude and inconvenient like the others, was always scrupulously neat and clean. Her benches and tables were sweet and pure, from frequent ablutions ; and her children, though poorly furnished and coarsely clad, were always clean. We enjoyed long and frequent conversations ; and I soon discovered that she was far from being pleased with the moral, or rather immoral, practices of the Mormons. Her husband and herself were among the first converts to the new doctrines. They had been deceived by the artful impositions of Smith, and his pretended power of working miracles. Impulsive, generous, and unsuspecting, both embraced the cause with ardor ; embarked their property in the enterprise, but found, when too late, that there was more pretence than reality—more appearance than substance. At least, such was the case with her.

The husband became imbued with ambitious views ; he aspired to become an elder and leader, and even fancied himself to be the favored recipient of divine communications.

"Oh, Mr. Murray," she said to him, one day, in my presence, after he had been relating his wondrous exercise of mind, "it seems to me that you must be deceived."

"Impossible," he answered, sharply.

"But it is very possible," she returned kindly.

"What should a woman know of such things?" he retorted.

Mrs. Murray was too noble and high-minded to weep or change countenance at her husband's taunt.

"Mr. Murray speaks rather slightly of the women," I remarked.

"Yes; it is a way he has acquired lately," she answered. "I sometimes fear that my happiest days are past. We are so differently situated from what we were; but maybe it is all for the best;" and she tried to smile.

"Of course, good may come out of evil," I said.

"I frequently think," she said, "of what our good old pastor told me. He was a venerable man, near eighty years of age. He had carried me in his arms a thousand times, that I know. He baptised me and my husband, both in one day. We had sat under his ministry, and partook of the bread of the Sacrament at his hands, for years; and he actually wept when he learned that we were going with the Mormons. 'For your sake, Mary,' he said, when he came to bid us farewell, 'for your soul's sake, my dear, lost daughter, consider well this thing; but more especially for the sake of your husband. Cast among that abandoned, outcast crew, for I must call them so, he will be exposed to temptations which you cannot understand, and of which, probably, you can have no perception. Oh, that you could be induced to remain with the friends of your youth! for much I fear that this day will be to you the beginning of sorrow.' My husband is no longer what he was," she continued. "He is dissatisfied with me, and angry at the children often and often, when I find it impossible to divine in what manner I have displeased him. He spends much of his time away from home, and not unfrequently two or three nights at a time."

A frightful thought seized me.

"Mrs. Murray, excuse me for the question," I said, "but is your husband a convert to the theory of spiritual wives?"

"Indeed, Mrs. Ward, I know not; but fear so."

"Then, you had thought of it?"

"Certainly; but I have no means of ascertaining. Neither

can I say that the knowledge would be agreeable to me. How could I bear to think of holding the second place in his affections? It seems to me that that doctrine is from the devil."

"And so are the other Mormon doctrines, in my opinion."

"At one time," said Mrs. Murray, "in the blindness of my enthusiasm, I attributed to Smith the power and attributes of a Divinity; but the scales have fallen from my eyes, and he seems to me an impostor of the vilest character."

"But would it be safe to speak thus plainly of him in public?"

"No; it would not."

"If it is discovered that one is disaffected, I suppose that he or she is excommunicated?"

"Something more than that is done with them;" and she approached so closely as to whisper the last sentence in my ear. I thought of Ellen's murdered infant, and asked—

"What is it, Mrs. Murray?"

"They disappear!"

"You alarm me, Mrs. Murray."

"As I said, they disappear—how, or in what manner, has not been ascertained."

"Are you certain of what you say?"

"Listen, and I will tell you; but remember not a word of it must be breathed to any one. A young man named Harrison, joined the Mormons some time ago. He was brave, upright, and intelligent, more so than ordinary. I perceived at once, that he had been deceived by their specious professions of piety, and meditated with myself on the result when he discovered their impositions. Everything went on smooth enough, for perhaps a month, when a regular breeze broke forth. I knew nothing about it, until Harrison came in here. His countenance was pale with suppressed passion, but he entered, though rather indifferently, into general conversation. At length, I inquired how he liked the Mormons, by this time.

"'Not at all, Mrs. Murray; indeed, I have come to the conclusion to leave them entirely; nor is that all, I design to expose them to the world. We had a regular breeze yesterday, Smith and I. I told him just what I had found him to be, a fool, knave, liar, and impostor. I talked pretty plain, I can tell you.'

"'And what did he say?'

"'He laughed; but such a laugh, it made me shudder. "Oh! you can laugh if you please," said I, "but you will rather quail to have your villainies exposed to the world, and exposed they shall be. Yes, sir; the world shall know all about you, your pretended miracles, your bank with lead instead of gold, and all the mean, contemptible trickeries, to which I have been a witness."'

"'You will wait until you have an opportunity to expose me, won't you?' said Smith.

"'An opportunity will soon present itself,' I answered.

"'Smith muttered something to himself, as he turned away.'

"'And where are you going, Harrison?' I inquired.

"'Back to my father's,' he answered.

"'Oh! how I wanted to warn him!' at length, I said.

"'You had better be careful how you offend Smith, and take good care of yourself.'

"'To be sure, I will do that.'

"He soon after took leave. The next day he started for his father's residence, and now read that"—as she spoke, she drew from her pocket a small piece of newspaper—"I picked it up along the street."

I read,

"FOUND DEAD.—A young man by the name of Harrison, was found dead in the woods day before yesterday. To all appearance he had been shot. We have no clue to the murderers."

I returned her the paper without saying a word, and she continued: "Another circumstance happened about eighteen months ago, which came more immediately beneath my knowledge. It was during a former visit of Smith to this place, that he brought to my house a beautiful young woman, and introduced her to me as a new convert. Her appearance was highly interesting, and she had evidently been accustomed to good society. Her name was Sarah Sweet, and she stayed with me, until I felt for her almost the tenderness that a mother feels for her child. One day I left her to call on a friend. When I returned she was weeping and lamenting bitterly.

"'Why, Sarah, what is the matter?' I inquired.

"'Oh! Mrs. Murray, what shall I do?' she almost shrieked, 'Smith has been here. The man whom I thought a prophet of the Lord, whose word I reverenced as of divine inspiration. And he seeks my ruin, soul and body; I dare not tell you all he said, but oh! I fear that I shall go mad?'

"'Compose yourself, my dear,' I said, 'you can go back to your parents, and with them you will be happy.'

"'Yes, I will do so,' she replied. 'Oh! what a fool I was to leave them; and once there, I will expose him and all his wicked practices, to prevent others from falling into the snare.'

"'Did you tell him so?'

"'To be sure I did, but he only laughed a hideous kind of laugh, and said "very well."'

"'Well, Sarah, my advice is, that you be very secret and cautious in your movements. How do you design to return to your father's?'

"'On foot, of course, there is no other way.'

"Sarah busied herself in making preparations to depart. Two or three women came in. 'What, Sarah, going to leave us?' said one. 'What's in the wind now?' inquired another.

"Sarah gave them little satisfaction, but they saw enough, Mrs. Murray paused, overcame with emotion.

"And how did it end?" I inquired.

"The poor girl started for her home, but never arrived there. She was found drowned."

At this stage of the conversation other visitors came in, and I took leave.

A few days after, Mrs. Murray called on me. After the exchange of compliments, "I have found it all out," she said, sighing.

"Found out what?"

"About my husband's spiritual wife."

"Then it was as I suspected?"

"Yes, and he told me of it himself, and even proposed to bring her to reside with us."

"And what did you tell him?"

"That if she came, I would go away; and he said, 'No, madam, you won't. Among the Mormons, husbands are lords. They have the privilege of punishing disobedient wives, and enforcing their homage.' Oh! that I had listened to the voice of my pastor; he foresaw all this."

"Who is the woman, with whom your husband has formed that connection?"

"Why, a woman that came with Smith, in your company, one Mrs. Cook."

"Is it possible?"

"It is, and oh! that I should live to see it, should live to feel myself occupying the second place in my husband's heart."

"Could you not return to your friends?"

"I would gladly do so, if I had the means, but it is the policy of these men, to keep everything like money out of the reach of the women; and then I suppose my fate would be like that of Sarah."

"It is more than probable."

"I could not leave my children," she said. "Oh! I am

sorely tried, but I feel, I know, that it is just, I am only reaping the reward of my doings."

CHAPTER VIII.

MORMON FAITH AND WORSHIP.

THE idea of a temporal millenium is one of the most important principles of Mormonism, and the one most cherished by the believers.. They speak of it on all occasions, and many of them indulge the most fantastic and absurd notions with respect to the state and degree of happiness to be enjoyed.

The Mormons are no exception to the general rule, that the character and temper of a people may be safely judged by their opinions of what is to constitute their happiness hereafter. Thus, the warlike Scandinavians placed the souls of the heroes in Valhalla, where they enjoyed the feast of victory perpetually, and never wearied of drinking mead from the skulls of their enemies. The Mahometan anticipates the balmy shades, cooling fountains, and black-eyed houris; while the Indian is to enjoy an everlasting season of hunting, and chase the wild deer with dogs swifter than the wind.

The Mormons, being generally devoted to simple customs, and agricultural habits, anticipate a millenium, in which the curse is to be removed from the earth, when all venomous beasts, and insects, and wicked men are to be destroyed; all poisonous plants and noxious weeds eradicated; and nature produce, in spontaneous abundance, all the good things of life.

Their opinions on other subjects are no less fantastic and absurd. Their standard of morality is different from that of other sects. To give money to the church, preach the Gospel, and have dreams and visions, were considered the most meritorious acts.

And judged by this system of morals they are all over-righteous. They are all dreamers, but the elders only have the privilege of interpreting. Smith, while he lived, monopolized the business exclusively. Many of them prophesy, but only the elders can detect whether they are moved on by a truthful or a lying spirit; and as to the preachers it is scarcely possible to discover anything like order or consistency in their discourses. They all turn on the everlasting hinge of living and reigning with Christ a thousand years.

Their worship is a strange mixture of Jewish and Christian ceremonies. Their civil polity resembles that of the Jews in many particulars. The head of the church is temporal governor, and they acknowledge the force of no laws save those of their own formation.

Mormonism is continually changing, and many doctrines are taught at present, which were unknown to the founders of the faith. Polygamy, was not openly advocated for some time. In the first place, the spiritual wife was said to be united to her husband, by a purely spiritual tie, independent of all sensual relations, and this once admitted, soon led to the other.

And then the temple, which was designed to be the seat of their worship in after ages, and occupied the centre of what they were pleased to denominate the Promised Land, was to be a sort of Mecca, to which the pilgrims of future generations were to resort. Mrs. Murray said to me one day:—

"I long ago became disgusted with the bombast and rant of the Mormon preachers, with their constant reference to dreams, and visions, and miracles; with their abuse of the heathen, as they termed our neighbors. Sometimes, however, these things took a ludicrous character. Old Mrs. Harris came to our house one day, in search of Smith. 'She had a marvellous dream the night before,' to employ her phraseology, and now was in pursuit of the interpreter.

"'And what was your dream, Mrs. Harris?' I inquired.

"'Oh! I would like to tell you, that I would,' said the crone; 'but the Lord has commanded, through the mouth of his prophet, that our dreams should first be told to him.'

"'Oh! well,' I said, 'it don't matter.'

"'But it does tho'. I want you to know what it is, and after it is interpreted I will tell you.'

"Smith made the interpretation of dreams a source of revenue; for the interpretation was not given till the interpreter was rewarded, and the reward was always proportioned to the wealth of the dreamer.

"For the same reason, I suppose, he endeavored to make them all converts to the doctrine of witchcraft. How well he succeeded will astonish no one who is acquainted with the superstitious tendencies of human nature. In an incredibly short time a multitude of children were bewitched, or believed to be by their parents and friends. Smith in all cases undertook the cure, but only for a handsome consideration.

"Trances were not at all uncommon. It was decidedly unfashionable not to have been in a trance. Almost every one could give a tolerably fair description of Heaven, could tell exactly how Abraham, Isaac, and Jacob looked, the seats beside the throne they occupied, and the robes they wore.

"Many of these descriptions were infinitely amusing. One old woman, who had been noted for industry, declared that Heaven, as it appeared to her, was a very nice cool room, where they had plenty of biscuit, and didn't have to work. Another said, 'she didn't see any biscuit, but they had very fine garments, and sat in rocking-chairs all day.'

"'But is there any night, Becca?' said a gaping listener.

"'Something like it ; kind of a night ; of course they want to rest.'

"'But they don't work?'

"'No; yet they sing, and shout, and march round, you know, and that's nearly as tiresome.'

"'But who did you see there, Becca?'

"'Oh! a great many, but they were all Mormons.'

"Smith here stepped forth and said, he supposed some good men had gone to Heaven before Mormonism was revealed. Indeed, he knew that was the case ; for once, and only a short time, too, after the blessed revelation had been made known to him, he was travelling alone in a wood, when he heard his voice called, and turning, beheld an angel. This angel was commissioned to carry him to Heaven, that he might preach the good news of Mormonism there. He consented, and in two days' time had converted all the heavenly inhabitants.

"Mormonism, perhaps, more than any other religion, is continually changing its phases. It has no stereotyped dogmas to which its teachers are required to give unqualified assent. It has no colleges, where its youth are trained to believe just what their elders tell them, and nothing more. If they will assert that Smith was a true prophet, the Book of Mormon a true history, and the Mormon people the only true church, little more is required of them. They are never asked, which is the most heinous, 'the sin of omission or commission?' whether the human heart is totally or only partially depraved? whether grace is free or restricted? or whether the saints can fall out by the way, or must persevere to the end.

"In short," said Mrs. Murray, "take away the dreams, and visions, and miracles, and very little remains. Its author had not sufficient genius to form a system really great or noble, or one that should be an enduring monument of human ability, but it addresses itself to the venal desires of men, encourages their superstitions, and gratifies their passions. Hence is the secret of its strength."

CHAPTER IX.

MORMON PROPHETS AND ELDERS.

IT is questionable if ever, since the time that Saul was found among the prophets, such a heterogeneous mixture of inspired men, or those professing inspiration, had ever been collected together in one place as frequently assembled at Mormon meetings. Great fat burly men, little short puny men—men who in shape and stature reminded one of ostriches, men with small heads and little sense, or great heads without any sense at all; men well-dressed and ill-dressed. Some had their lips stained with tobacco, the noses of others were smeared with snuff, and the breaths of not a few were rank with whisky. Different nations also were ably represented. Here was a thick-set square-backed Dutchman, eager to talk and take part in the meeting, and highly offended at everybody because they could not tell what he said. Not far off was a Frenchman gabbling and gesticulating, as only a Frenchman can gabble and gesticulate, to a tall raw-boned Irishman, who stood gaping and listening. These men were all elders and prophets. They used to meet together to discuss questions of business, but Smith, who always directed the meetings, would only propose the most indifferent and puerile subjects, and these being hurried over, he would call on them to rehearse their dreams or visions, as well as their success in working miracles.

As the sisters were usually permitted to be present, though generally forbidden to take part in the deliberations, I persnaded Mrs. Murray to accompany me on one occasion. To add to the interest of the meeting several missionaries who had been out preaching had returned, and were expected to give some account of their success.

Smith opened the meeting with prayer, then a hymn of thanksgiving was sung, after which the missionaries, as most to be honored, were requested to speak, beginning with the eldest. The words were scarcely spoken, when a little, puny, withered creature, who, to judge from his phrenological developments, was only a few degrees removed from the idiot, arose.

"Friends, prophets, saints, fellow-laborers, and co-workers," he began, in a sort of squeaking voice, that exceeded beyond all comparison the nasal twang of the Yankee, "I 'steem meself onered, greatly onered, in being ere this night, and, 'bove all, that I be permitted to 'dress this augush 'sembly. It duz me more good than I spress—duz, indeed. You know, brothren, you wern't willin' for me to go out preachin', but I felt it right here [and he laid his hand on his forehead], and here I felt it too [his hand was then applied to the region of the heart]. I knowed that I must tell the good tidings of our great Prophet here or be cursed—brothren, I don't say damned, because that is like the heathen, our enemies. Brothren, I sed I knowed that my duty called me to preach, but I didn't know that I should be called on to suffer martyrdom. Yes, brothren, a martyr and confessor both stands among you."

All eyes were turned to the little speaker, and a smile rested on several countenances.

"Brother Flitter will please be as explicit as possible," said Mr. Ward.

"Tell us of your converts," suggested Smith.

"It pleased the Lord and his Prophet," resumed Flitter, "that I should suffer martyrdom, and three several times I fell into the hands of the enemy."

Mr. Ward rather fidgeted in his seat, and I saw him direct several glances towards Smith, in hopes, I suppose, that he would put a stop to the absurd harangue, but the Prophet, who sat with two confederates behind the altar, seemed perfectly indifferent to the affair. Flitter proceeded:

"My first martyrization was riding hossback; I ain't use to riding that way, and it shook me up all over. I raly thought sometimes that my stomach would tumble out. I think it did get misplaced, and that's one reason why I can't eat corn-bread the way I did once."

"Eat more of it now, I reckon," said a voice.

"No; but just wait till I get through, as I am the oldest missioner, and the one what's suffered martyrdom. Where was I?—let me see?—Oh! I know. Well, the next time was from young chickens. You see, I guv out word that I'd hold a meeting at a school-house. Well, when I went there I didn't see anybody stirrin', so thinks I they hav'n't got here yet, but all of a suddent about twenty boys leaped up from behind the benches, and began firing eggs at me with might and main. I opened my lips to speak, when plump, splash came one right into my mouth. It didn't taste sweet, but that ain't the wurst of it, I hav'n't been able to smell anything since, my nose was so completely numbed with the odor. Brothren, I hope I'm too polite to say stink, but you all know."

Mrs. Bradish had sat for some time looking daggers at the speaker. At length she rose, and cried in a clear, ringing voice:

"Brother Smith, are you asleep?"

"Sister, Sister Bradish," whispered some of the elders.

She paid no attention, but kept her stern black eyes on the face of Smith.

"Brother Smith, are you asleep?" she called, in a louder tone.

"No, sister; I am not," he answered.

"Then, why do you sit there, and hear us insulted in this

manner," she said, "as if we cared anything about you fool's being martyrized with rotten eggs? Now, Flitter, just sit down, and stop your clack, and let some one speak who can do so in a sensible manner. Neither is that all : if you persist in allowing fools to go out and preach in our name, we shall become a laughing-stock among the heathen, if we are not so already."

Flitter seemed rather abashed at this speech, and took his seat in silence.

"Now," continued Mrs. Bradish, "if any of you have anything to say that is edifying, let's hear it."

No one spoke.

"Brother Pratt, please tell us what you have been about," said Mr. Ward.

Brother Pratt arose and looked around on the assembly, with great complacency.

"I cannot say," he began, "that any great success has attended my efforts ; neither have they been altogether fruitless. I have had the great satisfaction of baptising several into a knowledge of the truth. Several of my converts are making preparations to remove hither immediately. Bless the Lord !"

There was a general response of "Bless the Lord," and "Amen." Amid the murmurs of congratulation, Brother Pratt sat down The little Frenchman rose next. He had been on a missionary tour to a colony of French emigrants in a neighboring State.

"My friends,' he commenced, "I hardly know what to say of myself."

"Tell the truth," said Mrs. Bradish.

"Yes, the truth ; but the truth an't what I wanted it to be. Brethren, I done all I could, but it was very little. The miracle wouldn't work at all. I tried it over and over again ; and, because the miracle wouldn't work, they wouldn't believe ; and that's about all of it."

"But you made some converts, didn't you?" inquired Smith.

"Oh, certainly, some few women believed."

"Very well; convert the women—the men will be sure to follow; that's human nature," said Mr. Ward.

The accounts given by the other missionaries contained nothing new or striking; and then the prophets and dreamers were summoned to declare their exercises. It is scarcely possible to imagine greater absurdities, in the line of revery and imagination, than these men repeated as the solemn truths of inspiration. Some had visions of beasts of all imaginable shapes and sizes, with more heads than the hydra of Hercules, and more horns than the mystery of the Apocalypse. Many of them had been severely assaulted and tempted by the devil; and not a few had rejected very large bribes offered by his Sooty Majesty. To one he appeared sitting on a stump, smoking tobacco, with a rope in his hand; but the uses of the rope were not specified. One had even been favored with a vision of the Almighty, and informed by the Divine Personage that, if he would go on in the way he had begun, and take Rachel Allan for his spiritual wife, his way would be prospered.

Is not the reader weary of these absurdities? Certainly, I am weary of repeating them.

CHAPTER X.

MORMON CHURCH GOVERNMENT.

THE church government of the Mormons resembles that of the Catholic hierarchy, in many respects. Smith, while he lived, was pope. He put just what interpretation he pleased on the sacred Book of Mormon, fabricated just what new dogmas he thought proper to incorporate in the faith, and was never opposed, so far as my knowledge extends, by any of his followers. Though he professed to allow all the prophets and elders a voice in ecclesiastical affairs, the real business of the church was conducted by himself, with three assistants, and in these three was embodied the greater part of the learning and talents in the church. Mr. Murray had aspired to a seat of honor in the Mormon assembly, but he signally failed. Not discouraged, however, he determined to create a diversion in his favor, and there would, in all probability, have occurred a division in the church, had not the Mormons been required to unite against a common enemy, thus forgetting, for a time, their intestine difficulties.

In fact, the converts to Mormonism were, generally speaking, of the lowest and poorest class. Very few of the prophets or elders had enjoyed the advantages of an ordinary English education. Many of them belonged to that class of religious enthusiasts, who were so plentiful a few years ago, and the acme and aim of whose ambition was to preach. I remember several such. One was a young man who had been half-crazed at a Methodist camp-meeting, thus losing what little sense he had. After this, he used to roam about the country, trying to get school-houses, in which to hold meetings; or stopping at private-houses, and wanting to preach to the inmates. Sometimes he would fix himself in the centre of a village, and, standing there, would shout and preach at the passers-by. When the Mormons came about, he instantly adopted their sentiments.

Another, was one of two brothers, both of whom were smitten with a mania to preach. Both were extremely ignorant, and, even while members of a Seventh-day Baptist society, both were favored with dreams and visions. The eldest, however, succeeded in getting himself adopted pastor of the church, and then he opposed, by every means in his power, the preaching designs of his brother. And so, when the Mormons extended to him the right hand of fellowship, he could not resist their invitation to become an elder.

"The way of truth is so plain," said Smith, "that a fool can point it out just as well as anybody. Let those who are considered fools by their neighbors and relatives come to us—we will make them kings and priests."

And certainly a multitude of fools accepted the invitation.

"Let a man come to me, believe my gospel and preach it, and all his sins shall be forgiven. He shall have riches, honors, and all the wives he wishes for in this world, and in the next, life everlasting."

And thieves, and cut-throats, and swindlers accepted the offer.

Mrs. Murray one day gave me the history of several Mormon leaders of this latter class. One had served ten years of his life in the State Prison. He had been convicted of robbing the mail, but before he was taken had concealed the money, and when his term was expired joined the Mormons with his booty. Any one who brought gold to the coffers of the church was welcomed, and so this desperado was immediately taken to the embrace of the faithful, and two or three beautiful girls, or girls that would have been beautiful, with suitable dress and adornments, were bestowed on him for spiritual wives.

Another had been convicted of murder, though subsequently pardoned by the Governor of the State. Others had been convicted and punished for grand larceny and other crimes, but their delinquencies were forbidden to be spoken of, and every one was commanded to treat them with respect.

"How is it possible, Mr. Ward, that you can associate with such men on terms of equality? I pray that you will not bring them here to dine with me again."

"You are unreasonable, madam," he answered, "they are our tools to work with."

"I do not understand you," I replied.

"But you will, when we have won a kingdom, and find ourselves placed among the noble and great ones of the earth."

"Won a kingdom! Your language is still more mysterious," I answered. "Please be explicit."

"Do you suppose that we, the followers of a new faith, and the organizers of a new system, are always to be held in leading strings. Our policy is to become independent of the heathen, in civil as well as social matters. We will have our own laws, institutions and government."

"But how is all this to be accomplished?"

"By accommodating ourselves to all kinds of people that can be of any service to us when the struggle comes."

"But you do not meditate treason against the United States Government, do you? If such is the case, beware."

"What is the United States to me, that I should remain in obedience to a form of laws and state of society that my soul abhors?"

"But you are a subject of that government, and within its jurisdiction must be governed by its laws."

"That may be the case now; it will not be always," he answered. "We look forward to a state and condition of independence, peaceably if we can have it so; if not, by war. Such is the promise of God, and in that we confide."

The wildness of this scheme was only equalled by its temerity, and could only have originated in the brain of enthusiasts or fanatics. Subsequently I obtained a further insight into their views, as likewise what was to be the full development of Mormonism.

Mr. Ward and Mrs. Bradish used frequently to strengthen each other's faith in the good time coming.

I found that, according to their views of polity, all civil government should be administered by the church—that the officers of the church should be considered the nobles of the land—that the church offices should be held hereditarily by certain families—that treason to the church, and the murder of a brother in the faith were the only crimes they considered worthy of death—that a Mormon could not possibly, under any circumstances, be indebted to the heathen, because the world, and all it contained, having been originally intended for the saints, it was their privilege to appropriate whatever they thought proper. Such abominable doctrines were not long in producing their legitimate fruits. If a murderer or assassin fled from justice he was taken at once, protected and concealed by the Mormons; children were persuaded by them to abandon their parents, and silly women, for their sake, not unfrequently left their husbands and relatives.

Every child born of Mormon parents was considered a member of the church. Females were restricted from marrying unbelievers, by the severest penalties. Indeed, according to the rules and practice of Mormonism, are decidedly inferior beings, created to minister to the wants and passions of men, and only admitted to the communion of the faithful in this world and the next, in consideration of the husband. Hence the females were treated little better than slaves, were required to do all the drudgery, were frequently subjected to corporeal punishment, and painfully impressed with a sense of their inferiority in a thousand ways. Having occasion one day to go by the house occupied by the Prophet, Mrs. Clarke and Irene, I saw the former sitting lazily on the door-stone, basking in the sun, while the two women were at work in the neighboring corn-field.

I approached the fence, paused, and spoke. Irene continued her work, looking downcast and moody. Mrs. Clarke rested a moment, but glanced timidly towards her master, said she was in a great hurry—that she had designed to call and see me, but was forbidden to leave home. I bade her farewell, and she hurried on.

A few days afterwards I was sitting alone, when Mrs. Clarke came in. She looked so pale, wan, and disconsolate, that it made one's heart ache to see her. She took my hand, and burst into tears.

"Oh, Mrs. Ward, I am the most miserable creature alive," she exclaimed : "Oh, dear, why did I leave my husband ? why did I ever go near that vile impostor ? I am ruined, soul and body, indeed I am !"

"I hope not so bad as that, Mrs. Clarke."

"Oh, you don't know, you cannot know," she answered, bitterly.

"Mrs. Clarke," I said, "is your distress merely mental, or do you have to undergo physical burdens, for which your strength is incapable ?"

"Alas," she answered, "how is it possible for me to tell you all I suffer, all I have suffered ? How can I describe the bitterness of unceasing remorse ? My husband's countenance of despair and anguish is continually before me ; the cries of my children ring uninterruptedly in my ears. Then the cruelty of this man, for whom I have forsaken all, and the bitter hate of Irene, who employs every means to prejudice him against me."

"But, why should Irene hate you," I inquired.

"She flatters herself with the belief that if I was once out of the way, she would reign as the sole wife and favorite of the Prophet. It was her machinations that induced him to find a new husband for Mrs. Cook. She fabricated some infamous falsehoods about that woman ; accused her of being lazy, said she devoured the delicacies of the table which Smith desired to have reserved for himself. Smith attempted to chastise her with an ox-goad, when she turned on him, scratched and bit him severely, and blackened one of his eyes into the bargain. I think he would have had the worst of it, had not Irene hastened to assist him. As it was, they succeeded in fastening her hands, and confining her in the loft, where she remained until Smith induced Mr. Murray to receive her."

"How abominable!" I exclaimed.

"Irene hates me, and I am afraid of her. There is something in her countenance that puts me continually on my guard. I often see her looking at me with a fiendish expression that makes me shudder; but that is nothing, nothing to what I am forced by him to endure. Look here," and she displayed her arms and bosom black with hideous bruises, "see, these are the marks of beatings that he has given me."

"Oh, Mrs. Clarke, that is dreadful; but how did you offend him?"

"I was sick, and weak, and weary, and did not perform as much labor in the corn-field as he thought I ought to. Oh, my dear abandoned husband, what would you say if you could know my misery!"

"And yet you were delicately nurtured?" I said.

"To be sure I was," she answered, "and entirely unaccustomed to physical labor. Now I am compelled, by stripes and punishment, to perform the most menial drudgery. It really seemed, last winter, that it would be impossible for me to live till spring. I cannot tell you how much I suffered from cold, privation, and weariness. Irene took my best clothes, and then Smith made me wear her old rags. I had no shoes, and yet I was forced to go out in all kinds of weather to pick up and bring home wood, to beg an armful of hay for the cow, that seemed very near starving, as Smith would take no pains whatever to provide even the commonest necessaries of life."

"Well, Mrs. Clarke, I would advise you to escape from them if possible, and return to your friends. They would

5*

gladly receive you, even now, as the repentant prodigal," I said.

"Oh, I know that they would," she answered; "and heaven knows how earnestly I desire it. I could almost weep tears of blood, in my deep repentance, but 'tis all in vain, in vain!"

I looked at the poor woman, and how forcibly were the warnings of her husband recalled to my memory; yet he spoke not in anger, but sorrow. Did she remember it?—as if a woman could ever forget such a scene.

Mrs. Clarke soon after bade me adieu, and I saw no more of her for some time. Meantime, the winter set in exceedingly cold, with much snow. I had mentioned to no one the sufferings of Mrs. Clarke, as I feared to expose her to more rigorous cruelties, in the event of Smith's hearing of it, which I doubted not he would. Once I had seen her toiling through the icy mud and sleet, carrying a bag on her shoulders, which had the appearance of Indian meal.

I wonder that your Prophet is not ashamed of himself, to make such a slave of that poor woman; it is really too bad," I said to Mrs. Bradish.

"Why, what else is she good for?" said the lady; "she brought nothing to the Church. Then she is not beautiful, and he only keeps her for the sake of her services."

"And yet, Mrs. Bradish, he persuaded her to abandon a good home, to leave a husband by whom she was idolized, and almost break the hearts of her innocent children," I said, earnestly.

"So much the more fool she," said Mrs. Bradish, unfeelingly. "I have no pity for these weak, silly women, who cannot take care of themselves, but sit down and cry, baby-like, over wrongs and inflictions. But Mrs. Clarke had better be careful to whom she makes her complaints."

"Why so ?" I inquired.

"It won't do to tell everything you know," and Mrs. Bradish left the room."

About a week after this conversation, Mrs. Murray called one morning with the startling intelligence that Mrs. Clarke was nowhere to be found. "She came to my house yesterday," continued the narrator, "and I thought her senses wandering. She said she was going back to ask the forgiveness of her husband and die. When I told her it was a long distance, she faintly smiled, and said it was further to heaven. I tried to detain her, but could not, and Irene tells me that no one knows where she is."

"And Irene is delighted, I suppose?"

"She does not seem to be very sorry," resumed Mrs. Murray; "and, indeed, I cannot even conjecture what us women are all coming too," observed the latter, with a sigh. "My husband has now been absent a whole week. He ceased to make provision for our necessities some time ago, and we have become reduced to the last extremity. There is neither meat, milk, nor butter in the house; nothing but a small panful of Indian meal, and two or three eggs."

"But where is he all this time?" I inquired.

"Living with Mrs. Cook. The last time I saw him, he told me, that he had promised Smith to provide for Mrs. Cook; that he should do so, and that if I would not permit her to come and live in the same house with me, he should abandon me for her altogether. I told him that he could do as he thought proper, but that I was his wife in the eyes of God and man. This he denied, and when I required an explanation, he told me that the marriage ceremony performed between us was null and void, because we were unbelievers at the time of its celebration, and so I am to be repudiated. I understand that she has borne him a son, who has been named after their Prophet."

"They will not be apt to live happily together for any length of time," I remarked.

"And yet I do not wish them unhappiness," she answered; "I have not forgotten that he is my husband, and the father of my children, and how kind and affectionate he used to be."

CHAPTER XI.

MORMON OUTRAGES.

THE occupation of a considerable tract of land had been the Mormon policy; but instead of removing altogether beyond the boundaries of the white settlements, and taking possession of uninhabited districts, they chose a situation in a tolerably thickly-settled country. In this region they established a sort of outposts, communicating together by a line of Mormon families. These lines embraced the farms and property of many unbelievers, whom it became the interest of the Mormons to dispossess in some way or other. "To drive out the heathen," was a constant expression of their purposes. Some of the more zealous proposed that the Prophet should smite them all with death as the first-born of Egypt were smitten. This, however, he prudently declined on the ground of clemency. It was then proposed that their conversion should be attempted, but that plan, for some reason, failed, and the final decision was to plunder, harass, and distress them, until they were obliged to remove for the sake of peace. Smith asserted that it had been revealed to him, that all the grain, poultry, in short, that all the property, of every description, embraced within the established bounds of Mormondom, was designed by Heaven for the saints, and that they were ordered to go out and take possession. Some of the farmers, whose property was to be made a spoil, were able men, with abundance of grain and vegetables. They were entirely ignorant of the systematic plan of depredations of which they were to be the victims. Many of them had been very friendly to the Mormons, but that was nothing with the fanatics, who were quite as deficient in gratitude as the other virtues. The depredations were to be carried on secretly, under cover of the night, and the perpetrators were all sworn to secresy, all pledged to support each other, and, in all cases, to refuse to give any information before legal tribunals, or in any other way.

In fact, it was the regular organization of a banditti, with Smith at their head. Mrs. Bradish I found to be deeply interested in the affair. She beheld in this the furtherance of her ambitious schemes.

"I will be to the Mormons what Deborah was to the children of Israel," she remarked one day.

"But will the Mormons permit a woman to judge them, as Deborah judged Israel?" I asked.

"Under ordinary cases they would not, probably; yet the property which I have given to the church entitles me to the highest seat among its leaders," she replied.

"Are situations in the Mormon church proportioned to the amount of property bestowed by the candidates for ecclesiastical honors?" I inquired.

"They are," she answered; "but we can never rise to the state and dignity we desire as Mormon rulers, until the heathen are spoiled and driven from our midst."

Now commenced a regular system of depredation. Every night, particularly when the weather was dark and stormy, a company of the most daring and desperate would sally forth, like beasts of prey, on their nocturnal errands. Sometimes they would return, laden with plunder of all descriptions. At others, they obtained very little. Not unfrequently murders were committed, highway robberies perpetrated, and villanies of a still darker hue enacted. The whole country was alarmed, the newspapers teemed with conjectures, and rewards were offered for the perpetrators, by the public authorities, but without success. No one suspected the Mormons. They were quiet, and apparently peaceable. It was even proposed to them to join with the others in attempting to ferret out the villains. This was readily acceded to, from the supposition that being acquainted with the plans of their enemies, they could the more easily elude and lead them off on a false scent.

It had been decided on a particular occasion, to have a guard stationed around the domestic premises of every man in the neighborhood. As usual, the services of several Mormons had been offered and accepted, but the watches were all doomed to disappointment, not a robber appeared, not a single marauder was found abroad. However, when those who had come from a distance, returned to their homes, imagine their astonishment at finding everything in the greatest disorder, the women frightened, the barns despoiled, and the houses plundered. A barrel of pork had been taken from one place, a sack of flour from another, and a bag of potatoes from a third. A fat cow had been driven off and butchered in an adjoining wood. Several hogs and sheep likewise had shared the same fate. The agitation of the country exceeded all bounds, but no clue could be obtained to the perpetrators of the crimes. The Mormons, meanwhile, lived on the fat of the land, laughed at the mystification of their enemies, and augured from so good a beginning, a most auspicious end.

But a change came over the spirit of their dream. Mr. McDavit, a gentleman of wealth and respectability, detected a Mormon leader in his poultry-house slaughtering the inmates. McDavit attempted to detain him a prisoner, when the Mormon pulled out a pistol, severely wounded his assailant, and fled.

A civil process was immediately instituted, but the accused denied all knowledge of the crime, talked of being persecuted for righteousness' sake, and came into court fortified by a multitude of witnesses, who positively testified that on the night in question, he had been engaged with them in a religious meeting. He was accordingly discharged. Various occurrences of a similar character happened soon after, and suspicion settled on the Mormons.

The impossibility of bringing them to justice in the ordinary way, aroused the Regulators. These were a company of the most robust, brave, and resolute young men of the vicinity, who were regularly enrolled like a band of military, with officers of their choosing, and whose business was the cognizance and punishment of crimes and outrages that were beyond the reach of the law. Whatever may be thought of the illegality of their proceedings, it is certain that their presence was a great restraint to evil-doers.

One day I was standing before the door of our dwelling, when a Mormon prophet passed along, a beautiful young girl leaning on his arm. This prophet I knew as a man of family, but the girl was a stranger.

"Who is that girl yonder, leaning on the arm of Brother Hyde?" I said, addressing Mrs. Bradish.

"Her name is or was Corneilia Cornish," answered the lady.

"Where did she come from; I never saw her before?" I questioned.

"From some of the neighboring villages, I believe. Elder Hyde converted her, and brought her here, and now she lives in his family. He is very fond of her."

"Oh! Mrs. Bradish, do you regard such things as right and proper?" I exclaimed earnestly.

"Certainly I do, why not? Who has forbidden it?" she answered.

"Not Joseph Smith," I replied.

"And no one else, whose words are worth listening to," she said.

"Your own Bible favors such a system. And "——

"Mrs. Bradish," I said, "it is against the laws of the land, and now at least, it is our interest to conform to these laws; much I fear, that we shall render ourselves accursed.

"Have you no dread of the Regulators; you know well that the whole country is aroused against us."

"How should I know any such thing?" she asked angrily.

"How could you help knowing it?"

"But what has that to do with the Regulators?"

"Cornelia Cornish may have a brother, or cousin, or lover, who will not fancy her living with Elder Hyde."

"Look yonder," said Mrs. Bradish, suddenly, "there's Brother Clayton—sure as I'm alive—coming here, too!"

Brother Clayton was returning from a missionary tour.

"Well, Brother," said Mrs. Bradish, "I hope you have some good news to tell us. Things go on rather badly here. The heathen cannot be made to understand that only the saints are entitled to the good things of the land. But I trust that you have made many converts, and that we shall soon see them here, united with us."

"Generally speaking," said Brother Clayton, "I have had good success. The heathen were generally willing, and in some places anxious to hear the truth. Once only was I threatened with difficulty."

"How was that?"

"About twenty miles hence. I stopped at a small village, and gave out a notice of an intended meeting at seven o'clock that night, specifying also the place and the subject. I saw nothing in the least alarming or riotous, till about two hours previous to the time, when the meeting was appointed to commence. Then a company assembled, forced themselves into my presence, carried me from the room, notwithstanding my efforts to the contrary, mounted me on an old good-for-nothing horse, whom they drove before them for a mile beyond the village."

"Persecuted for righteousness' sake," said Mrs. Bradish.

"For a long time they refused to give me any satisfaction about the matter, till one more candid than the others, perhaps, pitying my degradation, observed :—

"'It is nothing that you have said or done personally, that has occasioned this. You may be a very good man, for what we know, but some months ago, as one of our citizens was walking out one evening, he heard a moan by the road-side. Hastening to the spot whence the sound proceeded, he found a poor woman lying on the ground, apparently in the last stage of exhaustion. He assisted her to rise and conducted her to his house. Though her mind seemed wandering at times, she told a very straight, connected story of herself, and how she came in that forlorn situation.'

"And this," said I to the narrator. "This is nothing to me."

"'Hear me out,' he said. 'This poor woman had been persuaded by the Mormons to leave her husband, had gone with them, and lived with their Prophet as his wife, two others sharing at the same time the same honor. Then he grew tired of her, and abused her shamefully; even then she bore on her back and person the marks of his blows ; and being seized with partial insanity, the result of her troubles and sufferings, she wandered off with the design of going back to her husband, that she might ask his forgiveness, and die at his feet. That,' continued the narrator, 'gave us enough of Mormonism ; we want nothing to do with it, or its professors, and, now sir, you must promise never to enter our village again.'

"I hesitated."

"'Promise,' he said, 'it will be best for you. I am a man of peace: I want no difficulty with any one. If you promise what we desire, well and good; if not, you will receive a complete coat of tar and feathers. What do you say?'

"I will make the promise that you require."

"And so they dismissed you without further violence?" said Mrs. Bradish.

"But did you hear what became of the poor woman at last?" I inquired.

"I believe they wrote to her husband, or something, but I can't tell the particulars," said Clayton, who took his leave soon after.

"Poor Mrs. Clarke," I said. "What a cruel destiny was hers."

"Yet it was her own fault," said Mrs. Bradish. "Why didn't she make the best of her circumstances, and if Brother Smith grew tired of her, content herself with some one else. She was continually puling about her husband—her husband. If she thought so much of him, what did she leave him for? I told Brother Smith, the first time I saw her, that she was a weak, silly woman, who didn't know her own mind two hours at a time, and who would probably disgrace the cause. Now you see that my prophecy has been accomplished."

CHAPTER XII.

REGULATORS.

AS I expected, and had warned Mrs. Bradish, Corneilia Cornish had a brother, a cousin, and a lover, all three, who were greatly displeased at her conversion to Mormonism, and her intimacy with the Mormon elder. Various plans had been devised to get her out of his hands, without a resort to violence, but the old fellow was too wide awake, and too chary of his bird for that. Every scheme was a failure, and disappointment only irritated them the more. Rumors of approaching troubles frequently reached us. Mr. Ward and Mrs. Bradish treated the matter with indifference. It was evident, however, that they felt much more anxiety than they thought proper to manifest. I made no disguise of my feelings, and being in nightly expectation of an outbreak, hesitated not to say so. I knew that a deadly hatred was excited throughout the country against the Mormons, and I felt that the revenge must be deep that could bide its time.

The spring had far advanced, when we were awakened one night by the heavy tramp of horsemen.

"The Regulators!" I whispered to Mr. Ward.

He sprang from his bed, hastily threw on his garments, and prepared to go out.

I attempted to detain him.

"What! stay and hide myself like a coward, when my friends and associates are being murdered! Impossible!" he said.

Mrs. Bradish came from her chamber, armed.

"Are the Regulators out?" she inquired.

"I believe so," said Mr. Ward.

"Let's go and see what they are doing, and who they are after?" said the heroic woman.

The words were no more than spoken, when a violent blow with a cudgel broke open our door, and in marched nearly a dozen men armed with muskets, rifles, pistols and bowie-knives. Mr. Ward made a sign to Mrs. Bradish, and advanced good-humoredly towards them.

"My friends, what is your errand here to-night?" he said.

"We want Jo' Smith, and we want that devil Hyde. We

want you, too, and all the rest of the Mormon vagabonds; and that ain't all, we'll have them too."

"Very well, take whom you can get," and he sprang through the window. The Regulators rushed after him with a loud shout. Mrs. Bradish declared that she would follow.

"But where will you go?" I inquired.

"Oh! round here, to see what they are doing," she replied.

I stood for a moment, and then determined to accompany her. I felt anxious about my husband, and knew, moreover, that the Regulators could have no motive to injure or molest me.

"Don't stand there trembling," said Mrs. Bradish, "but come with me, and know the worst of it."

I took her arm, and we sallied out.

There was no moon, and only a pale starlight. We saw lights in the distance, and heard strange and horrid outcries, mingled with oaths and blasphemies, and fiendish laughter. Approaching nearer we saw that Smith and Hyde were both prisoners. Corneilia Cornish had been mounted on a horse, behind a wild-looking boy. Her hands were bound, and she was otherwise fastened to the saddle.

"We've got two of the birds," called out one of the Regulators; "now we want the cuss that stole McDavit's hens."

"I don't think we shall find any more of them to-night," said another. "Don't you see there's nobody to be found but women and children. We don't want to hurt them poor devils, they have a bad time enough of it I guess."

In fact, confiding in the honor of the Regulators, the men had all fled, leaving the women and children.

"No; we won't hurt the women and children; but these fellows must have a touch. Where's the tar?"

"Take 'em to the woods," said one.

"No! no! Let these ladies see their Prophet transformed into an ostrich," cried another.

"Mercy! mercy!" shrieked Hyde, as he saw one approaching with a kettle of tar.

Mrs. Bradish could no longer control her anger. She held her pistol with a nervous grasp, the next moment it exploded, and the ball pierced the brain of the man with the kettle of tar. He reeled, and fell with a groan, saturating himself with the pitchy compound. The Regulators were astounded.

"Who done that?" they all cried in a breath, some hastening to relieve him, and others looking for the perpetrator of the deed.

"Here I am," said Mrs. Bradish; "I did it."

There was something sublime in her appearance, as she stood grasping the weapon, her head uncovered, her dark hair streaming in the night wind, and her brow unblenched, though surrounded by deadly foes.

The Regulators crowded around her. A fire had been kindled of some dry wood and brush, and I saw by the pale, red gleam of the light, that their companion was dead. The survivors gnashed their teeth with rage.

"Stand off!" she cried, as one approached to lay his hand upon her. "Stand off, or I will send your soul to show you knave the way to hell!"

There was something terrible in her voice and look.

"Do you think to frighten us?" said one, but his voice was unnoticed in the general tumult. They pressed nearer and nearer. "Take the pistol from her!" said one. "Give her a touch of the tar!" said another. "No, no! shoot her, as she shot him!" cried a third. There was great confusion, and a mingled uproar of voices. All at once, the countenance of Mrs. Bradish suddenly brightened. Her eye sparkled, and she laughed, oh! such a laugh of hate and defiance.

"Fools, knaves, villains!" she cried, "where are your prisoners? Where are the men for whom your tar was prepared?

Oh, ye are noble fellows! In your eagerness to maltreat a woman, your intended victims have escaped."

It was even so. Taking advantage of the confusion, Irene had cautiously slipped up to the prisoners, and being provided with a sharp knife, cut the thongs that bound them, when they fled to the woods.

"To the woods! to the woods!" shouted several in a breath. "To the woods! we must take them, dead or alive!"

And off to the woods they started, hallooing and hurrahing.

The brother of Corneilia Cornish mounted before her on horseback, and rode off.

It is impossible to describe the deep excitement and mental distress that I experienced on this occasion. The woods were near the village, and we could plainly hear the voices and menaces of the Regulators, and perceive the flickering and waving of their torches, as they hunted their intended victims. For Smith I cared nothing; I knew that he had outraged and insulted all woman-kind, in the persons of Ellen and Mrs. Clarke. I should have esteemed it an act of retributive justice, had some friendly shot interposed to put a period to his existence; but my husband was absent, and he, though a Mormon, had always been kind to me. My imagination pictured him as likewise an inhabitant of that forest. He might fall into their hands. The thought was horrible—and then the dreadful uncertainty. We listened; the sounds and menaces grew indistinct, the lights died in the distance, and we returned to our homes.

All the remainder of that night, and the next day, we passed in the greatest anxiety. I say "we," for Mrs. Bradish, even more than myself, gave way to gloom, and care, and despondency. I only feared for my husband; her concern was for the Prophet, the elders, and the Church. She trembled lest her air-built castles of ambition were to be suddenly overthrown. Through the day we received intimation that the Regulators were lingering in the vicinity, and that a guard was stationed around the wood.

"Then there is no hope!" I said bitterly.

"There is always hope," said Mrs. Bradish. "Do you distrust the protecting arm of Providence?"

"I have not your faith," I answered gloomily.

"Because you do not understand the gospel—because you are not a believer in the truth," she answered.

Mrs. Bradish was one of those singular characters, who unite to great resolution and intellectual power, a decided tendency to religious fanaticism. The world has seen many such—men and women—who, having imbibed a belief in some superstitious dogma, find all their preconceived opinions of right and wrong, good and evil, at once overturned; and in their stead, a deep and prevailing desire for the ultimate triumph of their novel tenets. Then, too, she was ambitious; she aspired to a place of distinction in the church; and who shall describe the resolute will, and deep, unconquerable strength of purpose, that arises from fanaticism united with ambition?

The hours passed away; night came, dark and gloomy. We retired to our chambers earlier than usual, but sleep was a stranger to my eyes. I am not naturally superstitious, but unusual terrors had taken possession of me. Strange noises echoed in my ears. Mutterings, chatterings, and solemn-toned night-calls, sounded through the gloom. More than once I fancied that screams of terror disturbed the silence; but overcome with fatigue and mental excitement, towards morning I fell into an uneasy slumber. I was awakened from this by a voice beneath the window—a real, veritable human voice. The tone was familiar. It was that of my husband.

"Be still as possible," he said in a low tone. "The Regulators are not far off. But go down and unfasten one of the lower windows."

"Why not the door?" I inquired.

"That would be dangerous. Open the window to the south," he replied.

I obeyed him, and the next moment he leaped into my arms.

"Where have you been? what have you suffered? why should those fellows be after you?" I inquired.

"Oh, Maria, I cannot tell you all!" he replied. "But I am very hungry; indeed, I am. I have had no food since yesterday."

"Your hunger shall be satisfied," I answered. "I prepared an unusual quantity of food, in anticipation of a visit from you." And I soon spread before him a very palatable meal.

CHAPTER XIII.

THE FOREST.

"MY dear," said Mr. Ward, when he had satisfied his hunger, "I will gratify your curiosity so far as I am able. Blood has certainly been spilt, but more of the Regulators have fallen than the Mormons; at least, so I think."

"Who have fallen of the Mormons?" I inquired.

"Well, two or three of the elders, with whom you were unacquainted; and Mr. Murray has been severely wounded."

"He has! but where is he?"

"In the forest. It is impossible to convey him home; and then he would not be in safety there."

"Does his wife know?" I asked.

"The last one does—the other does not. He requested me to

tell Sister Sally; and, notwithstanding the danger, I came round that way on purpose."

"And what did she say?"

"She didn't say much to it."

By this time, Mrs. Bradish had arisen, dressed herself hastily, and came to our apartment.

"The Lord has heard my prayers," she said fervently. "Blessed be His name! Faith and prayers can accomplish wonders. But now begin at the first, and tell us all that you have seen and heard. Where did you go when you fled, that night?"

"Of course I fled immediately to the forest: that was the only place of safety. The Regulators pursued me a short distance, and then returned. Anxious to ascertain what they were doing with you, I crept along stealthily behind them, and finally succeeded in concealing myself in a small clump of briar, where I could watch all their proceedings without being seen."

"Then, you saw when Brother Smith and Deacon Hyde escaped?" said Mrs. Bradish.

"I was a witness to your bravery on that occasion. Surely, if ever a woman deserved a crown, you do. And you shall wear one yet; you shall be a Priestess of the Most High—it has been revealed to me," said Mr. Ward. "When the Prophet and his companion escaped," he continued, "I followed them. We struck immediately into the thickest and most unfrequented part of the wood. In its deepest recesses, I knew a place of concealment, formed by the accumulated mass of fallen trees that a hurricane had overthrown. The trunks of some were lying prostrate over the limbs and branches of others, thus forming impenetrable cavities, in which detection would be almost impossible. Into these we crept, and, scarcely daring to breathe or stir, watched the approach of our foes. From our hiding-place, we could see them hurrying hither and thither—could hear their threats and imprecations, and were even witnesses to their savage butchery of one of our friends."

"And did you remain quiet, and see a brother slain?" said Mrs. Bradish.

"We could not have rescued him," returned Mr. Ward; "and the attempt would only have exposed us to the peril of sharing his fate. To-night I beheld another deadly encounter. Oh, that the enemies of the Lord and his people could be driven from the land!"

"Amen!" responded Mrs. Bradish, solemnly.

"You have all heard of Harry Hastings, who took such an active part against us, in the courts, last fall?"

We assented.

"Well, this Hastings was the leader of the Regulators. I saw him, and penetrated his disguise; I read, also, the deadly purpose concealed in his heart; but I feared him not, believing that the Lord would preserve his own. I was aware, also, that his animosity was chiefly directed against Brother Wilson, whom he accused of robbing his wife."

"As if a Mormon could be guilty of robbing," interrupted Mrs. Bradish. "As if the Promised Land, and all it contains, was not legitimately theirs."

"We hope to make it ours," said Mr. Ward, thoughtfully; "but matters look rather dark, now. As I was saying, however, when I was cautiously threading the forest on my way home, peering this way and that, through the darkness, and sometimes pausing to listen at the slightest sound, I discovered a man sitting on the fallen trunk of a tree, only a few yards from where I stood. The thick gloom of the woods prevented me from ascertaining whether he was a friend or an enemy, and I fell back into the friendly obscurity of a neighboring copse. In a few moments, I perceived the bright flicker of a torch, and heard several voices talking loudly. Peering through the bushes,

I beheld Wilson. The light enabled me to perceive and recognize his features; and near him was gathered a group of the Regulators. They were in disguise, as usual, but I knew the voice of Hastings, in a moment.

"'Will you promise to leave the country,' he cried, imperatively, 'you, and all your devilish set of rascals, if I don't shoot you?'

"'I can promise nothing,' said Wilson, 'because nothing has been revealed.'

"'Been revealed—indeed! I'll give you a revelation;' and he struck our brother a violent blow on the face.

"'Hold him!' cried another, 'while I cut an ox-goad; I fancy that will be the thing.'

"Hastings seized Wilson, and the other commenced whipping him with a large long stick. Wilson, though a less powerful man than his enemy, was, nevertheless, strong, active, and sinewy, and he twisted himself from the grasp of Hastings. Then, irritated beyond endurance by the pain of his wounds and bruises, he called him various opprobrious epithets, and said that he would yet live to see him in hell. A howl of rage burst from the Regulators, at these words, and Wilson, probably aware of the full extent of his danger, started off, like a frightened deer. He was closely pursued by Hastings, who drew a large, long knife. The fury of madness seemed to have taken possession of one, while fear lent wings to the other. The other Regulators attempted to follow, but were soon rapidly distanced, while I dashed off in an oblique direction, determined to intercept their route, and, if possible, save my friend."

"Bless you for that," said Mrs. Bradish.

"I could hear the heavy sounds of feet, and the crash and crackle of the underwood; then came the fall of a heavy body, and the next moment my hair almost stood on end, as a howl of terror sunk to a piteous supplication for mercy, and both were succeeded by a yell of fiendish triumph. By this time, I had reached them, and, without a moment's consideration of the consequence, I precipitated myself on the form of Hastings, grappling his throat in the desperate struggle. We rolled over and over together; but after that, I remember nothing."

"And Wilson was dead, murdered?" said Mrs. Bradish.

"Even so. When I recovered my consciousness, it seemed at first that I had been dreaming. The strange, the terrible events of the last half hour had nearly unsettled my reason. I stretched out my hand; it touched something. Oh! how cold and stiff. The chill of horror that thrilled my frame, told me too well what it was. But I arose and groped round in the darkness, and soon ascertained that two, and those deadly enemies, had gone to the bar of the Eternal Judge. And there I left them. What else could I do?"

"And, Mr. Murray?" said Mrs. Bradish, "I understand you to say that he was wounded."

"Yes; in a desperate encounter with one of the Regulators, he received a wound in the side. He slew his foe, however, and then succeeded in reaching us. We spread him a bed of dried leaves, dressed his wounds as well as we were able, and with suitable provision, he will probably recover."

"But you have no provision?" said Mrs. Bradish.

"Not much, certainly," answered Mr. Ward. "There is a cool stream near by, to which we resort for water."

"But you want something more than water," she said, interrupting him, "and you must have it, too; you said that the woods were watched?"

"Yes; strictly. I only made my escape by the merest accident," said Mr. Ward.

"But why does not Brother Smith exercise the miraculous power he professes to have, and vanish these enemies?" I inquired.

"He is merciful," said Mrs. Bradish.

"Not to his friends," I replied.

"The wicked must be permitted to run their race, in order that their transgressions may be full," she answered. "But that is neither here nor there, our friends must be supplied with necessaries;" and she sat a few moments in deep thought. Mr. Ward regarded her admiringly.

"This is my plan," she said, at length.

Both of us listened intently.

"You, Mr. Ward, must get two horses; smart, able horses. One of these horses must be laden with provisions and necessaries, and led by you, in company with Mrs. Ward. I will array myself in some of your garments, and mount the other. It shall be my purpose to draw off these fellows on a false scent. On which side of the wood do you enter?"

"On the north side," he answered.

"And where is the guard stationed?" she inquired.

"Their headquarters is that old shantee, where crazy Jim harbored."

"Very well, you must keep some distance behind me, and I will ride along there. They will probably challenge me. I will then put spurs to my horse. Undoubtedly they will follow. You will then advance and enter the wood."

"But why is my presence necessary?" I inquired.

"To return with the horse," she answered. "Mr. Ward must remain in concealment, and the horse, if left at large, would fall into the hands of the enemy."

"Your plan looks feasible," said Mr. Ward; "but the difficulty will be to get the horses. The village is closely watched, and it will be scarcely possible to get beyond its precincts without being discovered."

"Well, the attention of these fellows must be drawn to some other point; but you stay here while I go to reconnoitre."

"What means this masquerade?" I said, as Mrs. Bradish threw my husband's overcoat over her shoulders, and put on his hat.

"Ask me no questions, and I'll tell you no lies," she said, jestingly, and opening the door, she passed out into the darkness. I looked after her; there was a faint gleam of starlight, just enough, it might be said, to make the gloom visible. For a moment I caught a glimpse of her figure, but it rapidly disappeared.

"Oh! what a woman!" I said, shutting the door.

"A brave, noble woman," said Mr. Ward. "A woman who will do anything to advance the interests of the church."

Several minutes passed away, and still she returned not. I then went to the window, and looking out, discovered a faint streak of light, apparently a short distance off. It grew brighter and brighter as I gazed. Alarm seized me.

"Mr. Ward, look here a moment," I said.

He approached the window.

"That light yonder, what is it?"

He shook his head.

"Somebody's house must be on fire," I remarked," only see the flames how they mount upward, reddening the sky, and sending out showers of sparks."

"It can't be a great way off either," he said.

"I can plainly see the people running to and fro. And here comes somebody." It was Mrs. Bradish.

Instantly dismounting, she threw the reins of the steed she rode over a post, and rushed into the house.

"Quick! quick!" she cried, impatiently. "Now, while the rascals have employment yonder. Oh! I've given them something to do besides looking after us. It took fire nicely; was all in a light flame in two minutes. You ought to have seen how they run, and heard them screech and balloo. It was really laughable."

"And the horses?" said Mr. Ward.

"Oh! they belong to the Regulators. They were so deeply engaged, that they didn't perceive when I brought them off."

Mrs. Bradish actually flew from place to place, making preparation, and getting the food and clothing ready. Loading these on one horse, she re-mounted the other.

"Come, Mr. Ward, you must follow me carefully and cautiously."

"But is there any need of my going?" I said, shrinking from the darkness and exposure.

Mr. Ward replied in the negative, remarking that as the horses already belonged to the Regulators, he would turn them loose, when they had served his purpose.

"Good bye," said Mrs. Bradish, "I shall be back in two hours."

"Good bye," said Mr. Ward, affectionately saluting me.

A minute longer and I was alone with the sleeping children. Re-entering the house, I shut and fastened the door, and then sate down to meditate, and await her return. Thus, wrapped in a mournful revery of the past, and not very pleasant anticipations of the future, the time wore away. The day broke, the clouds changed from gray to red, and from red to crimson, yet Mrs. Bradish came not. I grew impatient, then anxious, and finally uneasy. Where could she be? What new scheme for the relief of the brethren, or the triumph of the Church, was being devised or executed? And, wearying myself with conjectures, I spent the day.

Near evening Mrs. Murray came. She looked pale and thin. "Have you heard of my husband," she inquired; "for I must still call him so, though he has cast me off for a younger and fairer woman. I cannot forget that we were once happy, and inspired with deeper affection for each other than most people in married life."

I informed her of all I knew, and concluded by inquiring if she had heard or seen anything of Mrs. Bradish.

"And so my husband is wounded; just what I expected," she said. "And Sally cares nothing about it—why should she? She never loved him as I have done, as I still do. It is not in her nature."

While we were yet conversing, a man came in; a total stranger, yet I saw at once, by his air and manner, that he was a Mormon, and soon learned that he came from a settlement of them about fifty miles distant.

"I had business with the prophets and elders," he said, "but I find that the saints have been sorely distressed by the heathen, even to the loss of life and liberty."

"Some of our friends have been slain," I replied. "Do you know of any that have been made prisoners?"

"I know not the name, but I was led to infer, from a conversation that I heard this morning, that one of the leaders, at least, was in the hands of the enemy."

"Will you relate that conversation?" I inquired.

"I was lying on a sort of rude settee, in the bar-room of the inn where I was stopping, when two fellows came in, and apparently without noticing me, called for liquor, and drank off a bumper to the success of the Regulators.

"'The Mormons are rather too much for them, are they not?' asked the bar-keeper.

"'They don't seem to have done much yet,' answered the man addressed. 'However, they drove the poor devils into the woods, where they intend to keep them for a while. And last night one of the birds fell into their hands.'

"' Did?'

"' Yes; it seems that he had been to the settlement to procure food, and such like, and came right on the guard of Regulators, as he was making for the woods. The boys gave chase, and, though the horse all but flew, they finally succeeded in capturing him, and now he is safely lodged in jail.'"

"That can be no other than Mrs. Bradish," I said.

"Not a lady," said the man.

"She was dressed in male attire, and probably was not recognized," I suggested.

This gentleman's name was Hale, and he seemed very zealous in the faith of Mormon; expressed unbounded confidence in Smith; related instances of his miraculous powers; and dwelt largely on their hopes of living and reigning with Christ a thousand years. He then proposed to go back to the village, obtain an interview with the prisoner, and ascertain in what manner he could be of service to her, if my suspicions proved correct.

I answered that thereby he would be doing great service to the church, and lay the friends of the lady under lasting obligations. After partaking of refreshments, he departed, promising to return the next morning.

"Mrs. Bradish certainly meets with all sorts of adventures," I said. "She has no fear, and is for ever running into danger."

"So it seems. I don't know what to make of her sometimes. She seems like a good clever woman, and yet she will connive at crime."

"You must be aware that her views of crime are radically different from those entertained by people less fanatical in their belief. She has brought herself to consider actions as good or bad, only with reference to the church. I pity her delusion."

"And she is much more to be feared than pitied. She would sacrifice her best friend, I fear, if by doing so she could advance the interests of Mormonism. Indeed, I have sometimes thought her to be the victim of a species of insanity. Have you not observed how her eyes will gleam, and her features writhe when she is agitated or excited?"

"I have observed it," I answered.

After much more conversation of a similar character, Mrs. Murray took leave.

CHAPTER XIV.

RETURN OF THE MESSENGER.

THAT night I passed alone. The next morning Mr. Hale returned.

"Your suspicions were correct," he said, seating himself. "The prisoner is the lady of whom you spoke. I obtained an interview with her, though not without difficulty, and heard her story, which was very romantic."

"She was captured by the Regulators, I suppose?"

"Yes; in attempting to divert their attention from Brother Ward, who was bearing provisions to the wounded and fugitive in the forest. They gave chase; she fled, but, unfortunately, her horse stumbled and fell. They were on her in a moment. She was taken, and pinioned, and when her name and sex were discovered, they called her a murderess, and chained her, without privilege of bail, in the felon's dungeon. But she bears her adverse fate with great dignity and composure. However, I think that something must be done for her rescue. It is dreadful to be tried for life, when judge, jury, and public are prejudiced against you."

"There would be but small chance of her acquittal."

"There would be no chance, whatever. The fact of the killing, she does not deny, but insists that the action, under the circumstances, was commendable. She wishes me to inform her friends. I promised to do so. Can you direct me to them?"

"I cannot to any certainty, but Mr. Ward will, I think, be in to-night. He rather reproved Mrs. Bradish, for her haste in shooting that fellow."

" He thought ill would grow out of it."

" And I was confident that such would be the case. For I heard one of those that bore away the body swear a dreadful oath, that after the men were done for, he would be revenged on her."

" They were exulting in my hearing," returned Mr. Hale, " on the prospect of hanging her. Indeed, the officers could only preserve her with difficulty from the grasp of the exasperated populace."

" When will her trial take place ?"

" In about three weeks."

" I should think that something might be done in that time."

" We must try," he answered. " But do you perceive any relaxation of vigilance on the part of the Regulators ?"

" I can scarcely tell, and yet, it strikes me that they have been visible much less frequently for the past twenty-four hours."

" These Regulators," continued Mr. Hale, " are very excitable characters, and as such, soon get wearied in their useless campaigns, and return to their homes. You will soon be rid of them altogether, probably."

" I hope so, indeed."

" As I anticipated, Mr. Ward came at evening. He said that the coast was clear, that the Regulators had dispersed, but whether for good, or only as a feint, he could not tell."

" It may be the latter, though I rather guess the former," said Mr. Hale. " These fellows are too impulsive to be persevering. They act merely from momentary excitement, and now that they have got that woman in their hands, can afford a respite certainly."

" But we must make an attempt to rescue her," said Mr. Ward.

" I think we ought to ; how shall it be brought about ?"

"What strikes me as the most feasible plan, is this. We will disguise ourselves as Indians, and while a part of the company attacks the village, and sets fire to the fences and out-houses, in order to divert the attention of the inhabitants, the remainder can force the jail and rescue the prisoners."

"That scheme is full of danger," I said. " Couldn't assistance be afforded her, so that she could escape without jeopardizing the lives of her friends?"

"Not likely," said Mr. Ward. "The gate is too strictly guarded; Mrs. Bradish has done much for us, we will now exert ourselves to do something for her. I cannot doubt that every true believer will be willing to assist according to his ability. It would be a lasting stigma on our name to suffer that sister to die on the gallows."

That night Mr. Ward stayed with me without molestation, and the next day the Mormons returned to their homes. Mrs. Cook, however, positively refused to receive her pseudo husband, and he was obliged to return to his first wife.

" Oh! how happy I am," she said, running into our house one morning, "my husband has returned to me. He even wept and asked my forgiveness. Oh! I would have forgiven him much more. It was all my fault, I suppose, because I was not sufficiently attractive. But I must hasten back to nurse and comfort him. You must, you will sympathize with me," and before I could assure her in the affirmative, she hurried away.

" I hope at any rate, that her husband will appreciate such love and self-denial," I said to Mr. Ward.

" It is not probable that he ever ceased to love her," said that gentleman, "but it was revealed to him that he must take another wife, and"——

"The revelation was certainly at fault," I answered, "in not directing him to a better and more amiable woman, than this Mrs. Cook seems to be."

Mr. Ward smiled in a peculiar manner, and turned the conversation to Mrs. Bradish.

"It is necessary, my dear," said he, "that the brethren should be extremely cautious. Our past encounter with the Regulators cost some valuable lives. However, they shall live again, and reign with Christ a thousand years, for they were martyrs to the truth. Yet we may not run unnecessarily into danger, and so I repeat, it is necessary to be cautious. You know there is a tribe of Indians about thirty miles from here."

"I have heard of them."

"They have had some difficulty with the whites."

"Indeed."

"Yes; and I hear that they threaten to attack the village, in the jail of which our sister is confined."

"Dreadful!"

"On the contrary, it will be exceedingly fortunate for us, should such be the case. The rumor itself is invaluable, as it will withdraw suspicion from us."

"It will, but oh! Mr. Ward do you not fear to be accessory to such dreadful crimes?"

"Crimes?" he repeated mechanically.

"Yes; crimes."

"There is no crime about it," he answered. "We are at war with the heathen, and all stratagem is allowable in such cases. Besides, we are to consider the interests of our church and its members, as paramount to all other considerations. Christ did not pray for the world, but only for his disciples."

A meeting of the Mormons was called that night. A special meeting, at which only four or five of the leaders were suffered to be present. The discussions and resolutions were all conducted with the utmost privacy, and the result could only be known by transpiring events. Mr. Hale, however, was speedily dispatched to the village of Hawthorn, to bear a message to the captive sister, and subsequently returned with a letter from that lady to my husband. I saw this missive; its contents thrilled my heart. It ran thus :—

"Mr. Hale tells me that you have a plan on foot to effect my liberation. Well, so be it. Heaven knows I have no wish to be put on trial for my life without a friend to speak for me. But one thing you must prevent if possible. Do not let our Prophet join the expedition. Indeed, he must not. If he does his death is certain. Yes, Mr. Ward, the husband of Mrs. Clarke is here, and his threats of vengeance are truly awful. The jailor's wife comes and sits with me sometimes. She was in here yesterday, and told me all about it. Of course I did not let her know that I had ever seen or heard of such a woman but as I know that Mrs. Ward will be anxious to hear from her, I will tell you as the jailor's wife told me.

"Mrs. Ward will remember Brother Clayton's story, and how he said that the people of the village where Mrs. Clarke stopped had written to her husband. That was the truth, and Mr. Clarke came on immediately to look after his poor distressed wife. He found her in a miserable condition; and, of course, attributes all her misfortunes to the Mormons in general, and Smith in particular, instead of her own folly and weakness He openly avows his intention of waylaying and shooting Smith, and he will do so unless circumstances prevent. I fear that there is trouble ahead. The loss of our leader would be dreadful just now."

"He that sows the wind must reap the whirlwind," I remarked. "I should not wonder if some terrible retributive justice were to overtake that man."

"The warning has come too late," said Mr. Ward thoughtfully.

Something more than a week elapsed, when Mr. Ward informed me that he should be absent that day and night, and how much longer he could not tell, but exhorted me to be patient and courageous, and, above all, to trust in Heaven. Though he forbore to give me any further information respecting the cause of his absence, I knew very well that it referred to the liberation of Mrs. Bradish.

CHAPTER XV.

THE LIBERATION, AND SOMETHING ELSE.

MR. WARD departed, and for two days I awaited his return. At last he came, but his countenance bore the impress of something terrible.

"Are you wounded, dear?" I inquired.

"No! Yes!" he answered.

"No! Yes!" I replied. "Rather indefinite. But pray tell me, Mr. Ward, is Mrs. Bradish killed?"

"I don't know," he answered, "Though I believe not; yet our Prophet is."

"What! Smith?"

"Yes, Smith, as you call him; I saw him die

"Shot by Mr. Clarke?"

"Even so," and Mr. Ward buried his face in his hands, and groaned aloud.

After remaining a few minutes in silence, Mr. Ward began:

"I will tell you all about it, Maria, because sooner or later you must know, and what is of more and greater importance, we must make preparations to remove immediately. 'Tis a case of necessity, for the country is rising against us."

"How dreadful to have provoked that rising," I said; "but how is it? what is it?—let me hear the whole story, and then I can judge for myself."

"Our plan to rescue Mrs. Bradish was this," said Mr. Ward. "Our Prophet, who had many followers among the Indians already mentioned, went down to solicit their assistance, and, if possible, enlist a goodly number of them in our cause. Meanwhile, I was to see that the brethren were armed and equipped, and the two divisions of our party were to meet and rendezvous at the Fords; beyond that circumstances were to direct. By some means, however, a rumor transpired that the Indians were about to attack the village. This was fortunate as diverting attention from us, though, at the same time, the villagers were thereby warned of our approach. You know the night chosen for our expedition, and how black and stormy were the clouds. This was favorable, and we marched up cautiously and silently to the outskirts of the town. Not a soul seemed aware of our presence, and we began to congratulate ourselves on the prospect of an easy victory. Here we divided the men. One division moving on in the direction of the jail, while the others remained as an outpost. All having orders to discharge a gun at the first alarm, on which the latter were directed to fire the outbuildings and fences near-them. I remained with this party, but Smith accompanied the other. In vain I protested against this arrangement, but he only laughed at me, and went on.

"We remained perfectly still several minutes, when a sharp, quick fire of musketry gave intimation that we were discovered. 'Fire the buildings!—quick!—quick!' I cried.

"In a moment it was done.

"'They will soon be here,' I said; 'let us now slip round towards the jail.'

"We moved onwards, but suddenly rising up before us, made visible by the burning sheds and grain-stacks, appeared a band of armed men. I heard the discharge of their deadly weapons, and felt a stunning blow on the head."

"How dreadful such things are," I observed.

"When I recovered, I found myself a prisoner. I was bound, and two men, whom I knew to be enemies, were watching over me. I remained perfectly silent, in order to gather what information I could from their conversation.

"'We were not looking for the devils so early in the evening, or they'd have got peppered other guess than they were. I don't know that we should have heard them at all, they came so plaguy still, if it hadn't been for my dog. Watch is allers up to sich things, and he heard them break the jail-door I expect, for he set up a dreadful barking, and just that minute Jim Smith comes in, and said that the Indians were on us. 'Twas raal dark and stormy, and we couldn't well see what was going on, but I knew by the noise that they were at the jail. Then the thought struck me that 'twas the Mormons, and I ran out, shouting with all my might, "The Mormons! The Mormons!" In less than no time a company was gathered, Clarke at their head.

"'The devils! Where be they?' he yelled.

"'At the jail,' I answered.

"'A light—a light! let's see what they are doing,' said some one.

"'A light was brought.'

"'Does anybody know Joe Smith?' cried Clarke.

"'That's him yonder, on horseback,' said I; 'and, sure as the deil, he's got that prisoner woman on behind him.'

"'They broke the jail open to get her out. She's the High Priestess,' said a man at my elbow.

"'This is for my wife, my poor, forsaken Laura,' said Clarke, as he raised the gleaming tube of death to his eye. It exploded. I heard a wild and piercing screech, and saw Smith fall from the horse. Then wasn't there a hurrah; and we rushed up to seize the woman, but, heavens! she fought like a panther—drove the horse right over us, before we could seize the bits, and got away.'

"'You don't say that?'"

"'Yes; I do, though. Old Sam helped her, I believe; but we took several others—some of the heads, too; and they won't get off without promising to leave the country.'

"'Well, was Smith actually dead?'

"'Dead as a door nail.'

"'Did you see the body?'

"'To be sure, I did; and it didn't look a bit different from any other body. Pshaw! he wasn't no prophet, no more than I am.'

"But I need not repeat their conversation," continued Mr. Ward, "nor my own harrowing anxiety. At length, I addressed my keepers, inquiring: 'How many, and who were prisoners besides myself?'

"'Oh, you've rousted have you, old boy?' said one. 'Well, 'twas time; I begun to think that you were sleeping your last.'

"'That's not answering my question,' I said. 'Who are prisoners besides myself?'

"'I imagine that you'll find out without much difficulty,' he said. 'We'll have you altogether in the morning, and make you promise and swear to clear out—the whole scrape of you—or, by G—d! we'll hang you on the first tree.'

"That was a long night, Maria. Oh, how long! I could not sleep; but I lay still and revolved in my mind the chances of escape. Yet, something whispered to me that I had better stay, and know the worst, even if such a chance presented. My presence would probably be consolatory to my captive brethren, who, now that their leader was slain, would feel like sheep without a shepherd. In the morning, we were all taken to the room usually occupied as the court-house, and there received our doom."

"And how many of you were prisoners?" I inquired.

"About twenty; and twelve of these were elders," he continued. "Our captors then bade us hold up our hands and repeat after them a horrible oath—binding our souls to the devil and everlasting torment, if we were not out of the country in the space of a month. I would have demurred at this, especially the shortness of the time, but saw that it would be of no use. We were there among them, poor, bruised, persecuted and wounded : they would have no mercy."

"And you took the oath ?"

"We did ; there was a dreadful penalty attached : our children to be slain, our wives polluted, our houses burned, and ourselves hung."

"And you could hear nothing of Mrs. Bradish ?"

"Nothing—only that she escaped. She will probably return to us."

"And now, my dear Maria," said Mr. Ward, "don't give way to grief or melancholy. Our journey will, indeed, be long and tedious ; but the scenes will not be devoid of interest and excitement ; and the country to which we go is utterly uninhabited, except by a few straggling Indians."

"And where is this country?" I inquired.

"Far on to the West, near the Great Rocky Chain, on the shores of the Salt Lake."

"But, Mr. Ward, do you suppose that we can ever live to reach there ?"

"Live to reach there ! certainly. As the Israelites crossed the Red Sea, we must cross the rivers—as they passed through the wilderness, we must journey through a desert ; and, as they possessed the good land flowing with milk and honey, so we will go in to possess that."

"I understand it," I replied ; "but who is to be the leader ?"

"We must choose one from among the elders," he answered. "There is to be a meeting this afternoon to decide the question.

It will be a situation of profit and honor for somebody ; and I hope that heaven will direct our choice."

"Amen," said a deep voice behind us. I looked around. Two or three Mormons had come in, doubtless, to discuss that interesting subject. Leaving them with my husband, I sought the residence of Mrs. Murray.

CHAPTER XVI.

THE NEW LEADER.

IT would be impossible to describe the grief, the horror, and consternation of the Mormons, when the death of the leader became fully known. Many of them were ready to take up the lamentation of the bereaved Mussulman : "He cannot be dead —our Prophet, our leader, and intercessor with God !" Others concluded that he might be dead, but would rise again ; and others, again, wept and moaned and lamented as if their hearts were broken. The elders and prophets, however, were too deeply interested about who should be his successor, to concern themselves much with the past catastrophe. According to accounts, the meeting was anything but an exhibition of a meek and lowly spirit. There was quarrelling, fighting, and even a throwing of missiles, with boisterous and outrageous language. At length, however, all resigned their claims but two, both of whom professed to have had a special revelation favorable to his own claim, and, consequently, adverse to the other. As usual, in such cases, a party adhered to either, and neither would resign his pretensions.

Towards night, the meeting adjourned, when Mr. Ward invited the aspirant, to whose party he belonged, to our house, and, for the first time, I was introduced to the since famous B—— Y——g. He was a good-sized, compact man, and would have been good-looking had he looked pleasant. As it was, his countenance wore a sort of sinister expression, anything but agreeable. He seemed never weary of extolling himself, professed miraculous powers, and said that God had audibly spoken to him, as he did to Moses, and commanded him to lead forth the chosen people; that in yielding his pretensions to that honor, he should be disobeying the Word of the Lord. His rival's name was White. He was much the ablest and best man. Subsequently, he moved to Texas with his followers, where they are living happily.

"This White," said Y——g, speaking of his rival, "is a prophet of the devil instead of the Lord. An angel opened my eyes to behold him as he actually was. He had an unclean spirit, like a frog, in his mouth, that gave him power to speak lying wonders. But I am not afraid of him. I heard a voice from Heaven, saying, B——m, you shall be Prophet and leader, and no man shall hinder you."

There was something infinitely ridiculous in this rhodomontade and the manner in which it was spoken. Was the man a fool, or did he look on us as such? Probably, the latter, for his cunning, scheming features bore the mark of more than ordinary intelligence, and his eyes, which changed color with every variable emotion, seemed to conceal a world of craft, and cunning, and forethought in their unfathomable depths.

And did such a man believe in Mormonism? He believed in it as a fable, that he designed to make profitable to himself. He saw in it an opportunity to rise to a situation of affluence and social importance. More than once such a temptation has proved too strong for a well-balanced mind. To him it was irresistible. His early education and habits had in them nothing remarkable, except, perhaps, a tendency to fanaticism, and total oblivion of moral purpose. Even when a child, he was untroubled with a conscience, and a great adept at lying. Subsequently, in his career of shopman, he exhibited the same talents for duplicity and meanness. The weights were all false, the measures scant. He adulterated the spices, mixed water with the rum, and sand with the sugar. Then, in the capacity of a pedlar he roamed around the country, vending useless articles of jewelry, damaged hose, lottery tickets, and similar articles; the whole and sole end of his endeavors being, as he expressed it, to "take care of number one," and deceive those with whom he trafficked as much as possible. At last, he became a devotee of the Methodist persuasion; exhorted the sinners, led in the class meetings, and shouted, sung, and hallooed times without number, until the sound actually made night hideous. But, as self had always been uppermost, it was so still. He was not allured by the beauty of virtue, or the love of truth. The fear of punishment in the next world was now the governing motive of his conduct. He was working out his own salvation, not by restraining his evil desires, but by the easier observance of prayers and meetings.

And many evenings, side by side with him in the class, stood a beautiful young girl, the daughter of a widow in the neighborhood, and apparently so artless, so innocent, so unsuspecting of guile, that no one, who retained a spark of humanity, could have found it in his heart to harm her. The serpent, however, found his way into Eden, and the pure are never safe from the machinations of the vile. Under pretence of visiting and caring for the loneliness of the widow, he readily found a way to excite the gratitude and sympathies of the daughter. And the old lady, in her ignorance of the world, never imagined that one who could pray so fervently, and sing so beautifully, and read the Scriptures with such a devotional spirit, could be otherwise than good. So she encouraged his intimacy with her daughter, and when he proposed marriage, gladly accepted the offer. "But Harriet must have a beautiful silk dress and a bridal veil," he said, "and, with the mother's consent, he would take her to the city, to select her outfit." The unsuspecting woman consented, but never beheld her daughter again, never saw nor heard from the perjured lover. What mother's heart could bear such a blow? hers could not. From a robust, hale, hearty woman, she gradually drooped, grew pale and thin, then a slight hacking cough disturbed her rest, and before the flowers of Autumn faded, or the songbirds had departed to a warmer clime, she died.

And the man who can thus betray a woman's confidence is capable of any treachery, and almost any crime.

At the time, I knew not our Mormon leader as such a man, but circumstances revealed him to me, as the destroyer of that beautiful girl, the murderer of her mother, and the father of an abandoned child. Nor was this the only hateful episode in his eventful life. Many a heart had he abused and trampled, winning its sweet wealth of affection, and then casting it from him, like a worthless weed. And did he feel no remorse? he was too utterly depraved for that. The Good Spirit had departed for ever from him, saying, "he is joined to his idols, let him alone."

From Methodism to Mormonism the transition was easy; not because there is any similarity in the doctrines, but because it is just as easy to act the hypocrite in one line as in another, when the only consideration admitted is, to inquire which will be most profitable.

The next day a majority of the Mormon church decided to receive B——m as their chief, Prophet, and spiritual governor, and invested him with such insignia of authority as he saw fit to prescribe. He was very haughty in his demeanor; fond of magnificent apparel; and more than once I half suspected that certain ideas of kingly dignity had taken possession of his brain. At any rate, he acted the part of sovereign Pontiff admirably, and presided over the Mormon worship with a state unknown before.

Coming into our house one day, he said, that it had been revealed to him that the body of the fallen Prophet must be rescued from the heathen, and be carried with them as a sort of palladium, to ensure their safety in their journey, as well as prosperity in the Promised Land. The Mormons, in their fright and consternation, had neglected the mortal remains of their leader, and, as it appeared, a hole had been dug in the ground by his enemies, and the body thrown in, without care or consideration. Several days had now elapsed, and it could scarcely be considered expedient to remove it, and so after much discussion it was finally decided that a coffin, with suitable inscriptions and adornments, should be procured, and being filled with the clothes and personal property of the fallen saint, should be considered as possessing the same efficacy as would pertain to his flesh and his bones. "Did the people believe in this humbug?" you inquire. "Do they not all the world over believe in humbugs equally as great? in relics and enchantments." Some of them do.

CHAPTER XVII.

GOING OFF.

A MONTH had nearly elapsed—a month of perplexity and anxiety in getting ready to move. As yet, we had heard nothing from Mrs. Bradish. B——m said that it had been revealed to him that she was still living, but thought it best to remain in obscurity. We made many inquiries of friends, who were continually coming to join us from a distance, but could obtain no information. Mrs. Murray protested against going any further from her childhood's home, begging and imploring her husband to permit her to return to her parents, taking her children.

This he sternly refused, telling her that all of them should accompany him, as he might need their services.

"But you can get another wife—have even now another," she answered. "You can do as you please, when I am gone, and I shall no more offend you with tears and protestations."

"You must go where I do," he said, "but you had better be careful how you comport yourself."

Mr. Murray was a man of exceedingly variable temper. At one time, he would be very affectionate and amiable; at another, cold, morose, and sour. Indeed, whatever happened to displease him, the effects of his ill-nature were vented on his wife. Was the weather too hot or too cold; was there too much or too little rain; if any disappointment occurred, his wife was sure to suffer for it. On the contrary, when everything pleased him, no man could be more gentle and conciliating. Mrs. Murray informed me that he grew more preposterous every day, and she attributed it to his irritation and disappointment in not being chosen to fill the place of Smith. Mrs. Murray, however, loved him exceedingly; and when he was kind and gentle, she was one of the happiest of women. On the contrary, his fits of caprice and passion would throw her into the deepest dejection.

Our new leader stalked around in his consecrated robes, with all the dignity and state imaginable, but contrary to our expectations, he left Irene in possession of the house occupied by the former Prophet. She likewise claimed the privilege of taking care of the holy relics of the deceased; and as no one interfered to prevent it, they remained in her possession—a circumstance which led her to arrogate a great importance to herself.

Two days previous to the expiration of the month in which we were to make our preparations for removal, our company was ready for departure. We were to rendezvous on the banks of a small creek, in order to await the approach of others, who were advancing from different sections of the State. We left our houses standing empty, our hearth-stones deserted,. our fields unsown, for a long, and it might be a disastrous, journey through the wilderness. The believers left their temple, but carried along, if not the bones, at least the relics, of their Prophet. Our order of march was easily determined, and we moved off like a small caravan, some riding on horseback, some in wagons, some walking, and one elder preaching loudly against the heathen, and ever and anon stopping to shake off the dust from his feet, as a testimony against them. How often it happens that something ludicrous will occur in the most trying situations, and while my eyes were filled with tears of sorrow and regret, I burst into a hearty fit of laughter.

After a journey of probably twenty miles, we arrived at the place where our first encampment was to be made. It was a beautiful and retired place, in a grove of cottonwood. We found several wagons already there ; and during the day and night many others came in. They were received with gracious condescension by B——m, who preached, and prayed, and exhorted ; saluted the sisters with a holy kiss, praised the babies, and flattered the men. I saw at once that he was likely to be extremely popular, and subsequent events substantiated my opinions. He soon found himself the centre of attraction on all sides. The best of everything was reserved for him. One sister neglected a pair of squalling children to embroider him a pair of slippers. Another took a dress-pattern, designed for herself, and made him a gown. He was continually receiving little presents of fish, flesh, or fowl, fruit, cake, or candy, which the new arrivals were bringing in. But the good sisters knew nothing of this man's true character, and very little of Mormonism, as it was subsequently developed.

The morning of the day on which our encampment was to be broken up, we espied a horseman approaching at a rapid rate, and waving a handkerchief, as if to detain us.

"I wonder what is wanted now?" said Mr. Ward.

"We shall probably know soon," I replied. "He is approaching rapidly." That instant, something familiar in the carriage and appearance of the person struck me. I looked again; it was Mrs. Bradish, dressed in male attire.

"Welcome, welcome, good friend and brave woman!" said Mr. Ward, advancing and offering her his hand. "We began to fear that you were lost or dead. Where have you been, true sister of the church?"

"Been?" she answered, "I have been to a good many places, and done some business, too. There are three or four wagons behind you; you must wait for them."

"Coming to join us?"

"Yes; they are my converts. I rode on ahead, as I thought that otherwise they would not be able to overtake you in time."

We stopped; and while the wagons were coming up, Mrs. Bradish related her adventures to the whole company, who were nearly dying with curiosity to hear. Even B———m came forward with his stately step, and requested an introduction to the distinguished sister, and then seating himself by her side, to the infinite envy and mortification of all the unmarried sisters, requested her to proceed.

"On that dreadful night," she said, "when these eyes beheld the fall of our holy Prophet, when he tumbled from his horse, shot, massacred by the heathen, and when I saw the sons of Belial crowding around me, with imprecations and menaces, some attempting to seize the reins of the animal, others trying to drag me from my seat, impelled by the strong instinct of self-preservation, I thought only of escape. Not that I cared so much for myself, not that the martyr's crown is ever to be avoided, from purely craven or selfish motives, but my thoughts referred to the church, thus suddenly deprived of her leader, and I determined to live, if possible, and contribute my small influence to her support in this fiery trial."

"Noble woman!" said B——m.

"My steed was powerful, and I urged him, plunging and rearing right against and over my enemies, and away we went with the swiftness of the wind. In the haste and tumult of the moment, it never occurred to me that I might be taking the wrong direction—that I might be rushing into the presence of my foes rather than escaping them. But on we went, over hill and dale, through forests and across the streams. Suddenly a light appeared in the distance. I directed my steed towards it, and soon alighted before the door of a small farm-house : knocking at the door, I heard a light step, and then a female, apparently middle-aged, opened it.

" 'My dear madam,' I said, addressing her, ' I have lost my way. Will you be so good as to tell me where I am.'

" 'Lost!' said the woman, with an expression of alarm and consternation. 'Then you had better come in here, and stay till morning. My child is sick, and I have been watching with him, which accounts for my being up so late. However, you can be hospitably entertained with us. I shall be happy to assist you in every way of which I am capable.'

"I thanked the good woman kindly, accepted her hospitality, and informed her that my horse was standing at the gate.

"'Well, we can tend to him, I guess,' answered the woman. 'There is no man in the house, my husband being absent on some little business.'

"And so my faithful steed was housed and fed, and myself comfortably entertained.

"When the lady invited me to retire, I frankly informed her that I should much prefer watching with her, as I had not the smallest inclination to sleep.

"'Oh, well, act your pleasure,' she said, with a smile, and then inquired whom she had the pleasure of entertaining.

"I frankly told her my name.

"She gave a slight start, and curiously regarded me.

"'Are you acquainted with the Mormons?' she inquired, thoughtfully, after a moment's silence.

"'I am.'

"'Excuse me, madam, I fear that my curiosity is getting ahead of my politeness, but are you the woman who shot the Regulator a short time since?'

"'I am that woman.'

"'Then I must inform you that you cannot possibly be safe with me, after to morrow morning. That man was my husband's brother. My husband is out now with the other Regulators. At sunrise he will return, and, should he find you here, I could not answer for the consequences.'

"I answered satisfactorily; and now, as we knew and understood each other, we conversed very pleasantly on general subjects, and, as is frequently the case, ended precisely where we commenced, on Mormonism.

"'I used to hear people speak of the Mormons in New York State,' she said, 'as I am an emigrant from that country. Indeed, two or three families of our neighbors became converts, but I never saw much of them, though I believe that they are living near us now.'

"'Their names,' I inquired.

"'Stillman,' she answered.

"'I have never heard of them.'

"'Probably not. I do not imagine that they ever publicly professed the faith of Mormon, though they were somewhat attached to it.'

"'I must go and see them.'

"'They live about five miles on the plain direct road.'"

"And you have been there all this time?" said Mr. Ward.

"Don't you interrupt me," exclaimed Mrs. Bradish. "In the morning, guided by the directions of my kind hostess, I soon found the residence of Mr. Stillman. The house was very ordinary in its appearance from the road, though bearing the evident marks of thrift and comfort. Everything looked sleek and happy—the cows, the pigs, and the poultry. Several children were playing around, but they soon paused to gaze and wonder, when they saw the strange woman approaching, and then rushed into the house. Presently a tall, amiable looking matron, came to the door, in whom, to my infinite surprise and astonishment, I instantly recognized Louisa Beardsley, an old schoolmate. The recognition was mutual, and she approached me, smiling through her tears, with extended hands.

"'Oh, Louisa,' I exclaimed, 'has heaven, indeed, reserved this great happiness for me?'

"'I am certainly delighted to see you,' returned Louisa, 'walk into the house.'

"And we went in together.

"'My family, you see,' said Louisa, 'consists of my husband and myself, these three boys,' pointing to some great, robust, hearty urchins, 'and that girl yonder,' here she made a gesture towards a beautiful girl who sat by the window sewing, and who looked up, bowed, and blushed at this allusion to herself.

"'But is that girl your niece or daughter?'

"'Neither; her story is very romantic; some day you shall be made acquainted with all the particulars.'

"The girl colored and trembled at this remark, and Louisa, who perceived it, changed the conversation.

"'You see that house yonder, just over the hills?' said Louisa.

"I answered in the affirmative.

"'That is where the family of my husband's father live. They were half inclined to be Mormons once.'

"'Indeed?'

"'Yes; the old gentleman still insists that there was something miraculous about it, and I am inclined to believe that nothing but their difficulties with the Regulators prevented him from searching them out and professing their faith.'

"'That should rather have been an inducement.'

"'Not with an old man like him, who is horrified at the least disturbance. And yonder,' she continued, pointing off in another direction, 'is where my mother lives. You were not acquainted with her?'

"'I believe not.'

"'Well, you must get acquainted; yet mother is deeply prejudiced against the Mormons.'

"'Have they injured her?'.

"'Never, to my knowledge,' said Louisa, laughing.

"I found Mr. Stillman to be a man very gentle, moderate, and easily persuaded, who was directed in all things by his wife. Not that Louisa aspired to command or rule her husband, but he found it easier to abide the decision of her judgment than to exercise his own. Old Mr. Stillman possessed the same character, and was positively uxorious in his love for his wife. I found that she had heard and read much of Mormonism, and, being in her youth very excitable, she still retained a spice of romance in her disposition, and was particularly delighted with some of the new doctrines and practices. The news that you were to be expelled the country soon reached us.

"'Well, Aunt Mary,' I said, 'why can't you and Louisa here just pull up stakes, and go too?'

"'Bless me! what—travel off through that great desert among the Indians and buffaloes?'

"'Certainly; the buffaloes make very good beef; and as for the Indians, I think it would be better than any circus to witness their manœuvres on the backs of the wild horses.'

"'And I think so, too,' said Louisa.

"'If it wasn't for the plague and trouble of moving,' said old Mrs. Stillman, 'I should be inclined to go.'

"'Yes; if it wasn't for the plague and trouble of moving,' said the old man, who had a habit of repeating everything his wife said, as if he were her echo.

"'That wouldn't be much,' said Louisa; 'but I hear that the Mormons indulge themselves in a plurality of wives.'

"'So did Abraham and Jacob, and David, the man after God's own heart.'

"Louisa said nothing.

"'If it was right for these ancient and holy men, who are held up as patterns and exemplars to succeeding generations, it cannot be wrong at the present day. You cannot find a passage in the Scripture where it is forbidden.'

"'That may be,' said Louisa; 'and yet, I should go mad to have my husband take another wife; I know I should. It must be outrageous to the feelings of any woman.'

"'I fancy you would care nothing about it. Why, Louisa, only think how it lightens the burdens of a family, for two or three to share them.'

"'I don't care; I should be tempted to kill 'em both.'

"'Your husband would scarcely wish to take another wife.

"'I don't suppose that he would,' said Louisa

"'I shouldn't be a bit afraid of it,' said old Mrs. Stillman.

"'I shouldn't be a bit afraid of it,' chimed in the old man, as usual.

"'Well, if I actually knew that he wouldn't, I should be tempted to go with them.'

"'Nonsense, Louisa. It is only under peculiar circumstances that Mormon husbands take more than one wife. There are many who never think of such a thing. Your influence over Mr. Stillman is too unbounded for him to ever give way to that temptation, unless, indeed, it was your request.'

"'I don't think it would be a temptation,' said the old lady.

"'I don't think it would be a temptation,' reiterated the old man.

"'I don't know as it would,' said Louisa.

"'At any rate, that need make no difference to you.'

"'It wouldn't to me,' said Mrs. Stillman, senior. 'I shouldn't be at all concerned about father, here, on that score, at least.'

"I soon discovered that the two women were almost persuaded to join us; and a little coaxing, and wheedling, and flattery soon brought their husbands to the same views. Mrs. Beardsley, however, opposed the matter with all her influence, and many were the arguments between her and Louisa.

"'But, mother,' said Louisa, 'the Mormons have never injured you—why should you be so prejudiced against them?'

"Because they are false teachers, false prophets, and co-workers of all iniquity,' said Mrs. Beardsley.

"'How do you know?'

"'Oh, I know—then they have two or three wives apiece.'

"'So did the patriarchs.'

"'Perhaps it was right, in that age of the world.'

"'Well, what is right in one age of the world, is right also in another, since the laws of right and wrong are immutable.'

"'Oh! my child, my child, remember your soul—your precious, immortal soul.'

"Mrs. Beardsley always endeavored to change the conversation, when she found herself rather worsted in argument.

"'What has that remembrance to do with the righteousness of a plurality of wives?' said Louisa, laughing.

"'You forget that I'm your mother, thus to turn me into ridicule,' said Mrs. Beardsley, in a dissatisfied voice.

"It has been conceded that opposition is the life of trade; it certainly is a great help in match-making, and in this case it rather promoted than retarded the arrangements. The three families were frequently together, and the conversation always centered on the Mormon emigration. The two Stillman families had concluded to join our company, and made all necessary preparations, and Louisa had determined to persuade her mother to go with them.

"Mrs. Beardsley, a widow in good circumstances, lived with two or three domestics, in a small house, which she had long talked of selling, and for which she had received a very fair offer. If there was anything at which she excelled, it was knitting. From morn till noon, and from noon till night, the knitting-work was in her hands. She knit stockings to sell, and stockings to give away. Woollen stockings, cotton stockings, and silk stockings. All the clergymen in the neighborhood, several of the school teachers, and not a few of the children, bore on their feet the testimony of her industry and benevolence. She kept a great pile of stockings in a closet, which were regularly taken out and aired once a month. Stockings of all colors, sizes, and descriptions; black, blue, green, white, yellow, and variegated; big, little, and middling. It was with no small degree of pride that the old lady would show and review her treasures; and she was quite as proud to be thus prepared to answer the calls of benevolence. If a beggar came along soliciting charity, she gave him a pair of stockings, and cared nothing about his muttering or looking displeased. On one occasion, however, the stockings were flung back in her face with an oath. If a tract-distributor or Home Missionary called, soliciting contributions, the pile of stockings formed a ready treasure from which to obtain a donation. One of these worthies, however, remarked when presented with the gift, 'That as the stockings were black, they looked too much like the devil to suit him,' and asked for money.

"'If my stockings look like the devil, money is the root of all evil, and I don't wish to bestow any evil gift upon a good man,' returned the lady.

"As I have said, the three families were together at the residence of Mr. Stillman, jun. That gentleman was seated in the door, playing with his youngest boy, who was kicking, laughing, and screaming in the very ecstasy of childish fun and mischief. Louisa was gliding about the room putting things 'to rights,' as she quaintly expressed it. Emily, the beautiful girl already mentioned, was sitting by the window, with some plain sewing in her hands. Old Mrs. Stillman occupied a stuffed and cushioned rocking-chair, making some lace into a cap. Mr. Stillman, sen., was seated near her, evidently regarding her matronly countenance with the deepest veneration. And Mrs. Beardsley was snapping her knitting needles with rather more spirit than usual, her bright, black eyes sparkling with uncommon ardor, and the most casual observer would have decided that an argument of no common interest was being carried on.

"'You are my only daughter, Louisa,' said Mrs. Beardsley. 'That you very well know, and if you prefer the Mormons to me, I've no more to say. I can go and live with your brother, but mind you'll get nothing of me.'

"'You'll give me a pair or two of stockings?' said Louisa.

"'No, I shan't, if you have no more regard for me than that.'

"' Well, it don't matter, but mother, you left your parents.'

"' I know that, but your grandfather was giving all his property to the boys. I told him only the week before we moved, that if he would give me a deed for ten acres of woodland, I would never leave him,' replied Mrs. Beardsley.

"' I don't see what that amounts to,' said Louisa, ' only that you thought more of ten acres of woodland than you did of him.' Mrs. Beardsley looked surprised; that was certainly a view of the case she had never taken.

"' Well, mother,' said Mr. Stillman, jun., ' get ready and go along. I don't doubt that there will be plenty of widowers, and bachelors in the company. Who knows what a match you might make ?'

"' Or,' said Mrs. Beardsley, ' there might be married men, who would think that an old woman might be useful to nurse babies.'

"' And knit stockings,' said Mrs. Stillman, sen.

"' However, mother, you must go with us,' said Louisa; ' that's the whole of the matter.'

"' Oh! yes,' said Mrs. Stillman, sen., ' get ready and go.'

"' Get ready and go,' echoed the old man.

" At this juncture of the conversation, a letter was brought in and handed to Mrs. Beardsley.

"' From my son,' she said, breaking the seal.

" She read a moment, threw down the letter, and went on knitting.

" Louisa picked it up, glanced over the contents, and said :—

"' Here is news, certainly.'

"' What is it ?' inquired Mr. Stillman.

"' Why, brother Henry has joined the Mormons, and is going to emigrate.'

"' Now, mother, you can have no excuse.'

" But I must bring my story to a close, for yonder are the wagons coming, and Mrs. Beardsley occupies one of them."

CHAPTER XVIII.

EMILY'S NARRATIVE.

PASSING over the events connected with the first few days of our journey, I shall only say that we had the usual quantum of cross, squalling babies, big, ugly boys, and dirty, boyish girls. Mothers scolded as they always will scold; fathers smoked and talked, and the preachers exhorted. Mrs. Bradish had introduced me to her friends, and I was particularly pleased with Emily's appearance. She was very beautiful, at least, so I thought, but beautiful women have been too often described by romancers for me to attempt it. One thing, however, was certain; our Prophet and leader evidently regarded her with deep admiration. The antiquated old ladies sought in vain to attract his notice, or share his company, he had neither eyes nor ears for aught but Emily. He walked with, he sat with her, he relaxed his haughtiness in her presence. How I trembled for her artless, unsuspecting innocence. She knew nothing, she did not even dream of the dangers in which she was involved. I had heard from Mrs. Bradish that some mystery was attached to her birth. She was probably an orphan; was it not my duty to attempt to shield and protect her?

One beautiful evening after we had encamped, built a fire, prepared supper and eaten it, Emily wandered off from the rest, and sat down on a grassy knoll. I approached, we entered into conversation, and she confided to me the events of her life.

"The first that I remember," said Emily, "is being in a

large old house, surrounded by groups of squalid children, and miserable-looking men and women. We were beneath the jurisdiction of a toothless old woman, who put us to bed at night, assisted us to dress in the morning, and gave us orders, which we never obeyed, in the daytime. Our days were passed in running over the fields and woods after berries, climbing fences and trees, hunting birds' nests, and hallooing at all the travellers. We were never sent to schools or meetings, never taught to pray or sing, or instructed to be good. In this respect, there seemed a vast difference between us and two other children belonging to the establishment. They might have belonged to a higher order of beings, and I soon learned, that in the mistress of the mansion they recognized a mother. We were never permitted to eat or play with them; and how strangely their white muslin dresses, ornamented with lace and embroidery, contrasted with our coarse homespun frocks. At length, reason began to dawn on my mind. I felt a strange, indefinable curiosity, a mysterious yearning of heart, which I could not analyze; but I wished to know something of myself and my parentage. A thousand times had I attempted to ask the old woman, whom we called, 'nurse,' but as often my resolution failed; for, in my ignorance, I knew not what language to employ. As I grew older, however, my timidity wore off, and I presented myself rather abruptly before her one day.

" 'Well, child, what now?' she inquired.

" 'I want to know whether or not I ever had a mother?'

" 'Why, I expect so; of course, everybody has a mother; but what put such an idea as that in your head?'

" 'And had I a father, too?'

" 'Why, child, what on earth—how did you come to think of that?'

" 'Because I wanted to know; wanted somebody to love me, and whom I could love.'

" 'Well, you mus'n't think of such things.'

" 'I can't help it; and then I want to know why mistress won't let us speak to Helen and Julia, and why she gives them pie and cake, and won't let us have any, and why'——

" 'For mercy's sake, child, you frighten me. Now run and play.'

" 'But you ha'n't told me yet.'

" 'Oh! I can't tell you. You mus'n't ask such questions.'

" 'At any rate, you can tell me, why there are so many more people here than I ever see at Mr. Mannington's? and why these men keep coming to bring all sorts of sick, and lame, and ugly persons here, just as if there wasn't enough such now.'

" 'Souls alive! this is the poor-house.'

" 'And what is the poor-house?'

" 'Why, it's where all the poor, and sick, and lame folks go to, to be took care of.'

" 'Did they bring me here?'

" 'You was born here, as near as I can find out.'

"After awhile I began to shrink from the presence of those with whom I had been accustomed to associate. I had a longing for higher pursuits and nobler pleasures. The imbecile and idiotic were the objects of my especial dislike; my mind had not been trained sufficiently to pity them.

"One of the women up-stairs had a small mirror, in which I was sometimes permitted to look.

" 'Child, do you know that you are beautiful?' she said to me one day.

" 'Beautiful; what is it?' I knew not the meaning of the word.

" 'Do you know that you are pretty, then? nice, sweet, like the flowers and humming-birds.'

"I caught a glimpse of her meaning.

"'No; no. I didn't 'spect I was, my clothes is old, and my hair tangled.'

"'Never mind that; you are a thousand times more beautiful than Mrs. Bassett's girls, with all their finery and ringlets. Your hair would curl beautifully, too, with a little care. I know it would. Come, sit down here at my feet, and let me try it.'

"I obeyed willingly, but it was no easy task that she had undertaken. The hair was tangled, matted, and almost felted; it had not been combed for a month.

"'This beats all,' she said, after tugging and pulling at the refractory locks. "Warn't your hair never straightened in the world? There, don't cry, child, or I shan't have the courage to go on with it; but such a mat I never did see.'

"I sobered up, determined to bear the infliction like a heroine, and have my hair curled once. What would the rest of them think when they saw me in ringlets?

"An hour probably elapsed before my hair-dressing was completed, then, with the assistance of some soap and water, my hands and face were cleansed and smoothly polished.

"'I declare, child, it does my eyes good to see you. Look here, and she presented the small mirror. I looked, and screamed with delight.'

"'Now go down, and let 'em see you.'

"I hesitated a moment, and then obeyed. A half-idiot woman was passing through the hall, bearing a huge tub of water, as I descended. At my unwonted appearance she gave a start of surprise, dropped the tub, and splashed the beautiful dress of the mistress, who was walking from the parlor, accompanied by a visiting lady.

"The servant stood pale and trembling; the mistress glanced around and beheld me. But the visitor had seen me first, and the varying emotions of pity, admiration, and surprise were plainly visible on her features.

"'Oh! it's you, you hussy; well, I don't wonder you frightened Sally, your hair fixed in that kind of style, exactly like—well, no matter; but don't appear before me again in that fashion.'

"'On the contrary,' said the visitor, 'I should be delighted to behold such a beautiful child every day—to have her always in my presence. Look here, darling; I never saw such beautiful ringlets and expressive eyes.'

"The last remark was unfortunate, for Mrs. Bassett's two daughters had approached, and were standing by their mother. She glanced angrily towards me, and then at them.

"'Go up-stairs, and stay till I send for you,' she said, and I obeyed with willingness.

"At dusk, I heard the passionate sound of sobbing in the family room. My curiosity could not be restrained, and I crept softly down to listen. Presently, a voice, which I knew to be Julia's, said, 'Oh! mother, it is too bad; I can't, and won't bear it. Only to think that lady said her hair and eyes were the most beautiful she ever beheld. Oh, dear!'

"'Don't cry, Julia. I'll take care that you are never insulted in that manner again, that I will,' and approaching the staircase, she cried at the top of her voice, 'Em, come here.'

"Trembling with apprehension, I came forward.

"'How dare you appear in my presence, with your hair in such a fix to-day—exactly like Julia? Didn't you know that it wasn't suitable nor fit for one in your condition?'

"'No, ma'am.'

"'Well, it isn't, and to prevent you from doing so hereafter, I shall cut off your hair. Go, Julia, bring me my scissors.'

"Julia was delighted to obey.

"'Now sit down here.'

"I sat down before her, and the operation commenced. In a

few minutes my hair was all cropped short, close to my head. Julia laughed outrageously.

"'There, Julia, hush,' said the mother. 'I'm sure it looks much more becoming and proper for a girl like you, whose mother was a'—— She stopped.

"'What was my mother?' I inquired.

"'Nobody; but now go to bed at once.'

"I retreated, and Julia remarked as I passed out: 'She won't look so beautiful to Mrs. Burney now.'

"I went up stairs, and met Betsey at the entrance of her room.

"'Sakes alive, child, what have they been doing to you?' she cried out.

"The lights were burning, and she could see very plainly.

"'Cutting off my hair.'

"'Heathens! Barbarians! Who done it?'

"'The mistress.'

"'What did she do that for?'

"'She said it wasn't proper for one in my station to wear her hair as Miss Julia wore hers.'

"'Station, indeed! better talk about station! Her father died in jail, and her mother was supported by the township for years; and this lady here, who talks about station, worked around the country at pot-wrestling, till Bassett, an old widower, with a small house, and a large family, took pity on her,' and Betsey was obliged to pause, and take breath.

"I stood listening, though unable to comprehend the full meaning of the words.

"'Betsey, what is that you are saying?' called Mrs. Bassett, from the foot of the stairs.

"'The truth,' replied Betsey.

"'Well, don't you never dare to speak such words of me again. I won't bear it, indeed I won't.'

"'Yes; you will bear it,' replied Betsey, whose dander was fairly up. "You will bear it, because you can't help it; and as for my telling it, I shall do that just when I please. Here, you've cut off this poor child's hair for no earthly reason, only because Mrs. Burney praised and noticed it. It's a real wonder that you didn't dig out her eyes, and smear corrosive sublimate over her face, to make her as ugly as your great red-faced, flat-nosed brats.'

"Mrs. Bassett had several times attempted to speak, but Betsey's eloquence effectually stifled her voice; and half the persons in the house, hearing the unwonted noise, came rushing to the scene of action, demanding what was the matter?'

"'Why; just look!' said Betsey, 'just look!' and she dragged me forth in plain view. 'Just see how she cut off that poor child's hair, because it was so much prettier than Julia's?'

"'Did the mistress do that?—what a shame!—what a shame!'

"Mrs. Bassett, provided with a long lash, which she laid lustily about her, finally succeeded in dispersing the crowd, when I retreated timidly to bed.

"The next day, Mrs. Burney called again, and inquired for me. I heard her pleasant voice, and Mrs. Bassett's reply.

"'Excuse me, madam, but what can you want with the child?'

"'I want her to go home with me; I have obtained a permit to take her, from the overseers.'

"'For a servant?' suggested Mrs. Bassett.

"'No; for a daughter. I wish to adopt her, and make her my heir.'

"'You certainly do not wish to adopt a child whose mother was a'—— I could not hear the remainder of the sentence.

"'Mrs. Bassett, I have said it. The child is good and pure, and exceedingly beautiful. Will you please to call her?'

"Mrs. Bassett hesitated, as if seeking some excuse, but finding none, she ordered me into the parlor.

"Mrs. Burney gazed on my shaven head with looks of mingled surprise and pity; then turning to Mrs. Bassett, she inquired:

"'Who wrought all that ruin?'

"'If you mean, who cut off her hair—I done it. I don't consider it proper for a child in her condition to wear curls.'

"Tears sprang to the eyes of Mrs. Burney, as she said:

"'Oh! Mrs. Bassett, how could you be so cruel? Come here my darling—but your curls will grow again. We will have some tonic to start it.'

"'Am I going home with you?' I said, nestling close to the kind lady.

"'Yes, darling; you shall go with me, and be my daughter.'

"'What is daughter?'

"'I'll be a mother to you,' she answered.

"'Will you? will you?' I cried, dancing around the room. 'Oh? I shall be so happy!'

"I had no experience of the love or tenderness of a mother, but yet an instinct of nature told me that it was something exceedingly pleasant and endearing."

The account of the residence of Emily with Mrs. Burney, and her experiences in that situation, must be deferred to another place.

CHAPTER XIX.

SUNDRY MATTERS.

IT is scarcely necessary to remark that with the demise of Smith, Mormonism took a new aspect in many particulars. This is chiefly to be attributed to the difference in the characters of the leaders. B——m, though professing to believe in miracles, rarely attempted the exhibition of them, and finally, ceased to talk of any such thing. Smith had introduced spiritual-wifery, under the pretence of a pure platonic, or rather spiritual affection ; B——m openly advocated polygamy ; and, in order that his precepts and practices might coincide, he espoused three wives in one day. Before the demise of Smith, however, polygamy was slowly coming into practice, though the sentiments of the ladies were divided on the subject. It was decided by the latter to be not simply a privilege, but a duty, and the virtues of the believers were estimated very much by the numbers of their wives. During the journey, however, they had little time for marrying, or giving in marriage.

Our guide was a young man, named Harmer, who bore the title of Captain, in consideration of his having once held that office in the Mormon legion, those first pioneers of that faith, who, in the service of the United States, had explored the region of the Great Salt Lake, in their overland route to California. It was chiefly through his representations of the health, and beauty, and fertility of the country, that the Mormons had been induced to emigrate thither. And Harmer seemed fully competent for the task he had undertaken. Hale, energetic, and robust, he appeared incapable of fatigue, and being endowed with great self-command, he readily acquired an unlimited influence over the minds of others.

We travelled for several days through a country sparsely inhabited by white people; over great rolling prairies, with probably a small house in the midst, like a solitary ship in a boundless expanse of ocean; along the banks of muddy, marshy streams, and beneath the shades of the imposing cotton-wood trees. Here we had few adventures worth recording—perhaps a wagon broke down, or a horse became lame. Not unfrequently we were entertained with the music of those family-organs, squalling babies. Sometimes a refractory mule refused to do its duty, or a cow parted from our company without saying " good bye." On the whole, however, we had a fine time of it, especially when compared with what was to come.

We numbered one hundred and twenty wagons, each wagon being drawn by four mules; fifty horsemen, and twenty-five led horses; besides a great number of cattle, sheep, and hogs, designed to be slaughtered on the way for food, or to serve for stock when we arrived at our journey's end.

When we arrived at St. Louis, we found several other wagons waiting to join us, and, after a short delay, proceeded to cross the Mississippi, and strike off through the uninhabited ocean of prairie. It may be as well to observe, in this place, that, in consequence of time and trouble, I have forgotten the names of many of the streams and mountains, and can only testify as to the general features of the country.

We took the Santa Fé road, however, and, continuing that day in the same direction, encamped at night on the borders of a small stream. During our journey, it was customary to encamp about an hour before sunset, when the wagons were so arranged as to form a sort of barricade, in a circular form, in the centre of which tents were pitched in military style. The mules and horses were then hobbled and turned loose to graze, in company with the stock, which the men watched and took care of by turns. At nightfall the horses, mules, and oxen were collected and picketed—that is, secured by a halter to a stake, one end of which was driven in the ground, while the cattle and sheep were brought into the enclosure. At day-break the camp was roused, the animals turned loose to graze, and breakfast prepared.

Mrs. Bradish was exceedingly busy, and professed herself to be in raptures with such a nomadic mode of life.

"Wasn't it nice and romantic," she said, looking round. "So many families all cooking and eating in the open air, exactly like gipsies."

"It looks rather strange," I said.

Mr. Ward brought in his usual comparison of the Israelites journeying to the Promised Land.

"And once there," interposed B———m, "we will show the heathen our power and independence of them and their devilish government. Yes, there" ———, and he nodded authoritatively.

We halted at noon, for an hour or two, to rest and dine, and on the second day of our route forded a small stream. While making our encampment at night, one of the women became frightened at a huge spider. Her screams terrified the horses; they commenced rearing and plunging, and finally broke loose, when they set off over the hills at full speed. Harmer and some others went in pursuit, but did not return with the fugitives till near morning.

Mrs. Bradish could not conceal her vexation. "Now 'see what you have done! I'd be ashamed of myself—'fraid of a spider. What if they should all get lost, and not return at all? Pretty times we should have without Harmer, wouldn't we?"

Mr. Ward said he anticipated no danger of such a catastrophe as that, yet he could not conceive what a woman saw in a spider to be frightened at.

Her husband scolded her severely, and even threatened to use his lash about her back, at which B———m smiled complacently. Indeed, I observed that the further we removed from the civilized settlements, the more tyrannical the husbands became, and I finally began to wonder what would be the end of it.

Towards morning it began to rain heavily, and as our tents were formed of light and thin materials, they afforded but slight resistance to the watery element, and a more deplorable looking set than we presented, when morning came, can hardly be imagined. We were all wet as drowned rats, to use a familiar expression, and, though sharing the misfortune of the others, I laughed heartily at their doleful appearance. Some seemed to enjoy the scene with me, others cried, the babies squalled lustily, and not a few of the men employed language that sounded marvellously like swearing.

"My young un's actually drowned," said a woman, coming forward and holding up a lean, pale child, that looked, indeed, as if it had been water-soaked.

"Hold it up by the feet, then," said one of the men.

"In that case its head will drop off," said another.

"Oh, dear, just look at my bonnet!" screamed one of the girls.

The bonnet had been stiffened with paste-board, and now it seemed a mass of wet paper and starch.

"Well, it's too bad," said Mrs. Stillman, sen. "I never thought such things could happen."

"I never thought such things could happen," echoed the old man.

Louisa said that she expected just such things, and much worse.

"Then you was a fool," said Mrs. Beardsley, "for ever starting on such a barbarous journey. Only to think of it, I wonder what will come next. Here's my knitting-work, wet as a hog. I can do nothing at all with it."

"But, mother, it will dry when the rain ceases."

"Rain cease, indeed!" said the old lady; "when will it ever cease? Why, I've heard say that it rained two or three weeks, right straight ahead, sometimes."

Harmer, who had returned, looked up with the utmost seriousness.

"Why, madam, that's nothing at all to what I've seen. Why, I've known it to rain for six months; and we even got so used to the water once, that we went diving and paddling about, like a parcel of ducks."

"Then heaven help me!" said the lady, "for I could never live through it."

But the worst of it was, we could not light a fire to get breakfast, and such provisions as we had, were thoroughly soaked. B———m took the thing with all the coolness of philosophy, or fanaticism. "The rain," he said, "was probably sent to try their faith and patience; and he hoped and trusted that they would manifest the spirit of true believers."

Mr. Ward suggested that a shelter for the fire should be made, by arranging in wigwam fashion some of the wagon-boards. This was soon done, and then one family after another prepared breakfast; but it was eaten without much pleasure. The men stood round, with the water running from their slouched hats; the garments of the females hung straight and dripping; five or six infants, who crept instead of walking, were spatting and plashing in the little pools; while the youngsters of eight or ten years were running, hallooing and whooping, like young savages, through the rain and mud.

At length Harmer burst into a loud, uncontrollable laugh.

"I declare, it's better than any show I ever witnessed, just to see how you all look. Do see Mrs. Beardsley's hair!"

The lady's hair, being false, had fallen down over her face, where it hung, dangling and dripping.

Towards noon the rain ceased, and the sun came out very warm, which gave us an opportunity to dry our wet garments. Here, likewise, an ox was butchered for food, and the meat equally divided among the company.

The consequences of the rain, however, lasted for some time. Several of the children, and some of the women, became sick. Fortunately, I had provided many little essentials of medicine and comfort, while in St. Louis, which were now extremely useful in ministering to the wants of the weak and diseased. Mrs. Murray was of the latter, but though she had so kindly administered to her husband, when he was wounded, on the present occasion he paid little attention to her, but employed himself in caressing and riding with Mrs. Cook. Oh, the vanity and perversity of men!

It cannot be denied, that the neglect of her husband, and the scorn of his companion sorely grieved her sensitive mind, and had a great effect in shortening her life. Indeed, I attributed her disease to this, more than to any other cause. She grew melancholic, and would remain a whole day without speaking or noticing any one. Then one of her children was seized with malignant dysentery. The mother looked up joyfully, and smiled. "My children," she said, "have been the only ties that bound me to earth. I thank my heavenly Father that he has heard my prayers, and is about to remove them first. Yes, Father, I thank Thee," she exclaimed, lifting her eyes and hands to heaven, "that in the midst of judgment, thou hast remembered mercy, and art about to take us to Thyself."

That night, the other children were attacked, and before the sunset of the following day illuminated the tops of the distant mountains, the three had fallen asleep. The mother neither wept nor murmured ; indeed, she looked radiant with holy joy ; and the spiritual expression of her eyes was a rapture to behold. I prepared the snowy garments for the dead, and they were laid out in their soft, cold beauty, beneath the thousand stars, and the quiet moonbeams. Their grave had been prepared at the foot of a grassy hill, on the banks of a small stream, beneath the shade of a grove of poplars. Three attendants stood near, with flaming torches, while two by two came the long procession, to gaze on their pallid faces. Mr. Murray approached, the mother of the dead children hanging on his arm. Surely, conscience was at work in his soul ; for his knees trembled, and throwing himself on the ground, beside the dead, he groaned aloud. Not so with the mother: she stood calm and collected for a moment, then stooped and kissed the icy brows, smoothed the death-damp locks, and then raised a clear song of thanksgiving and triumph, that her darlings had gone before ; that she was about to follow. 'Twas a strange and impressive spectacle : the night ; the gleaming torches, showing, fitfully and indistinct, the gathered multitude ; then the dead children—the open grave—the weeping father, and that mother, raising a strain of victory and immortal hope.

After the ceremony was concluded, I pressed forward to offer her my hand.

"Will you spend this night with me?" she asked ; "something whispers that it will be my last."

"I will, certainly, if you wish it ; but don't indulge in such gloomy reflections."

"Gloomy?" she said ; "Oh, they are ones of happiness to me!"

Informing Mr. Ward of her wish, I retired to her tent.

Mr. Murray came in and sat down in one corner, unperceived by her. She lay on a pallet, and now that the excitement of the past hour had worn off, she was pale and weak as a child.

"I wished that you should be present with me, Mrs. Ward, in this, which I firmly believe to be my last hour. I have long had a presentiment that my death was near, and the thought was one of rejoicing. I had nothing on earth to live for but my children, and now they are removed, and I thank God—I thank God!"

She lay still a moment and then resumed : " You have sympathized with me in my great affliction, an affliction which has been sanctified to my soul's eternal interest ; once I believed in Mormonism ; once I forsook the faith of my father, and forgot the dying admonitions of my mother. But the estrangement of my husband opened my eyes, and I felt—I knew—that a belief which sanctioned and promoted such sinful practices, must be of the Evil One ; and then I said, in the language of the patriarch, ' Oh, my soul ! come not into their secret ; to their assembly, my honor, be thou not united.' But circumstances forbade my return to the friends of my youth, for I must be weaned from my idols."

"You weary yourself, Mrs. Murray," I said ; "here, take this," and I administered a pleasant cordial.

"Feel my pulse," she said.

I did so ; there was not the least perceptible flutter. I saw that she was sinking rapidly.

"Joy ! joy !" she said. "I go."

Mr. Murray could contain himself no longer. He rose, and approached the bed.

"Sarah, my wife," he said, "have you no regret for me ?"

She opened her half-shut eyes, extended her thin, pale hand, and faintly murmured, "My husband, I pity and forgive you."

"And is that all ?" he said, choking with emotion.

"What more is necessary ?"

"Wretched man that I am," he groaned. "Oh ! that I had remained true to you and virtue."

Mrs. Murray seemed to have forgotten his presence. "Bend near me, Mrs. Ward," she murmured.

I stooped over the bed.

"My last request is to be buried beside my children; but don't let that man, B——m, come near me. I forbade his attendance at the burial of my babes. Yes; I knelt down, and implored and begged him to stay away. Oh! the Mormon faith will not do to die by."

"In what faith do you die?" I said, solemnly.

"The faith in which I was born, and here," she said, "here is a letter which I wish you to send to my venerated pastor, should an opportunity ever occur," and she drew from the folds of her garment a sheet of paper, delicately traced.

"You will send it?" she murmured faintly.

"If an opportunity ever occurs."

"Now read."

I opened a well-worn Testament that lay beside her on the bed, and commenced reading. Once or twice she attempted to speak, but her voice faltered. At length, I came to that inimitably beautiful passage, "I am the resurrection and the life saith the Lord, whosever believeth in me, though he were dead, yet shall he live; and whosoever liveth and believeth in me shall never die."

Summoning all her strength, she articulated, "Amen! amen! Lord Jesus receive my spirit."

There was a gurgling in the throat, a shadow passed over the countenance, and all was still.

"Let me die the death of the righteous, let my last end be like his."

Mr. Murray arose from his recumbent posture, gazed mournfully at the face of the dead, and prepared to go out.

"Will you call Mrs. Stillman to my assistance?" I asked.

He assented, and in a few minutes that lady came in. That

night we sat with the dead, and when the morning dawned, the children's grave was opened to receive the body of their parent. As no clergyman was present, I read over the grave the beautiful and affecting burial service of the Church of England.

Mr. Murray seemed deeply affected at the time, but his versatile mind could not long retain the impression of a painful sorrow.

CHAPTER XX.

FORDING A RIVER, AND ITS CONSEQUENCES.

AS yet, we had found no difficulty in crossing the streams. They had been wide, but shallow, with hard bottoms, and the mules had easily drawn the wagons over them. However, the evil was yet to come. We came one day to the banks of a deep, turgid, and rapid river, two hundred yards wide, with an apparently rocky bottom. There was a general halt ordered, and a consultation took place. Some proposed to unload the wagons, take them to pieces, and ferry the whole over in a small India rubber boat, that belonged to the company; others proposed to build a raft capable of supporting the wagons and their loads; while yet a third party were of the opinion that the mules could swim across, and draw the wagons after them.

"No such nonsense as that," said Harmer; "they'll certainly get tangled in the harness and drowned. I tell you, we must make a raft," and seizing his axe, started off for a poplar grove. He was soon joined by several others, and the raft was directly in process of construction.

"I'd like to know how we are to get over anyhow," said

Mrs. Beardsley. "Heaven knows, I wish I were back again. What a dreadful soaking we had the other day, when it rained. Poor Mrs. Murray and her children actually died of it. Mrs. Crosman says, she hasn't been well since, and that two of her children came very near having the inflammation of the lungs. It's dreadful to think of."

"So it is," said Mrs. Stillman, sen.

"So it is," echoed her husband.

Mrs. Bradish, as usual, was all heroism. She would go over on horseback, she said; and dressed in man's apparel, she rode up and down the stream to discover the safest place to enter. She even proposed that every horseman should take a woman behind him, and cross the stream with her, that being the safest and most expeditious mode of conveyance.

"Have faith, and all will be well," cried B——m; "as for me and my wives we could walk over dry shod, if I willed it; but I don't."

"I wish you would will it, and take us all over that way," said Mrs. Beardsley. "I'm sure I don't want my knitting-work to get wet again. It was two days drying, and in two days I might have knit a stocking."

"If there was nothing of more value than your knitting-work getting wet, small damage would be done," said Louisa.

Yet Louisa was wrong in her remark; for things are valuable only as they are esteemed.

"Can any one tell me what they are trying to make down there?" said Mrs. Stillman, sen., as she came round to the fire where I was preparing dinner.

"They are building a raft," I answered.

"What kind of a thing is that?" she inquired.

"Oh! I can't describe it; but you will probably see before long."

"Well, such work as we have I never did see."

"I never did see," echoed the old man, who had followed his wife.

"I don't see anything strange at all," said Mrs. Bradish. "It's nothing strange that there's a river, or that it has to be crossed, or that a raft should be built for that purpose. I made my calculations on these things."

The raft was soon constructed. It consisted of middling-sized logs, bound together by very strong ropes and chains, on which thick planks were laid, and fastened with iron spikes. One wagon only could be taken over at a time, and the process of crossing immediately commenced. Twenty-five horsemen were to go go over first, in order to carry the ropes attached to the raft. Mrs. Bradish declared that she would go with them, and insisted that twenty-five of the women should each choose her cavalier, and pass over on horseback.

"Don't think of such a thing," said a man by the name of Randolph, who had joined us at St. Louis, and who was infinitely fond of leading, directing, and giving advice. "Don't think of such a thing, ladies; you can go over in the wagons with much less danger of getting wet. Don't you think so, Brother B——m?"

Mrs. Bradish gave him a look that might have withered him.

"I don't see why you men must always interfere in the affairs of the women. I have decided on my course. What say the others?"

"Come, Emily, go with me; I'll carry you over like a duck," said Harmer.

Our stately hierarch approached, and advised Emily to wait and go with him.

"I prefer to go with Mr. Harmer," said Emily.

The two men exchanged glances. There was defiance and pleasure on one side, malice and envy on the other. From that day forth they were rivals.

Many of the younger women decided to go over behind the men on horseback—it was so romantic.

I preferred to remain in our wagon with my husband and his children. Mrs. Bradish mounted her steed with its sweeping mane and tail, and first plunged into the stream.

She was followed by Harmer and Emily, and after them came the rest. Several of the horses became restive, and some of them seemed actually incapable of resisting the strength of the current. They were carried imperceptibly down the river. This was especially the case with the one Mrs. Bradish rode. Then he grew mad and frightened at the unwonted exertion, and began to rear and plunge in the water, sometimes striking the rocks with his fore-feet, and throwing himself above the waves, and then almost entirely disappearing beneath the turgid swells. The lady, however, kept her seat nobly, though the steed grew more unmanageable every moment. Trembling and frightened we beheld her danger from the shore, but could not go to her assistance. The horsemen were too deeply engaged with their own restive animals, and the partners of their danger, to afford her the protection she required. At length a huge wave, sweeping directly against her waist, carried her instantaneously from the saddle. She retained sufficient presence of mind, however, to buoy up herself for a moment, and, springing forward, she caught the horse by the neck; neither did she quit her hold till both were safely landed on the opposite bank. She then took off her cap, wrung the water from her dripping hair and garments, and waved her handkerchief in token of success. A loud shout greeted her, and in a few minutes more we had the satisfaction to perceive that the whole company were safely over. The wagons were then drawn over, one by one, on the raft, though not without danger and difficulty, in consequence of the strong current.

"We're sinking! we're sinking!" said Mrs. Stillman, sen.; "didn't you feel it then?"

"Yes! didn't you feel it?" echoed the husband as usual.

"Feel what?" inquired Louisa.

"Why, the sinking! Lord help!—it's all going to pieces!" she cried.

The raft had caught on a sharp, jagged rock, and the utmost exertions were required to get it loose. Randolph persisted that everything went wrong because his advice was not followed.

"The raft, I tell you, wasn't made right in the first place. Don't you say so, Brother B——m?"

"Randolph, shut up," said one of the others. "Here mount this mule, take a pole, and plunge into the stream, and help to work the raft off. It's stuck on the rock fast as a roach."

Randolph said he should do nothing, as the whole affair had been transacted contrary to his advice.

"If you don't, by the devil," said the person addressed, "you may get your wagon over the best way you can, for I'll have nothing to do with it."

"Nor I either," said another.

"Nor I," "Nor I," shouted a third and fourth.

"Well, I think"— commenced Randolph.

"Who cares what you think? Stop your talk, and go to work."

Randolph turned away sullenly, seized the pole, and commenced operations. At length, after long-continued and great exertions, the raft was gotten clear, and the wagon landed.

"Oh! dear!" said Mrs. Stillman, rubbing her hands; how glad I am that we are safe. I expected to go to the bottom every moment."

"We expected to go to the bottom every moment," said the old man.

"That was very foolish," said Mrs. Bradish.

"What was foolish?"

"Why, to be afraid when there was no danger."

"Come here, mother, and warm yourself by this fire, and have a good cup of coffee."

While they were partaking refreshments, we went over, and the raft being carried higher up, we had no difficulty.

Mrs. Beardsley insisted on remaining till the very last wagon, because, she said, "if all the rest got over safely, there could be no danger for her."

But the night was fast coming on, and in their anxiety to get all over before the darkness closed in, it was decided to put upon the raft the two remaining wagons, with their accompanying loads. The raft had evidently sustained an injury on the rocks, for the minute it was launched the last time, it parted in the middle, precipitating the wagon in which Mrs. Beardsley rode into the foaming torrent. It was instantly submerged. One wild piercing scream rose from the water, it was answered simultaneously from the shore.

"Mother ! mother !" shrieked Louisa. "Oh ! mother will be drowned ; but she wouldn't come over when we did. Oh, dear ! oh, dear !" and rushing down to the water, she would have plunged in, regardless of the consequences, had not her husband prevented her. Twenty men were by this time in the water, and Louisa had the unspeakable satisfaction to see her mother drawn from the waves, though cold and insensible.

"She has only fainted," said one of the men, "she don't appear to have swallowed much water."

"With warming, and rubbing, and the application of restoratives, I think she will recover," said Mr. Ward.

We removed her wet garments, wrapped her torpid limbs in warm flannels, bathed her face with camphor, and applied hartshorn to her nostrils.

"Just the way," said Mrs. Bradish, "a cowardly person is almost certain to run into danger."

"But you are no coward, and I thought you were in some danger," I said.

"I in danger! not in the least. I felt no more frightened than I do this moment."

"It's something dreadful to be upset in the water that way," said Mrs. Stillman, sen.

"It was more of a setting down, I should think," said Harmer.

By this time she had recovered sufficiently to open her eyes and commence speaking.

"I shall never forgive myself in the world for persuading her to come with us, if she gets hurt," said Louisa.

"Hurt," said the old lady, looking at her daughter. "Did you say I was hurt?"

"I hope not, dear mother."

"But where am I? what is the matter?" she inquired. "Oh! I remember, the wagon tumbled from the raft into the water. Wasn't that it?"

Louisa nodded affirmatively.

"And I was wet, water-soaked, wonder if it'll kill me, like it did poor Mrs. Murray and her children?"

While we were attending to her, the men had succeeded in driving the cattle over, and all were safely encamped by the time that the young moon arose over the hills.

"And so I've been drowned and come to life again. It's a miracle of mercy. I can believe it," said Mrs. Beardsley, as myself and Mrs. Bradish entered her tent that evening.

"Nonsense," said Mrs. Bradish, "you were no more drowned than I was—you were only wet and frightened; that was all."

"Oh! you needn't talk that way. I was drowned. I know that my sensations were those of a drowning person exactly."

"And what were your sensations?"

"They wouldn't bear description," said the old lady, evidently a little piqued.

Mr. Stillman soon came in, and informed us that some of the scouts had returned with information that a large party of Indians were stationed on a neighboring hill.

"Are they enemies?" inquired Mrs. Bradish.

"To be sure they be," said Mrs. Beardsley, "Indians always are. Twice we've been drowned, now it comes our turn to be roasted; I only wonder what'll be next."

"It is impossible to tell whether they be friends or enemies; if the latter they will probably attack the camp to-night. It will be necessary to set a double watch, and be prepared for any emergency," said Mr. Stillman.

"I knew we should never live to get there, and I said so from the first," said Mrs. Beardsley.

"Did your knitting-work get wet?" inquired Mrs. Bradish.

"Yes; it did, and the color run, so it's spoiled."

"That's a great misfortune."

I proposed returning, and we went to our tent. We found Mr. Ward somewhat alarmed about the Indians. He said they were evidently a war party of the Sioux, who had been on an expedition against the Crows.

It will hardly be supposed that we slept that night. The presence of a party of marauding savages was anything but pleasant, and when I remembered all the horrid things they were capable of doing, my apprehensions became intolerable. Two or three times in the night we were alarmed by the screams of some night-bird, and the distant howling of a wolf, but the morning dawned, and found us safe and sound.

CHAPTER XXI.

WOMEN LOST OR CAPTURED.

"THANK heaven," said Mrs. Beardsley, while we were preparing breakfast. "Thank heaven that we are alive this morning. I expected to have been carried off bodily."

"I had faith that we shouldn't be attacked. I prayed fervently that the Lord would discomfit these sons of Belial, and the fervent effectual prayer of the righteous availeth much," said B——m, the leader.

"Pugh!" said Harmer, "I know better than that, what started off the Indians. They found out that we had discovered them, and so they have slipped out of the bag. Now they will probably hang around, and like enough attack us at some indefensible point unawares. These red-skins are up to all sorts of deviltry."

"Fiddle on the Indians," said Mrs. Bradish, "I ain't a bit afraid of them, and now that they are gone I mean to have a good canter over the prairie. The morning is fine, and I know that it will do me good after my wetting yesterday. Emily, you will ride with me, won't you?"

"The experiment will be attended with great danger," said Harmer. "Don't go."

"You think we can't take care of ourselves," said Mrs. Bradish, laughing, "we'll show you the contrary."

"I think," said Harmer, solemnly, "that the Indians are lurking about. It will be their policy to cut off stragglers.

"But I ain't a straggler," said Mrs. Bradish.

"The Indians might think you one, however, if they saw you alone."

"I don't intend to be alone. Emily is going with me."

We all used our best endeavors to dissuade Mrs. Bradish from her rash undertaking, but in vain. The very alarm we manifested seemed only to strengthen her resolution.

"My steed carries double finely," she said. "He is famous on a race, and will easily distance the Indians, should there be any about, of which I am doubtful."

"You will, possibly, find out to your cost," said Harmer. "If Emily could only be induced to stay."

"Oh, it's Emily you care about."

"I think you are running uselessly into danger," said Randolph. "Don't you think so, Brother B——m?"

"I have faith," said B——m, "that the heathen have all been discomfited by an angel of the Lord ; and that the sisters may go forth with perfect safety."

"There, there ; now you see," said Mrs. Bradish, laughing. "Come, Harmer, be my cavalier, and bring round the steed."

"Mrs. Bradish, will you permit some of the men to ride with you," said Harmer, approaching where the lady was saddling her horse. "If you persist in going, allow me, at least, to send a guard with you."

"With me !" and she laughed outrageously. "Indeed, Mr. Harmer, I think that you need a guard much more than I do. Timorous people, I almost said cowards, are always in danger."

Harmer reddened, and, turning round, left her without saying a word.

In five minutes more, she was scouring, with Emily, over the hills.

"She is rushing on to certain destruction," said Harmer, "but I can't help it."

"Well," said Mrs. Beardsley, "we have more dangers and difficulties to encounter than any other travellers ever had."

"Except the children of Israel, when they journeyed, like us, to the Promised Land," said B———m.

"I don't except any one," said Mrs. Beardsley. "It didn't rain where they were, and even that Jordan, a little foolish river, had to be dried up by a miracle, that they might pass over dry-shod. There was not one drowned, like I was, nor killed, like poor Mrs. Murray and her children."

"You didn't get injured, did you?" inquired the Prophet. "And I understood that you lost nothing valuable."

"Don't you call a great bag of sugar valuable?"

"Did you lose such a bag?"

To be sure I did. Sugar, too, of the finest quality, that I brought along on purpose to sweeten my coffee. And then only think of the disadvantage of having everything wet—my chest of stockings, all Louisa's little stores. Oh dear!"

"I hope that it will be made up to you ten-fold; I will pray that it may," and B———m walked away.

Mrs. Beardsley did not look as if she cared much about his prayers.

We halted for dinner on the banks of one of those small streams, which look like trenches dug in the prairie. The country around us was well timbered, and the air perfumed with the scents of innumerable wild flowers. I had long been uneasy at the continued absence of Mrs. Bradish, and could conceal my apprehensions no longer.

"Mrs. Bradish is certainly lost or captured," I said.

"It's trouble of her own seeking, but I pity poor Emily," said Harmer.

"Let some of the men on horseback go out to look for her," I suggested. "It will be no more than right, on Emily's account, if no other."

The name of Emily interested Harmer.

"Yes," he said, "let it be done for Emily's sake."

"A party of picked volunteers, well armed and mounted, started off in pursuit of the fugitives. We had made our evening encampment before they joined us, and then they brought no certain tidings of the women. In a valley, however, about five miles distant, a skirmish of some kind had evidently taken place. The turf was broken and torn, as if from the violent plunging and rearing of horses, and near by they picked up a knife that was stained with blood.

Harmer was nearly frantic, and Louisa wept in uncontrollable grief.

"Well, I knew it would be so," said Mrs. Beardsley. "My wonder is, that we hain't all been carried off. I shan't sleep a wink to-night."

"Oh, you're in no danger, not in the least. The Indians won't disturb us any more. They've had a grand dance around poor Emily's scalp before this time, I'll warrant."

"Couldn't some of the men go out and try to rescue them?" said Mrs. Stillman.

"'Twould be of no use," said Harmer. "The Indians roam over thousands of miles of territory. It would be impossible to even guess where they might be now."

"Oh, but you might possibly find them," said Louisa. "Do try, do, Mr. Harmer ; have pity upon me. Emily was dear to me as one of my own children. How can I ever think of giving her up so."

"But, after all," said I, "we do not know of a certainty that they have been captured by the Indians. They may have wandered off and got lost in the woods and interminable prairies, where some friendly hunter or trapper may meet them. We should always hope for the best."

"Heaven grant that it may be so," said Louisa.

"And if such were the case, how much better would it be?" said Mrs. Beardsley. "Not much, I fancy. They'd certainly starve, or be eaten by wild beasts, or" ——

"Hold! mother, hold!" said Louisa. "Don't torture me with such cruel conjectures. The God that notes even the fall of a sparrow, must be with them. Nothing can happen to them without His permission. He will care for and protect them. In Him is my trust."

"How silly you talk," said Mrs. Beardsley. "Don't you remember hearing of that poor child, whom the Indians cut into quarters, and roasted before its mother's eyes; or that man whom they skinned alive, and who was nine hours dying?"

"Oh, Mrs. Beardsley, stop, stop, for heaven's sake!" exclaimed Mr. Ward, "you will frighten the women out of their senses."

Louisa was weeping bitterly. Harmer was roaming about like one distracted; and that night all was silence and loneliness in the camp.

I watched B——m narrowly, and saw that though he evidently regretted the untoward fortune of Emily, he viewed the agonies of Harmer with a malicious pleasure. The next day we were agreeably surprised by the arrival of a friendly party of Cheyennes. Several of them brought us various esculent vegetables.; but Harmer only understood their language. They conversed with him some time, and their tones sounded strange and wild, harmonizing well with their appearance. The moment they left us he came to me, his eye flashing, and his whole appearance bespeaking pleasure and agitation.

"These Indians tell me," he said, "that the war-party of the Sioux, with the two women, are encamped about ten miles ahead on the banks of the Vermilion river. If that is the case, we can overhaul them easily to-night."

"But won't they slip off?" I inquired.

"No. They are waiting for a party of the Crows, who have been out on a plundering expedition against the Snakes, and who, according to their calculations, will return this way."

"But great caution will be necessary."

"Oh, certainly; indeed I think it will be best to keep the matter a profound secret until all our arrangements are made, though I wish to consult Mr. Ward and some others; but don't let Randolph know. We don't want his advice, and that is all he will be ready to give."

The day was already far advanced, and it was decided to encamp in a smooth, green valley, which would afford excellent pasturage for the stock, and send forward a scout to reconnoitre. This task Harmer undertook himself. "If I can only save Emily," he murmured.

"But remember that the liberty of Mrs. Bradish is quite as valuable to her friends," said Mr. Ward.

"I hope to be able to save both," he answered; and putting spurs to his horse, was soon out of sight.

"Where has Harmer gone?" inquired Louisa.

"To see if he can discover any traces of our friends."

"Bless him for that; I see he takes an interest in my Emily."

"I think so, and I trust it may save her from a snare."

"To what do you allude?"

"To B——m, the hierarch; he loves her, too."

"Impossible! He has three wives already."

"And would gladly take a fourth, provided she was young and beautiful."

Louisa's countenance changed, as she said, "Is not this horrid custom a dreadful temptation to men?"

"It seems to be," I answered.

"Oh, it is, it is; it must be," she exclaimed, passionately. "And it would certainly kill me if my husband should take another wife."

Harmer soon returned with the information that the savages were there in great numbers, and that the greatest precaution would be necessary to avoid a general engagement. Emily was tied to a tree, looking more dead than alive. He could not perceive that she had suffered any great violence at their hands. But Mrs. Bradish was fastened up with a small piece of board on her head, at which they were shooting arrows.

"And did they perceive you?" I inquired.

"No, indeed; I left my horse tied in a thick grove, two miles off, and approached them noiselessly and cautiously on foot. They seem to be well-armed and mounted, and we shall probably have sharp work."

"That may be; at what time to-night will you set out?"

"Not until after the moon sets, and the sky becomes dark, and the air very still, and then I wish to pick the men, and lead the expedition. Wonder if Mrs. Bradish will say any more about cowards?"

We kept the good news from all but Louisa, and those who were to join the enterprise.

Two hours past midnight, when deep, unbroken silence reigned throughout the camp, a party of fifteen, well armed and mounted, were observed to emerge silently from the shady covert of a willow grove, and disappear almost immediately in the thick obscurity of a neighboring valley. Hence they rode in silence for several miles, along the smooth bottoms and over the grassy hills, till one, who seemed to be the leader, reined his steed at the entrance of a grove.

"We will leave our horses here, and go forward on foot," he said, in a voice subdued to a whisper. "The enemy is encamped just over the hill yonder. Now, don't speak, nor fire a gun, nor raise the least alarm. They are probably sleeping, and should such be the case, we may possibly find an opportunity to release their prisoners without giving them any trouble." The company dismounted, tethered their horses to the trees, and advanced through the forest in the utmost silence. Once they were startled by the deep cry of a panther in the distance, and once some bird of night, roused from its perch by their presence, flew away screaming, otherwise neither sight nor sound indicated the existence of an animated being. At length, after rising a hill with unusual precaution, Harmer motioned to his companions to remain in the background, while he crept stealthily forward. Reconnoitering a moment, he then drew back, and beckoned for the others to approach. Cautiously parting the tall grass and shrubbery, they obeyed.

The Indians were all apparently sleeping around the embers of a dying fire, their arms stacked, and the prisoners confined in the centre. Two or three kegs, either containing, or having contained, whisky, were lying about, and appearances seemed to indicate that they had been holding a drunken revel. Some were lying on their faces, others on their backs, and not a few were doubled in apparently uncomfortable postures. The feet of some were towards the fire; the scalp-locks of others were evidently in danger of being singed. Once, when a breaking shrub made a slight noise, and he came fully into view. Harmer perceived one of the women raise her head, and glance around. It was a critical moment to him. A scream of surprise or pleasure would probably arouse the whole camp, but he made a gesture of silence, and sinking down again, she evidently communicated the pleasing intelligence to her companion. Creeping along the ground like a cat, in the stillest possible manner, Harmer reached the Indian who lay stretched between himself and the women. One blow with a tomahawk, which lay contiguous, cleft through crown and skull, and penetrating the brain, sent the savage instantaneously to his long account. He then cut the thongs which bound the prisoners, and assisting them to rise, the three made their way as expeditiously as possible from the Indian encampment.

"Harmer, I can't go without my horse," said Mrs. Bradish, "he is tied yonder ; I know where, and I must have him."

"For heaven's sake, hush," said Emily, in a subdued voice, though evidently in great alarm.

"I, at least, shall not go after him," said Harmer, in the same low tone. "Let her go if she chooses, but the peril will be hers. I shall stay with you."

"Of course, you will," said Mrs. Bradish. "And I desire that you should, but you will please inform me of the direction in which I can find our company ?"

"Due east," said Harmer, and Mrs. Bradish was out of sight in a moment.

"That woman is bent on running into danger," said one of the party.

"I shan't concern myself after her, if she gets retaken," said Harmer, "and I told her as much."

"You don't seem to like her very well," said Emily.

"Well, I don't."

It is scarcely necessary to repeat that this conversation was carried on in whispers, though Emily had assured her companions that the savages were too drunk to be easily awakened.

Hastily retracing their former course, they soon came to the grove in which their horses were tied. To loosen and mount them was only the work of a moment, and long before sunrise they had reached our camp. Mrs. Bradish came in about twenty minutes behind them. They were received with congratulations.

"I had a revelation, my dear," said B———m to Emily, "that you would be restored to us."

"Had you, father?"

"Don't call me father, that is not a suitable title."

Emily shrunk from his gaze, and Harmer turned away, muttering something between his clenched teeth.

As we had conjectured, they had been overtaken and surrounded by the savages, while galloping over the hills. Mrs. Bradish, true to her character, refused to surrender at discretion, and wounded two or three of her assailants. Being dressed in a sort of male attire, they were ignorant of her sex, and when made aware of it, seemed greatly to admire her bravery, saying, in French, "Squaw good shoot; squaw good shoot."

CHAPTER XXII.

EMILY'S NARRATIVE CONTINUED.

FOR a day or two nothing unusual occurred. We experienced the daily routine of emigrant life, little varied in its dull monotony, and diversified only by change in natural scenery, or incidents whose only charm consists in their novelty. Sometimes the streams were frequented by flocks of screaming plover, and other aquatic birds, while the smooth savannahs on their banks teemed with herds of antelope. Sometimes the prairie bottoms afforded us a very fair road; but the long grass actually teemed with myriads of mosquitoes and large greenflies from which the horses and cattle suffered severely. Generally, the weather was pleasant, and the cool breezes were redolent with the perfume of a thousand flowers.

One morning we came unexpectedly on an immense drove of buffalo, which were swarming, as far as the eye could reach, over the plains, where they had left scarcely a blade of grass remaining. In the presence of such a huge mass of animated beings, the beholder feels overcome by a strange emotion of grandeur. The continuous undulating motion, the dull, confused noise, unlike any other, and so admitting no comparison, struck us with awe and astonishment. Here a cow, separated a little from the others, stood quietly suckling her calf; there a huge bull would be rolling and tumbling in the grass; and, not far off, clouds of dust would prove the existence of an obstinately contested fight. Harmer and several others of the company were all exhilaration with the idea of a buffalo-hunt; and, as noon was approaching, it was decided to halt, thus affording them an opportunity. They did not return so soon as expected, and, as several of our oxen took it into their heads to join the herds of buffalo, we remained in camp the whole afternoon. Taking advantage of the favorable opportunity, I induced Emily to resume her narrative.

"My residence with Mrs. Birney would have been very pleasant," she began, "had the good lady been living independent of domestics, or had these domestics possessed her genial temper and kindness of heart. On my first arrival at her house, Mrs. Birney had introduced me to the servants, informing them that she had adopted me as her daughter, and that she expected them to treat me with all the consideration and respect that relation would authorize.

"'What! that little thing, there, from the poor-house?' said Matson, the maid. 'You haven't adopted her?'

"'Certainly, I have,' said Mrs. Birney; 'and don't let me ever hear an illusion to that poor-house again.'

"Matson turned up her nose, and left the room. I saw at once, however, that she would be an enemy. Probably she dreaded that my influence might supplant hers, in the mind of Mrs. Birney. At any rate, her taunts and sneers became the torment of my life, and even more intolerable than the perplexities I suffered at the poor-house.

"'They say you look like your mother, child; but that ain't much credit to you,' she said one day.

"'Who says so?' I inquired.

"I still felt a burning, unconquerable desire to know something of my parentage. Matson had discovered this, and now it was part of her policy to harass and distress me on that score.

"'Somebody that know'd,' she answered, sneeringly. 'Your mother was well known in these parts.'

"'Who know'd her?—for mercy's sake, tell me of one.'

"'Oh, I can't call names; and then her character was so bad, nobody would wish to be thought acquainted with her.'

"'And what did she ever do?'

"'That ain't telling. I often think, when Mrs. Birney is praising your beauty, and prides herself in dressing you so finely, that if she looked upon illegitimate children with the disgust that I do, she wouldn't have you about her house.'

"The cruel words of Matson rankling in my heart and festering in my brain, I sought the apartment of Mrs. Birney, and, walking up to her, requested to know the meaning of 'illegitimate child.'

"'Why, what put that in your head?' said the good lady, looking over her spectacles, and regarding me with an expression of sweet, yet curious benignity.

"'Because Matson says that, if you regarded such children as she does, you wouldn't have me about the house.'

"'Well, my child, Matson does very wrong to talk so. I wish you wouldn't pay any attention to what she says.'

"'But I can't help it. She begins to talk of my mother, and I long so to hear something about her. Oh! Mrs. Birney, do tell me of my mother. Matson says she was a bad woman, but she was my mother; and maybe her heart was right, after all.'

"Again Mrs. Birney looked up, and her eyes were filled with tears.

"'I can tell you all that I know of your mother, but that is from hearsay. Are you certain, however, that you wish to know?'

"'Oh! I do; I do!' and I clasped my hands, eagerly.

"'The curiosity of our first parents destroyed their happiness,' said the kind lady, 'and the knowledge of your mother's fate cannot be other than a bitter legacy.'

"'Not more bitter than this harrowing suspense.'

"'It may serve as a warning, too,' soliloquized the old lady; '"for, beauty provoketh thieves sooner than gold;"' then raising her eyes, she continued: 'Your mother was very beautiful. Like yourself, she inherited that pleasing, yet dangerous gift. She was the daughter of a widow, and they lived happily together, for many years. At length, a man professing great piety came to the neighborhood, and formed an acquaintance with the widow and the daughter. The old lady was pleased with his manners, and delighted that he preferred her child. He proposed marriage, and the offer was joyfully accepted. He then induced his betrothed to go with him to the city to purchase the bridal paraphernalia. There he refused to fulfill his engagements, or permit her to return to her mother, but kept her locked up in a house, whose inmates were lost to every sense of propriety or virtue, and finally left her without saying farewell. Indeed, she knew nothing of his departure, till the landlady came to turn her from the house, telling her that the gentleman who had paid her board said that he should do so no longer, and that she must take care of herself. We can only imagine her misery and wretchedness—thus forsaken in a large city, without a friend or relative or acquaintance to whom she could apply. But then, in that hour of utmost desolation, her confidence in heaven did not forsake her; and rising, without saying a word, she went forth into the streets.'

" Mrs. Birney paused in her narrative, and wiping her eyes, said, 'Child, the knowledge of your mother will be a bitter legacy.'

" Choking with emotion I could only articulate, ' Go on ; go on.'

"' Of course,' continued Mrs. Birney, ' a woman in her condition could only think of returning to her mother. She knew that the cruel, heartless world would only sneer at her sorrows, and insult her misfortunes ; but the mother would receive the poor lost wanderer with love and pity. And alone, and on foot, in the deep dark night, and through the rain, she started. Her strength, however, was inadequate to the successful prosecution of such a journey. She fainted by the roadside, and was found by a benevolent traveller, who lifted her to his carriage, and conveyed her to a neighboring inn. She was found to be violently ill, but her agonies were of short duration, and before the rise of another day, ' Her spirit had returned to the God who gave it." But she lived long enough to rehearse her pitiable story, and clasp you in her arms, with the request that you might be sent with a letter, which she wrote with her dying hand, to her mother. She was buried in the paupers' graveyard, and inquiries made respecting the old lady, her mother. It was ascertained that, overcome with grief and anxiety, she departed this life on the same day that her daughter died. Her property had passed into the hands of strangers, and you were an object of charity.'

"' And so they took me to the poor-house ?'

"' They did ; and now, child, one only chance remains for you to recognize your father should you ever meet him.'

"'What is that?'

"'That is contained in the letter of which I spoke, and which will be placed in your hands when you are of sufficient age to understand its import.'

"'Oh, that my mother had lived,' I exclaimed, passionately.

"'I will be a mother to you,' said the good lady, embracing me. 'And don't worry or cause yourself unnecessary trouble.'

"I thanked her for the information she had given me, and even felt much happier that now I knew the worst. My mother had been the victim of misfortune, not of crime. She was good, and beautiful, and innocent, and I could love and revere her memory. And so I used to go out by myself, and, seated in some solitary place, look far away into the deep blue of heaven, and fancy that I could catch a glimpse of the glory there, or a faint echo of an immortal harp. Then I would picture to my imagination the meeting of those two disembodied spirits who had been separated so long on earth; and many a time, carried away by the blissful and indescribable ecstasy, I threw myself on the ground, and, weeping tears of adoration and rapture, prayed that I might be permitted to join their blissful company.

"Then, from some source or other, I caught the beautiful idea that the spirits of departed relatives watched over and protected the living. Since then, it has always seemed that my mother is near me, that her presence surrounds me with a holy influence, that her breath is on my cheek, and her soft mild eyes looking into mine.

"At length Mrs. Birney became sick. It was spring; and the violets were just opening in the meadows, and the wrens building their nests in the little boxes which I had prepared for them; and the contrast between the pale wan mortal, hastening to dissolution, and the virgin freshness and beauty of nature, struck me as something inexpressibly painful. One day I made a remark to that effect in her presence, she smiled softly and sweetly, 'Then you think that dissolution and decay are dreadful things?'

"'Yes; dreadful,' I murmured, hiding my face in the bedclothes. 'Earth is so beautiful, and life so sweet.'

"'But we go to a place where the light is a thousand times clearer and richer than the sun's,' she said, in a clear ringing voice; 'to a land before whose beauties the most glorious scenes of earth are tame and insipid. What is this life to that immortality of blessedness which awaits us there? Oh! thanks, eternal thanks, be to God who giveth us the victory through our Lord Jesus Christ!'

"'But what will become of me when you die?' I cried, bursting into tears.

"'I have made ample provision for your support,' she answered.

"'You will have many friends, or many who will profess to be such, but never stray from the path of duty, never for a moment forget your God.'

"And she died?"

"'Yes; died like one going to sleep, and I wept over her. Oh! how long and bitterly. Then a strange man came and took possession of her effects. I told him that she had left a will. He smiled incredulously, and demanded the proof. 'Here in this drawer,' I said, going to the bureau. 'Here in this drawer, I saw her place it with her own hands.'

"'You can look, Miss,' he answered, nodding his head between each sentence, 'and if such a thing is found we shall see.' And I did look, and search, and rummage, while Matson stood by with her provoking tongue and insulting smile. 'Miss Pauper has no idea of giving up the title of heiress,' she said, 'but she may look till Doomsday and she'll find no will there.'

"'Matson,' I replied, 'if the will is not here, you have removed or destroyed it, because you only had the privilege of using the keys.'

"Her face colored to the temples: 'What motive could have prompted me to such a deed as that?'

"'Hatred of me; for you have always hated me, though I never did you any harm.'

"'That is little to our present purpose,' said the man, 'as the will cannot be found, if there ever was one, as the next of kin, I am lawfully entitled to take possession; you, Miss, can stay here, you can be of service to my wife.'

"'Well, I declare, the heiress sinks to a servant,' said Matson.

"Without noticing her cruel words, I thanked the man coldly, and told him that I would think of it.

"Mrs. Stillman offered me a home with her, which I gladly accepted; but yonder comes Harmer and the hunters, now for a supper of game."

CHAPTER XXIII.

FURTHER DEVELOPMENTS.

FOR several days nothing unusual occurred. The men amused themselves with hunting buffalo; the women with the common routine of a camp-life. Those who had babies to nurse had their hands full, as many of the juvenile members of our company had become sick. Those who had not, were never more disposed to thank Providence for the deprivation than on the present occasion. Mrs. Bradish went buzzing about from one wagon to another, like a bumble-bee among clover-blossoms;

consequently, she got all the news, and was made acquainted with every incident that possessed the least interest. She came to our tent one evening, after supper. I was sitting alone, Mr. Ward having gone to join a council of the elders.

"What on earth, Mrs. Ward," she began, "induces you to mope yourself in this manner? Do you consider yourself better, or not so good as the rest, that you shun everybody?"

"I didn't know that I shunned any one," I answered.

"Oh, well; may be you don't! but I've got a good piece of news."

"What is it?"

"There's to be a wedding in our company, before long."

"Who? Harmer and Emily?"

"What a simpleton you are!" she cried, laughing. "No; B———m wouldn't let that take place."

"Think not?"

"I know it; he intends having Emily himself; and then the man of whom I speak has one wife already, but wishes to take another—a perfectly reasonable wish."

"I don't hear anything about spiritual wives, as I used to."

"Oh, no; that's done away with. Brother B———m had a revelation that all true believers should imitate the example of the patriarchs, and raise up large families to inherit the good land, as well as to be able, at some future day, to go out against the heathen."

"I think polygamy to be an institution of Satan."

"On the contrary, I think it an institution peculiarly adapted to increase our numbers, and, consequently, our strength. I am deeply interested in the prosperity of the church, and so I advise every man to take all the wives that he can get."

"But suppose that you were married; would you be pleased with the idea of having your husband take another wife?"

"Oh, as to that, I can't tell. I should probably make a virtue of necessity."

"Poor Mrs. Murray died of a broken heart, at the unkindness of her husband; and I doubt not that the wife of this man of whom you have been speaking, will nearly go beside herself."

"Oh, she'll rave, I dare say, for she's spunk to the backbone!"

"Who is it, anyhow?"

"Mr. Stillman, jr."

"What! the husband of Louisa Beardsley?"

"Even so; but you needn't look so dumbfounded about it," said Mrs. Bradish, laughing heartily. "He can very well afford two, or even three wives. I told him so, myself. Indeed, I rather suspect the match was more than half of my making."

I never knew, before, what it was to be struck dumb.

Mrs. Bradish seemed really amused at my astonishment.

"Why, what is there in it, so dreadful, after all?" she said. "He will continue to love Louisa just as well, or probably better, than he does now. You know that a mother dearly loves one child, when she has but one; when the second is born, she loves that just as well, though no sane person would suppose that her love for the elder was in the least diminished. So a man may take a second wife, though loving and reverencing the first one with his whole heart."

"I can see no resemblance between the two cases," I said. "The love of a mother for her child, and a husband for his wife are very different things."

"Well, now that polygamy is incorporated in our system, the women will have to make the best of it, as it is not likely that the husbands, after once tasting its pleasures and benefits, will be likely to relinquish it."

"Does Louisa know?"

"I expect not. She has more than once made her brags to

me, that she wasn't one bit afraid that her husband would take another wife. I could hardly help laughing, then, at her ignorance of man's nature."

"Who is the bride to be?"

"One of the prettiest little girls imaginable—gay and sprightly as a humming-bird—full of life and fun as an egg is full of meat."

"I should hardly think she would suit him, then. He seems to be a serious kind of man."

"Have you never heard of the rule of contraries?" she answered. "Serious people are always charmed with your lively, versatile characters. Indeed, he is completely fascinated with her. I will tell you how it all came about. We were walking together, Mr. Stillman, Fanny, and myself. Fanny had been unusually interesting, and I never saw her look so beautiful before. Exercise had given unwonted lustre to her eyes, and color to her cheeks. The gaze of Stillman followed her, and I saw that she was exerting herself to please him. When she parted with us, I said:

"'Mr. Stillman, what do you think of Fanny?'

"'Why, I think that she is one of the most fascinating women that I ever beheld.'

"'I believe that she admires you quite as much.'

"'Do you, indeed? why, that is quite tempting. If I wasn't married already, I might profit by such condescension on her part.'

"'Married, to be sure you are; but that need make no difference. The church sanctions, and even promotes, the practice of polygamy. I think that Fanny loves you well enough to be happy even as your second wife.'

"He certainly looked pleased; then a shadow crossed his brow, and he said something, of which I only caught the last word, and that was 'Louisa.'

9*

"'If Louisa has the strength of mind, and the good sense that I give her credit for, she will see the expediency and righteousness of the measure.'

"He shook his head, and said nothing.

"'Louisa,' I continued, 'seems to be done bearing children. She should imitate the examples of Leah and Rachel, who, under the same circumstances, implored their husband to take other partners, in order, thereby, to raise up a numerous progeny.'

"Mr. Stillman was too deeply absorbed in thought to answer, and I left him, to have a talk with Fanny.

"'Fanny,' said I, 'Mr. Stillman is in love with you.'

"'In love with me, delightful,' said Fanny, clasping her hands, 'I made a dead set at our Prophet B———m, but little Emily yonder cut me out, though I know that she hates the old fellow like poison.'

"'Well now, Fanny, to be serious, do you really like Mr. Stillman well enough to become his wife, his second wife, for you know that he has another?'

"'As to that,' said Fanny, 'I concluded a month since that if I ever married, it would be as a second wife.'

"'Indeed, and what led you to that sage conclusion?'

"'Selfish conclusion, you might have said,' she answered, 'but little experience as I have had in the world, I am very well convinced that no man would be satisfied with one wife, where custom sanctioned the possession of two. Now it must be excessively mortifying to the first wife to have another brought in to share her empire and honors, and no less satisfactory must it be to the vanity of the second, to find herself preferred to that station. Then only think how jealous the first wife must be, while that very jealousy would be a matter of amusement to the second, as a tacit acknowledgment of her successful rivalship, and, consequently, superior charms.'

"'I see, Fanny, that you wouldn't refuse the addresses of Mr.

Stillman, and I think that he would make a very good match.'

"'I think so too, and then it would be fun alive to plague that proud wife of his. I always like to see your stiff, haughty things humiliated. Why, Louisa actually insulted me to my face the other day.'

"'How so?' I inquired.

"'Oh, it don't matter,' said Fanny, 'but I thought then that I'd get the better of her. Oh, 'twill be too good;' and she laughed and danced about like the very impersonation of mischief."

"And is it possible that you could encourage the match under these circumstances?" said I to Mrs. Bradish. "It will render Louisa, your friend, miserable for life, and I confess my inability to perceive who is likely to be rendered happier thereby."

"We don't expect happiness in this world, and whether or not we enjoy it in the next, depends on the self-denial we practise here," said Mrs. Bradish; and she walked away.

Several days passed away, and I heard no more about the wedding. I had observed, however, that Mr. Stillman and Fanny were frequently together, on which occasions, Fanny would invariably contrive to pass where Louisa could not help but see them. At length Mrs. Bradish came to me one day.

"She's found it all out," said the lady.

"Who? found out what?" I answered.

"Louisa, I mean, has discovered that her husband is about taking another wife."

"I could only sigh."

"You take it solemnly yet, and so did she, poor thing; Fanny, the rogue, rather overdid her part. In order that her triumph over Louisa might be complete, she told Margaret Shuff that Mr. Stillman sought her hand, and that she had promised to give him a decisive answer that evening. As Fanny anticipated, Margaret carried the news to Louisa, whose heart was already burning with hate and jealousy."

"'They had better take care,' said Louisa, looking like a thunder-cloud, 'Fan Simpkins is a little too mean and contemptible for anything ; if my husband had chosen a respectable woman I might'——; but she did not finish the sentence. Under any circumstances, the idea of her husband possessing another wife would have driven her nearly to distraction.

"And knowing this, as you did, Mrs. Bradish, how could you advise her husband to take another?"

"Because the happiness of an individual, especially when that happiness depends on a wrong estimate of the relative and social duties and privileges of life, sinks into comparative nothingness when compared with the prosperity and well-being of the Church."

"Oh, Mrs. Bradish, I can't bear to hear you argue in that manner, said I, it seems cruel and heartless."

"When the wagons halted at noon, it occurred to me that I had better call on Louisa, and if she mentioned the circumstance, endeavor to reconcile her to the match," she continued.

"Louisa was preparing dinner. Mr. and Mrs. Stillman, sen. Mrs. Beardsley and the children were beside her. She barely saluted me, and her eyes had such a wild, staring, ghostly expression, that I was half frightened."

"'Where is Mr Stillman?' I inquired, by way of breaking the ice, 'I see that he is not of your party.'

"'We see very little of him now,' said Mrs. Beardsley, snapping her knitting needles, and black eyes at the same time.

"'Well, it's too bad,' said Mrs. Stillman, sen., 'I'd no idea that so steady a man, and admirable husband, would ever give way to such a doctrine of devils.'

"'It's too bad,' echoed the old man, 'but as to its being a doctrine of devils, I don't know about that.'

"For the first time in twenty years the old gentleman had ventured to disagree in opinion with his wife; no wonder that her astonishment precluded a rebuke.

"'To what do you allude?' I inquired, in pretended ignorance.

"'Fan Simpkins, that despicable creature,' said Louisa, 'has betrayed my husband,' and that was all she could say; yet she didn't weep, didn't cry, nor sob, nor moan, but looked at her children like one demented."

"I don't know how you could have the heart to witness her misery, I said."

"'It's just as I told Louisa it would be,' continued Mrs. Beardsley, 'her husband was no better than other men, but she wouldn't believe me; said he was too much attached to her, and so on; men, however, are all alike.'

"'Not exactly, neither,' said Mrs. Stillman, sen., 'grandpapa here, wouldn't think of wanting a young wife, would you, dear?'

"'Oh, I reckon not;' but there was a tone of indecision in his voice that forcibly struck me, and I mentally exclaimed,

"Before a twelvemonth we shall see."

"'I tell Louisa,' continued Mrs. Beardsley, 'that now the worst has come to the worst—she'll have to make the best of it. If she'd took my advice in the first place.'—

"'But as it is, Mrs. Beardsley, it will work round for the best. We have the promise, and Louisa should not be so selfish as to refuse sharing the blessings of a good husband with a sister in the faith,' said I. 'We have no reason to suppose that Mr. Stillman has experienced any diminution of affection for her, though he finds it to be his duty to contribute more effectually to the prosperity of the church by contracting another connection.'

"Louisa moved round mechanically like one in a trance. I saw that some settled purpose had taken possession of her mind, though of its nature I had no definite idea. Mr. Stillman came up just as the two families were finishing their dinner. He seemed unusually merry, joked his mother about her cap, told Mrs. Beardsley that he had just made the acquaintance of a smart widower; asked Louisa what was the matter, that she had advanced ten years at least in age during the past two days. No one seemed to partake his hilarity, however, neither was any allusion made in my presence to his approaching nuptials."

Here Mr. Ward came up and told us that the scouts had descried an encampment of Indians a few miles ahead, but whether friends or foes remained undecided.

"And it don't make much difference which," said Mrs. Bradish. "Indians and buffaloes are the poetry of camp life."

The rumor that Indians were about excited no little agitation among the women. Usually gay groups of girls and children were out walking beside the wagons, or running over the meadows to botanize, or gathering pebbles and geological specimens from the hill-sides, or bottoms of the streams.

"Oh! dear Lord!" cried one. "Indians round, and my gals out walking. They'll be captivated—I know they will."

Another one, catching her sun-bonnet in her hand, ran a few paces from the wagons, and then stopping suddenly screamed, "Indians! Indians!" with all her might. Then, running on a short distance further, again stopped, and again brought her voice into requisition. The young people heard her (indeed she could easily have been heard a mile), and came flocking to the wagons like a bevy of young partridges, just as we discerned some dark-looking objects sweeping over the hills at some distance. There was an abundance of fresh horse-tracks, and several carcases of buffaloes, from which the valued parts had been removed, were lying about. We went on quickly and cautiously, Harmer, and the other horsemen, in advance, with loaded rifles. In a few minutes more the Indians were rapidly approaching on their half-wild horses. At first there did not appear to be more than twenty-five or thirty, but group after group darted into view on the tops of the hills, till all the eminences seemed in motion, and in a few minutes, three or four hundred were scouring over the plains. They certainly looked picturesque, adorned with paint and feathers, and the manes and tails of their horses nearly sweeping the ground. Harmer and his companions had levelled their rifles, and I was expecting to see a general, and, perhaps, bloody engagement, when Buckley recognized, and addressed the chief in his own language. The savage seemed astonished, and, swerving his horse a little, passed by at full speed ; then wheeled, and checking his steed, returned Buckley's salutation. They proved to be a Pawnee village, among whom Buckley had resided some time as a trader. We were soon in the midst of the band, and as several of our company understood something of their language, the conversation became general and exceedingly animated. The chief pointed out to us his village at some distance on our right, and showed us a herd of buffalo, just discernible, like a dark streak on the horizon, which he said they were going to surround. They had been making a large circuit in order to avoid giving the animals an alarm, when they discovered our approach. In ten or fifteen minutes the women came galloping up on their horses ; they followed the men to assist in cutting and carrying the buffalo meat. As the wind was blowing very strong and fresh, the chief modestly requested us to halt, as he feared that we might raise the herd. We therefore stopped ; the men dismounted, and, as the night was rapidly approaching, it was proposed to form an encampment. One of the elders interfered to prevent this, saying that he had a revelation that we were in danger from the Indians. Here B——m interposed that the saints were always in danger, but that it had been revealed to him that no harm should befall them on the present occasion, and so it was decided to remain.

Meanwhile, the Indians were busily engaged in the work of destruction. Having separated into two bodies, one party proceeded directly across the prairie towards the hills, in an extended line, while the other went off in an opposite direction, and instantly the chase commenced. The buffalo started for the hills, but were intercepted, and driven back, where they met the hunters approaching from the opposite direction. Clouds of dust soon covered the whole scene, preventing us from having other than an occasional view. At length the whole scene faded in the distance, and I turned away to busy myself in the domestic affair of preparing supper.

During my culinary operations Louisa Stillman came in, and, seating herself on a low chair, bowed mournfully with her face on her hands.

"You are in trouble, Mrs. Stillman?" said I.

"I am," she answered. "A trouble of which I never dreamed, deep, horrible and awful, has come upon me."

I could find no words in which to console or sympathize with her, and so remained silent.

"Mrs. Ward," she said, "I have come to ask a favor of you—a very great favor. You are not one of them, and hence I have confidence that you must feel for me."

"Indeed I do sympathize with you, Mrs. Stillman," I answered.

"I knew—I knew it! and so I have come to you."

"In what way can I assist you," I inquired.

"They tell me," she answered, "that my husband and Fan. Simpkins meet to-night to appoint a day for their marriage. Certain it is, that they are to meet in that little grove of poplars yonder. Now I wish to know the worst. This suspense is more dreadful than the blackest reality, and so I have come to ask you to accompany me to a place of concealment near by, where I can hear their conversation, and be made acquainted with their schemes."

"But, Mrs. Stillman," I began, for my mind rather recoiled from so dishonorable an act as private listening, "is there no other way by which your curiosity could be satisfied?"

"No other, no other," she replied, bitterly. "Nothing else will satisfy me. I must know what he says—what he says to her—yes, to her."

"And then?"

"If he loves me no longer,"—she hesitated, and her countenance assumed an expression that was frightful to behold.

"Well, Mrs. Stillman, I can go with you, if you so earnestly desire it, though I am doubtful whether the knowledge thus obtained will conduce to your happiness."

"It cannot add to my misery; then, too, I shall be relieved from this torturing suspense."

Tears sprang to my eyes.

"And Mrs. Bradish," she continued, "my old and valued friend, through whose persuasion and influence we were induced to emigrate, advised my husband to this step. That seems the cruelest of all."

"It is cruel," said I, "and how any woman can have the heart to look with such cool indifference on the miseries of another, is a mystery to me."

Supper was soon ready, but Louisa refused to eat, saying that she had no appetite. Mr. Ward endeavored to entertain us with some Indian anecdotes, but no one manifested any inclination to support the conversation, and so we relapsed into a gloomy silence.

At length the supper was over, the children put to bed, and the usual arrangements made for the night, when I informed Mr. Ward that I wished to go out. He consented, only requesting me not to be long absent.

Louisa took my arm, and we went out. The deep shadows of evening lay over the camp, whose large white tents and white covered wagons presented a strange and unique appearance. "This way," whispered Louisa "we can pass along here without being observed."

We descended into a deep, yet narrow hollow, probably fifty yards from the camp, and, following it for a short distance, came suddenly to the rear of a poplar grove. Concealing ourselves behind a huge tree, which the tempest had overturned, we prepared to await the approach of the lovers. We were not necessitated to wait long. Steps were heard approaching, then a light merry laugh burst on our ears, accompanied by words like the following: "Oh, fie, you don't expect me to believe that you, who have been a married man these ten years?"

Louisa trembled like a leaf.

"Well, what of that?" said a voice that I knew to be Stillman's.

"What of it? sure enough. You try to make out that my presence is necessary to your happiness. Haven't you never been happy? Your wife is beautiful, gentle, and loving. You have fine children. Can't you be happy with them, and without me?"

"Fanny," returned her companion, "how can you doubt my love? Ever since I first saw you—ever since I first thought of you, you have been my world, my heaven; your presence to me was what the sun is to the earth, and all is void and darkness without you. For your love, I would sacrifice my life,—I would change my very nature, if possible, if thereby I could render myself more agreeable to you. Wife, children, friends are nothing, nothing in comparison with your love."

I shuddered at these words, so deeply, coldly cruel, and fraught with such horrible treason against an innocent and loving family; but Louisa uttered one wild, thrilling scream, and fell over with her face to the earth. That scream!—I could never describe it; it was unlike any other human sound that I ever heard. It seemed the utterance of a long pent, unspeakable agony ; the wail of a heart bowed and broken in utter despair. No wonder that the lovers started from their seats ; and, turning round, Mr. Stillman beheld me and his prostrate wife.

"What's all this mean?" he said, in an angry voice.

"It means that your unpardonable levity has murdered your wife," I answered.

"And has my wife so far forgot herself as to act the eavesdropper?" he replied, tartly.

"Let's leave these pleasant people to enjoy the discovery they have made," said Fan, taking hold of his arm.

Mr. Stillman was turning away, when I called to him to stop. "Your wife, here, requires assistance," said I ; "Do you prefer that vain, haughty, coquettish thing, to the mother of your children?" He turned round, looking somewhat abashed. Louisa had not yet risen from the ground, but lay in a deathlike swoon. I raised her head on my lap, loosened her garments, and chafed her burning hands. At length she opened her eyes, like one just awaking from a horrible dream. Stillman had approached, and was bending over her, his broad bosom heaving with emotion, while Fanny stood, with a mocking curl on her lips, a few paces distant. "Is it you, my husband?" she said, faintly. "I dreamed that you had deserted me—that you no longer loved me. It is not so, is it?—say, dearest?"

"Oh! no, no!" said the miserable man, groaning with agony.

"You know," continued Louisa, "that we have not been married a great many years, and yet how happy we have always been, in our old home, there beside the beautiful lake, where little Ada was born and died? Methinks I see it now, with its beautiful green lawn and maple woods, intersected by well-worn paths? Don't you remember it, my husband?"

"Yes, yes!"

"And how sick I was, and how you watched over me, night after night, fearing, as you said, that I would die; then all your care and tenderness when I began to recover. Oh! my husband, I have not forgotten it."

There was a sound marvellously like weeping.

"Mr. Stillman," said Fanny, haughtily, "is it your pleasure to return?"

Louisa caught the words; half rising, she cried impetuously, "Leave us, leave him! you vile, wicked creature;" and then she continued talking to her husband, and calling up the memory of old times. "I know I was not worthy of such love and tenderness as you lavished upon me—that I was impetuous and passionate, and sometimes found fault without occasion, and I well know that I am plain, with very few of good looks to recommend me. I am not so bright and talented as some, and I am no longer young, and yet I loved you, my husband, with my whole heart and soul. I never knew what love, or life, or happiness was till I beheld you, and you have been the sum total of my world for years and years. There are many women far more beautiful, and rich, and gifted, yet they couldn't, they wouldn't love you as I have done."

He bent over her drooping form; it was too dark to discern clearly, but I fancied that their lips met.

"I often thought that I wasn't good enough for you, and yet I studied to make your home happy, and be to you all that a wife could be, and you were happy and satisfied with me, my husband; were you not?"

"I was, I was; Heaven knows that I was," he answered. "And we will be happy again. Fanny can never be to me what you have been, though her beauty pleased my fancy, and my vanity was excited by her preference; and then that woman, your friend, Louisa, advised me to take another wife."

"I know it, I know it," said Louisa. "Heaven grant that I may find it in my heart to forgive her."

I looked around for Fanny; she was gone.

"I cannot live to see you married to another," she said. "No, my husband, kill me outright ere you do this. It would be a mercy, a blessing to relieve me from such unspeakable misery."

"Well, you never shall see it," he answered, seriously. "No, my wife, I have done wrong, have been weak, and silly, and foolish, but they told me that you wouldn't care, that you cared nothing particular about me, and I suffered myself to be tempted and deceived."

Louisa still held him fast in her arms.

"And those cruel words you were saying," she whispered.

"What were they? I forget," he said. "I have been drunk, fascinated, intoxicated with a wild, unholy passion, but your words have recalled me to reason. The illusion has vanished. I find in your love something real and tangible, something that I never will sacrifice to a mere passing fancy for another woman, come what will."

"I blame myself more than you," continued Louisa; "blame myself that I ever consented to emigrate with this people, knowing their habits of polygamy as I did, and knowing, too, that I could never live to see you married to another. The idea of that is infinitely more painful to me than poverty or want could ever be. But I loved you so deeply, and placed such great confidence in your love for me, that I never dreamed such a thing could possibly occur. Oh! my husband, I judged you by myself, fancying that it would be quite as impossible for you to love another, as it would be for me."

Stillman was deeply affected. He had loved his wife with all the tenderness of which his heart was susceptible. They had lived very happily together, and now that her words had recalled the memory of the past, he felt how much and how deeply he had wronged her.

"I feel that I have wronged you, grievously wronged you," he said, his cheeks wet with tears, and his bosom heaving with deep emotions. "I ought never to have thought of marrying again, because, however right it might be to possess two wives, if it had been distinctly understood by all parties beforehand that such was to be the case, no man should insult a first wife, whom he had married with an express understanding, 'to keep himself to her, and to her alone,' by introducing a second to share her privileges and honors. I now see just where I stood," he continued; "and now, my dear wife, I love you better than before, better than I ever did. Put that love to the test; there is nothing that I will not cheerfully undergo to satisfy you; nothing that I will not promise as a recompense for the pain I have given you. Bid me swear that I will never again speak to Fanny, or propose marriage under any circumstances, to any woman whatever, and I will take the oath, nor ever break it while I draw the breath of life."

He threw himself at her feet as he spoke; I felt, I knew that he must be sincere.

Louisa embraced him tenderly, and took his hands within her own. "Oh! my husband," she said, "you make me too happy, too happy; you are, then, mine, and mine alone. And this is all that I ask of you: promise me, that while I live, you will never marry another; that you will always remain in deed and thought true to me."

He did as she bade him, and then, arm in arm and heart to heart, they sat in the cool shadows in all the blessedness of re-vivified affection.

Feeling that my presence might possibly be a constraint, I left them, and stole back to our camp alone and unnoticed, yet with a sensation of happiness altogether indescribable.

I found Mrs. Bradish conversing with Mr. Ward. She had been informing him of the wedding likely to take place through her auspices. "Why, bless my heart!" she exclaimed when I entered, "why, you look as if you had just come from a wedding. What remarkably pleasant thing has happened?"

"I have come from a scene better than any wedding," I replied; "the reconciliation of husband and wife. Louisa, your friend," I continued, addressing Mrs. Bradish, "is a happier woman to-night than she has been recently."

"Explain yourself," said the lady.

"I mean just what I say, that Louisa Stillman is a happy woman, and that Fan Simpkins may die an old maid. And that I am so delighted to think the abominable match is broken off."

"Broken off! Fan Simpkins' match broken off, when I proposed and advised it! Pray, Mrs. Ward, whose influence has interfered to prevent the consummation of my wishes?"

"Divine Providence, I believe, that opened Mr. Stillman's eyes to the heinousness of the crime he was about to commit."

"Pshaw! in two days' time he will change his mind. Fan can manage him, I'll warrant."

"On the contrary, Mrs. Bradish, he has taken a solemn oath never to marry another woman while Louisa lives; I was a witness to it."

Mrs. Bradish shook her head and murmured, "We shall see."

CHAPTER XXIV.

LOVE IN THE WILDERNESS.

LOVE in a wilderness—flirtations in a camp—how agreeably they diversify the monotony of a long journey. A courtship carried on among Indians and buffalo—on the banks of rivers, at the feet of mountains, and in the bosom of rolling prairies—possesses, at least, the charm of novelty. So thought Harmer and Emily. And then it seemed so natural—so like the birds and gazelles—to love under such circumstances. What heart could avoid it? they could not. When their cosy "*tête-à-tête*" was interrupted by some plumed and painted Indian, what could be more natural than for him to throw his arms about her, or for her to cling to him for protection? When the elders had retired to their tents, and the watch to their station, what could be more natural than for them to seek a cosy retreat beside a pile of burning embers, and whisper the soft nonsense, which, however silly to the lookers-on, is extremely interesting to all parties concerned?

"Come, Emily," said Harmer, "come sit down here by the fire. The brethren have finished their discussion on theology, and the old ladies their pipes and snuff."

Emily rather hesitated. The young man threw his arm around her, and drew her towards him.

"Come, I want to tell you something."

Emily suffered his embrace, and the whisper sounded marvelously like a kiss.

"Oh, Emily," he continued, passionately, "why do you keep me in suspense? Have I not sworn to renounce all my former tastes and habits and inclinations, because my wandering life was disagreeable to you? Have I not consented to make any sacrifice which you can demand? What more can you ask? You certainly cannot doubt my sincerity?"

"I have no doubts of your sincerity," said Emily. "Whew! what a shower of ashes;" and she sprang from the arms of her lover. The wind, suddenly changing, had blown a hurricane of sparks and ashes over them. Harmer quickly followed, and both took a position to leeward.

"What were you saying, love?"

"That I had no doubts of your sincerity, so far as the present time is concerned; but your mind may change—that is what I fear. My husband must be domestic—I should moan and grieve, and perhaps die in his absence; and you—you have become so deeply attached to a pioneer life, it seems to me impossible that you should ever settle down and be contented."

"Because you depreciate your influence, my love," he answered. "Oh, you can make me anything—anything. Your power over me has something of the miraculous in it. Say that you will be mine. Oh, say—— Confound the ashes!"

Emily burst out laughing; for the wind, having veered again, sent another shower of ashes and sparks directly in their faces. Again they found it necessary to change their positions; and, being comfortably seated, resumed the conversation.

"I am not rich," said Harmer; "I have neither gold nor silver nor fine houses. I can offer you nothing better than a hunter's lodge, at least till we get our farms cleared, and our dwellings made in that fine country to which we are journeying; and yet, Emily, the homeliest dwelling with love, is preferable to a palace without."

Emily sighed.

"Pardon me, Emily," he said, "but I have something on my mind which I must tell you. Two of the men were talking of you to-day."

"Of me! what did they say of me?"

"Be patient, and you shall hear. They said that B———m, our leader, was enamored of you; that you hated and despised him; but, notwithstanding this, you had consented to become his wife, for the consideration and importance that station would give you, as he had promised to exalt you above the others, something like chief sultana in the Turkish harems."

Emily laughed outright. "A very fine story," she said, "most admirably contrived. But were they the counsellors of the Prophet, or how were they made acquainted with his private affairs?"

"Emily, it grieves me exceedingly to see you turn such a serious affair into mirth."

Emily laughed still louder. "There's nothing serious about it; those fellows made it all up as they went along. Chief sultana, indeed—how ridiculous."

"But hasn't B———m ever sought your hand?"

"Oh, he has paid me much attention—has offered me several presents, though I always refused to accept them—has invited me to ride with him, and otherwise manifested a partiality for my company, though he never made a formal proposal for my hand."

"And, suppose that he had?"

"Well, suppose it."

"Would you have accepted him?"

"Pshaw! Mr. Harmer, you are not a priest, and this would make a strange confessional. Heigho."

A gust of smoke filled the atmosphere with insalubrious soot and vapor.

"But I want to know," said Harmer, "whether you would marry B———m, or not?"

"Fie! Mr. Harmer, you are getting jealous."

Harmer looked as if going into a fit of sulks. Emily had a spice of the coquette in her disposition. She dearly loved to tease and vex her lover; but she was fond of him, after all. She would tantalize him until he got angry, and then caress and coax him into good-humor.

"Now, don't get mad," she said, when his brow began to lower. "Don't get mad, and I will tell you all about it."

The gallant ranger slipped his arm familiarly around her waist.

"Now, what will you tell me?"

"That nothing on earth should ever induce me to marry that man, who has three wives already."

Harmer clasped her in his arms.

"Stay; I have not done speaking yet," said Emily. "I should fear to marry any man among the Mormons; because, in a few years, or perhaps months, he would weary of me and take another wife—that is something I couldn't bear."

"And you fear this of me?" said Harmer.

"Of you, of every man, who lives in a state of society where polygamy is admissible."

"Oh! Emily, then you doubt my love."

"Not exactly, but many men, and might we not say with propriety, that all men have a passion for variety? Your love for me to-day, is no proof of what may be the state of your feelings in years to come. Urge me not; I will be your sister, your friend, anything with honor that you wish me to be, except your wife, and that is impossible under the present circumstances."

"And your objection is, because you fear that some time hence, I might fancy that another wife would increase my happiness?"

"Even so," and Emily hid her face in his bosom.

"Well, I love you ten times better for it, after all," said the manly ranger, "ten times better. You want your husband to be all your own. You have no idea of sharing his caresses and affections with a rival. You are a true woman, and your woman's heart is worth possessing. Look up, love, and I will tell you what we can do."

Emily looked up, smiling through her tears.

"We shall soon be at our journey's end," he said. "When we have crossed those dark mountains which appear in the horizon, we shall enter the borders of the Promised Land. You know, love, that polygamy belongs essentially to the Mormon system, so we will leave the Mormons; we will go back to those States, where the laws have made bigamy a capital offence. There you can have no fears on that account."

"What! and travel this long distance over again."

"You object, then," said Harmer; "you do not love me."

"Be reasonable," returned Emily, "many things are to be taken into consideration. I have not objected; neither do I give an unqualified assent."

Harmer was a fine specimen of the Western Ranger, tall, stout-built, and athletic; accustomed to severe exercise, and passionately fond of buffalo-hunting and life on the prairie. He had never dreamed of love until the fair Emily crossed his path. At first, he thought her wondrously beautiful, and gazed upon her with much the same sensations as he gazed upon a beautiful bird or flower. This could not last, however, and long before he was aware of the true nature of his feelings, his eyes were for ever wandering off in search of Emily, and he experienced in her presence a new and indefinable emotion of bliss.

Emily could not be insensible to his preference, and her heart soon became deeply interested in the handsome Ranger, yet she remembered the fate of her mother, and took good care that her passions should alway remain subservient to reason and judgment.

"I can't possibly perceive what objection you can have to

returning with me to the settlements," continued Harmer, "I think you told me that Mr. and Mrs. Stillman are not your parents."

"They are not my parents.

"You were an orphan, then?"

"Yes; an orphan."

"And inclined to die an old maid?"

"Now you are getting silly again."

"No such thing; you refuse to marry in the Mormon country, but at the same time prefer to remain in it; what else can I make of it, only that you wish to die an old maid?"

"You misapprehend me altogether," said Emily, "but it makes very little difference. I trust we shall always be very good friends."

"Friends!" echoed Harmer. "Emily, is that all?"

Again she buried her face in his bosom. Dearly as she loved Harmer—and she did love him dearly, she almost feared to entrust her happiness to his keeping. Life on the prairies had little charms for her. Could she be contented in a hunter's lodge, living in Indian style, with none of the luxuries and very few of the comforts of civilization. Sleeping on skins, dressed in the rudest manner, feeding on roots and roasted buffalo-meat, a companion for female savages, and cut off from all intercourse with her race? Even for love, she could not consent to all this; true, he had promised to abandon his border life, but then the query arose, would he be happy and contented under such a change of habits? would her society console him permanently for the loss of all those pleasures, incident to a life of wild roving independence, and the spirit-stirring scenes of border strife? Would he not become wearied with the dull monotony of toil and agriculture? and would it not be her miserable fate to pine over his absence, or witness his dissatisfaction and discontent? Full of these thoughts, it is not at all surprising that she was never ready to return a decided answer to his suit, or that she mentally ejaculated times without number,. "Oh! I love the man, but not his way of life. Had he been some farmer's son, had he been brought up in entire ignorance of Indians and buffaloes, how happy we might have been."

By this time the fire had all burned out. There was neither coals nor living embers. Emily proposed retiring.

"Not yet, Emily," answered the lover. "I am so happy when near you, that I never wish to be absent for a moment. I love you so truly—oh! so truly—there is something so extraordinary and unexpected in my attachment, that it seems impossible that you should doubt its fervor and lasting nature."

"And perhaps," said Emily, though her heart belied what she was about to utter, "perhaps you have breathed the same vows to another before you saw me."

"Oh! Emily, how you wrong me; me, who scarcely ever spoke to a woman, and certainly cared no more for them than for female buffaloes."

"A true hunter's simile," said Emily, laughing.

"I never knew the language by which men of the world address the objects of their love," said Harmer. "I am utterly ignorant of all fine talking, and what I say my heart dictates; my words may be uncouth, or inexpressive, or unsuitable; yet they are, they must be sincere. Oh! believe me, Emily, I would lay down my life to make you happy."

"I do not doubt you," whispered Emily, "but a shower is rising, even now it begins to rain. Let me go to the tent."

"And you will meet me again to-morrow night?"

"Guess so."

And after kissing her hand, her arm, her neck, her bosom, and her eyes, he suffered her to depart.

CHAPTER XXV.

A WIFE'S TROUBLE.

WE rested several days in the neighborhood of some sylvan bluffs lying along the outskirts of a dark range of mountains. Rest had become actually necessary to preserve the lives of our weared and jaded animals. Some of these had already died from fatigue and over-exertion, others had been killed for food, a few had strayed, and several had been stolen ; so that our original number was greatly diminished. Some of the women, and many of the children, were sick, or rather worn out by the toils and fatigues incident to a long journey. Mrs. Bradish, however, was lively and active as at first. "She didn't want rest, not she ; she would much prefer going on. If people would only be resolute, and make up their minds not to become sick and wearied, they never would become so."

"And do you suppose that if they were to make up their minds not to die, that they would live for ever ?"

"That's quite another thing, and yet I believe that conceit has killed many a one. It requires the exercise of a strong will to be sure, but I have certainly performed many marvellous cures on myself, without the intervention of a drop of medicine. You need not laugh, the disease was actual and real, and so was the cure."

"What were the diseases ?"

"Cough, fever, dysentery, and such like."

I could scarcely refrain from laughing.

"You cured these diseases by the simple exercise of a strong will," I said.

"Yes; and working them off."

"Working them off?"

"To be sure; there is nothing remarkable in that. You know that I had servants, and consequently was not necessitated to ever lift a finger in any kind of toil, but when I discovered that my health was suffering, I went right straight at the hardest kind of work, washed, scrubbed, worked in the garden, and all such things, keeping my will firm and resolute meanwhile, that I would not be sick, and in this way I always recovered; and it was much better, too, than to sit in idleness, and swallow doses of nauseous medicine."

"To be sure it was."

"I think now that if all these sick and complaining ones would just resolve to go on steadily, they could do so as well as not. Why, I have come as far as any, and my strength hasn't failed as I can perceive."

"Mrs. Beardsley is very ill," I remarked.

"And Fan has made a dead set at Mr. Stillman, sen.," said Mrs. Bradish laughing. "She's determined to have one or the other."

"Impossible!"

"Why is it impossible? To me it seems very natural. Fan declares that she won't die an old maid, and that she won't marry any man who has not another wife."

"A strange taste truly."

"Oh! she gives the best of reasons."

"I should like to hear them."

"Well, she is a kind of coquette, you know, and she thinks it must be delightful to triumph over a first wife. I suppose she will esteem it a great achievement to make a conquest of that old man."

"Very like; and yet what an abominable disposition."

Mrs. Bradish laughed.

"You will persist in viewing things according to the old standard," she said.

"I hope and pray that Fan will be disappointed again, but what does poor old Mrs. Stillman say?"

"Oh! I can't tell half that she said, nor which felt the worst, she or Louisa."

"But how did it come about pray?"

"Why, Fan, of course, was mortified at her failure in securing Mr. Stillman, jun., not that she loved him, or cared anything about his affections, but she longed to humiliate Louisa, who she conceived had insulted her. She was outrageous at the result of Stillman's meeting with his wife in the grove that night, but swallowing her disappointment with admirably-affected indifference, she secretly vowed revenge. I inquired what she was up to, but she shook her head and laughed. You know how excessively fond the old man, Stillman, has been of his wife."

"He has always appeared fond of her."

"I always doubt such demonstrations of affection," said Mrs. Bradish. "The old man is really too weak and silly to feel much attachment for any one. Did you ever observe how he always echoes the old woman's words?"

"I have observed it."

"Wasn't it ridiculous? Yet the silly old coot couldn't think of anything himself; and never was a husband so decidedly henpecked, and at the same time in such blissful ignorance of it, as this same gentleman. It was a common talk everywhere and with everybody, that ' his wife wore the breeches," but he strenuously denied it, affirming that he always did on all occasions just as he pleased."

"' But papa is pleased to act in accordance with my wishes,' she would say complacently. 'Papa is aware that I always advise him for the best.' 'She always advises for the best,' the old man would answer, and no one ventured to dispute it. But if a man went there to purchase a cow, a horse, or, in fact anything, 'mother' must be consulted about the bargain. If any cash was wanted, 'mother' must be requested to get it, as she only knew where it was kept. If he went out of an evening, 'mother' must be informed where he is going, and just how long he would be gone, but the idea of his having a secret would have driven her at once into strong hysterics. I told Fan something about the old fellow's habit of subservience to his wife, and it tickled her amazingly. 'You know,' she said, 'that these silly old wretches are always excessively vain. I see a way to manage him famously, but won't the old woman explode, won't she blow up. I declare it's too good. The very thought half kills me.'

"'May be you'll get jilted again,' I remarked.

"'Let me alone for that,' she answered laughing.

"A short time after this," continued Mrs. Bradish, "I called on the Stillmans, and found that something unusual had occurred. Louisa, though so recently reconciled to her husband, was weeping violently. Old Mrs. Stillman looked indescribably, and Mrs. Beardsley was thanking her stars that she had no man to be worried about. They refused to admit me to their confidence, however, and I soon bade them adieu, and seeking Fan, demanded to know what new mischief she had been perpetrating. Her eyes sparkled with malice and pleasure, as she answered:

"'I have been sending that old fellow a billet-doux. The first that he ever received in his life, I presume. Probably the old lady has got on the track of it,' and she shook with suppressed laughter.

"I was really astonished at her boldness.

"'Oh, you needn't look surprised ; it was admirable, I assure you—filled with love from top to bottom. I copied it from a book ; here it is,' and she drew a small volume from her pocket. 'That one there, with the leaf turned down. Don't you think the old fellow's eyes snapped when he read it ?'

"'Shouldn't wonder, I replied,' perusing the precious epistle, which ended by asking an interview.

"'I knew,' said Fan, 'that the old booby wouldn't have any chance to write an answer. He says they watch him as cats watch a mouse.'

"'You have had some conversation with him already, then ?'

"'Oh yes ; we have met several times,' she answered, 'and I have petted and caressed him till his head is fairly turned. Was there ever a man that could resist a woman's caresses ?'"

"Well, Mrs. Bradish, whatever you may think of it, to me it seems abominable ; and a system of religion that tolerates and even approves such conduct, must be in the highest degree impure."

"It all depends on getting used to it," said Mrs. Bradish, "in the patriarchal age, the conduct of Fanny would have been considered virtuous. Witness that of Ruth. In these times, however, when the law, and public opinion both conspire to indulge women in their ridiculous habits of jealousy, the case is different. In Turkey, no woman considers herself slighted or insulted because her husband chooses to take another companion ; but yonder comes a party of Indians."

"Perhaps some of your old acquaintances."

"I rather guess not," she answered, "but I mean to go and have a talk with the chief."

They proved to be a war party of the Snakes, but what chiefly interested us was a beautiful Arapahœ girl, whom they had taken captive, and whom they expressed a determination to sacrifice. The poor creature had evidently been treated with the greatest rudeness, and huge scars on her back and limbs bore testimony to the violence and cruelty of her captors. They acted sulky, and we had occasion to suspect that they met with unusual losses. All our party sympathized deeply with the poor girl, and we endeavored to buy her ransom of the chief.

"Why, you haven't got nothing that a warrior wants" he said, "these, and these," pointing to the mules and horses, "ain't worth nothing."

We then offered him some tobacco and blankets, but he steadfastly refused, saying that they were accustomed to annually immolate a human victim to their deity, and that they must keep the girl for that purpose.

Emily, who had learned a few words of the Indian tongue, drew near the sufferer and commenced a conversation, partly oral, partly by signs. They presented a beautiful tableaux, these two girls, each a representative of a race. The time is night, the emigrant wagons and animals are in the back-ground. A bright fire of logs is burning, just outside a row of tents, and beyond gathers the party of plumed and painted savages. On the other side is a group of white hunters, leaning on their firelocks, with several large hounds crouching at their feet. Between the two stand the girls, Emily robed in the habiliments of civilization, her bright eyes sparkling, and every feature betraying unusual and sympathetic interest; while the young Indian, nearly nude, displays her wounded arms and graceful figure to the best advantage, and though perfectly conscious of the horrible fate that awaits her, remembers likewise that the blood of warriors is in her veins, and comports herself with the dignity of a princess.

. She informed Emily that her people had slain many of the Snakes, who came upon them suddenly; that she, the daughter of the chief, was captured while out gathering Yampah roots for food, that she expected to die, but would not weep. "No, Ethleen will sing the death song of the brave, and her fathers will welcome her to the happy island of the blest," she said.

"But you would rather live," said Emily, with tears in her eyes, "It is dreadful to die so young."

"Ethleen will sing the death song of the brave," she said with a dignified aspect."

Mrs. Bradish, who deeply admired heroism, was much struck with her manners and appearance.

"I say chief," she exclaimed, advancing to the foremost savage, whose one lock of hair was decorated with the feathers of the war eagle, while from a belt around his waist two or three bloody scalps were dangling.

"I say chief, that you must give this girl to me."

The chief shook his head, "Good squaw, can't."

"But you must," said Mrs. Bradish, "see here," and she displayed before him a keg of the fire-water.

The chief touched it contemptuously with his foot, "ugh."

She then brought forth a quantity of glittering beads and trinkets, and even added her valuable watch to the store of baubles; but the Indian was not to be seduced from his first resolution, and manifestly regarded her tempting treasures with the indifference of a stoic.

At length, wearied and disgusted with his resolute bearing, she abandoned the field with the determination to continue some scheme to rescue the prisoner by stratagem.

Indian women are, generally speaking, far uglier than the men. In many cases they are likewise more savage and barbarous. Ethleen, however, had a Spanish look, and appeared lovely even to civilized eyes. Mrs. Bradish sought the Prophet. She wished, for particular reasons, to obtain his approbation. The stately hierarch condescended to inform her, that it had been revealed to him, that the Indian maiden was worthy of rescue. She then summoned old Buckley, and a young man named Charley Moore, and the three retired behind the tents for consultation. The Indians, meanwhile, after receiving various presents, departed with their captive.

CHAPTER XXVI.

AN UNEXPECTED ENCOUNTER.

"I WONDER what that woman is up to now," said Mr. Ward, as he saw Mrs. Bradish coming and going among the tents. "I hope she isn't laying a plan to embroil us with the Indians."

"She would hardly do that," I answered; "and yet I suspect that she designs to form some scheme by which to extricate that Indian girl."

"She will hardly attempt so insane a project as that."

"There is no knowing."

"At any rate, I shall use my influence to prevent anything of the kind," said Mr. Ward; "I will go immediately to discourage it," and he left the tent.

He had been absent but a few minutes when Louisa entered. Her face was swollen with weeping, and she appeared excessively agitated. I readily conjectured the cause of her sorrow, and bringing a chair, invited her to be seated.

"I have not time really, Mrs. Ward," she answered; "I am looking for mother Stillman. Have you seen anything of her?"

I replied in the negative, and inquired how long she had been absent.

"For some time, and father is really concerned about her, as she is not in the habit of going out without his knowledge."

"It strikes me that her absence may be connected with the affair of Fan Simpkins. Had you not thought of it?"

"No," said Louisa. "How dumb I am; but here is a letter that Fan sent to father, and which I verily believe will afford a clue to the whole mystery. Here it is, I found it in mother's reticule, though I have no idea that father has ever seen it."

"Well, what is it?"

"It appoints an interview for this evening, by the spring, at the foot of the Bluff. Now, I shouldn't wonder in the least if mother had gone down there, with the idea of personating her husband, or chastising Fan."

"But would she venture out, when the Indians were around."

"It's a great chance if she ever thought of the Indians at all, she was so deeply agitated with passionate jealousy. However, if you will accompany me, we will go down to the spring, and see what is going on."

"Do you think it would be expedient under the circumstances?"

"Certainly; the Indians have all departed."

"But wouldn't it be better to inform your husband or father?"

Louisa shook her head. "I think mother would prefer that they knew nothing of the circumstance."

"Suppose, then, that I call Mr. Ward, I would prefer to have company."

But Louisa persisted that there was no danger, and in compliance with her urgent solicitations, I consented to accompany her. The spring possessed a remarkable character, being apparently imbedded in a large, smooth rock, about fifteen yards in diameter, where the water was bubbling and boiling up in the midst of a white incrustation, with which it had covered a portion of the rock. The rock was overhung by currant bushes, which bore an abundance of half-ripened fruit, while a great variety of chenopodiaceous shrubs were in the immediate neighborhood. The air was fragrant with a variety of sweet-scented blossoms, but the duskiness of the evening, and my apprehensions of an Indian ambush, prevented my enjoying the beautiful scene. I expected each moment to see a dusky warrior start from the shrubbery that environed our path, or to hear the horrid war-whoop re-echoing over the hills.

"Hush! hark!" said Louisa, "what was that?"

We both paused to listen, our hearts beating audibly.

"Murder! murder! help! help!" cried a voice, that we recognized as belonging to a woman.

"What shall we do?" said Louisa.

"Why, go on to be sure," for now that the first excitement was over, I began to be ashamed of my weakness. The moon had just risen, and a flood of silvery light came pouring down upon us, just as we entered the little cove, in which the spring was embosomed. The sounds still continued, screams, and trampling of feet. As we came nearer the words became clearly distinct, and we plainly heard a ringing sound of blows. "Oh! I'll give it to you, you hussy; I'll teach you to be teasing my man, and making appointments for him to meet you."

"'Tis mother," whispered Louisa.

"I guess so."

As we came nearer, the combatants became visible, and such a scene, it would be impossible to depict its ludicrous effect. Mrs. Stillman, partially disguised in a long, black cloak, with a black handkerchief tied over her head, was laying a huge rawhide with no trifling effect over Fan Simpkins's shoulders, interspersing her castigation with much spicy advice. Fan was kicking, struggling, and shrieking, but the old lady, who was a powerful woman, and a tiger when roused, held her safely by one arm. Neither noticed our approach, or that in their rencontre, they had advanced to the very edge of the basin of the spring. Fan was the first to perceive their situation, and springing suddenly forward towards her castigator, she precipitated Mrs. Stillman with great force into the water.

"Now, lie there and drown, old devil, and then I'll have your man without any difficulty," and Fan shrieked with a wild, savage laugh, and turned away.

This movement brought us into full view. "So you've come after the old jade. Well, its lucky; for I wouldn't lift a finger to keep her from drowning," and she passed on.

Mrs. Stillman was certainly more frightened than hurt, but the good lady, though an admirable housewife, and well skilled in the various branches of domestic economy, was entirely ignorant of hydropathy, or that sublime science which finds in wet sheets and bathing-tubs a sovereign panacea for all the ills that flesh is heir to. She had always entertained a mortal horror of getting wet; a damp stocking or apron would give her toothache or rheumatism for, at least, a fortnight. No wonder then that her surprise and consternation at finding herself thus suddenly engulfed in the spring, actually took her breath for a time, though her head and feet were both out of the water, being supported on either side of the rock. Her cloak and mask had fallen off in the melêe, though she still retained her lash in a death-like grasp.

"I don't know how we shall get her out," said Louisa, in a voice that slightly trembled, as I thought, with suppressed laughter. For my own part, I could scarcely restrain my risible propensities.

"I gave it to her, didn't I?" said the old woman, opening her eyes. "She'll remember it one while, I'll bet."

"I shouldn't wonder if you did, too," said Louisa. "But, mother, how are we to get you out?"

"I don't know."

"Can't you help yourself a little?" inquired Louisa.

Owing to the position in which she lay, with her back in the spring, it seemed impossible either for her to raise herself or for us to assist her to rise. The least movement might precipitate her extremities into the water, and we were utterly ignorant of the depth of the liquid element.

"Here, take hold of my hands," she said, extending her arms. "I think you can easily pull me out."

We grasped her hands, and partially lifted her out, when, by some mischance or another, Louisa let go her hold, and the frightened woman fell back, and this time with her feet and all her person in the water. Her clothes, however, buoyed her up, and, after an infinite amount of floundering, splashing, and tossing about, she succeeded, with our assistance, in establishing herself on terra firma.

"Oh, dear, I've catched my death this night," she said, panting with the unwonted exertion. "Fan Simpkins, the wretch, to plunge me in there so."

"But, mother," said Louisa, "what on earth could induce you to wander off here, alone, too?"

"Don't you never ask," said Mrs. Stillman ; "but, deary me, I can't walk with all these wet clothes hanging about me."

"Let us wring the water out," said Louisa, and, stooping down, we wrung the moisture from her garments.

"That wicked wretch, Fan Simpkins, that wicked wretch ; it's her what's brought me into this trouble."

"Never mind her," said Louisa.

"Never mind her, indeed ! think I'm going to put up with such impudence, and have my husband cajoled and persuaded .into bad practices, before my eyes ?"

"Who are these ?" said Louisa.

As she spoke, three horsemen emerged into view from the broad shadow of the cottonwood grove, and, without noticing us, struck off across the plain, at the foot of the hills.

CHAPTER XXVII.

A NEW CHARACTER.

THIS morning our camp was thrown into unusual excitement, by the absence of Mrs. Bradish, Buckley, and Charley Moore. Charley was a young man, about twenty-two years old, and the very beau ideal of a western ranger. When very young, he accompanied his father on various trapping expeditions into the Indian country and no one in our company was better acquainted with the manners, habits, and language of the aborigines. Then, too, Charley possessed all the accomplishments of a thorough-bred hunter, which, though widely different, are quite as diversified and various as those of a Broadway gent. If the latter must understand the exact manner of twirling a cane, or curling a moustache, the former must carry his rifle with a peculiar grace, and be able, at a moment's warning, to bring down a deer or mount a wild horse. Both are dressed in the extreme of fashion, but, in the one case the materials are broadcloth and velvet; in the other, they consist of a rich abundance of furs and moccasins, wide trowsers, and a blanket worn like a Mexican cloak. Both are fond of ornaments—one of rings, chains, and glittering bijouterie; the other of dirks, long knives and pistols thrust into a wide belt. One is enamored with splendid rooms, gorgeous furniture, and chandeliers brilliant with light and beauty; the other exults in a cosy nook among the rocks, with the everlasting mountains covered with primeval forests, mingling with the starry heavens above him, and dimly reflected by the blazing camp-fire at his feet. Both are fond of adventures—the one of breaking innocent hearts, and betraying the artless, confiding youth of the weak and unsuspecting ; the other of fording rivers, climbing mountains, peering over precipices, hunting grizzly bears, or racing with Indians. One is heartless, deceitful, hypocritical ; a lord of soaps and essences and lavender ; a connoisseur of gloves and neck-ties, an arbiter of dimples, and a leader of riot and dissipation. The other is an unsophisticated child of nature, bold, ardent, daring and honest. He is generous, for he will share his last morsel with a stranger. He will be the first to volunteer assistance for the weak and oppressed, and the last to give up an undertaking in which duty and honor are involved. He never forsakes a friend, never takes undue advantage of an enemy, never betrays the confidence of youth and innocence, and never wrongs the aged. Such was Charley Moore ; a hero in the estimation of his companions, and very generally known and beloved by the Indians. For even these savages can appreciate, as they always applaud, the nobler virtues of heroism, truth, and honesty. Born and bred in frontier life, accustomed to the spirit-stirring scenes of the chase, and passionately fond of all wild adventures, he had never found time to even dream of love. Though it is true that, in his calmer moments, a yearning for something, dearer and sweeter than he had known, would come over his spirit, and his bosom would heave and thrill with emotions he found it vain to attempt to analyze. Then he thought of his mother ; but he had never seen her. Though he could remember a little sister, with loving blue eyes and flaxen ringlets ; and how he used to gather all sorts of childish treasures for her, how he never wearied of her society, and with what pleasure he administered to her wants. Oh, the charm of gentleness, and how it tames man's rugged nature. Of all the world of memory crowded into the life of this strong man, of all the daring adventures he had known and witnessed, of all the scenes of excitement, and blood, and strife in which he had borne a part, his mind only loved the thought of that gentle sister, so mild in her soft, sad, spiritual beauty ; and when the past came back, with its thronging images, it was hers, and hers alone, that he waved to stay.

How well he remembered when she died ! He was but a boy ; and yet boys have strong affections ; and how often the passions of that youthful period cicatrize the heart with scars that are never erased ! They were several miles from civilized settlements—their hut had been the lodge of an Indian ; it was cold and uncomfortable, but he selected the nicest and softest skins for her couch, and then erected a sort of frame-work over the bed, on which he hung for curtains the clothes and blankets they had obtained from the traders ; and having heard his father tell of the comforts and luxuries of civilization, he induced a kind-hearted Indian female to stay with her, while he departed to obtain such necessaries as he fancied her invalid state required. With a delicate perception, remarkable in one of his age and habits, he brought for the sick child the identical articles that a skillful and experienced physician would have dictated. —Tea, sugar, oranges, confectionery, crackers, and a pillow— yes, a pillow—soft, warm and downy, with a white, snowy covering.

"What is this for ?" said the invalid child, lifting her eyes, now grown so large and bright, to his face.

"It's a cushion for your dear head," he answered. "Raise up a little—there—now, ain't that nice and soft ?"

"Oh, it is !" she said, "it is," as her head, with its superabundance of soft, shiny hair, half buried itself in the downy mass. And then when he displayed his other treasures, and their purpose, she did not weep, she did not even smile, but an expression of unutterable thankfulness, and love, and gratitude, illumined her features; and raising herself half up, she kissed him so tenderly and fervently, that the look and the kiss remained with him to his dying day.

And side by side with this, was the memory of her death in his mind—her death, so long looked for, and of which she was accustomed to speak with such tranquillity, that it awakened in him only the emotion of a gentle sorrow—a mild regret—altogether different from a passionate explosion of grief. One day, he was sitting, as usual, in the soft sunlight, by the door of their hut, when she called, in a voice so faint, so low and spiritual, that he rose, half-frightened, and went to her bed. Her eyes looked larger and brighter than ever, but her countenance had a pale and worn expression, that struck him as something new.

"I have lain here a great while," she said in a whisper.

"Yes, my sister," he answered, smoothing down the wealth of shining curls, and adjusting the pillow.

"Well, I sha'n't remain long, not much longer," she answered. "I am going to die; did you know it?" and a bright smile of intelligence flitted over her innocent face.

"I feared so," said the boy, half-choking with emotion.

"I used to think I might perhaps get well, and go out with you to play with the lambs, and gather flowers, when the spring came again; but I know better now," she continued, "for last night I saw my mother."

"You did?" said Charles, drying his eyes; "how did she look?"

"Very beautiful, with such a sweet face."

"How was it—how was it? Tell me just how it was, and why she came to you," he replied eagerly.

"Well," said the child, "I thought I was lying here sick, just as I am now, and that, though my eyes were shut, I knew that some one was hovering over me. Then I looked, and oh, such a pair of soft, mild eyes—so large and deep, and fraught with such an expression of love and tenderness! It was not like anything I had ever seen; her face, too, didn't look like earthly faces; and a soft, ethereal radiance seemed ever beaming from it, with a warmth that came right down here, into my heart."

"Did she say anything?" inquired Charley, with boyish curiosity.

"She didn't talk as we do," said the child, "and her voice did not sound like a human voice, but so much sweeter and pleasanter; and though she didn't tell me so, I knew right away that she was our mother, and that I was going to her very soon; and I felt, beyond a doubt, that all must be happiness where she is."

"I wished I knew what kind of a place it is," said the boy, in his straightforward manner; "and whether there be birds, and flowers, and sunshine there—whether they hunt beaver and buffalo, and sail over a beautiful lake, in canoes that can't overset, as the old Indian told me."

"I don't think that," said the invalid child; "mother didn't look that way."

"How then?"

She shook her head.

"Can't you tell me?"

Again she shook her head.

"I wish mother would come to me, too," said Charley; "I always wanted to see her."

"You are going to her, a little, every day," whispered the invalid.

"Oh, that I might go when you do!" he said, and burst into a passionate fit of weeping. "I shall be all alone then," he continued—no mother, no sister!"

"But you will have a mother and a sister both," said the girl, with wonderful energy. " We shall only be a little way off, and sometimes, nay, often, we shall be with, and around you. I believe that mother has often been with me."

Again the curiosity of the boy was aroused, and he exclaimed, wonderingly, " You do ?"

" Yes ; because I have felt a thousand times, when I thought of my mother, just such a happiness as I felt last night, when looking at her, and when she was breathing over me. And now, Charley," she continued, after a moment's pause, " I want you to lie down by me, for I feel very cold."

Charley hesitated. He had a faint perception that the cold of which she spoke betokened the presence of death.

" Oh ! do, Charley," she exclaimed, lifting her soft, supplicating eyes to his face ; " indeed, I shan't trouble you much longer. Lay down here by my side, and clasp me in your arms. I am cold and my heart is heavy."

Charley hesitated no longer. He laid his head beside hers on the pillow, wound his arms around her, but half shrunk from her cold clammy lips that met his forehead, in a last embrace.

" Now, be still," she whispered, " for I want to sleep."

And they lay very still, that brother and sister : he listening to her low breathing, and thinking of all she had been saying, until he finally fell asleep.

And they both slept, but wrapped in a different slumber. He dreamed of heaven and his mother ; and she—who shall depict the forms of imperishable beauty, the strains of unimaginable harmony, and the glorious reality of blessedness, that burst on her disembodied spirit?

The father had been out attending to his traps. He was a morose, unsociable kind of man, though good-hearted and fond of his children. He found the dead cradled on the bosom of the living—the blooming cheek of life pressed closely to the pallid one of death !

Was it a fancied resemblance to his sister, in Ethleen, that excited the sympathy of the youthful hunter, and determined him to attempt her rescue? It matters not. He was young, ardent, and excitable. She in her simple grace and beauty exceeded in lovable qualities many a damsel whose skin was fairer. He pitied and then admired her, and who is not aware that pity and admiration are near akin to love?

While waiting their return, we were somewhat alarmed by the appearance in our camp of a large party of Spaniards, Mexicans, and Frenchmen. They proved to be Santa Fó traders, who were making their annual peregrination through the country for the purpose of hunting, trapping, and purchasing furs from the Indians. They seemed a wild-looking set, talking a strange language, or rather a mingled dialect of four or five languages, and were accompanied by a number of Indian women, their wives as I supposed. They were all well mounted and armed, but several of the company appeared to be suffering from recent wounds. Their leader was a trapper noted in the West, and the horse he rode, and which he had named Charlemagne, was almost equally famous. It may not be generally known, and yet it is no less true, that many of these western trappers with their steeds and rifles, are quite as distinguished among their compeers, as, according to romance, the knights of chivalry were in the times of old.

B——m, our Prophet, came forth to meet and talk theology with the visitors, attended as usual by a large concourse of the elders and deacons. He informed the traders that we were journeying to the Promised Land, that our course through the day was directed by the revelation which he received in the night, and that with every step of our progress the power of the devil grew less and less.

"Stranger," returned the leading trapper, "as for the devil,

I don't know anything about him, though I have often thought that if such a being existed at all, he must be an Indian."

The Prophet shook his head, "You know," he said, "that Christ is to live and reign on the earth a thousand years."

"I don't know any such thing," said the trapper.

"Well, we know it, and so we are journeying from the land of the heathen, to establish a kingdom of the saints, and build a city in which righteousness shall dwell."

It was very evident that the thoughts of our visitors were much more interested in hunting expeditions, than with religious affairs, and the listlessness of their demeanor told their indifference to this strange homily.

They asked many questions, and among the rest, "Whence we came?"

B——m pointed with his fingers to the various points of the compass, and then proceeded to explain, that converts to the faith were coming in from all parts of the world. That Asia and the islands in the sea had received the good news, and would soon send a multitude of proselytes. "We shall have the greatest kingdom in the world, and a city that will be more glorious than all others," he exclaimed fervently. "And we shall increase abundantly, and eat the fat of the land. Our wives shall be fruitful vines, and our children like olive plants."

The women listened apparently with far deeper interest than the men. They mingled among us, examining our clothes, jewels, and domestic appurtenances with a strange mixture of surprise and curiosity. As I understand French, we had little difficulty in conversing, and so while the elders were discussing theology with the men, we readily entered into conversation with the women. They were greatly surprised on learning that a husband among us was permitted to marry all the wives he could get, and one of them expressed her eagerness to get away, for fear that if her husband heard of such a practice, he would follow it.

"And what would you do in such a case?" I inquired.

She drew a small glittering stiletto, and imitated the motion of stabbing with it. From her I learned, that they were only the advance guard of a large company, who were travelling much in the manner of an Asiatic caravan.

CHAPTER XXVIII.

THE FUGITIVES.

WE soon began to experience the deepest concern for the fate of Mrs. Bradish, and her companions. We could not for a moment doubt the object of the enterprise, but their prolonged absence filled our minds with apprehension and dread. It was proposed to send a party to look for them, but this Harmer steadfastly refused.

We were in a hostile country, surrounded by Indians and Mexicans of murderous habits, and, consistent with our own safety, could not diminish the number of our available men, by dispatching a party on such a wild-goose chase among the mountains. So he argued, and the more cautious and prudent, coincided with him.

"Charley Moore is a brave fellow, and can handle a rifle, break in a wild horse, and shoot a buffalo as skillfully as any man living, yet he is not so prudent as he will be when he gets twenty more years over his head," said Mr. Ward. "The enterprise was a dangerous one, but Mrs. Bradish seems actually fond of danger. I never knew such a woman."

"She certainly is brave to rashness," replied Harmer, "and

yet I don't like her. I don't like to see a woman affect the manners of a man," and he glanced towards Emily.

"Then you conceive cowardice to be a feminine accomplishment," she remarked, provokingly, "I shan't agree with you there. Nothing disgusts me so much as the silly habit some females acquire, of always being frightened at everything, and generally speaking, the fright is proportionate to the weakness and insignificance of the object. Thus a bug, a spider, or a worm, is quite sufficient to throw such delicate specimens of effeminacy into hysterics."

"I contend for a medium," said Harmer, laughing, "I do not admire bravery in a woman, yet cowardice is shameful in either women or men."

"Cowardice is shameful, and bravery not admirable, I am incapable of understanding the paradox."

"Well, I admire bravery on all occasions, and in in either sex," said Mr. Ward, "It is one of the noblest qualifications, when conjoined with prudence, which I regret to say is not always the case with the lady of whom we were conversing."

"I have been expecting all along that she would be out hunting buffalo," I remarked.

"Well, it would be fine pastime," said Emily, "I have been thinking how the stag-hunting English ladies would delight in it."

"Suppose you go out with me some day," said Harmer.

Emily shook her head, and said that she had not a trained hunter, "and then I should forfeit your good opinion by my boldness," she continued.

"And would you esteem that a very great loss?" he inquired.

"How can you ask."

"Because I wished to know."

"Well, your answer must be that I decline to hunt."

"But not to walk," he continued, "There are some beautiful specimens of helianthi and a great variety of other wild-flowers down in the valley yonder ; suppose we go and gather some, you are a botanist, and shall read me their language."

Emily smiled, "a hunter and trapper of the west, talking about the language of flowers."

"And why not?—the hunters and trappers of the far west have an eye and a soul that can perceive and appreciate the beautiful ; but come along."

"Mrs. Ward, you go too," said Emily.

Harmer looked rather displeased at this proposal, "Well, you go on, and I'll come presently," I answered, and they slowly walked away.

Agreeably to my promise, I placed a sun-bonnet on my head and followed. When I came up with them, Emily was holding an arm-load of flowering plants, from which Harmer was arranging a bouquet, while connecting a sentiment with each blossom, that, whether appropriate to the flower or not, was, doubtless, indicative of the feelings with which he regarded his companion.

"Oh, it is too ridiculous," said Emily, as I approached, "you ought to hear the sentiments Mr. Harmer attaches to these blossoms. This ammole (soap-plant) he says is indicative of my love,—is all grace, beauty and cleanliness. And this beautiful blue flowering lupine means, according to him, that my love is without spot or blemish."

"As Flora's interpreter, his sentiments are quite original, and very appropriate," I remarked.

"Oh, certainly, and this," she inquired, holding up a large poppy of a rich orange color.

"That means, 'my love is the chiefest among ten thousand and—altogether lovely,' I suggested, seeing that he had forgotten the sentence.

"Here is another," she said, selecting an elegant white flower, very sweet and fragrant, and much resembling a lily.

"That is, my love is all innocence," she said.

While engaged in this pleasant play, we were suddenly startled by a war-whoop, such as Indians make when returning from a victorious enterprise; and soon Mrs. Bradish, followed by Charley Moore and Buckley, appeared. Mounted behind Charley was the beautiful Ethleen, her long hair floating over her rounded shoulders, and every feature glowing with happiness. We returned to the camp together, when they informed us that after the departure of the Indians, with whom Ethleen was detained as a captive, they determined on pursuit, and mounting their horses, took the trail, which, after winding about in several narrow valleys, led directly into the mountains. That night they followed it by moon-shine till near morning, when the whole party became weary, and concluded to halt for refreshment. They kindled no light, but supped on some dried beef, and then, concealed among the rocks, laid down to sleep in silence and darkness. At day-light they resumed the pursuit, and followed the trail all that day, through narrow glens and along the foot of a considerable mountain range. Just at sunset they became satisfied that the Indians had encamped in the neighborhood; consequently, they were under the necessity of proceeding cautiously. As Buckley had the most experience in Indian habits and warfare, he volunteered to go forward when it became dark, while his companions remained concealed in the glen. Moore at first objected to this arrangement, but the old man finally succeeded in convincing him that the success of their enterprise all depended on wariness and caution.

"They are twenty to one of us, and we must outwit them some how, or the gal is lost," said the old man.

"And how are we to do that?" inquired Moore.

"That all depends on circumstances, but I think we can come it; Indians ain't quick-witted any way you can fix it."

"I thought they were up to all sorts of mischief and stratagem," said Mrs. Bradish.

"Well, they do try to be, but being and trying to be, are two things, you know."

"Certainly."

"You see, when I was trapping among the Ozark Mountains; but I won't tell the story to night."

"Why not?"

"Because it ain't a proper time, we must be on the watch for them devils."

And the old man bent his ear to the ground, and lay several minutes intently listening.

"I hear 'em," he said at length, "the devils are preparing for a carouse, I guess."

"Oh, God! for Ethleen's sacrifice," cried Moore, starting up. "Haste, haste, old man, we shall be too late."

"Never fear that," said Buckley.

"But I do fear it," said Moore impetuously.

"Young and hasty," answered the old man laughing, "just as I was when Bill Peters—but I won't tell it."

"No you shan't. I don't want any of your stories till Ethleen is rescued from her enemies. Come, what are you going to do?"

"Stay just where I be at least two hours."

"Then I shall attempt her release without you."

"And bring certain destruction on yourself and her."

"I shall try at any rate. I should hear her death-shriek for eternity if I sat here while they were building her funeral-pile."

"They are building it!" said the old man coolly, lifting himself from the ground.

"Old man," said Mrs. Bradish, "I shall have a very poor opinion of your bravery, and less of your humanity, if you suffer that poor girl to be sacrificed without making an effort to save her."

"And do you suppose, madam, that I would have come here for no purpose at all?"

"And yet you seem very easy about that purpose."

"Because I know my own know."

"You do indeed!"

"Yes, which is more than can be said of everybody. You see I knowed all about these Indian sacrifices, and just how they manage 'em. You see they'll get everything ready for their hideous pow-wow. They'll dance, and hoot, and yell to their heart's content, and until they are fairly tired out. Then the intended victim will be led away from the stake, and confined in a hut, or some other convenient place, while the devils will go to sleep, and by this means repair their exhausted energies preparatory to another scene. This slumber will be the time for us. If we can find the gal, we shall have no difficulty. It strikes me, however, that you had better stay here with the horses, and keep perfectly still, while I go on ahead. What do you say?"

They consented to be governed by his advice, when again putting his ear to the ground, he listened intently.

"I think it's time for me to be off," he said, rising up; and, divesting himself of all superabundant clothing, he disappeared noiselessly among the rocks. Moore looked after him long and wistfully, and then sunk down in an attitude of silence.

"I wonder how long he will be absent?" said Mrs. Bradish, to whom the suspense was dreadful.

Moore shook his head.

"An hour?" she continued, inquiringly.

"Two or three of them, probably."

"Oh, heavens! I cannot begin to wait that long."

"Unless you have to; but we must be still;" and both relapsed into silence.

Meanwhile, the old man pursued his way, sometimes striking

the trail, but generally guided by his ear, which he placed every few minutes to the ground. In this manner he proceeded a considerable distance, and having crept with more than usual caution over the brow of an eminence, he came suddenly within sight of the Indians. They were dancing, yelling and howling, around their victim, who was tied to a stake, and who seemed to regard all their preparations with a stoical indifference. At length one of the warriors suddenly darted from the circle of dancers up to the prisoner, and commenced brandishing his tomahawk over her head, motioning to strike, now here, now there—in the forehead, on the face, and over the throat. She never flinched, but regarded his actions with a clear, steady countenance, and calm unshrinking eye. Yelling horribly, he darted back to his place in the circle, and swept around with the others. In a few moments another seized a firebrand, and, rushing up to the girl, motioned to touch her with it on the eyes, the cheeks, lips and chin. This time she laughed derisively.

"You are no warrior," she said tantalizingly. "You don't know how to scalp an enemy. You are a squaw."

Enraged beyond measure, he was about to fire the pile, when a second warrior struck the torch from his hands. They were not ready for the consummation of their vengeance.

To describe these Indian dances would be impossible. No English words could possibly express the postures, the contortions and unnatural positions into which the performers throw themselves, and all this accompanied by yells, howls, screams, shrieks and noises, of the most terrific and horrible character.

Presently the dance became less animated, the voices less wild and shrill. One after another of the dancers dropped off, evidently overcome with fatigue. At length the chief sprung forward, and severing the cord that bound the victim to the stake, he led her off into a hut. Buckley, from the close covert of a thicket, beheld the movement. His eye sparkled with delight

11*

as he muttered, "They'll soon be quiet now." A few minutes proved his assertion, and the whole band were buried in the oblivion of slumber. Buckley crept cautiously towards the hut where he knew the girl to be confined. He understood perfectly the nature of his foe, and knew very well that no ordinary noise would awaken them, but he observed that the chief had a large dog, and, to judge from appearances, a sagacious one, which it might be difficult to elude. This canine warrior seemed aware of the proximity of a foe. Two or three times he had started up, snuffed the air, and barked loudly; then, running to his master, he began pulling and tugging at his blanket. The chief partly awakened, scolded the dog, and ordered him to lie down, a command which the animal manifested no inclination to obey. Buckley conjectured that the slumber of the Indians would continue probably an hour, when the victim would be again brought forth, and their horrible orgies consummated in her death. Every moment then was precious, but how was the dog to be quieted? One only scheme presented an appearance of feasibility. Raising himself up, and striking a light, he stood in the full view of his enemy, about one hundred yards from the camp. As he expected, the dog came bounding towards him, growling and gnashing his teeth. The old man received him valiantly with a drawn dagger. The struggle was violent, but brief, and Buckley beheld himself the master of the field. Gliding along to the hut without further delay, Buckley commenced removing the back side covering with extreme caution, and soon made an aperture through which he could scan the inside of the cabin. The girl was alone, and pinioned in a most uncomfortable position. Having satisfied himself of this, he recommenced widening the hole until it became sufficiently large for the ingress of a man.

Though Ethleen had detected the sound of his approaching footsteps, and even then, according to her statement, knew him to be a white man, she remained perfectly silent, conscious that her condition could not possibly be rendered any worse. Her heart bounded with exultation, when she read his features in the dim firelight, and heard the whispered words that assured her of the presence of a friend. With one stroke of the knife her thongs were removed, and she bounded to her feet like a young fawn. A moment after she was following him, with noiseless step, from the Indian encampment.

They had proceeded but a short distance, however, when they were startled by a tremendous whooping and yelling.

"They have discovered your escape," whispered Buckley, in the Indian dialect, "and will be down on us presently like so many devils."

"I think," said Ethleen, "that the noise we heard tells the arrival of a new party, who were coming in to-night."

"Probably, but even in that case your escape will be discovered."

Ethleen trembled like a frightened bird.

"Now dont be scary; your condition is not desperate," said the old man. "But we must keep our wits about us; can you climb a tree?"

"Like a squirrel."

"Well, then, betake yourself to that pine yonder; make no noise, let what will happen."

"And you."

"I will mount this one; but hurry."

Ethleen glided rapidly away, and Buckley ascended the tree he had chosen. It was a huge pine, thick at the top, with the growth of centuries. He was scarcely concealed among the branches, when a great demonstration of howling and yelling among the Indians, announced some new discovery—probably the massacre of the dog. The old man chuckled. "Don't it plague 'em, the copper colored devils," he muttered, unconsciously.

The Indians were examining the ground for his trail, which discovered, they pushed on vigorously. Buckley had anticipated this, and consequently had retraced his steps, walking backwards for a considerable distance, in which he was imitated by Ethleen. The Indians passed and re-passed, paused and hesitated, in their vain efforts to follow the trail, then finally abandoned the attempt, and went back to their encampment. Descending noiselessly from his hiding-place, he was joined by Ethleen, who fell on her knees and embraced his hands in unspeakable gratitude.

"Tut, tut," said the old man, "no time for that. Let's be getting away from the sarpents as fast as possible."

Ethleen rose, and the two were soon safely concealed by the mountain gorges, though in the nearest and most direct way to rejoin his companions.

CHAPTER XXIX.

WATER! WATER!! WATER!!!

WHEN the wounded men were sufficiently recovered, we recommenced our journey, and, notwithstanding all that the prophets and elders could say, and the encouragement they held out of our safety, peace, and happiness in the Promised Land, our people very generally had become low-spirited. B——m rated them soundly for this. "Would you, then, return to the flesh-pots of Egypt?" he said. "Would you dwell among the heathen, rather than endure the trials and difficulties incident to the possession of the Lord's goodly heritage? Oh! for shame, for shame! and I will pray for you, even as Moses prayed for the children of Israel; pray for you, that ye fall not out by the way."

Such exhortations, however, were illy calculated to produce a pleasant effect, under the multiplicity of discouragements that attended the emigration. Food had become scarce—that is, such as we were accustomed to eat. One after another, the poor worn-out oxen had been slain. Mrs. Beardsley declared that she knew it would be so, and said that she would rather die than eat a morsel of horse or mule flesh.

Mrs. Stillman, sen., was not certain about the dying, but protested that she thought it horrible, and even reflected rather severely on the first mentioned lady for exposing herself to foreseen difficulties.

The prophets counselled resignation, and dwelt largely on the example of the Israelites. ..

"Well, I can't see any resemblance at all," said Mrs. Beardsley. "The Lord sent them quails and manna, but he lets us take care of ourselves."

"We are under another dispensation."

"Another dispensation, is it!—then why talk of resemblances where none exist?" and the good lady snapped her knitting needles with redoubled vigor.

"I don't see that you have anything to complain of, mother," said Harmer, jestingly. "Your yarn seems to hold out well."

"Not so very well, either," she answered. "I haven't but six balls."

"Six balls,—and how many have you knit since we started?"

"Twelve."

"Why, mother, you will supply the whole colony with stockings."

"But we can't eat stockings," said Fan Simpkins, "and the trouble now seems to be to get something fit to eat. This dried buffalo meat is actually abominable."

It was so, in fact, being very little, if any, better than so much bark.

That, however, was only the beginning of sorrow, for in a few days we entered a sandy and barren region, where, to our other ills and inconveniences, that most intolerable of all, the want of water, was added. The streams were all dried up, the rivers disappeared from their channels, there was neither rain nor dew.

But, though the air seemed intensely hot, and the sky exhibited not a trace of clouds, there was a softness in the atmosphere at night, a resplendent glory in the stars, altogether incomprehensible and most delightful. And this region, otherwise so sterile, was filled with flowers of the richest perfume and the brightest colors. In many places, where it would seem, from the gravelly, sandy nature of the soil, that no plant whatever could take root, cactuses, literally covered with a profusion of large crimson flowers, thrived luxuriantly, thus presenting a remarkable contrast to the surrounding desolation. For one of the remarkable characteristics of this place, was the utter absence of animal life. Not a bird visited these resplendent blossoms, not a butterfly or insect enlivened the solitude. Neither hares nor pheasants lurked beneath their coverts. Even the Indians seemed to avoid the country. Once, and once only, we caught the glimpse of a troop of wild horses, skirting the horizon. It was only a glimpse, and yet I shall ever remember the graceful agility of their motions, and the sleek sparkle of their glossy sides. But sadder sights than these awaited us. I had descended from the wagon to walk, in order that I might examine the beautiful flowers. I was particularly charmed by two or three huge plants of the cactus species, which had grown so close together that they appeared compact. They were, at least, ninety feet in circumference, and large scarlet blossoms depended from the branches. But, while stooping to gather a bouquet, my fingers inadvertently touched a relic, the sight of which filled me with horror. It was a human skeleton; but the skin, instead of falling away, still clung to the bones, showing the veins, and muscles, and sinews, in a horrible state of preservation, yet with strict fidelity to nature. The long, lank, bony fingers, yet held a paper clutched tightly between them. Curiosity was stronger than fear, and I removed it. There were a few lines written with a pencil, which I had much difficulty in making out. They ran:

"We can go no further. My wife and five children—all dying for want of water! Oh, God! this death is horrible!"

The poor fellow had evidently sought the shelter of the cactus to shield himself from the burning sun; and there died from burning, intolerable thirst. But the wife and children—where where were were they? A little further on, in the same state of horrible attenuation, without decay. The mother yet clasped her infant in her bony arms, and the thin, tightly-drawn lips of the child were pressed to her cadaverous breast. Two of the children—a boy and a girl—had their fingers interlaced; while the other two were twined in each other's arms, as if they sought to solace the agonies of that horrible death by the sweets of congenial affection. And who shall say that they were not happier, dying thus, than multitudes have been who departed this life surrounded by all the comforts of wealth and luxury, but with hatred gnawing, Prometheus-like, at their hearts?

But the best of us were in no condition to speculate or philosophize. Thirst, intolerable thirst, was burning our tongues and scorching our brains. Our poor animals suffered as much, or even more than ourselves; and I half forgot my own miseries in witnessing theirs.

B——m, fond of instituting comparisons between ourselves and the children of Israel, began to talk about their sufferings in the wilderness. Mrs. Beardsley, whose asperity increased with the difficulties, requested him to step forth and imitate the example of Moses, by bringing water out of the rock. He declined the attempt, however, excusing himself on the ground that his followers had too little faith.

At length, after an inconceivably toilsome and weary march, one of the men discovered a spring. We crowded eagerly around it, both men and beasts, but imagine our sorrow, surprise and consternation, to find that the water was both salt and bitter. Truly, I thought of the waters of Marah, but no miracle interposed for us, as in that case, and while some murmured, and others prayed, a third party sat in sullen despair, and many wept. All around here were the skeletons of men and horses, which had not been able to find support for their lives.

Buckley, with his great sagacity, and knowledge of the country, declared he knew from infallible signs that water must be near. Accordingly, several of the men set off to look for it, and about a mile distant, found the bed of a stream, from which the water had disappeared, a little only remaining in holes, which was increased by digging, until we all received a comfortable supply. Our route the next day, was through a country equally dry and sterile, where the trail was literally paved with the skeletons of men and horses. These latter were continually giving out, some from thirst, others from crippled feet. A dull and sullen despair pervaded the company, and this was considerably enhanced from the fact, that many had lost their confidence in the knowledge and sagacity of the leaders.

"When, oh! when, will this ever come to an end?" said Louisa, one morning, as we commenced our weary march. "I had heard of the American deserts, where wild horses, rode by wilder Indians, roamed, but never thought to be myself a wanderer over its sterile plains."

Generally, however, the women bore their sufferings with a

fortitude far surpassing that of the men. Some of them even affected a cheerfulness they were far from feeling, in order to support the sinking spirits of the party. Fan Simpkins still carried on her ridiculous coquetries, much to the amusement of Mrs. Bradish, but to the infinite chagrin of the victims. Subjected to this annoyance, old Mrs. Stillman scarcely perceived the presence of other ills. When the old gentleman walked Fan would take his arm; when he rode, she would sit beside him; then she would present him with bouquets, talk to him, sing for him, and strive, by every means, to attract his attention. We might be hazarding too much, to say that the old man was charmed and fascinated, though it is certain that he was not displeased, and gave her far more encouragement than suited his wife.

"Mrs. Stillman cannot be a true believer," said Mrs. Bradish, "or she would see the expediency and necessity of these things, and cease her ridiculous opposition, accordingly. Does she suppose that her puny resentment is to change a practice incorporated with a system of divine truth?"

"It is impossible to tell what she supposes, or proposes. Indeed it is scarcely probable that she entertains the idea of any definite scheme whatever, but she hates and abhors the thought of sharing her husband's affections with a youthful rival."

Notwithstanding her errors and failings, Mrs. Bradish exhibited a strength of mind and purpose truly admirable. Under all the dangers and difficulties of our tiresome journey, she maintained the same serenity, counselled the same direct, straightforward measures; seeming to take the whole thing as a matter of course. When the others complained, she sung; when they wept, she returned thanks; when they cursed (for some of the men, notwithstanding their character of saints, did curse), she prayed; when they sat in sullen despair, she laughed and chatted, told humorous stories, and otherwise sought to divert their attention.

Then, too, she was kind and considerate, and, though in everybody's business, really counselled wisely. There are good points in every character; amid a multitude of vices there are always some virtues, and it frequently happens that the most glaring defects are associated with the kindest hearts. And this woman, so Amazon-like in her habits, would nurse the sick, especially children, with the fondest care. Above all others, she possessed the art so useful to nurses of getting the little rebels to take medicine. Was a nauseous dose of bitter tea to be administered, she must be called into requisition, and never failed, sometimes by coaxing, sometimes by scolding, and sometimes by other means, in getting them to drink it. She seemed to delight in making her influence felt; above all, she had a quickness of perception as to our necessities, with a ready skill in making the most of means.

But all her cheerfulness and care could not render the heat and thirst less intolerable, while journeying over the hot yellow sands of this elevated country. It could not make the bisnada any more palatable, or communicate a more grateful succulency to the leaves of the sour dock, with which we moistened our mouths; but when one day at sunset, we came to a bold running stream, we felt that Providence had not deserted us, for appearances led us to conclude that the wilderness of sand was passed.

We now came to the Indian country, and their hostile demonstrations were far from pleasant. As there was an abundance of water and good grass, it was deemed advisable to rest and refresh the animals for a day or two. This gave the savages abundant opportunity to harass and distress us. The men were obliged to keep arms in their hands continually. Towards evening they began surrounding the horses, which had been driven for pasture to a fresh hill-side. They were immediately driven into close quarters. During the night we were much troubled with them, but being desirious of peace, we simply acted on the defensive. The next morning multitudes of them were seen in every direction. Some on the bottoms, others on the hills; some silent, but many pointing at and haranguing us. Their language being probably a dialect of the Utah, Harmer could understand them very well. They were evidently hostile towards us, and we were not very well disposed to them. They were almost nude, without either hats or shoes. Their hair being gathered into a knot behind, was ornamented by the plumes of eagles, or tufts of horse-hair. Besides his bow, each man carried a quiver with forty or fifty arrows, partially drawn out. Besides these, each man held two or three in his hand for instant service. These arrows were barbed with a translucent stone, a species of opal, nearly as hard, and quite as beautiful as the diamond; and when shot from their long bows, were almost as effective as powder and ball.

In these Indians I was forcibly struck with an animal appearance. Their motions, their countenances, and the expression of their eyes, were those of a wild beast. One, who appeared to be the chief, with two or three warriors, came boldly into our camp. When shown the weapons of our men, "Well," he replied, twanging his bow, "these are quite as good."

"Pshaw!" said Harmer, aiming at a bird, which he shot dead.

The Indian gave a derisive laugh, and brought down another. Fearful of the consequences likely to result, Mr. Ward went forward to expostulate, and bestowing a small present on the Indians induced them to leave the camp.

These savages are a miserable and degraded race, infinitely inferior to their more warlike brethren of the Sioux, Pawnee and Snake tribes. They chiefly subsist on roots and lizards, and each man is furnished with a long stick, hooked at one end, with which they search for their favorite food in the crevices of the rocks. These they roasted and ate with great relish. Nothing delighted them more than to get hold of a worn-out horse or mule, the flesh of which, half cooked by the fire, and eaten without salt, afforded them a real luxury.

To the Mormons, who regarded the Indians as descendants of the ten lost tribes of Israel, these people offered a subject of curious and devout speculation, but though the Mormon Bible was brought forth, and its contents scanned with the closest scrutiny, no clue could be obtained to their origin, or the patriarch whence they sprung.

Buckley, whose views of religion and philosophy were somewhat original, declared that the Indians were a race by themselves; that they were produced in fact just where they were found, and not at all attributable to our first parents.

"How produced?" said Harmer, "you do not suppose that they growed like a tree?"

"Yes; exactly like a tree. Did ye ever read the first chapter of Genesis?"

All said that they had.

"Well don't you know that it reads there that God said. 'Let the earth bring forth grass; the herb yielding seed, and the fruit tree yielding fruit after his kind;' and it was so."

"But what has that to do with the Indians?"

"Nothing particularly, though it has something to do with the trees."

"So we perceive."

"Well, in another verse it says that God said, 'Let the waters bring forth abundantly the moving creature that hath life;' and it was so; now listen, in another verse still further on, we find that God said, 'Let the earth bring forth abundantly the living creature after his kind, cattle, and creeping thing, and beast of the field after his kind;' and it was so. Now what I want you to see is this, that the earth brought forth trees and animals, and that the waters brought forth fish, and such like, by the same process. Then if trees, and fish, and animals, were thus brought forth, why not Indians, too ?"

" Then you think that the Indians are beasts ?"

" To be sure I do, beasts just as much as mules."

" And have no souls ?"

"Souls are something that I, for one, don't know anything about."

The next morning B———m informed us that it had been revealed to him, that these savages were the tribe of God, and that their present degraded state was a judgment upon them, for their want of faith.

As no one could disprove the truth of this statement, it remained undisputed.

CHAPTER XXX.

OTHER DIFFICULTIES.

SAFELY beyond the sterile and desolate wilderness, and the hordes of wild, untutored savages, we began to congratulate ourselves on the prospect of future comfort, when a new difficulty presented, of a diametrically opposite character. We had been distressed with heat and the absence of moisture. We had experienced the dull monotony of arid plains, and now it was our lot to encounter the formidable obstacles of giant mountains covered with snow, and to feel the fiercer sufferings occasioned by wintry cold.

Mrs. Bradish looked at the mountains, but her eye never blenched.

"Is it possible," said Mrs. Beardsley, "that we are expected to cross these mountains?"

"To be sure, the land we seek lies beyond them," said Harmer.

"And lie beyond them it may," returned the old lady, "but for my part, I know that it would be utterly impossible for any man, woman, or child to ever get to it."

"You are greatly mistaken, mother," replied Harmer, "these mountains are not so formidable as they appear. We shall not attempt to clamber up the perpendicular ascent; far from it, but seek for notches, and gaps, and passes, and"——

"Go wandering about for months, get lost, and starved to death, perhaps."

"Oh, you are meeting trouble more than half way."

"No such thing, I am only making preparations for an emergency that will surely come."

"What makes you think so?"

"Because we are travelling the same road that other poor emigrants who perished have travelled."

"And yet that is nothing. The road we have already passed is strewn with skeletons; if others died, that is no proof that we shall."

I saw that blank amazement and apprehension filled the minds of many. Some openly murmured, but the greater number prepared to advance boldly into the mountains, and overcome the dangers, by facing them.

"Cursed be he that putteth his hand to the plough and looketh back," said B——m, "my friends and brethren I wish you to remember the fate of Lot's wife."

"I wonder what good that would do?" said Fan Simpkins, "we ain't pillars of salt."

"I wish that you was," said Mrs. Stillman, sen., emphasizing the "**you**."

"Why so, mother?" said Fan provokingly, "'tis strange that while you love papa better than anybody else, you are not willing for other people to love him too."

"Jezebel," muttered the old woman, and though hitherto considered of a very remarkably peaceable disposition, she made a motion that seemed very much like shaking her fist.

Emily, a great lover of nature, exulted in the picturesque scenery, and declared herself amply repaid for all her fatigue and suffering. She and Ethleen were inseparable, and the beautiful child of the desert was making a rapid acquaintance with the English language, under the tuition of her equally beautiful instructress; while she amply repaid the debt by teaching Emily the use of the bow and arrow. Moore united his instructions to those of Emily, and the susceptible heart of Ethleen readily acknowledged the claims of her deliverer. Side by side they wandered over the valleys and along the hills. Mrs. Bradish had designed for her a singularly beautiful and unique costume. It consisted of full Turkish trowsers of rich purple stuff, an orange vest or boddice, fastened with silk buttons, and worn over a chemisette of snowy muslin, to which was sometimes added, by way of full dress, a crimson sash. A delicately embroidered moccasin protected her graceful foot; while her long black hair was gathered into braids, and wound around her head in the form of coronet, to which were appended the brightest flowers and feathers.

"Oh, I would like to live here always," she said to Moore and Emily, one day when they had climbed a hill that afforded a beautiful prospect, "it is so beautiful, and looks so much like the scenery around my father's village.'

"What was the name of your father, dear Ethleen? you never told me," Emily said.

"My father was a chief and warrior," answered Ethleen, "his name is of no account."

The youthful savage had learned sufficiently of our tongue to understand that its definition with us would be ridiculous, and so she refused to reveal it ; it was simply the Buffalo's Horn.

" Had you any brothers and sisters ?" continued Emily.

" Two brothers, and one sister."

" And do you not wish to go back and live with them ?"

The poor girl made no answer, but burst into tears.

"Emily, how cruel you are," exclaimed Charley, "her relatives were all slain by these savages, from whom we rescued her. At any rate, that is what she told me."

"It was thoughtless in me," said Emily, " Ethleen, love, do not weep, you shall stay with us always, indeed you shall."

" With me," suggested Charley.

" Very well, with you, then."

Ethleen soon wiped away her tears, and they descended to the valley, where we were encamped.

This valley, which was about six miles wide, was bordered on either side by mountains from twelve hundred to two thousand feet high. On the north, broken and granite masses rose abruptly from the green sward, terminating in a line of jagged summits. On the south, the range was finely timbered, and at night luminous with fires, probably the work of the Indians, who were in the neighborhood. Among these masses, there were sometimes isolated hills and ridges, with green valleys opening between them, whose deep verdure and profusion of beautiful flowers presented a fine contrast to the sterile grandeur of the rocks, and the barrenness of the sandy plains.

The western part of this valley bore all the characteristics of an elevated plain, and the ground was completely whitened with saline efflorescences that shone like a lake reflecting in the sun. Advancing still further along, we came to a number of isolated cones about fifty feet high, consisting of layers of white clay and marl, in nearly horizontal strata. Several herds of antelope made their appearance, and a grizzly bear was seen scrambling among the rocks. As we passed along, we caught the glimpse of mountain torrent, and subsequently, encamped on the banks of a river which Buckley asserted was a tributary of the Colorado. Here we found an abundance of soft green grass, with beautiful flowers, that made the bottoms look gay as a garden. Several of our young people went out to gather bouquets, while the hunters departed to look for game. The spirits of the whole party seemed agreeably refreshed with the salutary change from sterility to a plentiful supply of grass and water, while the bracing mountain air acted like a charm on our weakened frames, but we could not be insensible to the fact that our provisions were daily becoming scarcer, and that we should probably have to encounter famine, accompanied with cold.

But it would be useless and tedious to follow our line of travel. One day we were traversing an undulating country, consisting of greyish sand-stone and fine-grained conglomerates; another, our route lay along a river valley, bordered by hills of moderate height; while, again, we were passing among primitive rocks, characterized by wildness and disorder, with impetuous torrents tumbling over them. Sometimes the tall crags were utterly sterile and naked, and sometimes they were partially or completely covered with aspen, beech, willow, and tall pines, nodding in magnificent grandeur over their summits. In several places, we discerned traces of beaver on the streams; remnants of dams, near which were lying trees which they had cut down. Sometimes we ascended hills, at others crossed ravines, or traversed deep valleys, filled with blocks of granite, mica slate, or milky quartz. We journeyed at frequent intervals over elevated prairies, whitened in occasional spots with small salt lakes, from some of which the waters had evaporated, leaving the ground covered with saline incrustations, while in others a bitter brine remained, standing about in little holes, or spread over a surface of considerable diameter, and probably two feet in depth. In this locality we made our fires of artemisia, which burned well, with a clear, oily flame.

At length, after a weary and toilsome ascent of one hundred and twenty miles, we came to what has been denominated the South Pass. In this there is nothing of the gorge-like passes characteristic of the Alleghanies, in America, or the Simplon and St. Bernard, of Europe, but the ascent is so continual and gradual, that the traveller finds himself on the summit without being reminded of any change. And thence we obtained a magnificent view, in one direction, over a broken and champaign country, covered at short distances by isolated hills. In another, the Wind River Mountains appeared on the horizon, like a low mountainous ridge; while directly before us we beheld the snow line of massive mountains, their white peaks glittering in the sun, and seeming to pierce the heavens. The air was extremely cold, the sky clear and beautiful, without a trace of cloud. The elders proposed a halt—and there, amid the wild magnificence of nature, with rocks and heights and mountains and granite boulders on all sides of us, they commenced a hymn of thanksgiving, and, whether or not we accede to the Mormon ritual, or have faith in the Mormon doctrine, all must conclude that the tune, the scene, and the occasion were particularly well calculated to inspire devotional sentiments, and all heartily joined in the strain. Never had the magnificent mountains witnessed such a scene before. The ancient rocks had reverberated thousands of times to the war-shout of savages, and the howls of wild beasts, but never to the worship of God. Then all bowed, and prayers were offered, the rude trapper fervently joining, as did every one else. Though Ethleen understood little of the worship, she appeared struck with its appropriateness and simplicity.

Just as we commenced descending the inclined plane of the

western side, we came to a pile of unhewn stone, which, considering the size and appearance of the boulders, had evidently been brought with much labor and difficulty together. While we were speculating on its character and purpose, Ethleen approached. She shuddered at beholding it, and was hastening on, when, observing her agitation, I inquired if she knew its use. She replied in the affirmative, saying that it was an Indian altar, where they offered to their gods such sacrifices as could be obtained, with now and then a captive taken in war.

Leaving this memento of an idolatrous belief, we passed on, and soon reached a river, said to be a tributary of the Colorado. It was broad and shallow, with a full, swift current, over a rocky bed. It was timbered with a growth of low bushes and dense willows, among which were very little verdant spots, affording fine grass for the animals, and many beautiful plants for my botanical collection. We crossed several other streams, in the course of a few days, generally mountain torrents, flowing impetuously over a rocky bed ; and passed some isolated hills of a remarkable character. The Indians, according to Ethleen, have some interesting traditional legends connected with these places. They regard them as especially under the power and influence of evil spirits, who, they assert, frequently make themselves visible, particularly on the highest one, in the form of a cloud.

We found the cold gradually increasing, and the air becoming purer and more bracing. Water froze at night, and fires were more comfortable. I am not over-fond of stirring early, but came out sooner than usual in order to witness the magnificent sunrises. The sky is inexpressibly clear and blue. The first rays of the sun have tipped with gold the lofty snowy peak of the mountain, though they have not reached us. In the east a long mountain wall rises abruptly two thousand feet, behind which snowy peaks, belonging to another ridge, are visible, though dark, and standing out clear against the glowing sky. A fog, just risen from the river, creeps along the base of the mountain at our feet. The scene becomes every moment more grand, interesting, and magnificent. The sun surmounts the wall, with a broad, glowing disc, and instantly effects a magical change. The river glows like molten gold, the valleys gleam, and the snowy peaks seem clothed in garments of silver. Though these mountains have never been famed in song and story, they have a character of grandeur and magnificence, and will doubtless find pens and pencils to do them justice. In the scenery before us, we perceive how much a forest improves a view, as the dark pines of the mountains were a source of much additional beauty. We were now approaching a huge mountain chain, and consequently soon became involved in very broken ground, among long ridges, covered with fragments of granite. Winding our way, with great difficulty, up a long ravine, we came, unexpectedly, in sight of a beautiful lake, set like a gem in the mountains, and which proved to be the headwaters of a large stream, tributary to Green River. The sheet of water lay transversely along the course we had been pursuing, and effectually blockaded all further passage. It became necessary to halt and call a council, and, as our jaded animals required rest, we encamped.

While the elders were discussing the best and nearest route to turn the flank of the lake, I amused myself in listening to the remarks of Mrs. Beardsley, and admiring the stately magnificence of the surrounding scene.

"Just as I knowed it would be," said the old lady, knitting away with redoubled energy; "I was confident that we should get lost."

"For my part," said Mrs. Stillman, sen., "I believe we have been lost all the time."

"I begin to think myself," said Buckley, "that we have come

considerably out of our way. I wonder what we have been thinking of all the time."

"Of nothing at all but foolishness," said the irritated old lady.

"Never mind, mother," said Louisa—"but did you ever see such magnificent rocks ?"

"I never want to see them again," said the old lady, who cared very little for the magnificence of nature.

The whole scene was one of surprising grandeur. With nothing to intercept or lessen the view, a mighty ridge of snow-capped mountains rose before us, pile upon pile, glowing in the bright refulgence of an unclouded sky. Immediately beneath them, and between two ridges covered with dark pines, lay the lake, glittering in the rich sunlight, its banks of yellow sand, and the light foliage of the aspen groves contrasting with the gloomy grandeur of the shadowy pines.

After a long discussion, it was decided that we should retrace our steps to the foot of the South Pass, and thence enter the valley which communicated immediately with the Green River, and thence inclining southward, led directly to Bear River, a tributary of the Great Salt Lake. A half-civilized Indian of the Black-feet tribe, who had been trapping for beaver among the hills, seeing our fires, came into the camp, and volunteered to be our guide. B——m at first refused to receive him, but the people began to murmur, and he was forced to accede. Our misfortune, indeed, was chiefly attributable to the headstrong Prophet, who persisted in opposing Harmer, and making his crude revelations the guide of the people, though it appeared that the others had become somewhat bewildered among the various intersecting trails.

CHAPTER XXXI.

BEAR RIVER VALLEY.

DURING our long journey I have had no occasion to allude to either Mrs. Cook, or Irene, the spiritual wife of Smith. The former, on the death of his wife, attached herself unreservedly to Mr. Murray. It was rumored that they quarrelled, and even came to blows: one thing, however, is certain, illicit connexions uniformly terminate unhappily, and she manifested the utmost indifference at his death. After this event she became exceedingly intimate with Irene, who manifested the utmost pride and stateliness, and gloried herself in keeping the relics of Smith. Every few days the precious garments were brought out and aired, and then returned to the place of deposit amid the perfume of musk and amber. During all this time Irene looked haughty and discontented, said very little to any one, and evidently regarded the wives of B——m with no friendly feeling. She absolutely refused to accord them the trifling deference that courtesy required, remarking that the surviving relict of the Father of Mormonism, should rather receive than bestow homage. This formed the subject of a good jest, and then no more was said about it.

But in our camp was one man, an elder, who had steadily, and from the first, opposed the election of B——m to the leadership and temporal head of the church. Rumor hinted that he aspired to the dignity himself, but being foiled, grew envious and malicious towards his successful rival. However this might be, he had been to B——m like Mordecai sitting in the king's gate to Haman, refusing to do him the outward homage which his heart refused. Doubtless, this was extremely unpleasant to one so tenacious of his dignity and honor, but he had the good sense to perceive that it would require punishment, if noticed, and this he was perfectly aware would place his enemy in a prominent situation that would augur well to his cause.

Lawrence made his animosity and dislike felt in a thousand ways, though it would have been a difficult matter to express in plain language any one act that was reprehensible. Every intelligent observer knows, however, that almost every passion or emotion of the human breast can be expressed without words. Who has not read indifference, disgust, and dislike, as well as love and tenderness, in looks. Then, how much may be implied in a shrug, a tone of the voice, or glance of the eye? What an insinuation of hate, or malice, or slander, may be couched under the smoothest words; and how much more certain are such of doing harm, since we imbibe the impression without being exactly aware of what it is? Then Lawrence was exceedingly cunning and diplomatic, affecting a taciturnity and reserve, altogether foreign to his character. He always kept himself in the back-ground, said little, took no part in discussions or altercations, and made himself familiar to no one, unless, indeed, we except Irene; yet, few that looked into the deep unfathomable recesses of his eyes; few that saw his brow wrinkled with thought, could keep from thinking that under this smooth exterior the pent-up fires of volcanic passion lay concealed. Recently he had paid more than ordinary attention to Irene. They had long conferences, took long walks, and associated together on all occasions. Mrs. Cook, though the friend and companion of Irene, was evidently a secondary personage with him.

Mrs. Bradish, always awake to everything that was going on,

observed this; and soon came to a definite conclusion, as to its tendency. Coming to our tent, one day, she exclaimed ; " Depend upon it, Mr. Ward, there is something wrong about Lawrence and Irene !"

" And what may it be ?"

" I can't exactly tell, though time will develop."

" That he wants a wife—a very natural want, to be sure," said Mr. Ward, laughing.

" And the mitre ?"

" I hardly think he has any designs on that."

" Well, we shall see. The fact is," continued Mrs. Bradish, " that B——m committed a great mistake, in not marrying Irene, himself. I told him so, at the time. She is excessively ambitious, and standing in so near a relation to the first Prophet, considers herself entitled to fill a corresponding place to the second."

" Is it too late, yet ?"

" To be sure it is."

" Think so ?"

" I know it. Yesterday, as in duty bound, I communicated my suspicions to him. He affected to treat the matter with indifference, though I could see that he really felt concern. When I mentioned Irene, and her former connection with the sainted dead, he smiled, and inquired if I supposed Irene considered herself insulted by his neglect ; to which I replied in the affirmative.

" ' Well,' he answered, complacently, ' heaven has already bestowed upon me three wives, and when we arrive at the Promised Land, I design to propose for another ; but, rather than have any difficulty about that, I will propose for Irene, likewise.'

" ' It is too late,' I replied ; ' she would certainly refuse you.'

"He lifted his eyes in astonishment.

"'Now, she would,' I continued; 'four or five months ago, it would have been different.'

"I saw that he was piqued, as he answered: 'Well, we shall see,' and walked off. And he did see. He went that very evening, and besought her to become his wife."

"And she refused him?" inquired Mr. Ward.

"Yes—scornfully."

"B——m has gained the ill-will of several of the party," said Mr. Ward. "He is, in fact, both selfish and obstinate."

It need scarcely be said, that there were murmurs, "not loud, but deep," when we began to retrace our march.

"I thought," said Harmer, "that we were going wrong, but, wrong or right, as the Prophet, there, urged his Revelations, I concluded that he might see where they would lead him."

Fan Simpkins asserted that it made no difference to her; it certainly did not to Ethleen, whose lover was continually beside her; but the others exceedingly regretted that even a day's travel should be spent in vain. It had been the custom of B——m to point out our direction, though, previous to his rupture with Harmer, he had been guided by his knowledge and experience of the country, but even that was rather limited.

The Indian, for a valuable consideration, undertook to be our guide to the Bear River Valley. He was a tall, athletic fellow, speaking English imperfectly, and professing great regard for the whites. Though he performed his duty manfully, pointing out the course, and assisting to remove obstructions, many of the more zealous Mormons considered it a great humiliation, to be necessitated to receive assistance from a heathen and idolater. Irene made herself very busy in disseminating and arguing such sentiments. Lawrence said nothing, at least publicly, though the two had several private conversations, of long continuance.

At length, night came on. We made our encampment, and prepared supper. While we were eating, a loud, wild shriek was heard. Instantly starting to my feet, I ran out, and met Emily, just coming to tell me that Lawrence was dead—that he died very suddenly, after having informed Irene that such an event awaited him, and requesting of her to be laid out in the sacred garments of Smith, as a revelation had informed him, that in that manner he would be restored to life.

I was not in the least astonished at this. Indeed, I had witnessed so much humbugery and jugglery, that I could not be surprised at anything, though I did wonder what new phase of deception was under way,

"The plot is developing," said Mrs. Bradish, when informed of the circumstance. "I want to see the dead man—where is he?"

"In that tent, yonder, with Irene," said a bystander.

Mrs. Bradish visited the dead man, but soon returned.

"He is no more dead than I am," she said. "He has brought on a state of syncope, or trance. Any one can do it, who pleases to, though, probably, some persons easier than others."

"I never heard of such a thing."

"Well, I have, and seen it, too," she answered. "I was once acquainted with a man, who laid a wager that he would die and come to life again. Some laughed; others were horror-stricken, at what they denominated his presumption and impiety. I determined to watch him closely. Having a mattress, he lay down on his back, folded his hands across his breast, and then remained perfectly still. After a few minutes, there was, evidently, a sinking of the system; the pulse rapidly declined; the heart beat slow and heavily, and the breathing grew shorter and shorter, until it finally ceased. Then the extremities became cold; the limbs stiff and rigid; the under-jaw dropped; the eye-winkers partially opened, revealing the ball turned upwards; and all the symptoms were those of death."

"Were you not frightened?"

"I was surprised and astonished, beyond measure; the more so, when, after lying in this state four or five hours, there were evident marks of returning animation. The countenance, which had been livid, gradually resumed its natural color; the eyes slowly opened, and the breathing became regular. After this, he recovered rapidly, sat up, and asked for food. Upon being questioned, he said that he could produce that state, at any time, merely by a strong effort of the will."

"But what inducement could Lawrence have, to produce this state?"

"In what light would you regard a man, who had risen from the dead?"

"As something wonderful, remarkable; something to be revered and honored."

"That is a sufficient solution of his motives. He requests the garments of Smith to be put on him, that is to give his wakening the character of a miracle. Then he will have to relate the wonderful scenes he has passed through, and the surprising revelations that have been made to him. This will give him the popularity that he desires, and I greatly fear will lead to a division in the church."

"This might partly be avoided by refusing to permit the sacred garments to be put on him," said Mr. Ward. "But I scarcely imagine that B——m would listen to anything I would say."

"Whether or not he listens to me, I mean to tell him," said Mrs. Bradish, and she started off.

In a short time she returned.

"Well, what result?" I inquired.

"After I had informed B——m of my suspicions, he went to the tent where Lawrence lay; Mrs. Cook sat at his feet sobbing, and Irene had buried her face in a remarkably dry handkerchief.

A large concourse of people, and several elders were standing or sitting around. The sacred garments had been removed from their perfumed resting-place, and were hanging up to air, preparatory to being put on the dead man, agreeably to his request. Without saying a word B———m walked into the tent, the assembled company involuntarily doing obeisance, which he coolly acknowledged, and then proceeded straight to the garments, gathered them up in his arms, and carried them off, before the spectators became fully aware of his intentions. He knew very well," she continued, "that there was no other way by which he could get them. They'll have a hard time to outwit him."

"Did they send for the garments afterwards?"

"To be sure they did; and Irene went herself, and coaxed, threatened, and scolded, but all to no purpose."

"He wouldn't give them up?"

"Not he; he told her that they were the property of the church, and that himself, as the head of the church, was their proper keeper. Then she raved and stormed like a fury, called him a thief, and demanded to know, by what right he refused to permit the miraculous virtues in the garments to be tested."

"And what did B———m say?"

"Nothing at all. He sat perfectly calm and collected, reading his Bible, as if nothing had happened to disturb his serenity."

After exhausting all her efforts to no purpose, she went back to the tent, and watched beside the sleeper. The next morning he began to recover slowly, exactly as Mrs. Bradish had predicted, but the absence of the consecrated garments divested his reanimation of the character of a miracle, though it did not prevent his relating a wonderful vision, in which he stated that he had seen Smith, and received information, that the founder of Mormonism was greatly concerned that the affairs of the Church had fallen into such improper hands, and finally concluded by asserting that he had been chosen and delegated to lead the saints to their destination. This announcement was evidently premature; no one seconded the measure, or seemed prepared to accept him in that capacity. Cries of "No! no!" resounded from all sides. "You are not a suitable person; you shall not be our leader."

"What God hath cleansed, you should not consider common or unclean," he said, "my vision! my restoration to life!"

"What proof have we of that?"

"I have always heard that seeing was believing," he answered.

"A great many people witnessed my dissolution, and now I stand here perfectly restored."

"It was all a trick, a jugglery, we have heard of such things before."

Mrs. Bradish had taken the pains to inform the whole company, that cases of suspended animation might be voluntarily superinduced, and nothing probably, but her knowledge and foresight had saved the Mormon Church from a revolution, so far as a new leader was concerned, and B———m from losing his dignified position in the Mormon hierarchy.

Overcome with gratitude, and probably thinking that such services merited a distinguished reward, he came to visit her that evening, and make his acknowledgments. After a long prefatory harangue, he said:—

"There is but one reward, my dear madam, which I can offer you, that is at all commensurate with the very important service you have rendered me, and it is altogether uncertain, whether or not that will meet your approbation."

Mrs. Bradish raised her eyes in astonishment, but finally remarked, that she neither wished nor expected a reward, having acted from the sole consciousness of duty, and being fully satisfied with the approbation of her conscience.

"That may sound well enough for you, madam, though it will hardly do for me. I do not choose to lie under unpaid obligations to any one. It scarcely becomes me; and so I must at least make you an offer."

"An offer," said the lady, "what kind of an offer?"

"An offer of marriage, to be sure."

"Of marriage to whom?"

"To myself," he answered, "but I see you despise me."

"Far from it, my dear sir," she said, offering her hand. "And yet I doubt much, whether a marriage between us would contribute to the happiness of either. You have three wives already."

"And that should rather be an inducement to you, than otherwise."

Mrs. Bradish smiled a meaning smile. "I fear," she said, "that my entrance into your household might not be relished by its present inmates."

"And what of that?" he replied, "you should be the first and greatest among them."

"No; that privilege belongs of right to the first wife."

"The husband has the liberty of conferring it on any one he pleases."

"The husband may assume that right, but I conceive that such an assumption of prerogative is unjust."

"The husband is the head of the wife; her temporal and eternal salvation depends on him."

Mrs. Bradish, though she had taught the same lesson to me and others, seemed to shrink when it was brought back to her. Then bursting into a laugh, she said, "You see, good brother, that we cannot agree even in a short conversation, and though I feel greatly flattered by your good opinion, must decidedly and at once decline your proposal."

"I have at least proved my gratitude," he said.

"Certainly, certainly; no one will dispute that."

"And we are still to be friends, the same as formerly?"

"Indeed, I hope so."

And the two separated, both better suited, and much happier than if they had been affianced lovers.

After a somewhat toilsome march over a rugged and broken country, we came at length to level, dry, uninteresting plains. Here we struck a trail, which our guide informed us, led directly to the Great Salt Lake, through a well-watered country, where fine timber and some game abounded. Our Indian guide, whose knowledge of the country was much more exact and accurate than that of Harmer or Buckley, or even both put together, related many wild and beautiful stories of the different rivers, with their wild wooded islands, and roaring rapids. Under his guidance, we progressed finely, and entered at length the high and broken country, which terminates in the Utah chain of mountains.

After several days' travel, in which nothing remarkable occurred, we crossed a mountain ridge at a pass of great elevation, and descended immediately into the picturesque and fertile valley of Bear River. From the summit of this pass, we had an extensive view over a broken and mountainous region, whose rugged appearance was greatly increased by the smoky weather through which the broken ridges were darkly and dimly seen. The ascent to the summit of the gap resembles, in many characteristics, the pass of the Alleghanies; and the descent on the western side, though rather precipitous, was tolerably good.

We were now entering a region which, for us, presented unusual interest. The Mormon Land of Promise, the Home of the Faithful, where they would be secure from the encroachments of the heathen; the Holy Place, where the saints should build up a kingdom, and where Christ should descend to dispense the joys of millenium blessedness, during his reign of a thousand years. All unpleasant thoughts were merged in the joyous anticipation of ending our journey so soon. The errors of

B——m were forgiven and forgotten, but the good Indian received a substantial token of our gratitude.

But independent of these considerations, the Great Salt Lake possessed, for me, a strange and extraordinary interest. It formed one of the most remarkable features in the geography of the country, and was the salient point around which centered innumerable traditional tales of hunters and travellers. Though Buckley had never visited its shores, he contended, that, according to accounts, it had no visible outlet, but that somewhere on its surface was a dreadful whirlpool, by which its waters descended, through subterranean passages, into the ocean. This Harmer disputed, and the Indian positively contradicted. However, it formed a theme for innumerable discussions, in which the women frequently joined.

"No outlet," said Mrs. Beardsley, "just like the Dead Sea in Asia; not just like it either, for Elder Scarow used to say that was the mouth of Hell."

"The mouth of Hell?" ejaculated Harmer.

"Certainly, but you needn't be so surprised about that; there's a Hell, to be sure, you won't pretend to deny that; and there must be somewhere to get into it. This Elder Scarow declared to be that horrible sulphurous lake, where the wicked cities of Sodom and Gomorrah stood."

"And how did he know?"

"Oh, he had a dream, or vision, that told him so."

"Well, who knows but what this lake communicates with the same place? Of course it would be necessary to have a passage on each continent," said Harmer.

Emily looked reproachfully towards him, and said:

"How can you talk so?"

Harmer only laughed,

"I don't see anything wrong in that," said Charley Moore, "the supposition is perfectly natural."

The old lady, however, seemed to think that they were making a jest of her, and retired.

Presently a little girl, the daughter of a woman in our company, who waited on one of B———m's wives, came with a note for Emily. I watched her countenance, and perceived that when she rose to obey the summons it contained, she appeared excessively agitated.

Harmer noticed this, their eyes met, and she thrust the letter into his hand.

CHAPTER XXXII.

OTHER EMIGRANTS.

THE valley of Bear River is from three to four miles wide, bounded on either side by mountainous ridges, rising suddenly from the plain. Shut out from the world, it reminded me continually of the happy valley, where the royal race of Abyssinia exhausted their lives in a round of endless enjoyment. These ridges, in some places, were sterile and naked; in others, they were thickly wooded with dark pine forests. Sometimes a stream would smoothly descend along a narrow, fertile, and picturesque valley; and sometimes mountain torrents would tumble impetuously over the rocks. Elk and antelope were abundant, and some of the hunters came suddenly on a trail of wagons and horses, by which we knew that another company of emigrants had passed.

"They are of our people," said B———m, "bless the Lord."

"I am not certain of that, though it may be the case," said Mrs. Bradish.

Journeying on over a small hill, we came suddenly in sight of them, encamped in a lovely situation, and joined them near night-fall. As our leader had anticipated, they proved to be Mormons, travelling to the promised land. We had a joyful meeting then, and the united companies sang the Hallelujah Chorus, with infinite animation. They had started from St. Louis a month subsequent to ourselves, by which we learned how much, and how far we had travelled out of our way.

They informed us that other companies of emigrants, principally Mormons, were reposing in a beautiful valley a short distance off, with whom they designed to unite. Our party concluded to do the same, and crossing a clear stream of water, about fifty yards in breadth, we ascended a wide ravine, between remarkable mountains, rising abruptly on either side. A few miles farther on, we passed the point of a narrow spur, and descended into a valley, whose picture of home beauty touched our hearts. For several miles along the river, the edge of the wood was dotted with emigrant wagons, whose white covers reflected in the sun. They were collected in groups at different camps, where the smoke was rising lazily from the fires, around which the women were busily engaged in preparing the evening meal, the children rolling and tumbling in the grass, and the cattle feeding in quiet security. They had been reposing for several days in this delightful valley, in order to recruit the strength of their animals, on its luxuriant pasturage, after their long and toilsome travels, and prepare them to finish their journey.

B—— passed around among the different encampments, and received the homage graciously awarded to him as their spiritual father. He rejoiced greatly in the goodly number of his children thus happily brought together, and compared the different divisions of them to the different tribes of the Israelites. They had come from several States, from Michigan, Indiana, Illinois, and

Beaver Island. "And they shall continue to come," said B——m, "from every part of the world—from Europe and Asia, and the islands of the sea. And we will build up a kingdom to the Lord, with a temple to which the nations shall come and worship."

It was proposed to hold a meeting in the open air, at which B——m was invited to preach. He consented, and the people all gathered, men, women and children. The pulpit was a platform raised on a wagon, beneath the wide-spreading branches of a green tree. The subject of his discourse, polygamy, which he attempted to justify from Scripture, and the example of the ancient patriarchs. His reasoning was something like this: That if it was right to have one wife, it was right to have two, or even more, since actions in themselves morally wrong—for instance murder, theft, or similar crimes—are not allowed, even in one instance. That the law of the United States, which allowed one wife to every man, and denied his right to more than one, was highly tyrannical; that in many cases the practice of polygamy was attended with many benefits, especially in cases of sickness, and where household burdens could not be otherwise than troublesome and onerous; that the purpose of marriage being the perpetuation of the human species, it followed that when the wife ceased bearing, or was otherwise incapable or unwilling to raise a family, it became the husband's duty to take another wife. This he proved by the example of Abraham and Jacob. David, he said, had several wives, yet the Lord never reproved him for it, and if it was right then, it remains so yet.

This doctrine, though nothing new to me, excited the surprise and consternation of many women. They were not prepared for such a state of things. They had been converted to Mormonism by the missionaries whom Smith had sent out, with instructions to deal only in the pure milk of the Gospel, by which he meant those parts of Mormonism the most conformable to the generally-received opinions of the day, reserving the meat—such things as polygamy and spiritual wifeage—for those more advanced in the knowledge of the blessings designed for the Faithful. It was easy to perceive that these doctrines were rather unpalatable to the majority of the females, though the men seemed pleased, and many of them really exultant. Not a few began immediately to direct their glances where stood a bevy of blooming girls, and greatly to the chagrin of their companions, four or five passed directly over to them, and commenced a conversation.

While resting in this beautiful valley, the time to me passed happily. We were divided into messes, three or four families in a mess, each being provided with a fire and cooking utensils, placed a short distance from their tents. When all were stirring, at meal times, we presented a very lively and animated appearance. Some were cooking, others eating, others preparing a temporary table, and yet others, somewhat behindhand, just kindling their fires. To borrow a fire was not at all uncommon. . Some families did all their cooking at borrowed fires. Perhaps a little blue-eyed girl would come bounding fawn-like over the grass :

"Mother wants to borrow your fire to get breakfast. Can she have it ?"

" Oh, certainly."

" And your pot, and tea-kettle ?"

" Very well."

"The spider, too ?"

"I reckon."

And the girl goes bounding back to report the success of her message.

Then a big boy, in tattered trowsers, and with a brimless hat, comes marching along with a huge armload of brush to replenish the blaze, followed by a woman in a gingham sun-bonnet, and coarse calico dress, bearing a great fat baby in one arm, and a dish containing some slices of raw meat with the other. Within speaking distance, the salutation would be given :

"Good morning, Mrs. Ward, I fear that we are putting you to a great deal of trouble, but it's so much handier to get breakfast by a fire already made, than it is to have to kindle one for yourself, that I told papa, seeing as how we were late, that I'd just come round here and get something to eat, though it's very little that we've got. How are you on it for coffee?"

"I have a little left, a very little, that I am saving until some of us get sick."

"Come, John, don't be all day filling that tea-kettle. Sit still bubby there on the grass. A little coffee did you say?— Well, it would do me good to even see some. Dear! dear! only to think what we have come to ; not a grain of coffee or particle of tea, and compelled to drink this slop—ain't it too bad, considering how we used to have all and everything?"

"It's neighbor's fare."

"So I suppose ; but that don't help it any. There, John, hang that kettle as it ought to be over the blaze. Now go and get the leaves I gave you yesterday, put them in the tea-pot, and bring it here ; the kettle will soon boil. There bub, you'r too noisy. I must get the meat broiling."

The emigrants supplied the place of tea, with a kind of wild sage, that made a palatable and nutritious drink.

The meat is put broiling, but "bubby" is determined to be noticed.

"Here, John," screams the mother, "come take 'bub ;' what's that you are saying?—shan't, eh? Don't talk your sauce to me. Come along, I say, here ; I can't leave this meat a minute ; 'twill burn up, certainly."

John, however, wouldn't come, and "bubby," shrieking with madness, rolled about on the grass.

Meanwhile, our breakfast is eaten—perhaps some boiled kamas or bitter root for bread, with fried or broiled venison, the flesh of the elk or antelope, and I rise up to put things "to rights." "Do you want this spider?" I inquired, raising my voice to the highest pitch, in consequence of "bubby's" excessive din.

"No," she answers. "I thought I should when Malvinai Matilda came round here, but I finally concluded that we'd drink our tea, and eat this meat, and leave the rest for dinner. Such good bread, and pound cakes and cookies as we used to have. Oh, dear!"

"We suffer great deprivations," I said, removing the spider.

"Oh, I never thought it was half so far. Do hush your racket. What on earth ails the child?—why, I cannot hear myself think. But what did you think of the sermon t'other night? I declare, I never was so beat."

"Thought it pretty good, considering the subject."

"And so did papa. He seemed really delighted with it, and actually declared that he meant to have another wife before a month."

"'Another wife, indeed!' I answered, sharply. 'I guess one wife is quite as many as you can take care of.'

"'Oh, I want 'em to take care of me,' he said, laughing.

"'Well, if you get another wife I won't do a hand's turn for you,' I replied.

"'Yes you would, you'd love me all the better, and be in constant strife with the others, to see who could do the most.'

"'Don't you believe anything of that kind;' but, here, I've been talking, and let my meat burn. It's done, I believe," and, putting it in the dish, she took up "bubby," who had screamed himself into a good humor, and walked off.

And such scenes were transpiring through all the valley. Meats were being dressed in an infinite variety of ways, or being eaten without seasoning or stuffing. Here, a group were using their utmost endeavors to masticate a boiled wild goose; and there, another company, seated on the grass, like so many Turks, were feasting on a loin of elk. Some were bearing water from the river; others carrying wood from the forest; some were talking politics, and discussing the temporal kingdom of Christ; while others were speculating on the quality of the soil, and its adaptation to agricultural produce.

The breakfast was readily got over, as there was little to cook, and consequently it was soon eaten. This done, the men sallied out over the hills to explore the country, some carrying their guns, others their fishing tackle, and some with neither. The young people amused themselves with roaming through the meadows, to search for edible roots. Lawrence and Irene, arm in arm, took a long walk, as Mrs. Bradish said, to plot new mischief; while the women gathered into knots and groups, talked about their babies, the recent sermon on matrimonial affairs, or fresh bits of neighborhood gossip; for no life is more favorable to scandal than the one we had been leading.

"That's a fine child of your'n, Mrs. Dallas," said one of those milk-and-water women, of whom I am always afraid, they look so sleek and beautiful, yet tiger-like withal.

"Eight months," said Mrs. Dallas, "and he's got four teeth."

"Four teeth! bless me, how smart he is, and beautiful too," she continued. "Well, I always did admire beautiful children."

The infant Dallas was one of the ugliest specimens of childhood, with little grey eyes, a pug nose, and red hair. Even the mother had never considered him beautiful before now. "Your husband never ought to think of taking another wife, while you bring him such beautiful children."

The women were seated on a low bench.

"My husband take another wife!" said Mrs. Dallas, starting. "Does he think of such a thing?"

"I don't know how he can help thinking of it, after hearing that sermon. I'm thankful that I'm a widow."

"I can't believe that my husband will ever want to insult me that way; for 'twould be an insult, now, wouldn't it?"

"An insult? I should think so."

"The very thought of it makes me weep," said Mrs. Dallas, and she burst into tears.

"I don't know as that will be the case, but then I shouldn't wonder if it was," said this prophetess of evil, and so, bidding the child comfort his mammy, and Mrs. Dallas not to care, she walked off.

Mrs. Dallas was one of those women who are always expecting evil and meeting trouble. She was very fond of her husband, and the words of this pretended friend filled her mind with the most dreadful apprehensions. When Mr. Dallas returned from the chase, he found her in tears, which she vainly strove to hide, and of which he determined to discover the cause. But all his tenderness and caresses were unavailing. She could not be the first to mention her horrible foreboding to him, and he left her at length, very much displeased.

It need not be supposed, however, that all the females entertained similar views of polygamy. Some declared that they were perfectly willing for their husbands to avail themselves of the privilege, and take other wives if they saw fit. Others said they knew not what to think of it, though the majority, it must be confessed, were anything but pleased with the proposition.

When the young people returned from gathering roots, Emily came to our tent. I saw that she had been weeping, and inquired the cause. At first, she hesitated, but a little persuasion overcame her reluctance, and she began:

"You know, probably, that I received a note from B———m the other day."

"I knew that you received a note, and circumstances led me to infer that it came from him."

"Well, he requested me to visit him immediately, as he wished to communicate with me on a subject of vital importance. I guessed its import, and nerved myself for a scene.

"The Mormon dignitary was seated in a large stuffed, and cushioned chair, with all the emblems of his dignity about him. He wore a long, loose robe, embroidered slippers, and a mitre, beneath which, his repulsive countenance showed to the greatest disadvantage. His wives retreated from the apartment at my approach; and he motioned me to a seat on the stool at his feet. I sunk down upon it, glad to escape the burning gleam of his eyes, for his whole countenance glowed with the fervor of an August noon.

"'You are very lovely,' he said, at length breaking the silence, and drawing back my head on his knee, he attempted to kiss me. I shrank from his touch, as from the sting of a serpent, and rising up, requested him to inform me of the business he wished to communicate, that I might depart.

"'Depart, indeed; why no, my charmer, your home is henceforth with me.'

"'No, sir,' I answered, 'you are mistaken there.'

"His countenance grew dark with suppressed passion, 'It is my pleasure to take you for a wife,' he said.

"'But it is not my pleasure to receive you for a husband, you are well supplied with wives already.'

"'Not so well as I wish to be, and then it was revealed to me that I must take you.'

"'Nothing of the kind has been revealed to me, and until it is, I must persist in declining your offer.'

"He seemed really surprised at my audacity, in placing myself in equality with him, and there was an expression in his countenance, and a gleam in his eye, that made me shudder.

"'And do women ever have revelations about these things?' he said, after a moment's silence.

"'I suppose so. I know of no reason why they should not.'

"'You require instruction, I see,' he said.

"'And shall be happy to receive it, provided it is of the right kind.'

"'And who shall be the judge of that?'

"'Myself.'

"He shook his head solemnly, and said, 'Your soul is in danger.'

"'And yours may be too, for what I know.'

"I no longer feared, though I hated and despised him.

"'This is all folly on your part,' he said at length. 'As my wife, your temporal and eternal salvation will be secured. You will be safe from the power of the devil, and beyond the danger of ever falling away. It is for your own good that I desire this, and now will you refuse?'

"'I will.'

"Again his countenance grew dark, and he inquired,

"'Do you not know that I possess the power to enforce your obedience; that no one, especially a woman, may thwart my will with impunity?'

"'But women have thwarted your will—Irene, Mrs. Bradish.'

"'Silence, I tell you, don't mention them to me,' he cried. 'These were different cases. It was mere expediency that influenced my conduct with regard to them, but you I have learned to love,' and he attempted to take my hand.

"I withdrew it.

"'I see how it is,' he said. 'Harmer has been inveigling you into a connection with him. Is it not so?'

"'By what right do you inquire? I did not come here as to

a confessional. If the important business you named relates to this, you will please suffer me to depart.'

"'Not till you have answered me.'

"'Well, then, he has not inveigled me.'

"'Has he not asked you to become his wife?'

"'He has.'

"'And you consented?'

"'I did.'

"'And you dare prefer him to me?'

"'I dare.'

"'But don't you know, that no marriage can be consummated among our people without my consent?'

"'I was not aware that such was the case.'

"A gleam of malicious pleasure twinkled in his eyes, as he answered, 'Well, it is the case, and you may rest assured that I shall never consent to your marriage with him. Heaven, everything, forbids it. And now I command you, by the right in me vested—a right which extends to the control and supervision of every female among us—that you cease to associate with him. Do you hear?'

"'I hear.'

"'And will you obey?'

"I made no answer.

"He looked threateningly, and muttered 'Beware!'

"'Beware of what?' I said, affecting a calmness and unconcern, that I was far from feeling.

"'Child,' he answered, and his countenance grew darker, and his voice sterner, 'what use is there in pretending all this ignorance? You know very well, that you are solely and wholly in my power. You have no parents, no relatives. These people with whom you live, have no legal claim over you, neither can they prevent the exercise of my undoubted right, to do with you as I please.'

"'But am I not under the protection of the laws of the land?'

"'Laws of the land! now that is too good—laws of the land! indeed, what laws of the land are there, but my will? What State? what government has power or authority here? No! my beauty, set your heart at rest in that quarter. Here I do as I please with my own. I consider myself amenable to no law, but the code of Mormon, and that places all authority in my hands.'

"'And you,' I said, 'what, are you, a leader of the saints, a priest and prophet of the Most High, thus taking advantage of my unprotected situation, to force me to a connection which my soul abhors? For shame, were you ten times more powerful than you be, I would hate and defy you.'

"'Because you confide in my generosity not to injure you.'

"'Far from it. You have no generosity; I know that you are as incapable of one true honorable feeling, as you are capable of perpetrating the grossest villanies; but because I can bear all the penalties of your wrath, whatever they may be, with pleasurable satisfaction, compared to the endurance of a state of vilest concubinage, such as you wish to impose upon me.'

"'And you call the holy state of marriage concubinage?'

"'I do, such marriage as you propose. Without love, without sympathy, without congeniality of mind, or appropriateness of age; sensuality on one side and compulsion on the other, what else could it be?' and I looked him directly in the face.

"'I see,' he said at length, 'I see that the true import of the marriage institution is altogether beyond your comprehension. These sympathies and congenialities of which you speak, are nothing, and only exist in the distempered fancy of silly young women. But you need a husband to protect and support you; a husband by whom you can be saved from perdition. As my wife, you will be honored and honorable; servants shall do your bidding—ah, and slaves, too.'

"'Slaves?'

"'Yes, slaves—negroes. Is there anything wonderful in that?'

"'Not that I am aware of, only I don't know how you are to get them.'

"'I can tell you. I left word with a slave-dealer in St. Louis, to send on thither a large gang of slaves. I presume they are coming now. Harmer cannot afford you any luxury; why will you cling to him?'

"'Because I am fond of his society, and have promised to become his wife. Let me go, I beseech you!'

"'Well, go; but remember what I said. I do not desire your final answer, now; that, I shall demand in one month from this date; but the wife of Harmer, you shall never be. You may go to the grave, but never to his bed.'

"'Destiny may decide otherwise,' I answered, and hastened away.

"And now, Mrs. Ward," said Emily, "do you suppose that this man possesses the omnipotence he imagines, or would have us believe?"

"That he possesses great influence, in many matters, is certain," I replied, "as he says, we are beyond the administration of the civil law; and yet, I should suppose that there were good and upright men among the Mormons, who would resent any great infringement of individual rights; especially, when that individual was a helpless female orphan, and on that account, if no other, entitled to consideration and regard."

"I never will be his wife, come what will!" said Emily; "I'll run away to the wild Indians, first!"

"What does Harmer say?"

"He raved like a madman."

"I should suppose as much."

"And now, Mrs. Ward, what am I to do?"

"The same as if nothing had occurred."

"And manifest the same preference for Harmer?"

"Just the same. He has given you a month to decide. Many things may happen in that time, of which, at present, we have not the faintest perception, and which may materially change his mind, or place you beyond his power."

"Heaven grant that it may be so!" said Emily, fervently.

Mr. Ward and several others came in, and the conversation changed.

CHAPTER XXXIII.

A HOME IN THE DESERT.

WE were alone in the desert—men, women and children. Many of us inspired by the most resolute fanaticism; others, imbued with sentiments of religious veneration for their leader; and all pledged to support a cause that, whether good or bad, whether conformable to their feelings or not, could not fail to redound to the glory of the Mormon hierarchy, and promote the interests and views of the church. Doubtless, the Mormon exodus was a matter of rejoicing to the enemies of that people, or it may be that they regarded the matter with absolute indifference: though to that very fact, is owing their unaccountable prosperity and rapid increase. That they stood alone, with no neighboring communities of a different faith, and possessing a social system founded on radically different principles, whose influence might retard their growth, or prevent the full development of their designs, was remarkably in their favor. They were at liberty to form such laws as suited them; to establish precedents and decisions, conformable to their own views;

and, above all, the utter impossibility of escape or appeal, exercised a wonderful influence over the dissatisfied, and aided, more than anything else, in causing them to abide by their fate, and conform to the circumstances in which they were placed. Had injured wives possessed the chance of redress by law, or even the opportunity of flying from the scene of such licentious habits, polygamy, even in its infancy, would have received a death-blow; but these, the ones most interested in its suppression, and upon whom fell the burdens of its intolerable evils, were constrained to abide by it, and, in most cases, without murmur or complaint.

The great influence which Mormonism has acquired in Utah, and the power by which it will yet make itself felt in the world, is solely attributable to the fact, that it has been left free to spread and develop itself, without any counteracting influences, which could not have been the case in a State where the laws were already established. In Utah, it became the nucleus, around which society formed itself, and thus entered, at once, into all the organizations of domestic and political affairs. The Mormons, from the first, were settled in communities; they were bound to each other by human sympathies, neighborhood attachments, and the ties of church relationship; consequently, there was no waste of influence; but a centre was created, possessing an attractive force, which could not fail of modeling, to a certain extent, all that came within its circle.

The Mormon exodus, though not regarded at the time in such a light, was a missionary effort on a grand scale, and in the most effective form. The Mormon Church, thus established, became the germ of a city, and planted the seed of all its evils and abominations around it. How far into the future this movement will reach, in its influence upon the destinies of the western portion of our continent, or even upon our Republic, it is impossible at this time to decide.

But it need not be supposed that all this has been accomplished without effort, and labor, too, of the most zealous and untiring description; and, in this respect, at least, other denominations of Christians might profit by their example. Settled in this wilderness, they have not only sustained themselves, but sent missionaries into every quarter of the world, and this without any of those appeals through the press, and without any of that system of begging which others habitually employ.

Thus, in a few years, Utah has become the centre of the Mormon world, the basis of a powerful State, and the stronghold of a church differing from Christianity in all its essential points.

Looking back over the past, it scarcely seems possible that so much has been accomplished, in so few years, or that such great additions are constantly being made to the Mormon fraternity. It is really marvellous in our eyes that, since we sat down, a band of hungry, half-starved emigrants, beside the Salt Lake, such great changes should have been wrought, as well in the physical features of the country as in the condition of our people. One, from an uncultivated desert, has become a region of great capabilities, budding and blossoming like the rose; while the other, for poverty have found riches, for weakness have acquired strength, are no longer despised, but feared.

Did we think of such a consummation, as we sat that night by the camp-fires, and meditated over the dangers we had passed or escaped? I, for one, did not. Blind and ignorant, indeed, we are, and incapable of perceiving what may be the result of our own actions. I had never been a believer in Mormonism, yet I loved my husband, and for his sake was willing to abide anywhere. Time, and the participation of danger and difficulty together, had wonderfully increased my affection for him. He was kind, considerate, and gentle, in his deportment towards me, and, though fully aware of the deceit that had been practised upon me in the beginning of our acquaintance, I readily forgave him that, and would have forgiven him ten times more, in consideration of my happiness, in loving and being beloved.

For many days after our arrival in Utah valley, the camp presented a busy spectacle. The site of the city, which was to be the centre of Mormonism, was first to be chosen ; then the lots to be measured off, subsequent to building houses. But the work progressed bravely, for all went at it with a hearty good will, and, in much less time than had been anticipated, we had comfortable homes. At first, two or three families were domiciled in one house, then the houses were increased to the number of the families, and finally, as the system of polygamy came into practice, the houses required to be multiplied to an almost indefinite extent. These houses were generally built of the adobe materials, though some were of logs, and large or small, according to the ability and taste of the possessor. Some of these dwellings were reared in picturesque and romantic situations, on the borders of beautiful streams, or the slight elevations of grassy knolls. Others were in the midst of broad fertile meadows, and all had an air of security and comfort that rarely belongs to a new settlement. Though far from the borders of the civilized world, and beyond the reach of railroads or steamboats, we possessed the necessaries, and in many cases the luxuries, of life. The abominable system of Smith, to purchase nothing from the heathen, had been generally relaxed. Indeed, Mormonism, under his successor, had taken an entire new phase. Most of the tricks and juggleries and impostures had been abandoned, though probably because there was no further occasion for their exercise. Traffic with the heathen was encouraged, on condition that we always got the best of the bargain, thus spoiling them, as the Israelites were said to have spoiled the Egyptians. Added to this, other companies of emigrants were continually arriving, who, generally speaking, were

13*

abundantly supplied with groceries; for, it should be remembered that several years had elapsed, between the first propagation of the Mormon creed, by Smith, and the exodus to Deseret, during which time many of the Mormon elders had done a large business in making converts. These had not been included in the restrictions imposed by the immediate presence of the Prophet, and, consequently, they came to us abundantly furnished with all things essential to living, with the exception of flour and potatoes. As a substitute, however, we obtained various edible roots, which, being baked, or otherwise prepared, were wholesome and nutritious.

Mrs. Bradish was lively and active as ever, and it will readily be believed that she found enough to do. Though always curious, and sometimes impertinent, she was really very useful, wonderfully attached to the church, and ready, at all times, to make any sacrifice to promote its welfare. Mrs. Beardsley was happily domiciled with her daughter, with the privilege of knitting for all the village. Her needles were never idle for a moment; never was woman so hurried before, for great numbers of little boys and girls were passing her door every day with naked feet; while Mrs. Stillman, sen., found a source of infinite vexation and trouble in the derelictions of her husband from what she believed to be his matrimonial duty.

"I declare," she said to me, a few days after our arrival, "I am completely bewildered; that detestable Fan Simpkins is the torment of my life. She told me to my face yesterday that she was Mr. Stillman's wife as much as I was; and that I might help myself if I could."

"Well, have they been married, Mr. Stillman and her?"

"That is what I cannot find out. When I question him about it, he answers indifferently or harshly; that it is none of my business, or something similar, and I can't nor won't bear it."

"But what will you do?"

"I would do anything almost to free myself from such a curse," she answered, "it is dreadful, horrible; a man of his age to be led astray by a blooming girl. Then, too, all she wants of him is to get his money."

"Think so?"

"I know it; you see he used to always give me his money to keep, and not a cent of it was ever laid out unbeknown to me. Now he manages entirely different; I am nobody to all intents and purposes. He never consults me on any subject, never gives me the money, never"——

"Oh well, Mrs. Stillman," I replied, "if that is all the grounds of complaint you possess, I don't see anything to prevent your happiness. Mr. Ward never gave me his money, or consulted me about his business, and yet I have been very happy."

"But I dont like it."

"It is a great thing, Mrs. Stillman, to conform to circumstances, and the sooner the women of Utah learn that, the better for them."

"But it is hard for old people to learn new lessons."

"I know it is, and yet what else can you do?"

From my heart I pitied the old lady, she was near sixty years of age; still good-looking and highly venerable in appearance.

She had been accustomed to the exclusive love and veneration of her husband. For nearly forty years they had been associated in conjugal relations. She had been his adviser and comforter, and now he turned away, bewitched and fascinated with the charms of a younger face. Night after night she was left alone, day after day she saw him not. When he came, his visits were short, and he was utterly unlike his former self. Who shall describe her utter loneliness of heart, her sense of deep humiliation; the harder to bear, because unexpected?

Leaving her to grieve and bemoan, we must take some further

notice of B———m. His house had been built in grand style, one hundred feet long, and sixty broad.

"I advise all the brothers," he said, "to build large houses, in order to supply the wants of their increasing families. Each brother should take at least four or six wives, and raise up speedily a pure and perfect generation for the Lord. In no other way can the kingdom of the saints be so rapidly established."

I presume that all felt the truth of this, but one inquired where the women was to come from.

"The Lord will provide them, even as he gave Eve to Adam."

"I hope, at any rate, it will not be by the same process."

"No danger of it," said Charley Moore.

"For my part," answered Harmer, "I would be satisfied with one wife," and he glanced at Emily.

The look was not lost on the Prophet, and he turned away with a frowning countenance.

"To judge from the size and appearance of his house," said Mrs. Bradish, "our leader intends to practise the precepts that he teaches, so far as raising a large family is concerned."

"I should think so."

"It is capable of entertaining four large families, at least."

"He probably designs to live *à la Turk;* each wife and her family separate."

"Most likely."

"His three wives wouldn't do very well together. They quarrel desperately, and I understand that it requires all his authority to keep them within bounds."

"Are they jealous of each other?"

"Not exactly, but each one wishes to take precedence of the others. The eldest fancies that her age entitles her to the place of honor. The youngest, because she is a beauty, and a favorite; and the middle-aged, on account of her wealth. They will not eat together, because each one wishes to sit at the head of the table; each one also aspires to superintend and direct the affairs of the household, while the others perform the labor. The husband promises them, that when the slaves that he has ordered, arrive, they shall all be exempt from household labor. That will probably make a difference, though it will scarcely remove all the heart-burnings and jealousies that render them miserable."

"And which are the natural fruits of polygamy,"

"Not exactly the natural fruits," said Mrs. Bradish, "because several women of my acquaintance view the matter with perfect indifference. Mrs. Leach says that she would delight for her husband to take a new wife, so that he would allow her a separate maintenance; that she had always worn the bonds of marriage as fetters, and would be glad at any moment to cast them off."

"But if I understand the subject, the marriage of another wife by the husband, would not release her."

"From his attentions it would, at any rate, in some degree."

"Does she desire such a thing?"

"So she says."

"Then she is certainly to be pitied."

"Not so much as those who rise up in opposition to the overmastering destiny, by which they will certainly be overwhelmed."

"Then how can you, a woman, argue in favor of, and approve of a system that is destined to bring misery on your sex?"

"Your slowness of apprehension, Mrs. Ward, is remarkable. It is not polygamy that renders them miserable, but the false and perverted views in which they have been educated. The daughters of these very women, so outrageous against that system, will grow up accustomed to it, and incapable of perceiving evil in it. It will neither offend their sense of right, nor seem degrading or humiliating. No one will shrink any more from being the third wife of a man, when the two former are living, than as though they were dead. It is custom and public opinion that regulate all these things. Under the Greek Empire it was considered disreputable to marry more than once. In more modern times, a man might lawfully take his twentieth wife, provided the nineteen were dead, which, in my view, is no better than to take the twentieth, the nineteen living."

"Were you a wife, you would probably think differently."

"Possibly, but the business of marrying and giving in marriage goes on rapidly at any rate, and will, probably, while there remains a marriageable unmarried female in the district."

"To me it looks extremely scandalous to see old withered white-haired men, walking the streets with young brides hanging to their arms, while at the same time an aged female, their true and lawful wife, is bewailing their absence at home."

"That may be, because you have not become accustomed to it."

"No, Mrs. Bradish," I answered, "you greatly mistake. It is the inconsistency of such a course, and even were it lawful, it cannot be expedient and proper."

"There you differ from Abraham, and Jacob, and David, and Solomon, who all thought polygamy expedient and proper, and practised it without reserve."

"Hush! here comes Elder Lucas."

The brother mentioned advanced to the door, and spoke. We invited him in. At first he refused, but Mrs. Bradish insisted.

"Yes, Brother Lucas, you must come in, and tell us about that wedding you went to the other night. There's been so much talk about it, that I am dying to know the particulars."

"Well, I've a fancy that it wouldn't please you much if you did know. It didn't me, however. I would much rather have been away: I'll never undertake such a job again for any man living."

"Why, what was there so dreadful about it?"

"Well, you see," he answered, "Brother Haley has contemplated taking another wife for some time, but could never screw up his courage sufficiently to tell Harriet of it, and so he comes to me the very day on which he was to be married at night, and says:

"'Brother Lucas, I once did you a favor—do you remember it?'

"'I do, and will return it, if it is ever in my power.'

"'It is in your power now,' he replied.

"'How so?'

"'I am to be married to-night. My wife knows nothing of it. I want you to go and tell her. Will you do so?'

"'But why haven't you let her know it before?'

"'I couldn't tell her. A thousand times I have longed to do so, but my heart always failed me.'

"'Will she care much?'

"'Not very much, I guess.'

"I looked at him steadfastly, and saw that his countenance belied his words.

"'You will go?' he asked again.

"'Certainly,' and I immediately set out.

"Mrs. Haley was busily engaged in her household avocations. She was singing a mournful song of her childhood's home, and her eyes looked red as if she had been weeping, but she received me cordially and kindly, and soon inquired if I had seen her husband, saying that he had been gone from home longer than usual.

"'And no wonder; he is detained by rather unusual business.'

"'What is it?' she quickly inquired.

"'Can't you guess?'

"'I don't think that I could; I am not familiar with my husband's business.'

"She looked towards me, and I made a feeble attempt to smile.

"'You are jesting,' she said.

"'I am not.'

"'Well, just tell me then. I am impatient under suspense.'

"'You know that Mormon husbands assume a certain privilege in matrimonial affairs.'

"The color forsook her countenance in a moment, her lips grew white and rigid. She clasped her hands till the blood half started from the clenched nails, and approaching me so closely that I felt her thick breathings on my face, she said in a hoarse voice:

"'Tell me all—instantly! instantly!'

"'Be composed, my dear madam,' I said. 'Your husband assures me that his affection for you is undiminished, but'—

"'He is going to take another'—

"The word stuck in her throat; she could not speak it.

"I nodded my head affirmatively.

"She clasped her hands to her head. I thought she was going to faint, but such was not the case. That blessed oblivion to sorrow was not for her. She sunk into a chair, not like Niobe in tears, for no tears came to her relief, yet such an expression of utter despair, such deep heartfelt misery, it is my prayer never to witness again."

"And you made no attempt to comfort her?" said Mrs. Bradish.

"Oh, yes I did, my dear madam. I said,

"'Don't lay it to heart so seriously. You will be very happy together, I presume. The lady whom your husband has chosen is every way worthy of him and you. She will make an admirable companion.

"She turned her head away as if the words pained her.

"'Please don't talk now—please don't,' she said.

"I sat a few minutes in silence, and then thinking to divert her mind, inquired, where she obtained that beautiful flower which was growing in the yard.

"She clasped her hands with an expression of agony that will haunt me to the day of my death. It was so utterly desolate and woe-begone. It seemed to say, how can you think of flowers, or aught beautiful and pure? Henceforth to me all is darkness and distress. But I continued:

"'I saw some beautiful scarlet blossoms of a new species blooming in the valley yesterday. If you wish it I will get them for you?'

"She shook her head, and a cold shudder ran over her frame.

"'You do not want them?' I said.

"'Oh, I don't know,' she answered; 'but don't talk to me, and about such things as that.'

"I saw then my stupidity; saw how futile would be mere earthly comfort; saw the husks that I had been offering to her bruised and wounded spirit, instead of the Bread of Life.

"'Shall we pray?' I inquired.

"She nodded her head.

"We knelt down, and I commenced—

"'Oh, not that way!' she almost shrieked; 'I can't bear that. Let me pray as I did in childhood.'

"I then recollected that she had been brought up in the ritual of the Established Church, and listened for the words of that litany which for pathos and fervor can never be excelled. But the petition which she breathed, though equally beautiful, was quite different,

"'Forsake me not, oh, Lord!' she prayed, 'in this my great extremity, but let me lean upon thee. Be thou my husband, my friend, and brother, and when all earthly hope fails, teach me to love thee more and more, to look to thee, and rest on thee.

And oh ! that it would please thee to sanctify this great affliction to my spiritual good ; that it might please thee to purify my heart from all vain and foolish desires.'

"A slight noise at the door caused me to raise my eyes. Haley was standing there ; his young bride leaning on his arm, but the injured wife, in the fervor of her devotion, heard nothing of his approach.

"'And above all, oh, Lord ! that thou wouldst forgive my husband for thus bruising and trampling on a heart that trusted in him, for betraying the confidence of one who loved and honored him above all others.'

"Haley stood like one transfixed with shame and surprise.

"'That thou wouldst forgive him for sinning against thyself, and making thy holy institution of marriage a means of licentiousness ; that thou wouldst forgive and pity her, his partner in sin ; that her eyes may be opened to the evil of her ways ; and that both may repent before it is too late.'

"Silently and stealthily the young woman drew her husband from the door, and the two disappeared around the corner of the house.

"Mrs. Haley finished her devotions, and arose calm and composed. Prayer has a wonderfully sedative influence, and when I came away her countenance had resumed its natural expression, only more sweet and sad.

"Haley has since informed me, that when he returned home, she said nothing to him on the subject, indeed, that she scarcely spoke at all.

"But where is the bride ?" said Mrs. Bradish.

"At her father's. She positively refused to go where Harriet lived ; said that the presence of such a woman would be a perpetual reproach on her, and that she couldn't nor wouldn't endure it."

"And so it would," I replied. " This polygamy is only

another name for the most abhorrent licentiousness, and no pure-minded woman would ever consent to have any part or lot in such a system. It could easily be broken up, if every woman would decide to remain in a state of celibacy, unless she could be united to a husband who had no other wife.'

"' And suppose the women have not the privilege of a efusal."

" I don't understand you."

" Well, then," said Mrs. Bradish, " the perfect development of Mormonism will restore women to their primitive condition."

" And what was that ?"

" A state of utter and entire dependence on their male relatives. These relatives will have the power of disposing of them in marriage as they see fit. The husband, instead of receiving a dowry with the wife, will bestow a gift on her parents or guardians, which will be handed over to the church."

" And so the church is to derive profit from the enslavement of its females ? Abominable !"

" You can call it enslavement, or whatever you like," said Mrs. Bradish, "yet you must be aware that the practice is sanctioned by patriarchal usage. Jacob paid for his wives, so did David, and Hosea, according to the Scriptures you venerate, while the Book of Mormon expressly authorizes it."

Brother Lucas soon after retired, and Mrs. Bradish departed to visit one of the elders, with whom she was becoming intimate, and whose mansion was shared by two buxom damsels in the character of wives.

CHAPTER XXXIV.

EMILY'S NARRATIVE CONTINUED.

LEFT alone for a short time, I was glad to see Emily coming down the street. She was dressed with unusual care, and I never saw her look so beautiful. As she approached, it struck me that something in her manners and appearance resembled B——m, yet the idea was new, and to an indifferent observer would have seemed ridiculous. He was considered homely, but it is a fact, that certain resemblances can be traced between the handsomest and the homeliest people, even as a caricature will bear a very general resemblance to its living original, though every feature is strongly and grotesquely exaggerated. A thought, which I dare not for a moment entertain, flashed into my mind. Her countenance had recently acquired a fixed and energetic expression, which made the resemblance more noticeable and striking, and I half determined to tell her of it.

After exchanging the usual compliments when she entered the house, she introduced the subject which seemed uppermost in her mind.

"You are aware," she said, " that B——m in my former interview with him, gave me one month, in which to decide whether or not I would accept him for a husband. The time expired some time ago, but he only demanded my decision yesterday, saying that he wished me to see how perfectly able he was to accommodate another wife ; that the best suit of rooms in his mansion was designed for me, and that he had the power, not only to punish me, but all my friends, if I adhered to my first resolution.

"And what did you tell him?"

"That he might punish me as much as he pleased, since I was determined to remain true to myself, and never marry a man who had another wife. That as to my friends, they were very few, but fully able to take care of themselves, so I entertained no fears on that score.

"'Take care how you despise my authority, or you shall feel it,' he said.

"'I neither despise you, nor your authority,' I replied; 'yet why should I fear it? you are no more than a man, and all the power you possess as head of the church, is liable to be wrested from you at any moment, if you make a despotic use of it.'"

"You were bearding the lion in his den."

"It don't seem so to me. I can't tell how it is, but every time I see this man, my fear of him grows less and less. It will disappear entirely, I think."

"I only hope that you will have no occasion to fear him; but what did he say to that?"

"That no one would interfere to prevent his doing with me as he pleased.

"'Have you then forgot that there is a Power who has promised to protect the fatherless, and whose promises never fail?' I inquired. 'In Him is my trust.'

"'But you refuse and deride His protection, in refusing me,' said my tormentor. 'You thwart His will, and forfeit His care, in not becoming my wife. He will do nothing for you; but to what other imaginary source do you look?'

"'To death.'

"The Prophet started wildly. 'Who speaks of death?' he inquired.

"'I do!' and I fixed my eyes on his face, with a calm, unshrinking gaze. 'I do; it is what we must all meet, sooner or later; it is something that equalizes and levels the oppressor and his victim—a sure and safe refuge against persecution, of whatever kind; and I should prefer that—yes, even that—the damp, cold tomb—to being your wife.'

"'But people cannot always have what they would prefer,' he said, mockingly; 'especially, when that preference is contrary to the will of heaven; and you would not dare—no, you would not dare—to rush, unbidden, into the presence of your Creator?'

"I made no reply.

"'Do you refuse to answer me?' he asked.

"'I do; such questions as that, you have no right to ask.'

"'But I have a right to ask; heaven has given me the right to know your most secret thoughts.'

"'Then heaven must give you the power to find them out, for it is certain that I shall never reveal them to you.'

"He seemed really surprised at my audacity, and doubtless was; but I had long before discovered, that the manifestation of a spirit of defiance was the only safe course to pursue with him. After a silence of several minutes, he said:

"'You, it seems, are averse to a marriage with me, because I am already married. Now, suppose you marry Harmer, or any other young man; you have no guarantee that he will not, almost immediately, take other wives; especially, when such a thing is considered a religious duty, besides its agreeableness and expediency. Objections on that score, are altogether invalid.'

"'My objections are many and great; polygamy is only one of them,' I replied. 'Will you suffer me to depart?'

"'If you will promise to hold no communication with Harmer.'

"'But I shall promise no such thing.'

"'You won't?'

"'No; and you have no right to exact such a promise.'

"'I haven't—eh?'

"'To be sure you haven't; and what is more, you have not the authority to enforce it. I shall talk with just who I please, notwithstanding your will to the contrary.'

"'Your boldness becomes you admirably!' he said at length, regarding my flashing eyes and defiant countenance; 'I never saw you look so beautiful. I am fond of variety, and after the endless smiles with which I am accustomed to be treated by my other wives, it would be delicious to have one whose pretty lips could pout, or even scold a little. One gets tired of sugar, and a little tartness, sometimes, would not come amiss.'

"'With your permission, I will depart.'

"'But my permission will not be given.'

"'Then I shall go without it;' and suiting the action to the word, I leapt through the window.

"The portly form of the Prophet prevented his following, though he looked and called after me.

"Passing around the house, and through a little gate, whence a foot-path communicated with the valley, I met a lady in whom I recognized one of B———m's wives. She looked distressed and troubled, and, offering her my hand, I inquired after her health.

"She politely answered that her health was good; and then coming at once to the subject that engrossed her thoughts, observed:

"'B———m wishes to make you his wife.'

"'He does,' I replied.

"'Well,' she remarked, surveying me from head to foot, 'you are much too beautiful, and I believe, too good, to be the wife of such a brute. Oh, Miss! if you knew him as well as I do, you would suffer martyrdom before consenting to become his wife.'

" My curiosity was aroused. 'Is he not, then, a model husband ?'

"'Model husband !' she answered bitterly; 'no man can be a husband to more than one woman; and much I doubt whether this man could be a husband to even one.'

"'Why not ?'

"'Because he is too selfish—too utterly devoid of all the finer and gentler feelings. He is incapable of sentiment, and degrades marriage to a mere means of propagating the human species.'

"'Is he fond of you ?'

"'How could he be fond of me, when duty, as he terms it, required him to divide his attentions between so many, and each wife was rigorous to exact her full share of his regards ? No; he cares nothing about any of us. He is for ever smitten with new faces; and that's the abomination of polygamy. Men are naturally inclined to variety, but habit, public opinion, everything, tends to restrain that inclination, in most communities. Among us, however, polygamy gratifies and encourages it. Wives may be multiplied like garments, and with every one that is worn, an old one must be thrown off. How I hate and despise myself, for ever sharing in such a system !'

"'But you were not acquainted with its evils, until you experienced them.'

"'And yet, I ought to have been aware that polygamy would destroy all that was holy, and beautiful, and tender, in married life. I ought to have foreseen how all the sweet and familiar confidence of that most endearing relation, when rightly considered, all the reciprocal sympathies, and tendernesses, and cares, which constitute, more than anything else, the true happiness of the conjugal state, must be necessarily wanting, where the affections were divided on so many objects, whose views, and feelings, and opinions could not be other than diverse.'

"'Does he treat you all alike?'

"'Pretty much; it would hardly do for him to greatly prefer one to another. He bought me a ribbon one day that wonderfully affronted Alice, and though he purchased a dress for her the next, she wasn't satisfied, but talked and scolded till he told her to shut her mouth, and never, while she lived, let him hear the word ribbon again.'

"'And did she obey him?'

"'She knew better than to disobey, but don't, for the world, let B——m know that I have said a word to you.'

"'No, of course not.'

"'He would punish me somehow, if he knew it.'

"'Are you, then, afraid of him?'

"'Perhaps you are not aware that those Mormon husbands, who have several wives, have a code of regulations by which they govern their famllies.'

"I replied in the negative.

"'Well, such is the case, nevertheless, and to each of these rules is attached a penalty, that varies in stringency according to the nature of the offence, and its heinousness in the eyes of the Mormon elders.'

"'But how does it happen that I never heard of this before?'

"'Because you reside in a family where polygamy, practically speaking, is unknown, and a great penalty is attached to the least revelation of household affairs. I am telling you this, under the risk of severe punishment.'

"'These rules; I wish to hear more about them,—what are they?'

"'The first one forbids the revelation of any incident that occurs in the household, provided it compromises the honor of

14

the husband, or any of his wives, or can have a tendency to bring the institution of polygamy into disrepute.'

"'And the penalty?'

"'Confinement in the cellar for a month.'

"'And have any of the Mormon wives been so confined?'

"'That is more than I can tell; however, it is not unlikely.'

"'And the second rule?'

"'Forbids all quarrelling and dissension among the wives; the one who commences the quarrel, to receive the punishment, which varies in degree from three lashes to twenty-five.'

"'And by whom are the lashes to be administered?'

"'Generally by the husband, though sometimes by a delegate whom he may appoint.

"'The third rule forbids one wife to injure or strike another, under the penalty of a dozen lashes, to be administered by the party aggrieved.

"'The fourth rule forbids one woman to strike, or otherwise correct the child of another, under penalty of receiving herself just as many blows, administered by the mother of the beaten child.'

"'And is that all?'

"'No, indeed; other offences of a similar character are classified and arranged with their penalties; yet all relate, more or less, to that abominable system, which makes the domestic altar a shrine of legal prostitution, sanctioned by the authority of a pretended revelation.'

"It need scarcely be said," continued Emily, "how much my abhorrence of that hateful institution was strengthened by this account, and now it is my fixed resolution, never, upon any condition, to enter the married state, while in the Mormon territory."

"Not with Harmer?"

"No, not even with him, unless a new state of things can be introduced."

"And that is very improbable."

"Though not impossible; at any rate it can be attempted."

"To what do you allude?"

"Never mind, you will find out;" and Emily soon after bade me adieu, and departed.

While meditating on her words, and what they were designed to insinuate, Harmer and Lawrence passed the window. They were conversing in a low, earnest tone, and then I remembered having observed them frequently together before. Mr. Ward that moment came in from an opposite direction.

"These men," said I, pointing through the window, "are becoming very intimate."

"So I perceive," he answered, "they are probably hatching mischief of some kind or other."

"Or they may be discussing something useful or good."

Mr. Ward shook his head, and the subject was dropped, as I did not wish to excite or strengthen his suspicions.

CHAPTER XXXV.

CHURCH AND STATE.

ESTABLISHED in Utah, as they supposed, beyond the cognizance or the authority of the government at Washington, the Mormons quickly developed a ruling principle of their religion; namely, the union of Church and State, which, as may be imagined, was an arbitrary and irresponsible despotism. B——m was temporal governor, and spiritual ruler; the maker and executioner of laws; the prophet, priest, and king, so far as real power and authority was concerned. It is true that he counselled with the elders, but then he acted precisely as he pleased; they might advise, but they could not direct. Certain it is, however, that many of his most important schemes were only confided to a few, and that messengers to various Indian tribes were coming and going, and that Indian chiefs were entertained, and mysterious treaties formed with them, of whose import, all but a select few were ignorant. Sometimes the ostensible motives was trade, though the most casual observer might have discovered something in this intercourse that indicated a deeper and more ambitious project.

Meanwhile every means was taken to strengthen the hands of the church, and by the church B——m clearly understood himself. Taxes were levied, and various measures taken to enlarge its revenues, and the funds thus obtained, after deducting a very small proportion to support missionaries, were disposed of in some incomprehensible way, or appropriated to some secret service. The missionaries, too, were compelled to travel, and preach. Unlike the same class in other denominations of Christians, they were never permitted to locate and remain in one place, at an immense expense and little profit. After the removal to Utah, they were particularly instructed to employ every effort to induce all favorable to the new faith to emigrate, and whether favorable or not, to point out the extreme beauty and healthfulness of the locality. They were directed to organize churches, baptize converts, and accept presents, which might contribute to swell the general funds, while at the same time no church should be expected or required to sustain a settled pastor, as every brother was presumed to be competent to preach.

The manner of their selection was rather original. The names of a certain number were written on small pieces of white paper, and these being put in a hat, with an equal number of blank pieces, the whole were well shaken up, when the oldest brother, and after him the others, drew out, each one a piece, and the men whose names were thus drawn out, were considered as destined, by the Holy Spirit, to preach, in turn. It was regarded as the height of impiety, to attempt, by any means, to avoid this contingency, but no one was required to speak a greater length of time than comported with his inclination and ability. Some would talk an hour, but others only five minutes. Some would take a text, and others only exhort.

This alternation, however, gave variety and interest to the entertainment. The missionaries to the heathen were chosen in the same manner, while those remaining at home were not suffered to remain in idleness, awaiting their turn, but expected to work at some kind of useful employment. Whatever might be his faults, B———m, in this respect, manifested a laudable energy. Ministers or elders, who presumed on their sacred calling, and wished to burden the church with their support, or to obtain a living independent of physical labor, he severely reprimanded, and if they remained contumacious, they were dismissed with contempt as drones and idlers.

"He that reclaims a farm from the wilderness, and brings up a family in the fear of God and the faith of Mormon, has accomplished a great work, and he shall live and reign with Christ a thousand years," he would remark, on all occasions.

"And what will be the condition of those who are restrained by nature, or misfortune, or untoward circumstances, from the performance of these duties ?"

"They are to be pitied and forgiven ; but let no one minister, elder, or brother, who is capable of assuming the responsibility, shrink from it, lest he be denied a right to share the fruits of the tree of life."

Under this discipline, the preachers found themselves necessitated to find employment. Many of them became the most active farmers. Others wrought at mechanical trades, and a few entered into mercantile affairs.

The Prophet and Governor sought to encourage all such

undertakings, and his manner of reasoning was correct and apt to the purpose.

"It is a fixed law," he would say, "that every man, with few and rare exceptions, is intended to live on his own earnings, and not on those of another. No man has a right to live, or eat his daily bread, without producing as much, on the scale of a life, as he consumes, and that, too, by some kind of honest physical labor. Indeed, it is every man's duty to quadruple himself in population, as well as to increase the fixed capital of the world for the next generation. A farmer should leave a farm cleared, cultivated, and stocked for the church. And if he has been a believer and preacher of the truth, so much the better. It shows that he has done his duty as an industrious and useful citizen. I praise and honor such a one, and my praise and honor is worth having. He shall be a king and priest to God ; it has been revealed to me."

It was the general policy of B——m to encourage preaching mostly, in those who were well off in temporal affairs. This obviated any necessity of assistance on the part of the Church. The rich men likewise monopolized the women, to a great extent, consequently, while one man enjoyed the honor of being a preacher and a rich man, with a house full of women, all loveable and lovely, waiting to do his bidding, another, quite as good, or better probably in mind and heart, though with less of this world's goods, was doomed to the cold and joyless trials of celibacy.

In this respect, however, it cannot be denied that some of the women were culpable, and that their conduct contributed, in no small degree, to the continuance of polygamy. Not a few preferred a rich man, with a dozen wives, to a poor one without any, and, though repentance must inevitably ensue, it would be too late. The Prophet encouraged this state of things, for various reasons ; indeed, he seemed to consider poverty as little short of crime, whose punishment consisted in the deprivation of social and domestic comforts.

It seemed to be the policy of B——m, to give the Mormon creed a consistency, or rather a systematized form, such as it had never taken under the administration of Smith. Besides the wonders of millennial glory, on which the preachers loved to descant, they were fond of expatiating on spiritual life. They professed to believe, and they certainly taught, that God had constantly on hand a multitude of little spirits, who want to come, and whom he has ordained shall come, and assume mortal bodies, and sojourn on earth for a time; human bodies being earthly tabernacles, temporary dwelling-houses for spirits. Yet, conjugal intercourse is necessary to accomplish the work, and hence, as God is very anxious that these spirits should be provided with bodies, and as the spirits themselves are very anxious to get down here, it became the duty of all true believers to lend their aid and produce the bodies as fast as possible.

And this doctrine, strange and ridiculous as it may seem, was openly taught from the pulpit as a defence of polygamy.

"It has been revealed to me," said B——m one day from the pulpit, "It has been revealed to me, that there are millions on millions of little spirits, all waiting and wishing for mortal bodies. And when they come to take bodies, they wish to be of Mormon parentage. Of course the higher order would be disgusted with a low, mean descent, the same as a righteous man is disgusted with a wicked one, or a neat, tidy person with one of filthy habits; hence, they would only be willing to go to the place where purity and righteousness dwell. The lower order of spirits will likewise go among the low and uncultivated, where the principles of virtue and integrity have been in part or wholly neglected. Good spirits do not want to partake of the sins of the low and degraded, hence they will stay in heaven until a way is opened for purity and righteousness to form a channel to which they can come and take honorable bodies in this world, and magnify that calling.

Let us take that course, and we shall draw the brightest spirits to honor our generations. Try this, and your offspring will be the fairest specimens of the work of God's hand. Let the servants of God maintain the principles of holiness and integrity, and marry a multitude of wives, and by that means draw in their train more of those spirits that will glorify the God of Israel, since we are very well assured that all the good spirits must necessarily be born in Utah, or among true believers. The Almighty will never send his choice spirits to the low and degraded people of the thirty-one States, who restrict the holy and virtuous to the possession of one wife.

Another argument which he advanced in favor of polygamy, was the idea of improving the stock.

"I have been looking about me," he said, "as I always am, and have seen how anxious many of our farmers are to improve their stock of cattle ; to make them of better blood, and thus be all the time improving : but it is not a common thing for men to wish to improve their own species. I wish you to think for a moment. I have seldom heard that subject agitated, when indeed it is the most important one that was ever investigated. Let us go a little further into the philosophy of this : a man by having many wives, and thus mingling his blood with a variety, can improve his species the same as we can improve any other portion of the animal creation. It is said that we bear the image of God, and now, don't let us dwindle down by the one-wife system to the physical and mental degeneracy of the monkey."

Blasphemous and absurd as these sentiments must appear, they were quite as new and ludicrous. The brethren, however, or all those who were able to take more wives, or to get them, seemed to think it was a capital idea. To Harmer it afforded a subject for an excellent jest, and whenever he heard of a brother who was about to marry his second or third wife, he would remark that such a one intended to improve his stock.

As the principles of Mormonism developed, it became evident that the females were to be regarded as an inferior order of beings. One by one the rights to which they had been accustomed, as well as the courtesies generally conceded to them, were taken away. When the husband died, his property reverted to the church, instead of going to support his bereaved family, a regulation which occasioned an infinite amount of trouble and difficulty. However, if the husband and father was particularly interested in making provision for the future support of his family, he could do so, by paying the church during his life-time a certain extra stipend, which would release its claim.

Many widows were thus actually necessitated to take husbands on the first opportunity, and many young girls, not exceeding the ages of twelve and fourteen years, became the wives of men old enough to be their grandfathers, to save them from the streets.

No family in Utah ever hires household service. Some few have slaves, but generally speaking when one wife is insufficient to perform the labor, another is taken, perhaps a third, or fourth, and so on, for the number is only limited by the discretion and desire of the husband.

In all cases where the father was living, his consent was necessary to the marriage of a daughter, even though that daughter was a widow and a mother. In the case of his death, the head of the church acted in the capacity of guardian, and his consent was indispensable. The fathers, from the instruction they constantly received, and other causes, paid little attention to the inclinations of their children, but were greatly influenced by the size of the nominal gift, though actually the importance of the price they were to receive. These bargains were not unfrequently the subjects of as much chicanery and intrigue, as if the object for sale was a horse, and the contracting parties two regular jockies.

One blustery windy day in autumn, muffled in a warm cloak, and otherwise protected from cold, I sought the residence of Mrs. Melton, in order to pay that lady a visit which I had long promised. Mrs. Melton's family consisted of herself, her husband, and two beautiful daughters. They were in tolerable good circumstances, but the husband was a scheming, discontented man, possessed with the idea of becoming rich. He had never married but one wife, because he considered them expensive. His sole remark when Mrs. Melton required a new dress or shawl would be : "these women will ruin us all by their extravagance ;" and, though he generally gave her the money required, it evidently came grudgingly, than which nothing can more deeply wound a sensitive mind. He was even more hard and churlish to his daughters, and their great natural beauty was seldom heightened by the aid of ornament in childhood; though, some years later, the father, who thought of nothing but making money, determined to cause their beauty to subserve his selfish ends. Accordingly he bought them dresses, and laces, took them to meeting, and exposed their charms to the wanton eyes of the old polygamists.

Of course they were soon noticed, and an old man, whose domestic establishment comprised a dozen wives and thirty children, came to the house while I was there to bargain for the eldest daughter. His appearance excited in the mind the most repulsive and abhorrent sensations. He was rude and ungainly in his manners, uncouth in form and feature, while his conversation was a rare mixture of vulgarity and ignorance ; yet, he was well off, a circumstance which gave him great importance in his own eyes, though his property had been acquired in the most degrading manner.

When he was an infant, his mother being left a widow, carried her son to the poor-house, and then travelled around the country with a begging paper, and thus acquired a sum sufficient to purchase a farm. This farm he managed to obtain by swindling his aged parent, whom he caused to be supported by the township until her death. After this he sold his farm, and with the proceeds removed to Utah, and became a very devout Mormon.

Mr. Melton and this man, on the occasion of which I speak, occupied an apartment contiguous to the one in which I sat with Mrs. Melton, but the door being ajar, and the gentlemen talking loudly, we could not help hearing the conversation. Mrs. Melton seemed nervously anxious, but said nothing. Several times I observed the tears trickling down her cheeks, as her husband enlarged on the various good points of the girls; and his companion, though eager for the purchase, rather dissented from the extravagant gift demanded.

"You see, Brother Weldy," said the father, "my girls are no common piece of woman flesh. You might search the society of the saints from one end to the other, and not find such others— so neat and trim, and handy at house-work, or any other kind of work, though, to tell the truth, they never done much at anything else, never earned me five dollars, while the expense of their bringing up has been great, very great, brother Weldy, consequently their husband must give me something commensurate. Beautiful girls like them should command rich husbands."

"I consider myself as well off as any man in Utah," said Weldy.

"Oh, certainly, you are well off, very well off, and consequently you can afford to give something handsome, especially as the girl is young, and yourself quite aged—excuse me, I don't think that any objection, but some folks might," and he endeavored to smile blandly.

"Why, yes," said Weldy, drawing his words, "I might give

something rather handsome, I s'pose, say that bay mare ; I'll give you her. She's a fine beast, very fine ; you don't see a better round these diggings."

"Say both horses, and its a bargain. They're just such a span as I've been wanting to get."

"Couldn't, positively couldn't, unless you let me have both the girls ; what do you say to that, eh ?"

"Both my daughters ! really, I don't know ; would it be lawful for a man to marry two sisters ?"

"Certainly ; the patriarch Jacob did, you know."

Mrs. Melton wiped her eyes, and I was actually dumb with astonishment.

"You would be welcome to the girls, both of them, provided you were willing to give me a suitable remuneration, but either one is worth both your mares, considering their age and beauty. I want to do well by them. I want them to marry a rich man, but I can't give them away ; that wouldn't look well—wouldn't look as if I had any regard for them."

"You mustn't be too hard on a fellow, now ; but I'm willing to do right about it. Say both the girls, and I'll throw in that Durham cow."

"That's more like it ; but it strikes me that if you were to see the girls, you'd be still more liberal. Let me go and call them."

Mr. Melton went out, but soon returned.

"They'll be in presently," he said, and the two men continued the conversation.

"You must be getting quite a family, brother Weldy ?" said Melton.

"Something of a family, it is true. I wish to do my duty in that respect, if no other."

"How many helpmates has it pleased heaven to bestow upon you !"

"At present I have twelve, and several more in view."

"Ah; but how do you manage to support 'em? These women are generally extravagant."

"I don't consider mine so, and as to their support, why a woman will earn her living, over and over again, in the course of the year. I carry on my large farm solely with their help, and it is much cheaper than to hire men. Why don't you take another wife?"

"I feared the expense of keeping them."

"Pshaw, keeping them, indeed; they'd keep you, if you wanted to live a gentleman. Generally speaking, they are much more active and industrious than men, much more trustworthy, too. It's one of the blessedest things in the world, to have the laws all made by the church. Polygamy, as I take it, is the legitimate offspring of the union of Church and State. The Church is more careful and tender of the interests of believers, than the State, when divorced from her, could ever be."

"Likely enough."

"Why, it is plain as day to me, and I bless the Lord for it. The heathenish statesmen, who make the laws of those States whence we came, care nothing about the church, the true interests of believers, or other things in which we are deeply interested. Mormonism can only flourish as a theocracy; but so long as the head of the church makes the laws we are safe. We ought to have a constitution and government of our own; we must have, too. It will never do for the saints to remain in virtual bondage to the heathen. They will come among us after a while, I expect, with the express purpose to deprive us of our superior privileges, because, of course, they won't be willing for us to enjoy what they cannot possess themselves. I regard polygamy as the chiefest of our blessings, and that will be what the heathen will attempt to root out and destroy. Independence is the only thing that can preserve us.

"It seems so to me."

"Yes, independence and a theocratic government. I have got enough of republics. I don't like this freedom and equality in name, where none really exists."

There was a sound of approaching footsteps, a rustle of female garments, then the door opened, and two girls made their appearance, arm in arm. Slightly abashed at the presence of Weldy, they were drawing back, when the father ordered them to advance. They timidly obeyed, when Weldy, without any recognition of their presence, raised his eyes, with a gaze of cool assurance, and surveyed them from head to foot; first one, and then the other. "Rather beautiful," he said, at length. "They can go."

"Leave the room," said the father; and they obeyed, but came, in great surprise, to the room where we were sitting.

"What is Weldy here for?" said the eldest to her mother, in a whisper, "and what does he want of us?"

"To marry you!"

"Oh, Lord!" said one of the girls, while the other ran from the apartment shrieking.

"Which of us, mother?" said the remaining daughter.

"Both!"

"Worse and worse! who ever heard tell of such a thing? but father will not consent? that horrible man, too, looks like an ogre."

"Your father has consented," said the mother.

The girl clasped her hands in mute despair. "Then we are indeed, lost," she said.

This conversation had been carried on in so low a tone, that the discourse of the men was plainly audible.

"They are perfect houris to my view," said the father, "and all that induces me to part with them is a regard for the church, and a desire that they may become mothers in Israel. It is my wish that every female should fulfill her vocation to the utmost, that thereby the number of the Faithful might become as the sand of the sea."

Weldy looked as if he understood perfectly the drift of such conversation, "Right fair girls, yet I don't admire such black eyes, and beauty after all isn't but skin deep. If I want 'em to work in the meadow, I dare say they'll be afraid of getting tanned."

"No, they won't; they never tan, some complexions don't, you know, and I'm really astonished that you shouldn't like black eyes; most people are partial to them."

"They are apt to be accompanied by a fiery temper, and quick tongue."

"Ah! you're mistaken there; many of the pleasantest women I ever knew, had black eyes."

"And your pleasant women are mere devils when roused."

"Well, if you don't want my daughters, say so; there'll be enough, that will."

"But I do want 'em; all is, I think, you ask too big a price."

"For the two best and likeliest girls in the settlement?"

"I do; it seems to me that I have made you a very fair offer. These girls are not half the use to you, that two stout hearty wives would be. You know that mere beauty is of but small account, it fades so soon."

"Well, considering all things, probably it is as much as I could reasonably expect," said the father.

"And we may consider the matter settled?"

"I guess so."

"And when can I have the girls?"

"Whenever you choose."

"Let me see; well, suppose I say this day week; will that be too soon?"

"No; I don't think that it will."

"You will endeavor to reconcile the girls, it they make any objections?"

"Certainly; but they have been reared in habits of obedience; there will be no difficulty with them."

Mrs. Melton turned her eyes to her daughter with a mute glance of despairing agony. The girl sat with her hands clasped, her cheeks bleached, the picture of utter despair.

I heard the men rise, and knew that Weldy was going. Mrs. Melton made a motion mechanically, as if to rise, and then sunk back in her chair.

"Oh! mother, mother!" said the girl, "you must save us from this fate."

"I would lay down my life to save you, darling, but the sacrifice would be of no avail."

I was ready to exclaim in the language of the patriarch, "Oh! my soul, come not into their secret; to their assembly, my honor, be thou not united."

Then I heard Weldy blessing that theocracy, or the power of the Church that, governing the State, conferred such privileges on believers.

CHAPTER XXXVI.

THE SELF-ACCUSER AND THE DYING HUSBAND.

SOON after our arrival in Utah, Charley Moore and the beautiful Ethleen were united in marriage. She was blithe and happy as a bird, and no one could doubt his perfect felicity. The handsome hunter, the rover of the prairie and the wilderness, had become suddenly transformed to the domesticated man, who always came home at night, and preferred the society of his wife to that of any other. They occupied a pleasant cottage on the brow of a hill, a beautiful garden in front, and a wide field, filled with various kinds of grain and edible roots, in the rear. Their fat, sleek cow pastured in the valley, and everything bore an air of quiet peace, and sweet contentment.

But leaving this pleasant abode of love and bliss, let us look in on poor Mrs. Stillman. It is late at night, yet the old lady is sitting alone. She seems lonely, sad, and disconsolate ; forsaken by the husband of her youth, the companion of her riper years, and the support of her age. She is thinking over the past, and memory brings back faithfully all the toils and trials, and privations they had shared together. The long, long years of endearing love and confidence ; the anxieties, and cares, and watchings in sickness, the constant companionship, and reciprocal attentions in health, and she felt from her inmost soul that he was her husband, and hers only ; that the ties which united them could only be severed by the hand of death, nor even by that, but that their spirits would meet and mingle to all eternity. She was no longer excited by passion ; jealousy, hate, madness, had all disappeared. She knew that a ceremony of marriage had been performed between her husband and the woman she had hated and still despised. She knew likewise that he had provided her with a house, and money to furnish it. She knew likewise that the greater part of his time was spent there, and that he was completely fascinated and bewildered with the attractions of his new bride, yet she reviewed the subject in all its bearings with comparative calmness, and mentally inquires, "what is it best for me to do ?"

A small fire is glowing on the hearth, and she sits in the shadow of its dim uncertain light. There is a cricket on the hearth, and its cheerful chirp, chirp, chirp, reminds her so forcibly of the past, that she almost wishes it would hush. Yet there is something so companionable to the lonely, even in the chirp of a cricket, something so home-like and domestic, that it soothes and solaces the weary and suffering.

Then came a gentle tap at the door, and the next moment Louisa entered, with a countenance that looked even unhappier than that of her mother-in-law.

"Sitting here alone in the dark, mother, and father off with that bad, bad woman? Oh! it is too bad. Why will you not come and live with us altogether? I feel concerned to have you stay here alone. You might be taken sick suddenly and die, before any person could find it out."

"No, Louisa, I prefer to remain here," said the old lady solemnly, "he comes once in two or three days to see how I am getting along, and though his visits are short, they reconcile me in some degree to his absence, because they show that I am still remembered."

"Such remembrance as that would not satisfy me," said Louisa, "it would be provoking rather than otherwise."

"I think not, if you could feel as I have felt."

"Why, mother, what has come over you?" inquired Louisa, "it really astonishes me to see you so calm and collected. What have you heard? what has happened?"

"I have heard nothing, and nothing has happened, only that my mind has changed in some respects at least, and I no longer look on things as I did once, and that, though in the conduct of your father there may be something to forgive, there is also much to excuse."

"Goodness, mother, I hope you will never attempt to excuse polygamy, under any circumstances."

"Heaven forbid, and yet, though polygamy is inexcusable, the polygamist may be, or it seems so to me."

Louisa shook her head.

"He is my husband," continued the old lady, "he has always been kind, and gentle, and considerate; I shall never forget that.

He was so particularly tender and careful of me when I was sick or a little ailing, that I would speak lightly of his faults, and regard them rather as human infirmities, than willful errors of heart or mind."

Louisa was half tempted to look on her mother as demented; the whole tone of her conversation being so different from what it had ever been before.

"It is but right," resumed the old lady, "that you, who have known my anger, my jealousy, and hate, should know also of my better feelings, should know how heartily I have forgiven them, and that my best wishes are for their welfare."

We may be sure that Louisa opened her eyes in supreme astonishment; "But not till they have repented?" she said, "not till they change their mode of life?"

"Yes, even now, because it is our duty to pray for the unjust, even more than the just; to love our enemies as our friends, and though to bid an evil-doer God-speed in his wickedness might make us partakers of the evil deed, we should wish for his welfare, and that he might do well."

Louisa said nothing; she could not find it in her heart to forgive a woman, whose fascinations had once bewitched her husband.

"I have become aged," said Mrs. Stillman; "I was never beautiful or clever. My conversation was ordinary and commonplace. I had no education, and little talent, and my wonder is that he should ever love me at the first, that he loved me so many years, that he submitted to my authority as he did, conscious all the time of my defects, for he must have known them. It is strange that he never discovered before that I could not make him happy."

"You are all wrong, mother, in thus undervaluing yourself," said Louisa. "So far as talents, or education, or cleverness are concerned, you are much his superior, as everybody acquainted with you must acknowledge. He was never a smart man, though, till now, I always accounted him a good one."

"And he is a good one; heaven forgive me for not sooner finding it out. As I was sitting here alone," continued the old lady, " here alone, in the dull, dim shadows of the waning firelight, thinking in the bitterness of my spirit how he had deserted me, and of all the wrongs and sufferings that I had endured in consequence, I fell asleep and dreamed of my mother."

" Of your mother ?"

" Of my mother ; she has long been dead, but methought she stood before me, just as she looked in life, only more radiant and beautiful. Then she questioned me of my trouble, and I told her all from first to last. Her countenance assumed a mournful expression, and she inquired, ' Didn't it never occur to you, my daughter, that a large proportion of the wrong was on your side ?'

" ' On my side ?'

" ' Even so, your heart will tell you what I mean, examine it well,' and I saw her no more."

"Was the vision real?" questioned Louisa.

"Whether or not the vision was real, the result of it was. My eyes were opened at once to my long course of usurped authority and haughty exaction. I had aspired to rule and domineer over him, not by the gentle influence of love, but the pride of an overweening ambition. Not because it was for my good, or his good, or the good of our family, but because I loved to rule, and have my own way. I see it all now, the little consideration I paid to his judgment, the preference I always gave to my own pleasure, my blind perversity to his desire. Imagining myself possessed of his affection, I prized it little, and took no pains to secure and preserve it, hence it has passed from me, and nothing is left but the knowledge of my loss, and regret for the years of folly that caused it."

It was a pitiable sight to behold that old woman, with her pale, wan face, and snowy hair, thus bringing home to her heart the errors of her younger years, and finding in her own derelictions from duty, an excuse for the infirmities of her husband.

"I was told yesterday," she continued, "that Fanny pets and caresses him. Heaven knows that I never thought of doing such a thing; that she talks to him of love, and apparently lives only in his presence; while I made him feel always that his company was irksome to me, that his conversation displeased me. I have told him a thousand times that I regretted my marriage; that if I were single again, nothing should ever induce me to enter that state; that my burdens of house-keeping and family were troublesome, and that I would willingly be released. Such things, I begin to perceive, must necessarily alienate a husband's heart."

"But, mother," said Louisa, "all women are guilty of these things, more or less."

"Then the more shame be to them."

"But they don't see it in the light that you do. Their tempers become soured with a multitude of petty cares and vexations, and though the husband may not be to blame, he is the readiest object, and generally the victim on whom the wife vents her complaints."

"I see," continued the old lady, "now that my husband has gone from me, I see, what I never understood before, that his society was a great comfort and blessing to me. True, he wasn't much of a talker, and rarely gave an opinion contrary to me, yet the consciousness of his presence and protection, so lightly regarded then, seems to me now to have been a great thing. If he didn't speak a word I wasn't lonely; and then how strange that I never knew, that I never ascertained during the forty years of our companionship, that I loved him as I do."

"As you did," said Louisa.

"As I do," said the old woman sharply. "But only to think that I remained so long blind to the state of my feelings, even while we sat daily at the same board, and nightly by the same hearth, and participated hourly in the comforts of the same home."

"The home he has now forsaken," said Louisa.

"The home that his presence blessed, that his industry and forethought preserved from want, the home which but for him had never existed, and which his generosity and kindness made a quiet sanctuary for the stranger and the weary; a seat for the exercise of holy and gentle virtues; the centre of a thousand influences and associations, which bless and purify all within their reach."

"And yet, mother, I could not thus plead for him."

"Because you have never known him as I have; because you can never apprehend how everything around me speaks of him. He has been familiar with every place that I have; he has beheld the same countenances, and heard the same voices. Yet, he was more beloved than me; I could see that plainly. Eyes that looked coldly to me, beamed pleasurably on him; nor was it a wonder, he was gentleness and honesty, fearful of giving offence, and ever ready to do a kindness. And all this time," she continued, "I was well aware of his worth, but never laid it to heart. I understood perfectly well that he was grieved and wounded at my fault-finding, though he never said so, yet I delighted in it; it was making him feel my power, and power was the only thing on earth that I ever coveted."

"But now," answered Louisa, "now that it is too late to make amends, the remembrance of these things, doubtless exaggerated by distempered fancy, comes to aggravate your affliction. What is done cannot be undone. No self-accusation can ever obliterate an action."

"But actions if not obliterated may be atoned for."

"Sometimes, and yet you can hardly make atonement to your husband."

"Why not?"

"Because he has placed himself virtually beyond your reach."

"Beyond my reach, when he visits me every two or three days?"

"Certainly, since you would scarcely humiliate yourself to begin the subject, considering the manner in which he has treated you."

"The manner in which I have treated him is what concerns me now, and were the humiliation ten times greater than it is, I would cheerfully bear it, in order to make him some amends," replied the old lady.

"Amends to him, mother, for what?"

"For all my folly and wickedness."

"What folly and wickedness?"

"That which has been a part and parcel of my conduct all my life; which shadowed and blighted the happiness of our marriage; and which has finally driven him to the arms of another."

"How can that be the case?"

"Because if I had conducted myself with moderation and considerate gentleness; if I had trusted to his good sense of consistency and right, instead of my own violence, he would have treated her with the contempt she deserved."

"I knew nothing of any violence."

"Of course you did not. Outsiders rarely know what sights and sounds the domestic hearth witnesses."

"You didn't attempt to give him a taste of the lash, as you did Fan?" said Louisa laughing.

"No; my violence with him was all in words, and yet that is bad enough for a husband. Many men I believe would prefer stripes of the two."

"That might be."

"I didn't consider that the exhibition of my unlovable qualities was so much gained on her side; that my sulkiness and silence contrasted extremely unfavorably with her cheerful humor; that my selfishness, my everlasting desire to be pleased and waited on, was so different from her constant service and attendance, and desire to please, that no human heart could help being charmed with it."

"And what do you design to do?"

"Make him all the reparation in my power, which will be little, though enough to show my motive and good will."

"I hope that he will be satisfied now," said Louisa, "and not want to take another wife. It is such a common thing, when the barriers are once overleaped, to keep on, that I fear he will aspire to increase the number."

"If he is lost to me," said Mrs. Stillman; "if I cannot win him back, why it won't make much difference."

"Win him back! mother; how strangely you talk. Of course you can't undo the marriage ceremony which has been performed between them, and I can't see, under the circumstances, what he can ever be to you again."

Mrs. Stillman, sen., was about to reply, when a sudden and violent rap at the door engaged her attention.

The friendly "come in" was answered by the entrance of Harmer. He was evidently in great haste.

"What's the matter?" demanded Louisa, the first word.

He looked first at her, and then at the old lady.

"You come with bad news; what is it?" said Mrs. Stillman, sen.

"Your husband is lying at the point of death, and wishes to see you."

"At the point of death, and wishes to see me?" she repeated mechanically, as if unable to comprehend the full meaning of the words.

"Such is the fact," said Harmer. "He is in great distress, and able to converse only a minute at a time."

"Has he been sick long?" inquired Louisa, while the old lady was trying to find her bonnet and shawl.

"No. He went out this afternoon to gather roots, and found one very large, and looking so good, that he tasted it, and finally ate nearly the whole. It proves to be a mortal poison, and he cannot survive the effects."

Mrs. Stillman, with the first knowledge of her husband's danger, had lost all her presence of mind; and her eager, anxious haste, as is usual in such cases, defeated her purpose of immediate departure. She had flown to the cupboard for her bonnet.

"Why, mother, you don't keep your bonnet in the cupboard," said Louisa, scarcely able to repress a smile. "Here, sit down—you are trembling, now, so that you can hardly stand. I will get your things. Don't suffer yourself to be overcome."

Louisa, whose cool head and practised hand soon made the necessary preparations, concluded to go with them.

"Your husband is there now," said Harmer. "I called, on my way here, and informed him of the situation of his father."

As they approached the house, several persons were coming and going, while lights were glancing about, and now and then a deep, heavy groan indicated the mortal agony of the sufferer within.

"He is not yet dead?" whispered Harmer to an attendant beside the door.

The person shook his head, and Mrs. Stillman drew near, but her tottering limbs refused her support, and she fell heavily across the bed.

"Room! room!" cried a bystander; "a lady has fainted."

But she did not faint.

15

"My husband! Oh, my husband! can you ever forgive me?" she faintly murmured.

He answered not, for he was seized that moment with a frightful paroxysm of pain. His features grew livid; great drops of cold sweat started from his forehead, as intense agony scorched and racked each shuddering limb. It passed over in a moment, however, and he spoke and smiled at the recognition of his wife, and then requested all but her to leave the room. Two or three of the elders hesitated, saying that he was not in his right mind, and did not understand the purport of his language.

"He is in his right mind," said Harmer. "He is just coming to his senses, I believe," glancing at Fanny, who sat near the head of the bed. "He wishes to converse privately with his lawful wife. Will you go, or must I put you out?" he continued, while they still lingered.

"Leave us alone!" shrieked the dying man, starting up in his bed; for that moment the agony returned.

They rose and left the room, all but Fan.

"You, too," he said, motioning to her.

She obeyed mechanically, casting a look of hate and contempt on the favored wife.

And the two were left alone with God.

What transpired; what words were spoken; what tears shed; the bliss and agony of that meeting, reconciliation, and parting, it is not in the power of my weak pen to describe. When the attendants again entered the apartment, Mrs. Stillman was kneeling by the bed in silent prayer; and with him the bitterness of death had passed. The wild and burning agony that, an hour before, coursed like fire through his veins, had been succeeded by a torpid numbness, the precursor of immediate dissolution. A tranquil smile had settled over his countenance, and he seemed like one falling into a pleasant slumber.

"Have you nothing to say to me, father?" inquired Fanny, approaching the bed.

He neither opened his eyes, nor answered her inquiry, and soon breathed his last.

CHAPTER XXXVII.

A SCENE.

MRS. DALLAS, we have already said, was disposed to meet and anticipate trouble. There was no evil that flesh is heir to, that she had not apprehended as likely to fall on herself or her family. If the children were playing out of doors, she was in a state of nervous expectancy that they would be bit, or poisoned, or charmed by toads, spiders, or snakes. She never enjoyed a visit or a ride, on account of the liability of their house to take fire, or for fear that the children would tumble from the windows, or fall down the well, or experience some other accident, of which there was not a particle of danger.

But now, everything else was forgotten in the probability that her husband would take another wife.

"But what makes you think so?" inquired Mrs. Merry, to whom she had been unburdening her mind. "He is no likelier to marry again than my husband, and I have scarcely ever given the subject a thought."

"Oh, but he is, Mrs. Merry—a great deal likelier!"

"Why so?"

"Because your husband is devotedly attached to you—everybody can see that."

"I never thought that he was."

"You didn't?—that is strange."

"But Mrs. Binder, whose husband has just married his fourth wife, informed me that Mr. Binder was never so clever, and so fond of her, as when he contemplated a new marriage."

"The hypocrite!" said Mrs. Dallas. "But I know perfectly well, that my husband will marry another. I am well satisfied that he has already decided on the person."

"You are?"

"To be sure I am. I have noticed his looks and glances all cast in a certain direction. Isn't it too bad, when I have borne him so many children; and Mrs. Hope declares that they are the most beautiful flock of little ones that she ever beheld."

Mrs. Merry smiled blandly, and inquired who was the person favored with Mr. Dallas's regards.

"That great, ugly, heathenish-looking thing, who goes sailing about with a red shawl and bonnet," said Mrs. Dallas.

"What, Polly High?"

Mrs. Dallas nodded her head mysteriously.

"Well, I don't wonder so much that you are worried, if that is the case," said Mrs. Merry. "Why, I shouldn't never have thought it. Such a low-lived, vulgar creature; and such a bad reputation, too! I wonder what the world is coming to, when respectable men marry such women?"

"Respectable men," said Mrs. Dallas, sharply, "no respectable man would marry more than one woman; I don't call my husband respectable, I don't think there's a respectable man in Utah; I know well enough that there isn't."

"There are several men in Utah who remain true to their first wife."

"But how long will their truth continue,—till they can get other wives, and not a moment longer. Women are getting scarce in Utah, the best ones have already left the market. I heard they were about to send to California for a fresh supply."

" Of what ?"

" Women, to be sure."

" Abominable !" said Mrs. Merry, lifting her hands and eyes. Mrs. Dallas put on a patient, resigned expression ; " I long ago made up my mind," she said, " to bear it the best that I could, but when I think of that smirking, hateful creature, with her red dress and bonnet, my blood fairly boils."

" How long is it since you first ascertained that Mr. Dallas was paying attention to her ?"

" I cannot exactly tell, but not very long."

This conversation continued for some time, and finally Mrs. Dallas began to weep, Mrs. Merry tried to soothe and quiet her, which only caused her to weep the harder. Another neighbor came in, who of course received intimation of the astounding fact, that Mr. Dallas was about being married to Polly High.

" Well now, if that don't beat all, Polly High—who would ever have thought of such a thing ; I don't wonder that you are nearly killed about it," said this Job's comforter, " but really, much as I would like to, I cannot stay to condole with you," and the good neighbor walked off to unburden her budget of news ; Mrs. Merry soon followed, and Mrs. Dallas was left a lone to receive her husband.

Though this woman had not the least ground for the suspicion or conjecture that preyed on her mind, and actually made her life miserable, she had communicated it to her friends in such a manner, that they received it as a settled fact, and told it as such ; everybody wondered at it ; the women raved, but the men laughed, and said that the intended bride deserved a good husband. Polly was certainly a favorite with the male portion of the community, which sufficiently accounts for the horror she inspired in their spouses.

"If my husband was to marry such a thing as that," said one, a sort of virago, "I'd actually take the butcher-knife to both of 'em, that I would."

"No you wouldn't," said the husband, "I'd take care that you didn't hurt her."

"But I would hurt her,—if you don't believe what I say, just try it."

"That's what I'm going to ; if she wasn't spoke for, I'd go straight there now."

"Maybe you'd be preferred to Dallas, I'd go and see," said the wife, mockingly.

"Guess I'd better," he said, and rising, he took down his hat from the peg where it hung near the door, and went out whistling a Mormon melody :

"Charley had a buxom wife,
Charley thought he'd take another."

Walking down the street, he saw Dallas just returning home.

"The women are all in hot water about you," he said, approaching the other.

"About me, what about me ?"

"Why, because you're going to marry that High gal."

"High gal, I don't understand you."

"You needn't look so dreadful innocent," said Poorly, bursting into a loud laugh, "I never seed a feller sham astonishment so d—— natural before, in my life."

"There's no sham about it, I am astonished, and no mistake ; what is it that you have heard ?"

"Ha'n't I told you ?"

"No, you've been hinting at something that I know no more about than the man in the moon."

"It came from your wife at any rate."

"What did ?"

"That you and Polly High were going to be married."

"My wife never told that."

"She did, though."

"Who did she tell it to?"

"Mrs. Merry, and I don't know who else."

"I can't imagine why she would tell such a story as that," said Dallas, "you must have been misinformed."

"It strikes me," said Poorly, "that you need another wife; it would certainly save you a good deal of running about after hired girls; your wife always wants to keep one, don't she?"

"Yes, she would have one continually if she could."

"Then, all you have to do is to get another wife; she'll work for her keep, which will be much cheaper than hiring girls; then you'll have the pleasure of her society—on the whole it will be a first rate plan."

"Like enough," said Dallas turning his face and his feet towards home.

Dallas had never seriously thought of marrying another wife before in his life. True, he lived in a community where the thing was common, but one woman seemed determined to make him the patriarch of a numerous flock, and now it occurred to him that it would be an act of benevolence to the overburdened wife to bring in another to share her labors and responsibilities. It would be much better than to depend on hired girls, with little chance of ever getting one to stay more than a day or two, it certainly would, and he walked towards home full of the new idea.

"And suppose my wife does find fault with it," he mentally ejaculated, "she's apt to find fault and worry about nothing, so that on the whole, it won't make much difference, she'll get used to it, and be pleased with it, especially when she sees its advantages. Then, when she was sick there would be somebody to nurse her, without my spending all the time of her illness in looking for help. If the baby was cross, there would be somebody to assist in taking care of it. Upon the whole I think that the plan would be a good one." He could not decide to mention the matter to his wife, however. " I know just how she'll do," he continued, " cry and cough, snivel, and blow her nose, that's the way she always works it ; I never know whether she'll be pleased or not, though the chances are against it. She's for ever meeting trouble and expecting it, even when there's no likelihood of its coming, so, of course, I shan't make much account of her opposition one way nor t'other."

Mrs. Dallas, as usual, was weeping when her husband entered the house. He was naturally a lively, volatile man, and the sight of her tears almost sickened him. Not because he was hard-hearted or unfeeling, or indifferent to her sorrow, when she really had occasion to grieve. But tears and murmurs and apprehensions of evil, when perpetually indulged in, weary and disgust the best of husbands.

Dallas had found his wife in tears, probably twenty times, during the last two weeks. At first he kindly and affectionately inquired, " What was the matter ?"

" Nothing," accompanied by a great sob.

" Was she sick ?"

" No," with another sob.

" Did she want anything ?"

Another " no," and another sob.

" Then what did ail her ?"

" Nothing," again.

" But I know better ; something is the matter ; either tell what it is or quit crying."

" She was sorry if people couldn't have the privilege of shedding tears whenever they chose. She had long known that husbands wished to rule the tongues of their wives, but had hoped that the privilege of weeping would never be meddled with or infringed."

After this rebuke, Dallas questioned her no more. She wept, or let it alone; and he said nothing. He whistled, or sang, or read, while she sat sobbing; but, on the evening already mentioned, he naturally gave way to a burst of impatience.

"I shall make it a bargain with my second wife that she never weeps. I am getting to hate the very sight of tears," he said. "It's a mystery to me what good it can do women to be always crying about nothing."

Mrs. Dallas sobered up sufficiently to remark, that "men were not expected to understand the cause of a woman's tears."

"And faith, I never want to understand them," he answered.

"No one supposes that you do; but when is this madam to make her appearance?"

"Pretty soon, I imagine, if you don't stop this everlasting snivel. I'm tired to death seeing it. I can't have a minute's rational conversation with you once a month, and, as for anything like mirth, I might as well expect a grave-yard to laugh."

"Your cruelty is killing me," she sobbed.

"My cruelty killing you; you are killing yourself, more like, by this foolish way you have got of grieving over imaginary troubles. What is it that I have done?"

She made no answer.

"Tell me, madam, what it is that I have done."

Still silent.

"Well, I shall tell you what I am going to do, and that quickly, too. I'm going to marry another wife. I will have somebody to chat and converse with when I come home—somebody that will look on the bright side of things, and not try to plague and discourage me as you have done."

"I have not tried to plague and discourage you."

"Well, you know that it does plague me to always find you weeping about nobody knows what. I want a wife for her society, but heaven knows that utter loneliness were preferable to constant tears."

"I presume that your next wife will entertain you much better than I can hope to."

"It is hopeful that she will better than you have."

"Especially while she is a new thing."

"New or old, I never like this crying over imaginary evils."

"But the evil isn't imaginary."

"What is it, then?"

"Why, ha'n't you just told me that you were going to marry another? and wouldn't that make any woman cry?"

"But I never thought of marrying again before to-day, and you have been crying, off and on, this two weeks, though as to the matter of that, you have always been at it."

Again Mrs. Dallas was silent.

"Who told you that I was going to marry another," he inquired, presently.

"Nobody."

"Then how did you know anything about it? Such a thought had never entered my head, till I understood that you had reported it for a fact."

"That was a mistake."

"What did you say, then?"

"That I suspected it, feared it; nothing more."

"Didn't you say that I had been paying attention to Polly High?"

"Her name was mentioned, not exactly that way, though."

"How then?"

"I don't know what necessity there is for repeating the whole of our conversation. Indeed, I can't remember half that was said."

"A fine gossip, no doubt ; but I must be entertained with silence and tears. However, since you have made me think of it, I have concluded that it would be a good plan."

"I made you think of it—think of what ?"

"Of having another wife."

Mrs. Dallas opened her mouth to speak.

"Not one word," he said ; "you are always a prophet of evil—always expecting misfortune of some kind or another, and I wish you to hear me."

"I have no desire to hear you," she answered ; "and what is more, I will not hear you, if you think or attempt to excuse this diabolical system of polygamy."

"Capital," said Dallas, laughing ; "your anger becomes you mightily. Well, a woman may storm and rave and scold just as much as she pleases, so she won't cry and snivel ; I'll think it first rate. But now, wife, I wan't you to consider this thing, and how nice and sisterly it would be to have some one to help you always—how nice it would be for me."

"No doubt of that," interposed the wife.

"I shouldn't have to be running all over the country, vainly endeavoring to hire girls."

"You'd have to run more than you do now, like-enough. You'd have to hire girls to wait on both wives instead of one."

"No, I shouldn't ; because one wife could wait on the other."

"You wouldn't expect me to wait on your other wife ?"

"If she needed it."

"You'd expect something, then, that wouldn't ever transpire ; I'd never lift a finger to save her from perishing ;" and the sparkling eyes and animated countenance of Mrs. Dallas, told how much she was under the influence of passionate resentment.

"Ah," retorted Dallas, "wives can be managed, if husbands are resolute. I should teach you better than that."

"Doubtful."

"Besides, when one wife's mad, another would think it for her interest to be pleased, when one scolded, the other would laugh, when one sulked and cried, the other would chat and be merry; so you would be certain of fair weather from some quarter; a blessing not often experienced here."

"What did you ever marry me for?" said Mrs. Dallas, energetically, "I never sought your attentions, never run after you through heat and cold, never coaxed and implored to be blessed with your love," and she looked him sternly in the face. "I knew then that 1 shouldn't suit you long, knew that our dispositions were so different there could be nothing reciprocal between them, but you persisted in believing the contrary. I shed tears even, while consenting to be your wife, because I felt that our married life would be unhappy. I shed tears on our wedding day, because the same evil presentiment haunted me. You say I have met trouble, though that would have been impossible, if the trouble had not also met me. I have experienced the very evils that I anticipated, and you, the author of them, would refuse me even the luxury of tears."

"Because I have become weary of seeing you weep."

"And don't you suppose that I am weary of weeping, weary of having anything to weep about?"

Dallas sat several moments in deep meditation, "I see it all now," he said at length; "our marriage has been unhappy, because I didn't sufficiently consider your temper and inclination in the first place, but now it is too late to repent. The ties between us can never be obliterated without crime on one side or the other. We must make the most of our bargain, and to do this, it is absolutely necessary for each one to conform his or her disposition to that of the other. I have had a pretty hard trial sometimes, harder than you may imagine, to buffet along with the world, and provide the comforts of life for my family, but I have always tried to keep up my spirits, to look on the bright side of everything, and to hope for the best. Neither have I ever distressed or troubled you with forebodings of evil ; I have never come home with a cloud on my countenance, but you have met my smiles with tears, my hopes with presentiments, my delights with anticipated ills. When to-day has' been bright, you have lost all the pleasure of it, because there might be clouds to-morrow, and thus it has always been."

Mrs. Dallas sat perfectly silent, her face buried in her hands. She could not help feeling that his accusations were, in a measure, true, and that she had wearied him with tears and reproaches, for which there was really no occasion, but pride prevented a concession of that kind, and she only said, after a long silence :

"You ought not to have been so importunate to marry a woman so reprehensible in temper and conduct."

"I know it," he replied, gloomily, "I have often thought so lately."

"I hope you will look out better next time, and that the coming bride will be a paragon of perfection," she said bitterly.

"And so do I."

Again there was a silence of several minutes, at length he spoke :

"But, my dear wife, can't you restrain, in some degree, these faults of temper which are so aggravating to me ? Can't you cease this everlasting weeping, and meet me, when I return from my toils at night, with a smiling countenance ? Can't you let me see that my efforts to make you happy are duly appreciated, and not utterly and totally of no avail ?"

"I shall make no promises," she answered, "because I am not confident of my strength to keep them."

Dallas arose without uttering another word, and left the room. One week from that day, he brought Polly High to share the burdens and responsibilities of his household.

CHAPTER XXXVIII.

EMILY AGAIN.

"HAVE you seen anything of Emily?" inquired Harmer one day, as I met him along the street.

"Seen Emily? no, not for several days."

"Well, I'd like to know where she is, anyhow."

"Why, is she lost?"

"Something has gone of her."

"You astonish me; isn't she at Mr. Stillman's?"

"Louisa knows nothing about her. She says that it is nearly a week since Emily started to go to your house, and she has seen nothing of her since. Mrs. Beardsley is certain that the Indians have carried her off, and only wonders that they have not kidnapped somebody before."

"Have there been any Indians about?"

"Not very recently; and what would the Indians want of her?"

"The Indians are friendly, they wouldn't spirit her away."

Mrs. Bradish approached, "What are you discussing, good people?" she inquired.

"I will answer that question by asking another; have you seen anything of Emily?"

"Not lately."

"Who has, I wonder."

"I can't tell, indeed. Is she among the missing?"

"So it seems."

"I saw her last week going out to botanize in the valley, and I well recollect that our Prophet entertained some Indians that very day, because I saw them coming out of his house just after I parted with Emily."

"Are you sure of this?"

"I am."

"Then Mrs. Beardsley must be right; the Indians have probably carried her off, thinking to obtain a ransom. We must find out to what tribe they belonged. Can you recollect what day you saw them?"

Mrs. Bradish thought she could recollect, and volunteered moreover to go at once to B——m, and inform him of the circumstance.

Curious to hear and see for myself, I decided to accompany her. He received us graciously, listened with apparent astonishment to our narration, but seemed perfectly at ease with respect to the Indians; supposed that Emily was well enough off, probably visiting somewhere, and would return when she got ready, did not think there was any probability that a misfortune could have happened to her, and counselled us to have faith, and all would go well.

Mrs. Bradish was evidently dissatisfied with his cool manner of dismissing the subject.

"Whatever you may think to the contrary notwithstanding, I am perfectly well convinced myself, that the Indians are at the bottom of the mischief, and it seems strange to me that you refuse to inform us of their tribe, or the name of their chief."

"Because, madam, I fear that something might be said or done, that would embroil us with these people. It is for our interest to keep them friendly, and as there is scarcely a possibility that they know aught of the matter, I prefer that the names and tribe of my visitors should remain a mystery."

"But somebody must know," said Mrs. Bradish.

"You have no evidence even of that."

"Then what has gone of her?"

"That is a question which I am unable to answer, though I have no apprehension on her account. She is able to take care of herself."

"It is possible that she has wandered off, and got lost among the mountains."

"Oh! I guess not," replied B——m coldly.

"At any rate, I shan't rest," said Mrs. Bradish, "until I find out where she is. I can't. She was my particular friend, so good, and so beautiful; excuse me, sire, but I fancied that the tender regards you entertained for her, would have made you sensibly alive to her danger."

"Her danger? I am not apprehensive that she is in danger," he said. "You have no faith."

I regarded the countenance of this man, so calm and sinister in its expression, and mentally inquired, if it could be possible that his indifference and unconcern arose from a knowledge of the place of her concealment. But I could scarcely find it in my heart to believe that such depravity actually existed, and forbore to mention or encourage such a suspicion.

Leaving the habitation of the Prophet, who at parting exhorted us not to grieve or worry ourselves, for God and the angels would take care of our innocent and youthful sister, and doubtless restore her to us unharmed, though Mrs. Bradish the moment we were out of hearing, declared that he had used us shabbily, and that she didn't like it, we found Harmer waiting to hear the result of the interview.

"Nothing! nothing!" said Mrs. Bradish, anticipating his inquiries. "He refuses to tell us anything, though I marvel whether he knows himself; takes the matter amazing cool, thinks she'll come back when she gets ready, and such like."

"The villain!" ejaculated Harmer; "but I have found out, and no thanks to him. Charley Moore saw Emily go into the valley to gather flowers, the Indians were a tribe of the Utahs, their chief's name is Walker, and the lands they infest are in the immediate neighborhood of the Wahsatch mountains; I start to go there this night."

"Do nothing rashly," I said, for the thought forced itself on me, that Emily might be found nearer home, but having no evidence I feared to communicate my suspicions.

"At what time will you start?"

"When the moon rises, which is near midnight."

"Well," said Mrs. Bradish, glancing at the sun, "between now and then, I will visit every house to alarm the inhabitants and make inquiries. You stop at Mr. Ward's. I will be there to report the result."

He assented to the proposal, and she departed immediately to execute her plan. Returning home, I met Louisa dreadfully agitated. "Have you seen aught of Emily?" she inquired anxiously.

"I have not."

"It beats all; I supposed her to be at your house until a short time ago. I thought, too, that she was making rather a long visit, and several times had it in my mind to come round there, but something hindered. Harmer, however, grew impatient, and started off to hunt her up, and I guess it was well he did."

"She came to our house, I suppose, in my absence, and then went to the valley to gather flowers."

"And has not been seen since?"

"Not that we can ascertain."

"She must have been kidnapped by the Indians."

"Or lost among the mountains."

"In which case we shall never see her again," said Louisa, bursting into tears.

"B——m says that if we have faith all will be well."

"How did he take it?" inquired Louisa, wiping her eyes.

"Cool as a cucumber, and even opposed our taking any measures to discover her."

"Why, that's strange."

"It looked so to me, after the regard that he has professed for her."

"But as she has always refused his addresses, he may be indifferent to her misfortunes, through a motive of revenge."

"Or, or he may know more about the matter than he chooses to tell."

Louisa looked surprised, and a gleam of intelligence passed over her features.

We separated, and I went directly home. Of course my thoughts were with Emily, and her unaccountable absence. Then, too, the calm indifference of B——m would rise to my memory, and overwhelm me with astonishment. Notwithstanding my endeavors to the contrary, I would find myself mentally forming conjectures as to his possible implication in the affair. Mr. Ward said that the Indians were probably the perpetrators of the outrage, or that she had become lost and bewildered in the deep intricacies of the hills and valleys. He related instances of people having become lost even amid the most familiar scenes. "One lady of his acquaintance had started to visit a friend, who lived on the opposite side of a narrow piece of woods. She travelled some distance along, as she thought, the accustomed paths, when she came in sight of a house that looked both strange and familiar. She noticed likewise the cows, the poultry, and the general appearance of things, how much they looked like those belonging to her, and, having become conscious by this time that something was wrong, she determined to enter, when, to her infinite surprise, she ascertained that it was her own home. Instances of females thus becoming lost were of almost daily occurrence, and it would not be in the least astonishing if such was the case with Emily."

"A week in the mountains ; she can hardly be living then."

"Never indulge in such forebodings as that," said Mr. Ward. "She could live many weeks in the woods, as the weather is very mild, and there seems to be an abundance of roots."

"Which she would scarcely dare to eat after their fatal effect on Mr. Stillman."

"Hunger would banish fear, I imagine," he answered, just as Mrs. Bradish came in.

My first words were :

"What success ?"

"None at all," she replied. "Nobody has seen or heard tell of her that I can find."

"And what do the people think ?"

"Some say that the Indians have taken her, others that she is lost in the woods. Of course there will be different opinions. A party of men are going out to-night to look for her—I never saw them so excited."

Harmer soon came in, accompanied by Buckley and Charley Moore. Buckley had made preparations to depart for California across the Sierra Nevada, but postponed his journey until the fate of Emily was ascertained. Consequently, they had both decided to accompany Harmer. They were well armed with rifles, pistols and knives, and provided with an abundance of ammunition.

"God speed and prosper your way," said Mrs. Bradish.

There was a hearty response of "amen" from all assembled, which comprised quite a number of young and old. It had been decided that the young men should go with Harmer, as the

Indian trail led directly through the valley, where she had last been seen. They were furnished with horns, whistles and dogs, and were evidently sanguine of success.

"I doubt if her strength would hold out to travel a great way," said one.

"We shall find her not far off, but overcome with fatigue, and sleeping in a cave," said another.

"She may have found some Indian settlement," suggested a third.

At length the moon showed her broad bright disk over the adjacent hills, and the farewells being said, the party set off.

CHAPTER XXXIX.

MARRIAGES.

"A VISITOR, ma," said our youngest daughter, now grown to be a woman.

"Indeed! Who is it?"

"Mrs. Melton, I believe."

The lady soon entered, habited in deep black.

I involuntarily glanced at her unusual apparel. She noticed this, and not being a person to stand on ceremony, immediately began the relation of her troubles.

"I have dressed in mourning, Mrs. Ward," she said, "and yet no outward form or ceremonial of sorrow can shadow forth the poignant anguish that weighs down my heart. It is dreadful to lay a child in the damp cold earth, yet more so, much more so, to have her immolated on the altar of Mammon. And such marriages as are tolerated and approved here seem to me actually horrible. I have argued and reasoned with Mr. Melton, and used my utmost endeavors to get him to relent, but all in vain. He is determined to sell the girls to Weldy, and nothing but death will prevent the consummation of the sacrifice," and the poor mother began to weep.

"What do the girls say about it?" I inquired.

"Henriette is nearly distracted. Margaret said a good deal at first, but finding that her father was resolved, she relapsed into her gloomy and moody habit. She has all along been subject to fits of melancholy, and I suppose that they will return on her now with accumulated strength."

"We never knew that she was subject to such spells."

"Few persons do know it, because we always tried to keep it still, but it will have to become public now, if she's going into all that family. It all comes from the cruelty of her father."

"How so?"

"He refused to let her marry an amiable young man, who was deeply attached to her, and whose passion she reciprocated. It nearly proved her death at the time, and she has never entirely recovered from its effects."

"But why did Mr. Melton refuse to permit her to marry him?"

"Because he was not able to bestow a valuable gift in return."

"I can scarcely understand what the man must be thinking of."

"Of money, to be sure—money, that everlastingly fills his thoughts by day, and his dreams by night. He looks on his daughters as legitimate subjects of speculation, because, he says, that they have cost him so much. Heaven knows how, and it would puzzle any mortal to tell. Henriette knelt at her father's feet, and implored him with tears of agony to have pity upon her, and save her from such a dreadful fate, but he spurned and reproached her, accused her of ingratitude in not consenting willingly to his choice, especially when it brought such valuable gifts to his hands. At this she grew exasperated, and threatened to leave his house and protection, and go off among the Indians. He replied that he would find her, if he had to search the world over, and that she should be married to Weldy, if she went to the altar in chains. Henriette's temper being fully aroused, she asserted that they were all barbarians; that the religion of Mormon was from the devil; that polygamy was an abominable institution, and that though they might compel her to stand up with the man she hated, she would never by word or deed signify her assent to the contract—never.

"'Then you dare to disobey me?' he said.

"'I dare to disobey any man, who seeks to make me a slave, and whose tyranny would embitter my whole life. When you ask me to marry that hideous old man, who looks like an ogre, and acts like a fool—a man whose home is shared already by a dozen wives, good, bad, and indifferent, two or three of whom are Indians, others Spanish, and several Dutch—is it possible that you expect me to consent willingly—more horrible still, when this same old man that wishes to become my husband, desires to take my sister in the same day—to purchase us, giving in exchange horses and cows, can you expect us to conform, unless by actual compulsion?'

"'Henriette,' said Mr. Melton, 'you are certainly old enough to know that all this is folly. It makes no difference how many wives he has. Solomon married a king's daughter, though he had taken wives from all the nations about Judah. Do you fancy yourself superior to that princess of the royal house of Egypt. I am really ashamed of you.'

"'And I am ashamed of my father,' interposed Margaret, vehemently, 'ashamed that any man, professing to be influenced by a divine spirit, should make the marriage of his daughters an occasion of enriching himself ; and such a marriage, too ; my soul is sickened by the thought of it.'

"I told the girls subsequently that, though their father remained inexorable, it was possible that they might hope for release from the generosity of their lover, if such a heart could be considered capable of such a feeling.

"'I would just as soon,' said Henriette, 'trust to the compassion of a hungry lion.'

"Margaret, however, said that she was willing to make the attempt, and volunteered to commence the subject herself.

"'Here comes Weldy, now,' said Henriette, looking from the window.

"'Now, then, is your time, girls, now that your father is absent,' I exclaimed, 'and Heaven grant that you may soften his iron heart.'

"Weldy came in, saluted the girls with apparent fondness, made an attempt to compliment their beauty, which proved exceedingly awkward, and then inquired for Mr. Melton.

"'He is not at home, Brother Weldy ; and we consider his absence rather fortunate than otherwise on the present occasion. We wish to appeal to your good sense and generous feelings, as a man of honor and principle, to withdraw your suit for the hands of these girls, who are too young to assume the responsibilities of married life, and altogether unsuitable to your circumstances.'

"'Excuse me, madam,' he answered, 'but I must dissent from your opinions. These young ladies, in my house, at least, will have no responsibilities to assume. My establishment is well governed and directed, by older and competent heads. Nothing will be required of them, but gentleness and obedience, and that deference which youth is always expected to render to seniority.'

"Here I informed him that my girls had always been accustomed to have their own way.

"'Yes,' said Margaret, 'and I am the last one to bow to hoary hairs, when they cover a fool's skull, as is frequently the case.'

"'I shall neither be gentle nor obedient,' said Henriette, 'because I loathe and despise both you and your wives. I won't do nothing that you wish me to, not a single thing. I expect you want me to be a sort of nurse and waiter, to run after your thirty young 'uns, but I shan't do it, I shan't touch the squalling, yelping brats. I never could bear 'em, I can't yet, and I won't have nothing to do with 'em.'

"Weldy laughed at this, a regular loud horse laugh. He did not seem the least bit angry, as I expected that he would, but fairly shook the rafters with a hearty roar.

"'No, my beauty,' he said, 'I don't expect any such thing. You're much too slender and delicate to be hiking a great child about; I know that very well. No one shall impose such duties on you, and I shall not wish you to do anything contrary to your pleasure, rest assured of that.'

"'And don't you wish me to do anything contrary to my pleasure?' she inquired, quickly.

"But Weldy was not to be caught that way.

"'I shall not, my dear, when you are mine—legally mine.'

"'Mr. Weldy, I beg, I entreat of you, to give up all design of marrying us,' said Margaret. 'You cannot conceive how much, how much and how deeply, we loathe and abhor the situation you offer us. Our ages, your circumstances, everything precludes the possibility of happiness for either in that state. We cannot love you, neither can you love us, and marriage without love must be unhappy.'

"'Pshaw, half the marriages in the world are consummated from motives of policy, or expediency,' said Weldy, and then he went on to argue the point, that 'marrying for love was an antiquated notion, altogether unsuitable for this utilitarian age; that he had married for love once, and but once, and that the wife he then obtained had proved the least lovable of any one of the dozen, and he thanked heaven for the lesson it afforded him; that, generally speaking, those marriages in which there was the least of what was romantically and sillily called love, were always the happiest; and that, for his part, he anticipated the greatest amount of real, solid, steady-going bliss from his approaching nuptials, with two such beautiful and accomplished ladies.'

"'But, Mr. Weldy, can't you, won't you give us up? Won't you tell father that you have changed your mind, and no longer want us? Do, do have pity upon us, and we will bless you for ever.'

"'Have pity upon you, have pity upon you, my charmer, and why should I pity one so young and beautiful. I love, I adore, I admire you; I would pity you and myself, too, as to that matter, if anybody else was to have you, because no one can be so sensible of your attractions as myself. Nobody else could ever prize you as you deserve to be prized,' and he attempted to embrace her.

"Margaret sprang from his outstretched arms with a scream, and Henriette reminded him that he had just declared that he never made but one love match.

"'Which was the truth,' he answered, 'though it's a clear case, that in marrying you, any man would have to marry for love, because every man must love you at first sight.'

"These silly and unmeaning compliments greatly disgusted the girls, and Margaret called out, 'Weldy, I believe that you are a fool.'

"'If such is the case, it's all attributable to you,' he answered. 'What is the penalty when a girl turns the brain of a man?'

"'Whether or not your brain is turned, Mr. Weldy, I believe that my girls are perfectly innocent of it. Here you are, old enough to be their father, and with a dozen wives already, dealing your balderdash compliments. I am sick of it, sick of such nonsense, and impertinence, and folly. I had hoped something from your generosity, but I see that I was mistaken in the man.'

"'Really, Madam,' he replied, 'you make this marriage with your daughters very expensive; I have come down handsomely to your husband. Did you desire a new shawl or dress?'

"I was so offended at this pretended misunderstanding of my wishes," continued Mrs. Melton, "that I was half inclined to take the broom and drive him from the house."

"I wonder that you didn't," I remarked; "such impertinence!"

"Wasn't it though, really outrageous; when all I desired was to preserve my daughters from such an unnatural union?"

"He just said it to tantalize you," I exclaimed.

"I knew that very well, and replied, that though my shawls and dresses were less stylish than might be, I regarded them as of no consequence, compared to the happiness of my children; and then he had the impudence to assure me that their felicity would be secured by marriage with him.

"'Why, Madam,' he said, 'I am astonished at your objections, they are so trivial and frivolous. You have nothing to say against my moral character, or that I am ineligible in a pecuniary point of view, because you are aware that on all these points I am good as the best. But you talk about age, as if many young wives hadn't been perfectly happy with old husbands, and as if what had happened once, couldn't happen again. I only expect them to honor and obey, and as I am not a man of sentiment, I shall be perfectly satisfied with that. Well as I love them, I neither ask, nor wish them to love me. All is, they mustn't love somebody else, that would set the house on fire at once.'

"A thought struck Margaret, and she said, 'Suppose we confess to you that we love another now?'

"'I should know the confession was false, because your father told me that you had never had a lover.'

"'Then my father told you a falsehood; mother, here, shall decide.'

"'You have, my child,' I answered, addressing Margaret; 'I don't know that Henriette ever had.'

"'Oh, well, it is nothing; all I ask you to do is to honor and obey me.'

"'And that I shall not do.'

"Again he set up a roaring, screaming laugh, in which nobody joined; when, greatly to our surprise and confusion, Mr. Melton entered the room.

"He looked rather astonished, and said, addressing Weldy; 'You, sir, must find my wife and daughters very good company.'

"'Oh, very good, charming; but don't you think they have been trying to make me believe that our intended marriage will be unhappy, and all that sort of thing.'

"Mr. Melton glanced angrily from one to the other; 'I have forbidden any such suppositions or conversations,' he said, 'and yet they persist in disobedience.'

"'Women have been willful and perverse since the days of Adam,' replied Weldy.

"'Then what do you want so many of them for?' I inquired.

"'Oh,' he answered with a leer, 'they are dear creatures, notwithstanding all their willfulness and perversity.'

"'And these stiff-necked and disobedient girls would refuse the honor you offer them,' said Mr. Melton, 'they deserve a severe punishment.'

"'No, don't punish them,' said Weldy, 'I wouldn't, on any

account, that a hair of their beautiful heads should be injured, much less for any contumely that they may offer me. Of course I am not worthy of them ; no one can be more sensible of his unworthiness, and for this reason, perhaps, more than any other, heaven has blessed me with so many wives, and seems to intend blessing me with more.'

" 'I should think,' said Margaret, ' that probably the other personage had more to do with it than heaven. Heaven only bestowed one wife on Adam in Paradise ; it would scarcely give a greater number to sinful men in their fallen state.'

" 'What do you know of such things ?' inquired Mr. Melton.

" 'I had ought to know something about them, considering the circumstances in which I am placed.'

" ' As for me, I think that the less a woman knows the better. Knowledge is not suitable for women, it makes them opinionative and consequential. They are not so easily governed, and the proper government of the women, is the foundation of all domestic peace.'

" Weldy laughed, and such a laugh, that his coarse ungainly features only looked uglier and more repulsive. ' You can know but little about women, however, you, whose domestic experience has been confined to the possession of only one wife.'

" ' But now I am going to turn over a new leaf,' said Mr. Melton, glancing at me, 'I have been married this afternoon.'

" ' Been married this afternoon, Oh, Lord !' screamed Margaret, ' what will come next.'

" ' Your own happy nuptials, I suppose,' said Weldy ; and going to Mr. Melton, he congratulated him on the prospect of happiness for the future, with a hearty shake of the hand ; said he was always glad to see his friends evince a determination to enjoy life, and finally concluded by asking who might be the happy bride."

"And was that the first intimation you received that your family was to have an addition?"

"The very first."

"And you didn't faint, nor grow sick?"

"Oh, no; I thought, even then, more of the horrible fate to which my children were destined, than of what misery might result to me, under any possible circumstances."

"Mr. Melton then condescended to inform us that, being likely to get rid of the burden of providing for his daughters, he fancied that he could support another wife in tolerable comfort, especially, as she possessed a good round sum of money, which was to be placed in his hands, at the expiration of a month.

"'Well, you are one lucky dog, anyhow,' said Weldy. 'Now, here I have to pay you for these girls, while you go right off and bargain for a wife who has money. That's the advantage of marrying a wife who has no relations.'

"'Ain't it, though?'

"'I reckon you'll be for getting another, won't you?'

"'Not at all unlikely, if I could come across one with money.'

"'You always look out for the main chance.'

"'Don't I? Well, who has a better right?'

"'Nobody.'

"And thus they continued talking for a long time," continued Mrs. Melton, "and I discovered that on the same day when my daughters were to leave home for the house of their husband, Mr. Melton designed to bring his bride to fill their place—their place, indeed, as if my heart can ever receive, or look upon her, with any feelings save those of dislike and contempt."

"I am astonished that Mr. Melton should take another wife. I did not even suppose that he would entertain the idea of such a thing."

"Why, Mrs. Ward, there is not a man in Utah, who has not seriously revolved in his mind the expediency of such a course. Of course, they must think of it, when it is made the basis of sermons and conversations. Men are continually inquiring of one another, what they think of it, how they like it, and all such questions. And Mr. Melton, if he imagines that another wife will add to his happiness, I am perfectly satisfied that he should try the experiment; but my poor, dear girls"—and the mother burst into tears.

"It is possible, Mrs. Melton," I said, "that your girls may be much happier than you anticipate, though it is not at all wonderful, that you, or any person of rightly-constituted mind, should regard such an incestuous connection with horror. Weldy, even now, seems less heartless than Mr. Melton; and I presume these girls might exercise twice the influence over him, that they could over their father. They are young and beautiful, and"—

"But the sin, Mrs. Ward—the wickedness of living in such a state; that is dreadful in my eyes; for, whatever they may say to the contrary, it is—it must be—a sin. I wish my daughters to be pure in heart; I brought them up to virtue, and now that this must be the consummation, almost drives me mad. Sometimes I have been tempted to act the part of the Roman matron, and at others, have been ready to arraign the justice of heaven, that thus permitted one portion of mankind to trample on the happiness and rights of the other."

"It is all, I suppose, for some wise end."

Mrs. Melton shook her head doubtingly, and soon after rose to take leave.

CHAPTER XL.

A CONSULTATION.

CONTRARY to the expectations of nearly all the village, the party who had accompanied Harmer in pursuit of Emily, returned, without having obtained any information of her. There was nothing in the valley to indicate that she had ever been there. There were no traces in the soft mud, by the brook-side ; neither broken flowers, nor shreds of garments. All concluded that, had she passed that way, there would have been something significant of the fact. Hence they determined to prosecute the search in another direction.

Mrs. Beardsley declared that she had known, all along, that they would not find her. To be sure, they wouldn't ; wild beasts, or Indians, or something else, had destroyed her, long before this time.

" May be not," said Mrs. Stillman, sen., who had taken up her residence with Louisa, since the death of her husband.

" If it had been Fan Simpkins (for I will never call her Stillman)," said Louisa, " I actually wouldn't have cared at all ; but Emily—so beautiful, and amiable, and innocent—for such a dreadful thing to befall her, almost makes me doubt the goodness of Providence."

" She must be somewhere," said Mrs. Stillman, sen. ; " because these fellows did not find her, is no proof that she has not been lost ; and even if Harmer does not discover her among the Indians, who were here that day, it will be no evidence to me, that she has not been kidnapped by some of them ;" and after delivering these quaint and incontrovertible opinions, the good lady felt as if she had discharged an important duty.

Mr. Stillman had formed a company of twenty men, with whom he intended to explore the gorges and ravines around the foot of the great Salt Lake, as he fancied that, becoming bewildered, she might have wandered off in that direction. The preparations were all made, and the party assembled, when a messenger arrived from B———m, forbidding them to depart, and ordering each man to go to his work. Mrs. Bradish was in the midst, encouraging the enterprise, and urging them not to abandon the prosecution of the search until they had found her; consequently, this sudden and summary arrest of a proceeding, that she considered just and necessary, filled her with the deepest indignation ; and, notwithstanding her deference for the Head of the Church, she was not slow to manifest her displeasure. The men were equally dissatisfied, but they stood around in sullen silence, while she advanced boldly up to the messenger, and demanded the reasons for so extraordinary a proceeding.

"He gave no reason, madam," said the messenger, "only that you were on a fool's errand ; that he would guarantee any pledge, that Emily was perfectly safe ; and that the men should go to work, instead of wandering about the woods."

" But how does he know that she is safe ?"

" He has had a revelation."

Mrs. Bradish shook her head, and looked as if she doubted it.

" What do you say ?" inquired one of the men, turning to Mr. Stillman, " are we going or not ?"

" I should go," said Mrs. Bradish decidedly ; "no one can entertain a greater respect for B———m than I do ; that is, in his legitimate sphere, as our spiritual leader ; but when it comes to interference with personal privileges, when he wishes to restrict us in the exercise of individual liberty, I hold that resistance is a necessary virtue."

Mr. Stillman said, that though he entertained the highest regard and deepest reverence for the lady who had just spoken, he was compelled to dissent from her opinion. That their spiritual leader was likewise their temporal governor, and that to disobey him in one respect, would show their want of confidence in his judgment and good sense.

"I give it up," said Mrs. Bradish, "who can tell? probably he knows more of Emily than we have imagined. It seems marvellous to me that he is so utterly indifferent to her fate."

"It may be best to wait till Harmer returns," suggested Mr. Ward, "he may bring some information of her, though I hardly expect it."

"But he may be gone two or three days yet," said a bystander, "and the exposure and hunger of two or three days more, may cost Emily her life, if she be not already dead."

"I move that we go, whether he wants us to or not," said another.

"So do I," ejaculated a third, "it is none of his business, no how."

"I don't know how it can be, we were not working for him."

"Go, go, by all means," said Mrs. Bradish, and she made a motion towards the windows of B———m that looked to me like snapping her fingers. Could it be in defiance? but no one will dispute that her resolution and independence of spirit were remarkable. "If you hesitate," she continued, "I will collect a party of women and go myself."

"A party of women, indeed, you'd all get lost," said one of the men; B———m, who could see from his windows the hesitancy of the company, came slowly forth, and approaching the group, accosted them in consolatory terms; something like the following:

"I can give you an earnest and hearty assurance, that our young sister is comfortably provided for, and what is more, that she has withdrawn from us voluntarily, and for reasons perfectly satisfactory to me, as they should be to you."

"But where is she?" "What be they?" "How do you know?" was anxiously inquired.

"Where she is, and what were her reasons for going away, are secrets which I am not permitted to reveal, and I know by the spirit that is in me, to read secret and hidden things."

"If that is the only way you know," said one, though in a low tone, "I wouldn't give much for the knowledge."

B——m had recently lost much of the prestige of his power and influence; his revelations had become too common and absurd to attract much notice, or win any confidence. Then, too, his character for lying, sensuality, and hypocrisy had disgusted many of the best men in the church; many wished to have him deposed, and some even went so far as to talk of it, but no measures had been taken to effect the purpose. True, he likewise had many friends, generally speaking, those who derived honor or profit from his elevation, or those who were connected by marriage with him.

It must be conceded, however, that much of the machinations against him was fomented by the animosity and envy of Lawrence. This man, whose character seemed a compound of mean duplicity and selfish cunning, took every occasion to enlarge on the faults and infirmities of his successful rival, descanted on his weaknesses, and actually turned his sermons, as well as his style of preaching into ridicule. When B——m appeared in public, he usually managed to be somewhere not far off, and he always made it a point to criticise most unmercifully the language and sentiments of his opponent. On the present occasion, he was standing in the midst, and this time with Irene leaning on his arm; they had, it seemed, been out walking together, and seeing the gathering, had approached to ascertain what was going on. They obtained the information that they desired from a bystander, when Lawrence began his remarks.

"And he forbids your going to look her up?"

"I believe so; he says that she is in safety."

"If he knows that, he must know where she is."

"He does, probably," suggested Irene, "I presume that he has her secreted somewhere in his house."

"Think so?"

"To be sure, I think so; if such is not the case, why is he so indifferent and unconcerned?"

"I will volunteer to lead a party to search the house, and see who is concealed in it," exclaimed Lawrence.

"No, no," cried several voices.

They had lost all confidence in B———m, it is true, but Lawrence was almost equally unpopular.

"I have not the least doubt," said Irene, "that this woman, whose absence has struck you all as something remarkable, is now confined in that hypocrite's dwelling, and I have good reasons for what I say."

"What be they?" "What be they?" demanded the listeners.

"I have not time to relate them, but if you wish to find Emily, follow my husband, and search that house."

During this scene, B———m stood like one amazed; his countenance changing from surprise to apprehension, from apprehension to anger. Two or three seemed inclined to second her proposal to search his house, though the most influential were evidently opposed to the perpetration of such a deed of violence. He was a skillful physiognomist, and the expression of the surrounding faces was not lost on him. He determined, therefore, to treat the accusations of Irene as the ravings of a maniac, and addressing one of his friends and confidential advisers, requested him to look after that woman, thus become suddenly insane. This request, made in a voice sufficiently loud to attract the attention of all assembled, caused them all to look round, and several women screamed at the bare supposition of being contiguous to a mad-woman.

"Who is it?" inquired Irene, "who is it he means?"

"Yourself," said Hyde, the designated friend, "come along with me."

"With you, I am not crazy."

"Certainly you talk like a crazy person, you must be taken care of," he replied.

Irene, who possessed little courage or resolution, was overwhelmed with astonishment and consternation; all she had ever heard or imagined of narrow cells, straight-waistcoats, chains and mad-house-scourges, flashed across her memory, as she clung shrieking to Lawrence, and entreated him to save her.

"No woman in her right mind, would ever give way to such unlikely and unaccountable suspicion. I received intimation that she was mad some time ago, though I have never before to-day seen any exemplification of it," said B———m, with a demeanor as cool and as calm as if nothing had happened.

"Take me home," said Irene, clinging to Lawrence. "Take me home; do, do."

"Take her home," said B———m authoritatively, "and keep her there. Home is the place for her; and that is not all, remember that I will not overlook or forget her insults, and if she puts herself in my way again, and stigmatizes me with such language another time, she will be taken care of in a manner that she won't fancy."

Irene hurried away trembling.

Mrs. Bradish, deeply as she was concerned for Emily, could not refrain from laughing heartily at the singular incident.

"What do you think of Irene's suspicion?" I said to her that evening, when we were in conversation about Emily.

"What do I think?" she answered.

"Yes; don't it seem to you, as if there might be a possibility that her conjecture is correct?"

She nodded affirmatively.

"It seems so to me, and everything tends to confirm the suspicion," I said.

"I shouldn't wonder at all, if Emily was confined in his house."

"Nor I either."

"I never thought of it, till a short time since," said Mrs. Bradish, "but his coolness and indifference do look like it."

"And his objections to having her sought, with all his assurances that she is safe and well off."

"I have a great mind to undertake the matter myself," said the lady. "If he has got Emily stowed away in some place of concealment, I'd soon bring her to light."

"How so?"

"He has got many wives, and these wives must some of them know about her. By intriguing with them the whole mystery could be unravelled."

"Probably."

"No doubt at all of it," she replied. "To-morrow I mean to commence operations."

I could not help regarding her with surprise. She had always been an advocate of polygamy, and never expressed the least sympathy or regard for its victims. Perhaps she read my countenance, or herself felt the contradictory nature of her conduct.

"Emily," she said, coming close to me, "has always been my loved and valued friend, and Anna Bradish prides herself on never forgetting to do good to those who have done good to her."

"That's the rule you go by, is it?"

"The rule I go by, is always to treat people precisely as they treat me. If they use me well, I will, if possible, use them better, but if they injure or insult me, I shall not promise what kind of treatment they'll receive in return."

"Then you don't go by the golden rule?"

"The silver rule is good enough for me," she answered, laughing.

"And what is that?"

"Why, haven't I just told you? to treat people as they treat you."

"Has B――m ill-treated you?" I inquired.

"His treatment has not been very kind."

"But I thought that you were the best of friends."

"So we were for a time, but not now."

"That is strange, anyhow."

"You know, Mrs. Ward," she observed, after a moment's thoughtfulness, "that Mormonism is continually changing its phases. Under the rule of Smith we had dreams, prophecies, and miracles. Spiritual wives were likewise in vogue. Since then, the characteristics of our faith have been polygamy and revelations. Now, it long ago occurred to me, that the absolute temporal and spiritual authority, which the leader and Head of our church exercised, might be wisely shared by a female of age and experience, whose moderation and judgment could scarcely fail of having a happy effect on the masculine counsels of her colleague; Smith was favorable to such a scheme. He even proposed it to me as an inducement, when I hesitated about uniting with his church. 'Because,' he said, in plain words, 'that the sister who made the greatest sacrifice, embarked the most property, and manifested the most zealous attachment to the faith, would of course be promoted to that situation.' I am naturally ambitious of distinction, and consequently I lent a willing ear to his flattering overtures, forsook my friends, abandoned my principles, and in more than one instance, connived to conceal his practices of vice, in order to share his authority at some future time. His death precluded the possibility of that, and though circumstances deprived me of the privilege of assisting in the choice of his successor, I had little doubt that my claims would be recognized, and the avowed purpose of the sainted dead respected in a proper manner.

"You know, moreover, that B——m acknowledged himself under obligations to me, and offered me his hand in consequence."

"Which you should have accepted, if you wished to share his authority."

"There you are mistaken again; a wife according to the code of Mormon, can have no authority, her very existence being lost or merged in that of the husband. I didn't choose to resign my identity to so distinguished a man as our Prophet, but I did choose a few days since to inform him of my expectations, and the elders and leaders of the church were favorable to my plan."

"And what did he say?"

"Commenced a long tirade about the unfitness of women for authority, and advised me to fulfill the design of my creation, by taking a husband and bearing children. Could anything be more insulting?"

"To some women it would have been good advice."

"But I am not like other women. He knows that, so do you, and everybody. He couldn't have frightened me, as he did Irene yesterday, the silly fool," and she laughed at the remembrance of Irene's fright. "After all, he's a cunning old fox," she resumed, "but it's a long lane that has no turn."

CHAPTER XLI.

DIFFERENCES.

AS Harmer's absence lasted much longer than had been expected, many of us began to be concerned about him. B——m, however, took the matter very coolly, barely remarking that those who depended solely on their own sagacity and foresight, could scarcely expect the blessing of God. The fact was, neither Harmer nor his companions had consulted the Prophet, or asked his advice, and that, in his view, was a crime. As day after day glided by, and they came not, it was proposed to send an expedition after them. This reached the ears of the master, and he forbade it, to the no small chagrin of the men.

"They went forth without us, and rejoicing in their own strength," was his characteristic answer; "let them return in the same manner."

Mrs. Bradish meanwhile strove to ingratiate herself with the wives of B——m. This was quite an undertaking; the number having increased from three to twenty, of different ages and conditions, and it certainly required all her tact to manage the affair with sufficient delicacy, chiefly because she had no means of ascertaining which wife was the favorite and confidant.

"All my hopes are centered on filling an important situation in the church," she said to me one day. "It is for that I live and act. B——m has slighted and insulted me, but he may feel my power when he least expects it. He is losing friends. I desire to gain them. I have effected that purpose in some degree already. If I succeed in finding and releasing Emily, Harmer will owe me a weight of gratitude—don't you think so ?"

"I do, certainly ; but there is a mystery attached to Harmer's continued absence. After she is found, he will have to be looked up."

"Many of the elders are favorable to my scheme," resumed Mrs. Bradish. "They say that a woman should by all means be associated in the government. Lawrence is highly pleased with the idea."

"But he would wish to confer the dignity on Irene."

"No ; Irene is now his wife, and consequently could not be associated with him in that capacity."

"Does she know that ?"

"I don't suppose that she has ever thought of it," said Mrs. Bradish ; "but I have. You know," she continued, "or whether you know it or not, it is no less a fact, that the Mormon leaders design to build here in this place a fortified city, that shall be the centre of a kingdom, over which the elders of the church will rule with absolute authority. The chief magistrate being sovereign pontiff, and the functions of king and priest both exercised by one person, or, according to my calculations, by two, a male and female, associated in the regal dignity."

"But have you any hopes of succeeding in such a wild scheme ?"

"We have a positive certainty of success ; that is, if all could be brought to coalesce and unite as one man."

"That will be the difficulty. Half the men in Utah will aspire to the situation of leader, while very few will be willing to serve, much less obey, consequently your strength will all be frittered away in factions. Every aspirant will be at the head of a party, and these parties will war against each other in deadly feud. It is folly for the founders of Mormonism to dream of, or aspire to any separation from the government of the United States. The thing is morally impossible. That government, you well know, claims all this territory as public land, and exercises supervision over the Indian tribes."

"The right of which supervision the Indian tribes have never acknowledged," she said, interrupting me.

"It makes little difference whether they acknowledge it or not, since they have not the means for successful resistance," I answered.

"These means will be furnished them," she said. "Again I repeat, that all we require to ensure success, is union among ourselves."

"The very thing the most difficult to be obtained," I answered.

"And then the Government at Washington has recognized Utah as a territory of the Union, under the protection and amenable to the rules and regulations of the other territories."

"Which shows how little they know of us, and our intentions."

"Or knowing, how little they regard them."

An expression almost of anger flitted over her countenance, and she said:

"We are too many to be despised."

"Certainly; and yet compared to the Union, the strength of Utah is nothing at all. At the most you could only cause difficulty and dissension. You might cut off straggling parties of emigrants, and, probably, harass and distress the frontiers, yet what more could you do?"

"That depends on circumstances."

"Not altogether either. Under any circumstances strength must be superior to weakness."

"You are not sufficiently acquainted with our circumstances to form a correct estimate of our available strength," she replied; "but it is not possible for us to agree, and so this subject might as well be dropped."

Mrs. Bradish soon after left me, to join, by special invitation, a meeting of the elders and leaders of the church.

I had long suspected the Mormon leaders of disloyalty to the Federal Government. I well knew that the whole creed and code of their religion was opposed to republicanism in temper and spirit; that their favorite hobby was a theocracy, and their most admired characters those of king and priest. How far this might lead them into overt acts of hostility against the government, remained to be seen.

Mr. Ward had attended the meeting. He was in unusual good humor, and, contrary to my common custom, I inquired what business had been transacted.

He smiled, and answered that I would soon see the result of it, as they had decided to build a factory in which to make powder, and another for the manufacture of fire-arms.

"And who is to be the proprietor of these manufactories?"

"The Church."

"And the artisans?"

"Are expected next month. Our faith is doing wonders everywhere," he continued; "and I find, by recent accounts, that only a few of the believers emigrate. We shall soon have MORMON churches in all the principal cities. This I consider as very desirable."

"Why so?"

"Women are not to be trusted with secrets," he answered, laughing.

Not deeming it wise to question him further, the conversation ceased.

Mr. Ward was generally reserved. Perhaps he considered it necessary to be so. He well knew that my regard for him was the only tie that bound me to Mormonism, consequently I could hardly be trusted with the private affairs of the church. Yet, he could not prevent me from seeing and understanding that much was being actually transacted which no civilized community could approve.

The Mormons had wandered off to Utah, for the avowed purpose of being beyond the surveillance and influence of the laws which governed the established States. Neither did they wish for any intercourse with the heathen, or those who could see no virtue in polygamy, no beauty in the enslavement of women, and no political consistency in a government administered by one person, in the capacity of king and priest. Consequently, their chagrin can be better imagined than described, when the overland route to California was made through their territory, and trains of emigrants and travellers frequently arrived, and stayed for days with them.

Of course they regarded these travellers in the light of intruders, and, really having something they wished to conceal, it is not strange that every inquiry, and the least manifestation of curiosity, were considered as the result of espionage. Yet, being well aware that any manifestations of hostility, at that time, would be premature, and might probably lead to the defeat of their purposes, they treated these visitors with a cool, yet dignified hospitality; though it is certain that measures were concerted to prevent their coming, and turn the tide of emigration into another channel. One thing which particularly displeased them, was the establishment of military posts by the United States, and the occasional vicinity of the troops and officers belonging to the National Army. Mr. Ward and Mrs. Bradish were both equally opposed to it, and both declared that it must be stopped, though, even then, I was such a novice in Mormonism, that the means to be adopted never crossed my mind.

Among the Mormons at this time, were many worthy and

estimable men and women, who had been seduced to embrace its doctrines by their specious appearances, without fully understanding to what they led, or their actual foundation. These were quiet and well-disposed citizens, who took no part in the business of the church, and knew nothing of the designs of its leaders. But not a few were characters of a different cast. Some were real desperadoes, and ready tools to execute any design, however vicious. These were men of no property, and generally without families; old bachelors, whose youth had been spent in the midst of associations and connections that precluded marriage; or runaways and outlaws, who had embraced Mormonism for the sake of living in human society. Bands of these men, numbering from ten to twenty-five, were accustomed to go out, ostensibly for the purpose of hunting, though it was rare, indeed, that they brought in game. For a long time, my suspicions were unawakened, but, when aroused, I determined to take particular notice.

"These men are not very successful in hunting," I said one day to Mrs. Bradish, as the party, returning from an expedition, passed the window.

" Are not?" she said, with a knowing smile.

" I don't see any game."

" The game is probably left behind."

" I don't understand you."

" Don't you?—well, no matter, probably it's quite as well that you shouldn't," and she turned away.

" It seems to me that these men are assassins and robbers; that their trade is blood; that they, in fact, are the reputed Indians, of whom the emigrants have complained so much."

Mrs. Bradish made no reply, but slowly promenaded the floor.

" The suspicion seems too horrible to be entertained for a moment, and yet I find myself unable to divest my mind of it," I continued, looking steadfastly in her face.

She came close to me—so close that her breath touched my cheek. " Did you kill a spider yesterday ?" she inquired.

" To be sure I did," I answered, in a tone of surprise.

" And why did you do it ?"

" Because the insect came in my way."

" You never go out in the fields and woods to hunt spiders and destroy them. You never meddle with them unless they intrude on your premises."

" I never do."

" And if they do, you consider it justifiable to remove them ?"

" I do."

" Well, that is exactly the case with us. We have come off here purposely to be by ourselves, but these people follow us up, intrude their presence on us, and seek to ascertain, for the purpose of betraying, our plans. Now, I hold that it is perfectly right for us to free ourselves, if we can ; to connive at their removal ; to cause them, in fact, to disappear ; to treat them exactly as you treat snakes, spiders, and venomous reptiles."

" But reptiles and men are different."

" Both reptiles and men were created by the same hand ; it is the will of God that both should live ; then by destroying the life of an insect, you infringe the design of the Creator quite as much as you do by destroying the life of a man."

I was silenced, but not convinced.

Now that my eyes were fairly opened, many things transpired daily to convince me that much more was going on in Mormondom than a casual observer would perceive or appreciate. The factories for the manufacture of gunpowder and fire-arms were in process of building, though three-fourths of the people in Utah were utterly ignorant of their purpose or design. The emigrants never dreamed of their projected use.

One day a company of emigrants arrived, almost immediately after the return of a party of the pretended hunters. They had been attacked and severely handled, several of their animals being killed, and the men wounded. They bivouacked near our house, and, as Mr. Ward had informed me that they came from that part of New York State where I had formerly resided, I determined to visit them in the evening. These emigrants, it should be remembered, were not Mormons, but travellers on their way to Oregon or California. I found a lady, very social and communicative, who gave me many interesting particulars concerning my friends, and, at my desire, related the events connected with the attack on her party. What she regarded as especially remarkable, was the fact, that the Indians talked English. "They do not generally understand our language, do they?" she inquired, with such an innocent, unsuspecting manner, that I mentally felt degraded by an association with such monsters as I believed our people to be, but, controlling my feelings, I answered, "Not generally."

"So I thought," she replied, "Indians, too, have voices unlike white men, whereas these fellows conversed with just such tones and articulations as are common to our race. Wasn't it strange?"

"They had probably learned English at the military posts," suggested Mr. Ward.

"Or were white men in disguise," replied the lady's husband.

I observed that Mr. Ward regarded him with a scrutinizing look, and probably satisfied with the observation, he said:

"That must be very unlikely; but the Indians are becoming so hostile, that I wonder the emigrants persist in following this route."

"Because they can find no other, where the mountains and rivers are passable," answered the gentleman; "other routes have been attempted time and again, but always without success."

"Yet there must be another way; the difficulty is in finding it."

The gentleman smiled sadly, "Most people," he said, "prefer a known route, and to encounter known dangers, rather than unknown."

"What amiable people," I said to Mr. Ward, "but it really seems strange that the Indians have become so hostile of late."

"The Indians, yes, yes, rather strange ; but the emigrants must choose a new route, and the American military officers, too. We cannot have a system of espionage in our midst."

"Have any American officers been here ?"

"Not exactly here, but near enough. The Indians waylaid and destroyed them, too."

"How does it happen that they never attack the Mormons ?"

"The brethren are under the protection of heaven."

That answer settled the question, of course.

CHAPTER XLII.

THE NEW WIFE.

IF a place was designed to take precedence from the variety of occupations carried on within its boundaries, Utah would certainly have risen high in the scale. Every dissimilar view and opinion was being industriously propagated. Schemes for individual and church aggrandizement were being hatched and fomented. Projects for a coalition with the Indians, in opposition to the measures of the Federal Government, formed a favorite hobby. But while such pursuits occupied the time and attention of the zealous aspirants for church authority, another class were employed with equal zeal in marrying and giving in marriage ; not the least remarkable part of this affair, being, that the bridegrooms were mostly middle-aged men, many of whom were already blessed with several wives, and a multitude of children ; if an institution could be called a blessing which made a home much more resemble a hospital or asylum, than a quiet scene of domestic peace.

Mr. Slocomb had been a thrifty inhabitant of the Empire State, the owner of a fine farm, stocked with fine cattle, and plenty of them, the husband of a thrifty, prudent, industrious house-wife, and the father of a fine lot of boys, of several ages, from two to twelve. Mr. Slocomb had been possessed with a mania for emigration several years. Like most people well to do in the world, he was dissatisfied, not with what he had, but because there were some things which he had not. He dreamed of a large estate, with five hundred or a thousand acres, which might be equally divided between his boys, when he was done with it, his usual manner of expression, giving to each one an estate larger than the one he occupied.

Mrs. Slocomb opposed the measure for a long time. She was attached to her home and friends. She prized the school-house and the church, and thought that they might enjoy happiness without going so far to find it. But, though distinguished for virtue and integrity, and immovable on all subjects connected with moral principle, she possessed one weak point,—that of easy credulity in religious matters. Had a Chinaman or Mussulman come to her neighborhood, preaching his religious tenets, ten chances to one, he would have found in her a devout listener, and ultimately a believer, so far as their tenets did not interfere with her preconceived ideas of moral right. She had been a firm adherent to the doctrines of the Second Adventists, but the failure of their prophesies rather shook her faith, when the Mormons came. These attracted her greatly ; she invited them to her house, and listened with wonder and credulity to their glowing accounts of the Promised Land. Mr. Slocomb proposed immediate emigration; the Mormons united their entreaties to his, and she yielded to the promptings of an enthusiastic fanaticism. But even in Utah, and notwithstanding the fervor of her faith, she retained many of her old Eastern manners, and preserved the full integrity of her moral principles. She was, moreover, one of those who fear contamination by association with those she did not like, or whom she regarded as vicious. Of polygamy she had never heard, until her arrival at the Land of the Saints, when her surprise and horror were inconceivable. They went directly to the house of a brother, whose fervid faith and zeal had won for him honorable mention in the East. He received them graciously, bade them welcome to the hospitalities of his house, and introduced Mrs. Bee, a stately and dignified matron, with a large fat child in her arms. They exchanged salutations, when the good brother directed her attention to a much younger lady, who also had a child, and whom he likewise styled Mrs. Bee. Presently a third came in, looking still younger, but apparently in an interesting situation, and Mrs. Bee was presented again. Mrs. Slocomb began to conclude, by this time, that the good brother was demented, or herself in a dream, it might be difficult to decide which.

One by one, other ladies to the number of fifteen made their appearance, who were severally introduced to the astonished guest as Mrs. Bee. Too polite to make any inquiries, she sat in a maze of doubt and perplexity. It was impossible that all these females could be the sisters or daughters of their host, and that she had mistaken the title Miss for Mrs. It was equally impossible that he could have so many brothers whose wives were domiciled in his house. As the dinner-hour approached, and the multitude of children came thronging in, her curiosity grew intensely painful. She observed that most of the children were evidently neglected, with faces and hands that seemed never to have known the vicinity of water, and hair that hung in matted elf-locks around their ears. Many of the boys, eight or nine years old, still wore frocks, while the girls seemed to have dressed in anything that came to hand. Though addressing the different women as mother, she noticed that they all called Mr. Bee "father ;" that, however, might be by courtesy. There seemed little cordiality or sociality among the women, and it struck her that the whole party were laboring under unnatural restraint.

At length she found a solution of the difficulty, according to her mind. These were doubtless orphan children, whom Mr. Bee, in his benevolence, had undertaken to keep till they would be supplied with suitable places. Of course their mothers were poor widows, and the names—she might be mistaken in them. She forebore remark until after dinner, when the gentlemen walked out, and though all the various faculties of wonder, astonishment, surprise, and indignation, had been respectively called into exercise at the glaring want of anything like order or method at a gentleman's table, she supposed that in a new country, on the very outskirts of civilization, it might be customary to dispense with all formality and ceremony. It seemed to her that an infinite amount of useless labor had been expended in producing dinner, because every one thus employed refused to harmonize her actions with those of the others. One, who had been busily engaged setting the table, left the apartment for a moment, when another approached, removed the dishes and the cloth, restored them to their place in the cupboard, and proceeded to array the board in another cloth, and much inferior dishes. The first one returned to find all her arrangements superseded, while her anger was met by a scornful laugh. The same contrariness prevailed in the culinary department. Instead of assisting, each one seemed disposed to hinder and embarrass the others. A dish almost prepared by one, would be hastily thrust aside, and its place supplied by something another one was fonder of. Mrs. Slocomb was half disposed to disbelieve the testimony of her ears, but sounds marvellously like those of blows and kicks came not unfrequently from the adjoining apartment, and one of the women passed hastily around the house, her eyes red with weeping.

When dinner was announced, one of the younger ones rushed hastily forward, nearly overturning the matron with the fat child, and established herself at the place of honor—the head of the table—while two others, the least prepossessing of the whole number, came bounding along, and took places right and left of Mr. Bee. He paid little attention to them, but evidently wished to withdraw the notice of his guests from their ill-mannerly and ungracious conduct. Then commenced a great scramble with the children. Crowding beside their mothers, the ragged urchins demanded bread and butter, potatoes, cake, or milk. If one obtained more than another, blows followed, attended with kicks, and screams of no common power. At length the confusion and uproar increased, until the host could neither hear his own voice, nor those of the guests, when he arose, pale with anger, took a large ox-goad from its place of concealment, and laying it about among them zealously, he soon succeeded in clearing the apartment.

"Haven't I told you over and over again not to feed the young 'uns by handfuls while we were eating?" he said, glancing at the women.

No one answered, and Mr. Bee being too well-bred to manifest further displeasure, the cloud passed over.

As there seemed little opportunity for conversation in the house, where so many children were partaking their meal, Mrs. Slocomb proposed taking a walk to the matronly lady, whose superior gentility seemed to indicate that she was, or ought to be, at the head of the establishment.

"I should be happy to, indeed," she replied gracefully, "and will when my children are done eating; if I should leave them now, they would get no more food. It is the practice here for every one to supply her own children at the expense of the others."

"Will you tote that great young 'un?" said one in an insulting tone.

"It's likely," replied Mrs. Bee.

"I guess you will have to," replied the other, "for none of us will keep him."

More and more surprised, Mrs. Slocomb ventured to remark to the first speaker, that she didn't seem very accommodating.

"There's no accommodation here," she answered; "every one has to look out for herself."

"Are you boarders, then?" inquired Mrs. Slocomb; "or is Mr. Bee a relative?"

It was now the turn of the women to be surprised.

"Boarders!—a relative!" they repeated, looking at each other.

Mrs. Bee came forward, with an expression of painful perplexity resting on her countenance.

"Our friend, Mrs. Slocomb, is unacquainted with the customs of Utah," she said. "These ladies are all the wives of my husband, Mr. Bee. The faith of Mormon sanctions polygamy, the same as the ancient faith of Moses."

Mrs. Slocomb stood like one transfixed with horror and astonishment. Could it be possible that she had come to such a place as that, that the religion which she had embraced sanctioned such practices; that she had been sitting and eating with such degraded women? Their presence seemed a contamination, as she regarded them with a look of pity and contempt.

"You needn't look so haughtily, madam," said one of them saucily. "You'll have plenty of such companions by-and-by. I'll warrant your husband will not confine himself to one woman, no more than the other men."

Mrs. Slocomb deigned no reply, but hastily demanding her bonnet, bade Mrs. Bee farewell, and left the house in the most unceremonious manner.

Mrs. Slocomb was devoutly attached to the institution of marriage, as it existed in the Eastern States, and the bigamist, in her estimation, was quite as reprehensible as those guilty of crimes which it were an offence to mention in polite society. In her view, the residence of Mr. Bee was no better than a house of ill-fame, and she felt degraded by having entered its doors. She came directly to me, in a state of excessive agitation, and when I questioned her on the subject, she told me of all she had seen and heard.

"And such scenes, I regret to say, are common among us."

"How have I been deceived!" she said. "I considered Mormonism all truth, and purity, and beauty. I never dreamed that anything so hideous and revolting could be concealed beneath an exterior of so much piety. But we must leave Utah; I can never consent to stay where such practices are tolerated."

"But your husband," I suggested.

"My husband," she replied, "will be quite as much disgusted with such practices as myself. I shouldn't wonder if he was even more, if such a thing were possible; but here he comes."

Mr. Slocomb approached the house, his usual gaiety changed to a sedate and thoughtful expression.

"Why did you run away so unceremoniously from Brother Bee's?" he inquired, in a half-amused, half-angry tone.

"That, you know, quite as well as I can tell you. It seems to me a degradation, that I ever went there. Only to think of sitting and eating with such women!"

"Why, they seemed very modest women, and some of them were decidedly beautiful," said Mr. Slocomb. "My friend tells me that he was never happier. It seems so patriarchal!"

"Is it possible that you can find it in your heart to excuse such an abominable practice?"

"There's nothing abominable about it, that I can see," said Mr. Slocomb, and his countenance fell.

Mr. Ward soon came in, and the gentlemen commenced a discussion on theology, which ended, as such discussions generally did, on polygamy. Mr. Slocomb, it was evident, regarded the institution with favor, rather than otherwise.

"You see" I said, addressing her aside, "that your husband entertains very different opinions from what you anticipated."

She nodded her head, and shed tears.

"We never know of what men are capable, until they are tempted."

She signified assent, as before.

Notwithstanding the wishes of his wife, Mr. Slocomb refused to remove from Utah. He was well suited with the people and the place, he said, and wherefore should he remove, to gratify the whims and caprices of a woman? Bee was his confidential friend and adviser; and just two weeks from the day that they commenced housekeeping in Salt Lake City, Slocumb took home his second wife. Of course, Mrs. Slocomb regarded her in the light of an intruder, and as a depraved and abandoned character. These sentiments she had no wish to disguise, and in a few days, the two women were mortal enemies. Mrs. Slocomb uniformly designated her rival as "Bets." The boys caught her spirit, and the new wife became the object of their unmitigated contempt, and many practical jokes, of which the maliciousness could be much easier detected than the wit. Mrs. Slocomb was blindly attached to her children, and since her husband's second marriage, her infatuation seemed to have increased. She attributed their ill-behaviour to fondness for her, and chagrin at the ill-treatment which she had received; consequently, if not positively gratified, she was not displeased with their exhibitions of contempt and dislike.

According to the code of Mormon, the wife who corrects the child of another, is subjected to a severe penalty. Elizabeth knew this, and refrained from giving them even a gentle reprimand; but, when utterly wearied, and provoked beyond all forbearance, she went to Mr. Slocomb with her complaints. For a time, he heard her patiently, and threatened the boys with "straightening up things, and settling the hash;" though what was meant or understood by such threats, remained a mystery; and, as the boys were great favorites with their father, nothing serious was apprehended by them, to judge by the little effect it had on their conduct.

"Why don't you make the boys behave?" said Mr. Slocumb, one day, to his wife. "Elizabeth is continually complaining of them. I'm really tired of hearing it."

"Tired of hearing it, are you?" said Mrs. Slocomb, turning her large, black eyes on her husband's face, and winding her long, bright hair around her head, in the form of a coronet; "tired of hearing it; then silence her tongue!"

"But, madam, it is hardly right, that the boys should be indulged in such pranks as they practise on her."

"To what pranks do you allude?"

"Why, pulling away the chair, when she attempts to sit down; hanging buckets of water over the doors, through which she must pass; calling her names; pinning labels to her dress, when she goes to church; and otherwise distressing her. I am astonished that you permit them to act in such a manner!"

"And I am astonished, that you permit such a vile, abandoned creature to harbor about your house."

Mr. Slocumb looked surprised. "Do you call Elizabeth vile and abandoned?" he inquired.

"What else can she be?—the despicable thing! The very air seems contaminated by her presence—living with another woman's husband!" and the countenance of Mrs. Slocomb was quite as expressive as her tongue.

"But another woman's husband is her husband, likewise."

"That is false, Mr. Slocomb; the thing is impossible. No marriage ceremony can sanctify a connexion which God has not authorized, and which nature forbids. I will not call you by the name you deserve, nor her by the epithet she justly merits; but *you well know, that in a civilized community, your crime would have met its reward in the penitentiary."

"Go it, pumps!" said the oldest boy, snapping his fingers.

At length, the discussions between Mr. and Mrs. Slocumb took the form of bitter altercations. On one of these occasions, he informed her that she was generally disliked; that her conduct had produced a disagreeable impression on the minds of the people, which he exceedingly regretted.

"And of which I am very glad," she answered; "I don't want any society or intercourse with such a set, and what is more, I won't have, neither."

And she was good as her word, never associating with, or noticing any except these women who were the first, and in her view, the only wives of their husbands.

But after all, Mrs. Slocomb was more to be pitied than blamed. A woman of her rigid principles could not look on polygamy with the least allowance, and she flattered herself that Bets might be worried out, and driven off.

"I hardly think you will succeed in that, Mrs. Slocomb," I observed, when she informed me of her plan.

"Not if we render her situation intolerable, like Sarah did that of Hagar?"

"You wouldn't treat her cruelly," I answered; "your husband is, after all, the most to blame; I have heard say that she

17*

was mild and inoffensive in her disposition, and an orphan with no father's house to which she can go."

"Let her find a place, then."

Mrs. Slocomb was so blinded by passion and prejudice that all appeals to her better feelings were in vain, and yet, no woman could be more tender-hearted, gentle, and considerate, than she was on ordinary occasions.

One beautiful afternoon, we were walking together near her dwelling, when a loud noise of blows, screams, and angry words attracted our attention.

"Oh, that hussy," said Mrs. Slocomb, rushing to the house; I followed, when a scene painfully ludicrous was presented. Elizabeth, standing in the middle of the floor, was holding the oldest boy by one hand grasped tightly in his hair, while with the other she was belaboring him most unmercifully with the hot pudding-stick, just removed from a pot of samp that hung boiling over the fire.

"Oh, you miserable scamp," she cried, "I'll give it to you, that I will, your father told me to, you've tormented me long enough; I'll give you a lesson, you "———

"Do you dare to strike my child?" cried Mrs. Slocomb, springing to the rescue.

"Yes, I dare," answered Elizabeth, turning about and facing her antagonist, with eyes gleaming like those of an irritated panther; the boy sprang to his mother shrieking.

"Bruised, battered, and burned," said Mrs. Slocomb; "wretch, you'll pay for this."

"No, I shan't pay for it," said Elizabeth, "your husband, my husband, madam, told me to defend myself, and he would clear me from all blame."

"Liar, hateful, abandoned creature," said Mrs. Slocomb, wiping away the tears of her child.

"I am no more of a liar, no more hateful, or abandoned than

yourself ; I have been married, and Mr. Slocomb is my husband just as much as he is yours. What do you want to act the fool for ? and now, I'll tell you what it is, Mr. Slocomb has given me the liberty, and I can prove it ; and every time that your great, odious, abominable boys disturb me in any manner, they'll get a good beating ; I will bear their sauce and impudence no longer, that I won't."

"Then, clear out."

"That I won't ;—clear out, indeed, leave my home and my husband, just to please you, and your abominable brats ; no, I'll stay, and, before many years, dance over your grave, that I will."

Mrs. Slocomb was not prepared for such an outburst of passion, as Elizabeth was generally mild and unresisting.

"You needn't think," she continued, "that because I have borne your insults so long, I am going to bear them for ever ; from this time forth, I'm going to take a new start, and my word for it, your boys will find the odds."

Weary and disgusted with such a scene of household folly and disorder, I left them and went home.

The next week, Mrs. Slocomb came to our house ; I was her confidant, and she never hesitated to inform me of all her troubles. She really appeared sad and depressed ; said her life was a burden, and her habitation a continual scene of discord. Elizabeth and the boys were fighting and quarrelling from morning till night ; Mr. Slocomb would not, in fact could not, preserve order, as he had given Elizabeth permission to take her own part, and the boys were absolutely ungovernable.

"You can't effect any compromise ?" I suggested.

"Compromise, no," said Mrs. Slocomb, "I must and will be mistress in my own family ; as to Elizabeth, however, we might possibly get along if it wasn't for the boys. She won't bear the least from them, and they won't take a word from her ; and so it goes. The other morning Bets was stooping over to cut up the meat which had been fried, and was swimming in hot fat in the spider which stood on the corner of the hearth; William said something which she did not like, and taking the knife out of the boiling gravy, she struck him with it on the side of the face. He then grabbed her by the hair, and held on, while she nearly chopped his naked feet into mince-meat with her knife and fork; and so it is every day."

"I believe it impossible for happiness to exist in a family where there are several wives."

"Oh, dear," said Mrs. Slocomb, "yonder comes one of the boys after me, I wonder what new thing has happened?"

The child was crying, Mrs. Slocomb met him at the gate, listened a moment to his story, and without bidding me farewell, and even leaving her bonnet, started off in the greatest agitation towards her home.

While I was wondering at her strange demeanor, a messenger came with information that Mrs. Slocomb wished to see me immediately. Surprise and curiosity led me to obey the summons.

She was sitting by the bed, weeping; one of her boys laid on it, presented a picture of death; while Elizabeth sat sullenly in a corner.

"Oh, Mrs. Ward," she cried, on seeing me, "I am the most unhappy woman in the world; look there," and she pointed to the child who lay in a state of stupor.

"What is the matter with him?" I inquired.

"That hussy," and the voice of the poor mother was drowned in sobs.

"I gave you fair warning," said Elizabeth.

"You have not killed the child," I said, turning to Elizabeth.

"I neither know, nor care; they'll have to learn to let me alone."

It appeared that while Elizabeth was washing the floor, the

boys as usual began their capers, when she became angry and struck one of them over the head with the mop handle. There was a nail in the end of the stick, of which, however, she was ignorant, but the iron penetrated to the brain, and no hopes could be entertained of his recovery.

Mr. Slocomb had been sent for, and soon came. He gazed a moment at the dying child, and turning to Elizabeth inquired,

"Is this your work?"

"It is," she answered calmly. "You have told me not to come to you with complaints, but to take my own part; I have only obeyed you, you see the result, yet I had no intention of killing the child."

"You had, you know you had," almost shrieked Mrs. Slocomb. "You have threatened time and again to kill us all."

"Not if you minded your own business, and let me alone," said Elizabeth, with the greatest *sang froid*. "I'll engage to hurt none of you in the first place, but you mustn't begin a batter."

"You are all to blame," said Mr. Slocomb.

"It is with you that the blame rests," retorted his wife, her words interrupted by sobs and tears. "We lived happily together, till you went and brought that thing here. She will kill us all I expect."

"Why don't you send for some one, or do something?" said Elizabeth, in a softened voice.

"It is too late," I whispered.

"Yes; too late, too late," groaned the mother. "Willy, dear, look up; don't you know mamma? Oh! my sweet lamb that you should die thus!"

A faint smile played over the boy's features; he tried to speak, but failed. A shiver passed over his limbs, a shadow darkened his countenance, and we stood in the presence of death.

"Did they hang Elizabeth?" says the reader, "or send her to the penitentiary? or what did they do with her?"

They did nothing at all. She was not even reprimanded by the church. The men, and all the women, except the first wives of their husbands, affected to believe the murder accidental, and said that the boy ought to have behaved himself, and many even hoped that it might prove a warning to the children, and cause them to treat all the wives of their father with deference and respect.

"Did they continue to live together?"

Of course they did, and since the death of William, Elizabeth ruled the house. The boys were afraid of her, and Mrs. Slocomb seemed overwhelmed by sorrow. She lost all her wonted energy, and upon two or three occasions, I detected in her look and manner decided symptoms of insanity. She talked continually of her murdered child, and would sit for hours weeping over his grave. Then she complained of the desertion of her husband, said that he no longer loved her, and that her daily prayer was to die, that she might go to her mother.

I conversed tenderly and feelingly with Mr. Slocomb on the situation of his wife; told him that she was on the verge of insanity, and entreated him to send Elizabeth away.

He treated the subject with indifference, but said, "that he would think of it—that Elizabeth was a very good girl, and now that Mrs. Slocomb's health has failed, he didn't know what they should do without her."

It was evident that Mr. Slocomb was willfully blind. He desired the society of Elizabeth, and rather than practise self-denial in that particular, would let misery and disunion reign in his family. A practice common with the husbands in Utah.

Some days after, the whole village was thrown into great excitement. Mrs. Slocomb had committed suicide, after causing the death of her two youngest children. The three had been found weltering in a pool of blood over the grave of William, the mother grasping in her cold hand a gory knife. Her gleaming eyes and incoherent words had been a subject of general remark.

Mr. Slocomb continues to live with Elizabeth, and has added two more wives to his domestic establishment.

CHAPTER XLIII.

ETHLEEN'S ADVENTURE.

AMONG Indian females apathetic indifference to the absence of their husbands is the prevailing fashion. The squaw must comfort herself with pride and dignity, which preclude the idea of shedding tears, or manifesting anxiety about any one, however near and dear. Ethleen retained many of her Indian customs with tenacity, and forbore remark, though all else were wondering at the continued stay of Harmer and his friends. However, it was easy to perceive that her indifference was feigned, and that she really suffered all the tortures of agonizing suspense.

"Ethleen has gone," said Mrs. Bradish, whose visiting propensities gave her all the news.

"Gone where?"

"Nobody knows. She requested Louisa to milk her cow, and taking her bow and arrow, started for the mountains nearly a week ago, since which time no one has seen or heard of her."

"Shut up her cottage, I suppose?"

"Of course; it looks lonely enough round there now."

We concluded that Ethleen had gone to look for her husband,

and as Moore was a general favorite, to say nothing of his connection with Harmer, and the moral certainty that information of one would make us acquainted with the fate of the other, all wished her success.

Some of the young fellows protested, that had they known her purpose, they would have accompanied her. Many said that she would perish and never return; others declared that her native Indian sagacity would preserve her. It was talked of in every circle, for a week, and decided according to the inclinations and dispositions of the party. Then some new incident, or adventure occurred, and Ethleen was, for the time being, forgotten. Mrs. Bradish came to me one day, in a great state of vexation and perplexity. "I am completely discouraged," she said.

"Why so?"

"I find it impossible to obtain any information of Emily. Where on earth she has gone to, is a mystery of no common magnitude. I begin to fear that she is dead. I have sounded all the women in the harem of the Prophet, and they either don't know anything about her, or else they are adepts in concealment."

"Probably the latter," I suggested.

"It may be; and yet I am inclined to think not."

"Time will probably determine. If Harmer was here"——

"He is here," said a manly voice we had no difficulty in recognizing. Sure enough, there stood the tanned and weather-beaten voyager, with Ethleen looking over his shoulder.

"Where have you been all this time?" said Mrs. Bradish. "We thought something had befallen you."

"And something did befall me."

"Where are your companions?"

"Dead!" A faint cry from Ethleen told how much she was interested in the answer.

"And Emily."

"Has been spirited away to some place of concealment by B——m."

"Certainly?"

"Yes, certainly. I saw and conversed with the Indian who assisted in the business, but he would give no clue whatever by which we might be enabled to find her."

"Then you did find the Indians?"

"Not those which I started from home with the design of visiting," he answered. "However, it will be necessary for me to begin at the first, and relate all my story, to satisfy your curiosity."

"That is just what we wish you to do."

"Well, then, we met with no adventure worth naming, till on the second day of our journey, when we came suddenly on a trail, which Buckley said he knew to be that of white men."

"How did he know that?" inquired Mrs. Bradish.

"Because the toes of the right foot were evidently turned out in walking, which Indians never do," he answered; "but don't interrupt me again."

We did, however, for Harmer having sat down on the doorstep, I missed Ethleen, and asked what had become of her.

"Yonder she goes over the hills," said Mrs. Bradish, and sure enough she was just disappearing in the valley.

"What does the girl mean? that isn't the way to her home."

"You'll never see her again," said Harmer.

"Never see her again; why not?"

"Indian nature," he replied. "The ties that bound her to the whites have been broken by the death of her husband. She is disgusted by the rules and regulations of Mormonism, and, if I mistake not, will henceforth associate with her race. But to my story. Following this trail, we found ourselves suddenly surrounded by a company of mounted Indians, armed with rifles.

Escape was impossible, and, seeing their purpose, we determined to sell our lives dearly as possible. But Moore and Buckley fell, shot dead. I was overpowered by numbers, and severely wounded, when, what was my astonishment to discover that my assailants were Mormons, instead of Indians. No wonder you look surprised. They were acting under orders from head-quarters, but one of the number, whom I had befriended, interceded for my life. They took me with them to a cave, where they changed their garments, painted their faces, and assumed their Indian disguise."

"In order to attack the emigrants travelling through the territory, and prevent their visiting the holy city?"

"Just so."

I glanced at Mrs. Bradish, but she remained perfectly silent, and Harmer continued. "Those men had received imperative orders to procure my death, though I am not at liberty to reveal whence the murderous mandate emanated. I heard the debate, the more blood-thirsty wishing to shoot me, the others to take me off into the mountains, where there could be little prospect of my ever discovering the settlements of white men. I joined my entreaties with theirs, and we prevailed. They carried me, blindfolded and on horseback, a four day's journey, into the wild, inhospitable wilderness, then compelled me to drink a sleeping potion, from the effects of which I awoke to find myself alone."

"A dreadful situation."

"Dreadful, indeed, but I was not discouraged. Even then and there, I thought more of Emily than myself, and determined for her sake to live. My chief desire was to fall in with a roving party of Indians, and my wishes were gratified on the third day after my abandonment. They were friendly and hospitable, and carried me with them to their village. Here I had an interview with their chief, who, upon learning whence I came, immediately began to talk of the schemes and plans of my father, as he styled B———m.

"I pretended to be well informed of them, and thus encouraged the Indian to talk on."

"Which was wrong," said Mrs. Bradish, the first she had spoken.

"No, madam, it was not. This man had attempted my life, and I had the score to settle with him."

"Well, what did you find out?"

"That emmissaries from B———m were continually coming and going among the Indian tribes, whose business it was to excite them to hostility and rebellion against the Government, by representing that the said Government wished and intended to dispossess them of their lands. I ascertained, too, that some of the most powerful tribes had actually entered into a treaty with B———m, to furnish him so many warriors on an emergency, in return for a large quantity of powder and fire-arms."

"And what, Mr. Harmer, does all this amount to? You have known, from the first, that the Mormons intended to be free from the heathen, and to build up a city which should be the glory of the earth."

"But I never did know that they intended to resort to murder and midnight assassination to carry out their schemes. I never did know, till then, that they designed to instigate the savage Indians to attack the harmless emigrants, and even join in the unfeeling butchery of women and children. No, Mrs. Bradish, I never dreamed that this was to be the consummation of their designs."

"It is not the consummation of their designs," she answered, interrupting him, "but only a means for their accomplishment."

He laughed, scornfully—"Vaulting ambition overshoots itself."

"The Federal Government, Madam, will receive information of all the schemes hatching against its peace and prosperity."

An expression of the deepest indignation and disappointment crossed her countenance. "How now, do you mean to act the traitor, and betray us?" she inquired, rising and going towards him, "if so, your life is not worth a farthing."

"Spare yourself all trouble of that kind," he answered, "it would do you no good at all to kill me, but be only hastening your own destruction. During my absence, I visited a military post, was introduced to the United States officers, prepared dispatches for Washington, in which all your secrets are laid bare; and now what can you do?"

She threw up her hands with a gesture of utter despair.

"That is something you didn't expect, isn't it?" he continued. "If you kill me to-morrow or to-night, it will not help you; if you let me live, I have done you all the favor I can; for, Mrs. Bradish, all your plans of aggrandizement and independence, must ultimately have failed, and you would have appeared in the characters of murderers, assassins, and traitors to your government."

"Don't talk to me of traitors," she almost shrieked, "who is, who can be a greater traitor than yourself?"

"I am not a traitor, and whoever calls me so is a liar," he said passionately; "I have never joined these schemes, nor had anything to do with them. I have never plotted against our government; didn't I help to uphold its banners in Mexico? haven't I always been a true and loyal citizen? did I ever promise any adherence to your iniquitous plans?"

"But the government at Washington is ten thousand miles away; and it is doubtful, even then, whether or not they give credence to the news."

Mrs. Bradish was well aware that the Federal Government, once informed of their secret desires and machinations, would take such measures as to effectually preclude the establishment of their theocratical independence. Their designs were not yet ripe, that she well knew; and she caught at the merest straw, in order to support her air-built castles, and sustain her sinking hopes but a moment longer.

"The distance is nothing," resumed Harmer, "and one of the officers told me that rumors of secret conspiracies among us were common at the East, and that the appointment of a governor for our territory had been recommended to the President."

"A heathen governor, to spy and inspect our proceedings? then, indeed, are we lost."

"Saved, rather," reiterated Harmer, "I never saw nor heard of conduct more heathenish than is practised and approved here. Crimes that would send a man to the penitentiary in any of the States, are openly applauded with us, or you, as I utterly disclaim all connection with your church henceforth, and had it not been for Emily, I should never have returned to such a nest of devils; in fact, if Ethleen had not come to my assistance, I know not whether I should ever have succeeded in getting back.

"The Indian, Walker, who seems to be well posted up in all matters pertaining to the plans of B———m, detained me in captivity many days. My hands and feet were bound with thongs, and two young savages, stationed alternately at the door of the hut, kept watch over me. Another brought me a scanty pittance of food and water; but it is an ill-wind that blows nobody any good, and my confinement here resulted in a vast increase of information, which I have faithfully transmitted to the Federal Government.

"Ethleen, who came direct to the Utah country, possessed all the sagacity and cunning for which her race are distinguished. She loitered in the neighborhood for several days, and, not wishing to be discovered, remained concealed among the hills. By one of those presentiments, for which it is impossible to account, it occurred to me that a friend was in the vicinity, and while debating in my mind who it could be, I thought of Ethleen, and her probable anxiety for the fate of her husband. Consequently, I was not in the least surprised when the son of Walker introduced her into my presence. He had first noticed her foot-prints in the sand, and following them, came suddenly upon her while she was sleeping. Struck with her beauty and youthful appearance, he loitered near till she awoke, when the preliminaries for a further acquaintance were settled. Learning her errand in their country, he brought her to me, though without the knowledge, and contrary to the wishes of his father.

"With true Indian stoicism she received the news of her husband's death, made no remarks on his virtues, nor even inquired where the event took place; but I soon learned that she was intriguing with young Walker for my release. The savage hesitated several days, while Ethleen continued her importunities, when one evening a large flask of whisky was provided for my guard. The temptation proving too great for his sobriety, long before midnight he was wrapped in a drunken slumber. I heard his heavy and suppressed breathing, and soon perceived a light form gliding through the gloom. Then the thongs that bound my limbs were cut, and a well-remembered voice bade me arise and be at liberty.

"Young Walker furnished us with a couple of horses, and comforted us with the assurance that we need not fear pursuit, as the warriors were just preparing to set off on an expedition against the Great Santa Fé Caravan.

"It was necessary, however, to avoid my Mormon enemies, and so we took a new. and undefinable route, in which the sagacity of Ethleen, as displayed in following courses, and ascertaining distances by the appearances and positions of the planets, was truly remarkable. The monotony of our homeward route was diversified by one adventure only. We came suddenly on an emigrant party, who had been attacked by Indians, and of whose number several had been wounded, and the best part of their goods carried off. They seemed greatly surprised that Indians should understand the English language so well, and resemble white men so exactly in all but color."

CHAPTER XLIV.

THE GOLD FEVER, AND ITS EFFECTS.

LIKE the breaking out of an epidemic in New Orleans, or some other city of the South, the gold fever broke out, and raged with unparalleled violence, with this difference, however, that epidemics are mostly local, or confined to particular localities, whereas the gold fever extended into all the cities, in fact over all the districts of the Federal Union. Commerce languished, agriculture was suspended, and all political, or other business, gave way before it. Of course Utah was no exception to the general rule. The news came that large deposits of gold had been found in California. It ran through the country like wild-fire. The people were electrified, and many of them forsook their farms and mechanic-shops, to search for, and wash gold. The hunters found this more profitable business than prowling on the trail of emigrants. The establishments for the manufacture of gunpowder and fire-arms, came to an immediate stand-still from a dearth of hands, since all the available workers flew off to the "diggings." In vain B——m commanded them to stay, inveighed bitterly against the love of gold, and talked of sacrifices in the cause of truth. His exhortations were attended with little or no influence, seeming only to prove the aphorism that opposition is the life of trade.

Even Weldy, who received the wonderful information on his return from the church, where his marriage with the two Misses Melton had been solemnized, made immediate preparations to leave his home and bevy of wives, for the new-found El Dorado. Pursuant to this, he called up his family on the morning after his double marriage, and, informing them of the golden land lying just across the Sierra Nevada, declared his intention of visiting it, and recommended his youthful brides to the respect and consideration of the elder ones.

"Won't I make 'em stand round when he is gone?" said one of the younger wives, who, with neither beauty, nor wit, nor talent to recommend her, was certainly the tyrant of the flock. Her coarse manners, and cruel disposition, made her an object of fear and hatred, though Weldy, in consideration of the wealth she had brought him, was obligated to treat her with something like deference. Notwithstanding the rules of Mormonism, she tyrannized without mercy over all the children, and such of the women as she could bend to her purpose. Weldy had been too much occupied with money-getting to maintain order in such a large family, besides, he hated trouble; he hated when returning from the cares and turmoils of a business life, to be entertained at home with the clamors and complaints of his wives, demanding justice against each other. He soon came to view them as all alike culpable, and hesitated not to tell them so.

"Now I'll tell you just what it is," he would say. "I don't want to hear any more of your fusses. You can all live together well enough if you have a mind to, and you shall, too. If I hear any more of your complaints, I'll give you a whipping all round—my word for it."

This summary manner silenced the complaints in a great

degree, though it failed to remove the cause of them, and discord, confusion, and misery, reigned supreme. Now, we have no idea of blaming the husband for all this. It was something that he could not, from the very nature of things, prevent. The dispositions of women are altogether beyond the control of men. Many husbands find it extremely difficult to get along reasonably with one woman. Then, what can one man do with a dozen, or fourteen women, all in one family, considered as equals, without any legitimate head?

On the morning in question, the Mormon father and patriarch, standing in the midst of the floor, took his farewell leave of each member of his family separately, and delivered to each one his parting benediction and advice. The women lingered around him, many of them the ugliest specimens of womanhood in existence: some large, and others little; some with blue, or black, or grey eyes. Some with babies; others with none, but all alike watching with jealous eyes to detect any little token of esteem, by which preference to one more than the others might be manifested.

Het, the tyrant of the household, was a bouncing dame, with a waist like a molasses-barrel, a face of the dimensions of a pewter-platter, freckled and blotched with moles, to say nothing of squint eyes, green in color, and hideous in expression. She hated beauty in anything; but beautiful people were her especial abhorrence.

"Now, Hetty, be good," said the husband, "and don't abuse the weaker ones."

Hetty's eyes twinkled, but she did not speak.

"You will do right, won't you, that you may live again after death, and reign with Christ a thousand years?"

There was really an expression of concern on his countenance as he made the interrogatory; for he well understood her hateful disposition.

"Perhaps I will ; perhaps I won't," she answered.

He barely touched her hands, but there was neither shake nor pressure, nor any salutation with the lips. She was evidently angry, but said nothing, and gave her place to another.

"You are a woman of judgment, Eliza, do the best you can," he said.

"Which will be bad at the best, considering," she answered.

The hand was lightly shaken.

And thus the farewells were taken. There was little trace of feeling or emotion by any of them, or on either side. Polygamy, besides proving the ruin of all domestic peace, had been the destroyer of all household affection. It was the natural result of that abominable system. The last wives only, those wedded the day before, were saluted with a kiss. The children were not honored with a separate recognition and parental leave-taking, but told "good bye," and commanded to be good while papa went to get gold.

"And so," said Het, before Weldy was out of sight, "and so the old boy has left us to our own destruction. Now, I mean to be queen, and have everything exactly my own way. You'll have to walk the chalk now ;" and she looked round on the assembled faces, her eyes gleaming with malicious pleasure.

Het made immediate arrangements to take possession of the best room in the house, and form a sort of court, appointing some to perform the household drudgery ; others to look after the children ; and yet, others to watch the cows ; reserving four or five to wait on herself. But her subjects were stubborn and rebellious ; few consented to abide her authority, and these were mostly children who had experienced the power of her vigorous arm. Blows were not unfrequently exchanged, hair flew by handfuls, and many a face was bruised and battered till it bore little resemblance to the human countenance. With the exception of the two sisters Melton, who had both been brought to this sink of iniquity on the same day, the women hated and disliked each other, and generally acted as spies on each other's conduct. This afforded a fruitful source of altercation and crimination, and eventually led to ruin and death.

Hetty, ugly and despicable as she certainly was, had a lover, whom she was accustomed to meet in solitary places; for it is necessary even here, that wives should conceal their infidelity, since husbands have almost unlimited power of punishment, such as disgrace, exposure, expulsion from the church, divorce, which includes refusal of support, banishment from the country, stripes or confinement; indeed the wife is thrown completely on the mercy of the husband, in this as in other cases.

Hetty, however, had been discovered in the society of her lover, by two Indian women, likewise the wives of Weldy, who watched the cows. The knowledge of this discovery held her in awe of them, until the departure of her husband, and the commencement of her unrestrained authority. These Indians possessed all the characteristics of their race, especially that of never forgiving injuries; and one day, suffering the best cows in the flock to stray, they were severely reprimanded by Hetty, who threatened them with stripes. They retorted; accusing her of infidelity to her husband, before the whole household. This aroused her indignation to a perfect storm of passion, and seizing the girls by the hair, her usual manner of proceeding, she gave them both a violent beating, with a promise that if they breathed such a word again, she would drown them in the lake.

Whether or not, she would have ventured to put the threat in execution, is a matter of doubt. The Indians, however, did not design to give her a chance; yet, they went out as usual with the cows, and no one dreamed of the horrible thoughts concealed in their breasts. But all day long they were carefully looking and searching through the valley for a plant known by them to possess the power of rendering the partakers of it raving mad, reveal all their secrets, even to the most infamous crimes, and finally, die, after suffering years of horrible torture. This, to these half-civilized children of the forest, seemed a vengeance, exquisite indeed ; but the plant capable of producing the extraordinary malady was scarce, and only to be found in particular localities. Then, too, the remarkably pungent and aromatic odor it exhaled, would render the administration of it peculiarly difficult, if not dangerous. They ascertained, however, that the root dried and reduced to powder, while retaining all its poisonous qualities, lost its peculiar exhalation, and, sprinkled over food, might be readily mistaken for pepper or mustard. By searching several days, they obtained a considerable quantity ; I saw one of them with quite a bundle of it in her arms ; the dark red flower, and broad serrated leaf arrested my attention. To my inquiries of its name and properties, she answered vaguely, and with a hideous leer ; I felt disgusted with her, and passed on, retaining a portion of the leaves in my hand. These leaves applied to the nose had precisely the effect of hartshorn on the olfactory organs ; but if continued in, a strange, wild, inconceivable exhilaration of the mind occurred ; no one could describe the sensations experienced, or the remarkable phantasms that torture every sense.

Having made their horrible preparation ready, one of the Indian women feigned sickness, as an excuse for staying at home. Her assistance in the kitchen was tendered, and accepted without the least suspicion of her design. In the absence of the cook she managed to spread the powdered root profusely over nearly every article of food, and this with the perfect knowledge that all the household women and children would partake of it. Excused from eating, by her pretended illness, she beheld her rivals and enemies with a countenance of malicious satisfaction, devour the poison, and chuckled inwardly over the idea of her horrible revenge. A few minutes after eating it, the victims began to be aware that something was the matter ; but though all were more or less affected, the symptoms in the different ones, were different, owing, probably, to the constitution, or the quantity eaten. Some complained of shooting pains and dizziness in the head, and then began to hoot, halloo, tear their garments, break dishes, and act all sorts of imaginable freaks. Others crouched in the corner, grinning and chattering like monkeys. The children raced and screamed, and tore through the house, and out, and off, and down the street to the infinite dismay and horror of all sober people, who fancied that everybody's children but their own, should be trained to habits of sobriety.

Mrs. Bradish, who visited all the houses in regular rotation, had called at the establishment of the Mrs. Weldy, with the design of spending the afternoon with them. Her astonishment at the scene before her, can be better imagined than described. Is it any wonder that she became frightened, and fled from such a complication of horrors, leaving the poor sufferers to themselves ?

There is something in lunacy that, in all cases, inclines the patient to wander. Sleep, good natural balmy sleep, they never know. Physical fatigue and exhaustion may, after a time, induce a state resembling repose, though having little of its influence, and producing less of its effects. The inflamed and heated brain must still act and think—dreams, even more horrible than the waking fancy could produce, torture the restless victims, the most terrible of nightmares haunts and torments them, and death were a thousand times preferable to a life of such agony.

Mrs. Bradish came directly to our house. Mr. Ward she said must go with her to see what could be done. The case was so extraordinary, we were half tempted to disbelieve the story, and consider the narrator herself as a little out of her head.

"When you went there they were perfectly well?" said Mr. Ward, interrogatively.

"Perfectly well, to all appearance, and just sitting down to eat dinner."

"And what were the first symptoms of insanity?"

"The one that began eating first made all sorts of mouths and faces, and then sprang up and began dancing as if she had been bitten by a tarantula. Mercy on us! yonder goes one of them now," she continued, looking from the window.

Sure enough, tearing along the street, whooping and hallooing, was the beautiful Henriette Melton.

"There's no use in waiting any longer, Mr. Ward, go with her and see what can be done," I advised.

Mr. Ward rose, took down his hat, and invited me to accompany them. I felt a curiosity to do so, and readily complied. We found the house deserted by all but the Indian women, and they were up stairs, talking and jabbering in their native tongue. The table remained standing in the midst of the floor, the plates and dishes on it just as the victims of the dreadful poison had left them. The meat, however, had acquired a remarkable stain, and emitted a peculiar odor. Mr. Ward cut off a small slice and threw it to a dog belonging to the house. The animal ate it, and almost immediately exhibited the effects, howling, barking, jumping up in the air, and making all sorts of antics. We could doubt no longer that the food was poisoned, and our suspicions rested, of course, on the Indian women.

By this time, quite a concourse of people had assembled, and the criminals were instantly secured. They were rummaging the trunks and chests, and packing up the best and most available articles, previous to their meditated flight from the place. At first they sturdily denied any participation in the horrid act, but, finding themselves disbelieved, openly and freely confessed it. The people demanded their immediate execution, without any of the forms of law, and they were taken to a tree in the valley, and there hung, without mercy and without regret.

Their fate was horrible, yet incomparably less so than that of their victims. There were neither asylums, nor poor-houses, nor hospitals in Utah ; while some of the wretches had friends, and some had not. Many of them ran off wild, into the woods, haunted the dens and caverns of the mountains, and fled in inconceivable horror from the face of man. Some died, and their bleaching skeletons were found by hunters. Others, in their weakness, became the prey of wild beasts. The effects were less perceptible and violent on the children, some of whom are yet surviving, but stunted in body and deformed in intellect.

Weldy returned from California to find his lands overrun with weeds and briars, his flocks wild in the woods, and his house the abode of owls and bats. Had there been proof of his death, his property would have been confiscated to the use of the church, but, as it was, everything was suffered to go to, wreck.

"No use in grieving over spilt milk," was his characteristic expression, when informed of the circumstances. " I have lost my women, but I have got gold," and he slapped his pockets. And the gold procured him wives. Fathers with marriageable daughters, would inquire of him why he didn't take another wife, because they were aware that he was able to pay handsomely. Many mothers—in justice to the especial truth and purity of woman's nature—did object to such heartless arrangements, but their objections elicited only reproach.

CHAPTER XLV.

REVELATIONS.

FORTUNATE it was for all concerned, that the timely discovery of gold in California diverted the attention of the Mormons, and withdrew so many of their available men. These men, once beyond the influence of the governing High Priest, found their zeal for the church and the propagation of their principles remarkably cooled. Even the leaders, finding their projects foiled, and their schemes circumvented, grew ashamed of their crimes, and many of them adopted a more healthy state of feeling and sentiment. This was especially the case with Mrs. Bradish, whose really strong mind soon recovered from the shock of blasted hopes and disappointed ambition, and who, by a reaction of views not at all remarkable, awoke as from a dream, to a clear conception of the fallacious character of the desires and aspirations in which she had indulged. This change of sentiment was attended by the deepest remorse. The true character of the Mormon leaders, with whom she had associated, in whose deceptions she had partaken, and whose crimes she had assisted, rose up before her in all their hideous deformity, and bitter were her tears of repentance and regret.

"And your pecuniary loss, my dear madam," I said to her, one day, when she was discussing the subject; "your pecuniary loss must be considerable, since I believe you told me that your fine property was mostly embarked in the church."

"My loss of property has been what most people would consider great," she replied, "yet that is nothing to loss of uprightness, integrity, and peace of mind; nothing to the loss of confidence in yourself. I was the dupe of a miserable villain, while firmly believing myself to be exercising shrewdness, and executing the schemes of a lofty ambition. The early Mormon leaders possessed a singular and fascinating power, which they practised on all that came within their influence, by which they pretended to cure diseases and work miracles, and which"——

"Is now popularly known by the name of Mesmerism," I said, interrupting her.

"Even so," she answered; "and that mysterious influence, so little known at that time, contributed, in no small degree, to his success, and that of those engaged with him."

"The mystery of it is, how Smith came to possess the knowledge of that magnetic influence, several years anterior to its general circulation throughout the country."

"That is no mystery to me," she replied. "Smith obtained his information, and learned all the strokes, and passes, and manipulations, from a German peddler, who, notwithstanding his reduced circumstances, was a man of distinguished intellect and extensive erudition. Smith paid him handsomely, and the German promised to keep the secret."

"And you?"

"I learned the whole affair in my intercourse with the elders. I was present when Smith instructed Mr. Ward in the art. You, madam, were subjected to its influence. So have ten thousand others been, who never dreamed of it. Those most expert in it, are generally sent out to preach among unbelievers. When a person becomes identified in name, and standing, and character, with us, its exercise is not so necessary, and is generally suffered to fall into disuse."

Mrs. Bradish covered her face with her hands, and sat several minutes in silence. "Poor Ellen!" she said at length, "what a fate was hers!"

"And Mrs. Clarke?" I suggested.

"I sinned deeply against them in more ways than one, and, Mrs. Ward, I have sinned against you."

"Against me?"

"Against you. Do you know this letter?" and she drew from her pocket a missive, which I remembered as the one that I had written and indited to my friends, so many years before. Great, indeed, was my astonishment; but she gave me no time for remark. "This letter, of course, was never sent, as you supposed. Yet, you must be aware that one very near and dear to you was the instigator of the deception."

"I perceive it."

"He met you in the stage, admired you, and commenced a systematic plan of deception, to secure you to himself. Can you forgive him?"

"I can; for this deception has been overruled to procure me the happiness of loving."

"Can you forgive more than that?"

"I think so."

"Could you forgive the man who imposed upon you by a false marriage? Could you forgive that?"

"Torture me not with such questions. Our marriage was not false and spurious."

"And for that, you may thank me; for your husband designed, and even believed, for some time, that he had thus imposed on you."

"Is it possible?" I inquired, overwhelmed with grief and horror at this treachery.

"Don't you recollect your astonishment at not being called on to sign the deed of conveyance, when Mr. Ward sold his landed estate?"

"I remember."

"And that proves my assertion, that he did not then regard you as his lawful wife. Mr. Ward, however he might love you, loved the interests of Mormonism better, and it was his policy to prevent, in this way, your claim to dower, in the event of your surviving him ; because he desired that his property, when he was done with it, might go to the church."

"And you discovered this?"

"I was the confidant of all his schemes, and determined, from the first, that justice should be done to you. It required a little art and address to procure a real magistrate, instead of the false one he intended, without his discovering the cheat. However, I succeeded, and you were really married."

"Does he know it now?"

"Certainly ; and when I informed him of the truth, he thanked me a thousand times, and said that I had made him happy, and removed a weight of guilt from his mind. The fact is, when Mr. Ward united with the Mormons, he entertained ambitious views, and wished to be a leader ; consequently, it was his purpose to embark all his pecuniary resources in the enterprise. Failing in this, and the feelings of his better nature being brought into exercise, he began to consider the wrong practised against you, which, through my contrivance, had been averted."

I thanked her for the interest she had manifested in my behalf.

"'Tis nothing," she answered ; "and yet, I could wish that you would remember me with kindness, when I am gone."

"Gone? Where are you going, then?"

"To California, the Land of Gold."

"But what employment can you find there?"

"I should suppose, a plenty, from all accounts. The Stillmans and Mrs. Beardsley are going likewise. Harmer, too, though he wishes to first find Emily."

Here a light, clear, silvery, ringing laugh burst on our ears. Looking towards the door whence it came, we detected a female form, half hidden behind a large bush of Mexican roses. "Show yourself," said Mrs. Bradish, playfully catching the stranger in her arms, and withdrawing the hands from the blushing face.

"Emily! is it possible; where have you been, child?"

"Not a prisoner, certainly, to judge from the radiant countenance," said Mrs. Bradish.

And sure enough, her face was the very picture of happiness. Mrs. Bradish drew her into the house, and seated her in a chair.

"Now tell us where you have been," she said.

"Indeed, I cannot," she replied.

"Well, we know something of it already," I said. "You were carried off by the Indians."

"Who became weary of keeping you, and so brought you back," said Mrs. Bradish. "But it cost us all an infinite deal of trouble and perplexity, and resulted in death to some."

It is not necessary to give here the long conversation that followed, or the mutual explanations demanded and accorded on both sides. But Emily was silent on many points which we were extremely curious to have explained.

"I cannot tell you, indeed, I can't," she said. "Because it seriously implicates my father."

"Your father?"

"Yes; among my other adventures I have discovered him."

"And he is no other than the renowned and redoubtable Mormon leader, B———m," said Mrs. Bradish; "I have long suspected it."

"Even so," said Emily, "a circumstance which causes me to both rejoice and weep. I no longer feel that overpowering sense of loneliness, which used to accompany the remembrance of my forlorn and unprotected condition, for he owns and acknowledges me as his lawful and legitimate daughter. He was legally united to my mother, though report at the time affirmed the contrary, and yet I am, I must be, filled with grief and horror and astonishment at the circumstances under which this discovery was made."

We besought her to relate the particulars, but she steadfastly refused, and then we learned that B——m only ascertained his relationship to her the day before, while pressing with unwonted ardor his claim for her hand, and that the letter left by her mother was considered by him sufficient proof to establish the fact beyond a doubt.

"And you were really in his house," said Mrs. Bradish, "and his wives knew nothing about it."

"I was in his house, a part of the time at least, and they did know all about it," said Emily, "of course they durst not reveal the secret, and living in that house as I have, I am more than ever convinced of the sin and shame of polygamy. From first to last it is evil, abominable and disgusting."

"And yet I have heard several women approve of the system," said Mrs. Bradish.

"Yet you should recollect, Mrs. Bradish," said Emily, "that very few women who may have experienced the evils of polygamy are at liberty to express their real sentiments. For instance a woman, who, to my certain knowledge, was burning with abhorrence of the system, was entrapped into sending a long letter to her mother at home, in which her situation was described as most desirable, though her husband had several wives. And that same letter got into the newspapers, went the rounds of the Union, and even came to Utah, with her name attached to it, though she was utterly ignorant of its existence in any such shape."

"We all know that wives are kept in the background."

"And the worst of it is, they have no legal redress. The most, in fact the utmost, that a woman can do, is to conform to her circumstances, and be satisfied with her lot. Who would complain, when conscious that the complaint would only make matters worse? To appreciate polygamy, we must have a view of its practical operation, we must come face to face with it, sit at the same table where a dozen women and a multitude of children, all the wives and offspring of one man, partake their daily meals; we must observe the rivalries, the jealousies, and heart-burnings; we must hear their bitter recriminations, which the utmost authority of the husband, which the dread of stripes, imprisonment and divorce cannot wholly suppress."

And yet the whole tendency of Mormonism is to perpetuate the system."

"It certainly is, and that by reducing females to a helpless and dependent state. Even now, a woman, if she expects to live, must have a husband or a father on whom she can depend for food and clothing. The avenues of employment are shut against her. Wages are out of the question. If a man wishes female labor performed, he will take another wife who can expect nothing but personal support. If a wife grows dissatisfied with her lot, the husband divorces her; how, then, is she to live? She must beg, but there is a law against begging, there is a law against assisting vagabond and divorced wives; not a public law, a law to fall beneath the notice of the world, and be criticised, and its justice examined, but a rule of the Church, quite as potent, and even more dangerous, because secret."

"Yet you will take a husband, and become a wife," said Mrs. Bradish, "no doubt, with the expectation that your beloved will be so good and loving as never to insult you with the presence of another wife."

"I will place it beyond his power to do so," said Emily. "I leave Utah for California now in a few days."

"And Harmer goes with you?"

"That is the calculation."

"Then you have had an interview?"

"Of course, business called him to my father's this morning. I was sitting at his feet in the general reception room. He inferred from our apparent intimacy that the union to which he was so deeply opposed had been consummated. But rising instantly, and extending my hand, I introduced him to my father. His surprise can be easier imagined than described; this, however, gave way to the liveliest emotions of pleasure when the old gentleman promised to sanction our union, and even seemed glad of a pretext to get rid of us so easily."

"Does he know of your proposed removal?"

"He does; and not only assents to it, but said that he hoped all the disaffected to his administration would accompany us, as he wanted none but believers to inhabit the City of the Saints."

"Heaven grant that everything may transpire as you wish, yet I may be pardoned for having my doubts. All in this world is uncertain," I said.

Mr. Ward and others now came in. They all congratulated Emily on her acknowledged relationship to the Governor and Prophet, wished her all happiness in her approaching marriage, and the prospect of her future residence in the land of gold. Mrs. Bradish appeared more lively and cheerful than I had seen her for some time, talked of her probable adventures in scaling the Sierra Nevada, and her success in amassing her fortune when she arrived at the "diggings."

CHAPTER XLVI.

MYSTERIES.

SINCE my residence among the Mormons, I had as little general intercourse with them as possible, rarely went to their meetings, and knew nothing of their political business or church affairs, except such information as circumstances threw in my way. I was not, and never had been, a believer in their doctrines, and unless I had absolutely closed my ears and eyes and understanding to all passing events, I could not fail to perceive that the whole system was founded on arrant jugglery and imposture, and that all sorts of secret arts were employed to entrap the weak, the unsuspecting, and the unwary. But there was one thing I could not fathom, one mystery utterly unresolvable, and though I am not naturally suspicious, or prone to indulge unreasonable conjectures, I found it impossible to banish all thoughts of foul play from my mind. Indeed, several circumstances, all light and trivial, taken separately, yet of considerable importance in the aggregate, had inspired me with a sort of vague indefinable suspicion, that the Mormon Church was the centre of a secret organization, whose plots and plans were of the blackest description. I had known for many years that the scum of society, the refuse of prisons, and criminals hoary with all sorts of sin, were freely admitted and registered in its ranks. I had been aware of political machinations, and plundering expeditions against the helpless and unsuspecting emigrants, and yet had fondly imagined that such things arose rather from the turpitude and evil dispositions of the Mormon leaders, than from the absolute and unchangeable nature of the principles of the Mormon Church. I knew that a thing pure and heavenly in itself, might be perverted to favor the purposes of designing men, but after awhile I began to suspect and ultimately discovered that the root of the evil was in Mormonism itself; that a Mormon, if he acted out the principles of his church, must be hypocritical, sensual, devoid of all conscience, and devilish.

Was my husband of this class? "Speak well of a bridge that carries you safe over," is an old adage, and so far at least he had always treated me with kindness and affection. Then I remembered the disclosures of Mrs. Bradish, and the deception he had employed in our first acquaintance, which only seemed an additional proof, but no matter. It is not becoming in a woman to speak ill of her husband.

I had noticed on several occasions the mysterious and unaccountable disappearance of several persons, not my particular or intimate friends, or those belonging to the circle in which I was accustomed to move, but people that I knew by sight and reputation, whose faces I had encountered in the street, and whose names were familiar. Yet these sudden disappearances never elicited remarks or inquiries; that is, among those who should have taken the matter in hand. They were gone, and that comprised the sum of the matter; but where they were, or who had spirited them away, was quite another thing. In all cases, however, the persons thus mysteriously removed, were enemies of the person or administration of B——m, and sometimes it appeared they had been aspirants to supplant him, or share his rule.

Lawrence and Irene were two of this number. They had dwelt together in a small house, and Irene might be seen daily walking with him in their little garden. But all at once the door of their cottage was closed, the garden was solitary, their domestic animals ran wild to be reclaimed by order of the church, but the church made no inquiry concerning their owners, Mr. Ward said that they might be off on a journey. He didn't know why any one should ask of him where they were, as he was not their keeper.

Almost precisely the language of Cain, but I banished the thought. Equally mysterious had been the disappearances of others. An amiable young man, who had visited Utah in company with an emigrant train, became deeply enamored of a young girl belonging to a Mormon family, though not a daughter of the house. His affections were returned with ardor by the lady, whose hand had been demanded by a Mormon elder, already the husband of nine wives. Ignorant of danger and intent only on the gratification of his passion, the lover remained in Utah while his friends prosecuted their journey. Arabel, from the commencement of his attentions, had been strictly watched, yet love laughs at locksmiths, and they had concerted a plan of escape. This by some unaccountable means was betrayed, and the eloping lady leaped from the window of the room in which she was confined, not into the arms of the youth, but those of the man she loathed and hated.

But where went the lover?

To this day no one knows, that is, if their words are regarded as the truth, but there are those whose cheeks will blench at the mention of his name.

Several women disappeared in the same manner, generally disaffected wives. B——m very laconically explained the matter in a newspaper published by his direction, and under his supervision, by stating that Indian Walker was passionately fond of the Mormon women, and that unless husbands were more careful of their wives in future, they would lose yet more of them. But Mormon husbands are careful of their wives with a vengeance, and it seemed remarkable that the Indians should only meddle with such as had become obnoxious to their husbands.

A young and very prepossessing lady came with an emigrant train bound to Oregon. She became acquainted with a man, apparently a gentleman, who represented himself to her as being single, and possessing a large property. Other arts and intrigues were brought to bear upon her, and she finally consented to become his wife. The 'marriage took place in the morning, and the same day her friends resumed their journey. But judge of her consternation and astonishment, on being conveyed to his home, to find it tenanted by one wife, whose appearance betokened her a perfect tigress. She took no further notice of the new wife, 'than to order her into the kitchen, and bidding her remember that henceforth that was to be her place. Julia looked at her husband.

"Margaret is right, my dear," he said. "You must always obey her; indeed, on that condition only, she consented to my bringing you here."

Julia was too deeply grieved to speak, and retired to the kitchen, and from that hour a system of tyranny and cruelty was practised by the first wife on the second that almost exceeds belief.

Julia applied to her husband in vain.

"The wife's first duty was obedience," he said.

" Obedience to yourself," suggested Julia.

"Obedience to me, comprises obedience to her likewise," answered the husband, "because it is my command that you obey and serve Margaret; but don't bother me with your fusses."

And so Julia was constrained to perform all the household drudgery, and not unfrequently was subjected to physical punishment of a cruel and revolting kind. For, though the rules of Mormondom actually forbid the exercise of authority or punishment by one wife over another, the husband is at perfect liberty to suspend these rules any moment when he sees fit.

Julia found the trials and miseries of her lot increasing every day, and she finally informed her husband that she had made up her mind to leave him with the first emigrant train that came along, and one was then expected every day. The husband approved her plan, said that he would give her money, and seemed perfectly satisfied. But two or three evenings subsequently she disappeared, and was never seen or heard of afterwards. Nothing, however, was done about it. Some few of the women expressed surprise, but were silenced by a Mormon elder, who assured them that Satan had carried her off bodily, because she presumed to be discontented with her happy lot among the children of God.

Another source of mystery and terror in Utah, was the almost constant exercise of Lynch law ; and, of this too, women were mostly the victims. Let a woman, if she dare, commit such acts as would be likely to bring polygamy into disrepute, expose the weakness or sensuality of an elder, or manifest a disapprobation to the existing state of things, and some hideous punishment would be sure to be hers—when, where, or what, it would be impossible to tell, though none the less hideous and certain—that is, if information of it ever reached the ears of the elect and sanctified.

In this respect, matters daily, and almost hourly, grew worse. On our first arrival at the Salt Lake, and some time subsequently, we enjoyed a tolerable degree of freedom, but the reins had been gradually tightened, until it seemed that our very thoughts were under a secret surveillance. And the worst feature of the case was the deep and unfathomable mystery attending it. Punishments were inflicted for words lightly spoken, long after the words and the occasion of them were forgotten. Lynch laws were summarily executed on helpless victims, entirely ignorant of the crimes of which they were accused. Few women thus punished ever recovered from the effects of it to their dying day, and many were rendered nervous, and half insane, from apprehension of the like.

One poor woman, who had told an emigrant, in the hearing of a Mormon elder, that polygamy was a system of abominations, and who repeated a few of her troubles and sufferings, was taken one night when she stepped out for water, gagged, carried a mile into the woods, stripped nude, tied to a tree, and scourged till the blood ran from her wounds to the ground, in which condition she was left till the next night, when her tormentors visited her again, took her back to her husband's residence, and laid her on the door-step, where she remained till morning.

Could any woman be expected ever to recover from such treatment as this? I think not. She remained sick for a long time. Her husband's other wives refused to nurse and care for her, and she finally died, after lingering something more than a year.

Another female was suddenly snatched up by a man on horseback, when returning to her home in the dusk of the evening, carried to a retired place, and her mouth and tongue seared with a red-hot iron, though they refused to inform her in what she had offended, and she could remember nothing.

Such things were not solitary acts, but of frequent occurrence, and the female part of the population were in a state of constant apprehension.

It was a long time before I became fully convinced that all these things were the result of a systematic plan. Husbands, I knew, possessed almost unlimited discretion as to the punishment of wives, but this Lynching business, which was quite a modern improvement, inspired every one with tenfold horror, from the mystery connected with it; and once coming into vogue it soon superseded all the former modes of punishment by divorce, stripes administered by the husband himself, or solitary confinement. At least this appeared to be the case, for after the Lynching became fashionable, we heard very little of domestic punishments, and this certainly looked as if the whole thing was managed by preconcerted arrangement. No wonder that the bravest women were actually nervous with constant dread and apprehension.

In this state of doubt and conjecture, it cannot be wondered at that I had my secret fears and misgivings, that the party making such preparations for a start to California would be suddenly cut off by some remarkable and mysterious means. Once I ventured to express this apprehension to Mr. Ward. He looked at me with a searching and inquiring glance.

"Why, do you fear that?" he said.

"Because others have disappeared so suddenly and strangely, and because"——

"What?"

"I hardly know, I cannot tell, a presentiment, or something like it, perhaps."

"I don't believe in presentiments," he said sternly, and the subject was dropped.

Some few days after this, he came to me where I was sitting alone in my little parlor, and said; "Maria, I have something of importance to say to you. It is necessary for your own safety and happiness that you listen to me."

A thousand vague indefinable fears, a thousand horrid fancies and suspicions flashed through my brain; my head grew dizzy, I felt sick, and darkness surrounded me, when my husband sprang forward and caught me in his arms. "You need not be frightened," he said, in a soothing voice, "I only wished to give you some advice; Maria, my wife, you have been all along rather free with your tongue."

I felt that there might be truth in this, though I was too deeply agitated to speak.

"Nay, Maria, do not tremble so, dear, no one is going to hurt you," he said; "but, Maria, you know something of Mormonism?"

"Something, very little," I whispered; "you know I seldom attend their meetings."

"You know something, and conjecture something; is it not so?" and his eyes sought mine.

I could not endure their gaze, but answered; "'What should I conjecture?"

For a moment his countenance grew angry, then changed to a grave and serious expression.

"This play of words is worse than folly, and it is utterly useless to attempt deceiving me. I know well what you suspect, and now answer me truly, have you told these suspicions to any one?"

"I cannot positively recollect what I may have said, yet I think not. But suppose I had, what then?"

"I cannot tell exactly," said Mr. Ward; "and, my wife, having eyes, you must be blind, having ears, you must be deaf, having a mind, you must be utterly devoid of understanding. Whatever you may suspect, never breathe that suspicion, whatever you may imagine, never give it a tangible form. It is the only course that you or any one else can pursue with safety."

"Mr. Ward, will you tell me why?"

"I may not, my dear, yet, depend upon it, such is the case."

"No doubt; and Mr. Ward, may I ask you yet another question?"

"Yes, my dear, a dozen if you please."

"And you will answer them truly?"

"Probably, if it is consistent; but, Maria, I am under obligations that I may not, must not explain; you must not even tempt me to their infringement, because—because—well, no matter, there is a reason, and one so important that I hesitate about telling it."

"You know, Mr. Ward, that there have been many sudden and mysterious disappearances. In fact it seems that persons can hardly venture from their doors after night-fall, without something befalling them. Is not this so?"

"Enough like it," said Mr. Ward, burying his face in his hands.

"Many poor women have been treated very cruelly, without knowing for what they suffered, or who were the executioners. Now, what I want to know is, whether these acts are the work of irresponsible men, acting from motives of personal malice and revenge, or whether the church instigates and directs them as part of its policy to force obedience."

"That, Maria, I cannot tell."

"Don't you know, Mr. Ward?"

"Granting that I do know, I must not tell."

"Then it is the Church; because if the guilt rested on irresponsible shoulders, you would be ready to say so."

"You reason from false premises, and jump at hasty conclusions," said Mr. Ward, "but beware of curiosity; it was the fatal sin of Eve."

"But how can I help having curiosity, when such strange things are being transacted."

"It is not such a very strange thing in Utah, for refractory wives to be punished, is it?" said Mr. Ward, rather seriously.

"No, Mr. Ward, it is not, and the constant recurrence of such punishments has filled me with the direst apprehensions."

"And yet, my dear, you must know that the wives are not such patterns of amiability and obedience as they should be. Think of Mrs. Foster, and the hideous crime she committed. Was not that deserving of punishment?"

"The husband was first to blame, for exposing her to the liability of committing the crime."

"No, no; such reasoning as that will not do."

"It will, it must do, because it is the truth. Mrs. Foster was brought up, educated, and married in a country, where public opinion, law, Gospel, everything, regards polygamy as a great crime. She discharged all the duties of a wife, well and nobly, while her husband remained true to her. But he must remove her here, and outrage her sense of justice and propriety by taking another wife, and that wife a weakly, sickly creature, incapable of taking care of herself, or the children she was yearly bringing into the world. And so Mrs. Foster was required to do all the household drudgery, nurse her rival, and be the slave of that rival's children. There was no chance of escape, no possibility of change, except by death. Some women would have killed themselves, Mrs. Foster preferred to remove the cause of her trouble. She did so, was detected in the crime, and hung privately, after being tortured by severe scourging, as a wholesome example to other wives."

"And other wives required the example."

"That is your opinion."

"And it must be yours, or if not, you had better be careful not to manifest your opposition. This much I will tell you, that suspected persons are watched by the authorities of the church, and such punishments as the church appoints, are meted out to offenders. Yet the utmost secresy is a part of our policy, and the knowledge you now possess, were you known to betray it, might cost you your life."

"Mrs. Bradish and Harmer will hardly keep your secrets when they arrive in California. Emily, too, knows more than I do. How about them?"

"When they get to California," repeated Mr. Ward.

The words were simple in themselves, but the tone, the look accompanying them, filled my mind with a dreadful suspicion.

"Yes, when they get there, Mr. Ward, or will that consummation of their wishes be prevented?"

"How should I know? A thousand things over which I have no control may prevent them. Heaven may order otherwise, if they design to do injury to the church and the saints. But, after all," continued Mr. Ward, "though they may conjecture much, they know very little, and of our most secret and intricate business they cannot even have an inkling. We soon learned to distrust Mrs. Bradish, as we saw from the first that she designed to rule in the end, and knowing that, we judged, and circumstances have proved the justice of our judgment, that her schemes once thwarted, she would immediately forsake us."

"How I wish that we could go with them;" I said.

"You are not unhappy, be you?" he inquired.

"Personally I am not, yet relatively I am. This place is a perfect Sodom, of that you must be beware. How unhappy and miserable are the women, how degraded the children. And your two daughters here, in this abominable sink of iniquity, to be perhaps the tenth or twentieth wife of some sensual animal, who only lives for licentious gratification."

"Softly, softly, speak softly," said Mr. Ward, "such language used to some others would subject you to punishment."

"And that is the reason why I wish to get away."

"Even that wish, if known, would be considered a crime."

"What then are we, poor women, to do?"

"Be contented with your lot."

"And if that is impossible?"

"Be silent, Maria; more than once your conversation has been reported, and I have been obliged to employ all my influence in your behalf, and that, after a time, will be of no avail. I mention this that you may be on your guard, and not expose yourself to punishment."

" But who reported my conversation ?"

" I know nothing about that. No informer is known by our rules of judicature."

Here company came in ; a Mormom elder with his girlish and seventh wife. The lady soon departed, however, though the husband remained to have a discussion with Mr. Ward, and I retired to my room.

CHAPTER XLVII.

LIGHT.

THE rooms were on a floor, and only divided by a thin partition ; hence though it was not my purpose to listen to their conversation, I became unintentionally acquainted with the subject of their discourse. It was not theology, but the revelation of a crime, the atrocity of which rendered me breathless and horror-struck.

A young American officer had visited Mormondom, some time before, on business or pleasure, I am unable to say which. A small party accompanied him, and they were hospitably received and entertained by the Mormon elders. Gunison, the leader, was a man of talents, a shrewd observer, and he possessed likewise no small share of that feminine quality, termed curiosity. He knew that polygamy was in vogue among us, but he seemed rather dissatisfied with the accounts given him by the masculine portion of the community, and their praise of the system, and employed various endeavors to get the judgment of the women upon it. His designs becoming known, he was subjected to the strictest scrutiny, and not a woman permitted to speak with him. Some of his men, however, were more fortunate, and two of them discovered distant relatives, who gave their opinions of Mormonism and polygamy unreservedly, with the stipulation that they should be immediately taken away, as their condition was unendurable, and they would rather bear all the hardships, and fatigue, and exposure incident to their long journey back to the world and civilization, than remain any longer with the Mormons. Perhaps these women were ignorant, or in their ardent desire to escape, did not sufficiently and prudently consider the danger to which they were exposing their friends. Perhaps they trusted to chance, or providence, or fate, but by the employment of stratagem they escaped successfully from the Salt Lake City. Their absence being discovered at the same time when Gunison went away, of course, their abduction was laid to him. The rage of the elders, when aware of this, knew no bounds. They honored the gallant and his companions with the most opprobrious epithets, and a meeting was summoned immediately. This much I knew at the time; but the result of that meeting, and the assassinations to which it led I learned from the conversation alluded to above. It appeared also that Gunison had otherwise rendered himself obnoxious to the Mormon saints, by the discovery of some of their secret designs. At any rate, it became their murderous policy to attempt his destruction.

Coolly, and with all the complacency imaginable, did the Mormon elder proceed to relate the story of their sanguinary deed. How the party sent to cut off Gunison, prospered on the way, how the Lord directed them to his trail, and how they followed it many days, and finally discovered him, with his companions, encamped on a hill. How the Mormon leader, seized with sudden inspiration, ordered his men to choose every one his man, and when their rifles were discharged, to rush in with their knives and tomahawks, and kill the wounded, declaring that the curse of God would rest on them if they left one alive, except the women, who were to be reserved for a more cruel fate.

"And what did they do with the women?" queried Mr. Ward.

"Took them to the nearest river, tied their garments over their heads, and drowned them," said the elder. "The Lord prospered us in that, and he will prosper us in this, too, never fear."

Thus I found that their success in the horrible massacre of Gunison's party, was being employed as an argument that success would attend them in some other equally horrible.

"Doubtless the Lord will prosper us," said Mr. Ward.

I knew his voice, and actually shuddered at the profanation of that holy name. And it is one of the greatest horrors of Mormonism, that its votaries pretend a divine sanction for all their sins; that they have a "thus saith the Lord," for their most palpable wickedness. According to their accounts, He prospers them in murder, assassination, licentious intercourse, and the torture of helpless women. Blessed are the eyes that have never gazed on their villainous faces, and let all at a distance take up the language of the patriarch, "Oh, my soul, come not in to their assembly; to their secrets, my honor, be thou not united; for in their anger they slew a man, and in their self-will they digged down a well."

No wonder that I lost a part of this delectable conversation. It is a wonder that I listened again, when a new subject was introduced.

Pursuant to the policy of the Mormons, to suppress all information of their plans and doings, and prevent any accounts, not favorable to their moral and religious character, from reaching public view, they had taken for their rule of conduct the old adage, that "dead men tell no tales," and the knowledge of a great state secret, in the most despotic government on earth, could not have been more fatal than it was among them.

It must not be supposed, however, that all the Mormons were cognizant of this state of things, or guilty of participation in such crimes. Some were mere passive spectators, who took no pains to inquire into the actual causes of many events transpiring around them. Others, whatever they might think, took good care never to express their thoughts. And some, I would fain believe, were really ignorant.

It may seem strange, that a society of men could carry on a scheme of premeditated villany so many years, and the public remain in ignorance of it, especially when emigrant trains were passing through the country at intervals, and conjecture might reasonably infer that where so much obnoxious existed they would be likely to discover something.

And one party of emigrants did discover something, but which they never revealed. It was late in autumn, when a company, numbering eight wagons, ten men, twelve women, and a little multitude of children, halted at Salt Lake City to rest and refresh themselves and their animals, preparatory to crossing the Sierra Nevada. The men were shrewd and observant, the females inquisitive, which gave considerable umbrage to the Mormon elders, though the hypocrites forbore to express an open dissatisfaction.

We have all heard and sympathized with the runaway slave, who is tracked by bloodhounds; in Utah, guests and visitors are tracked by spies quite as cruel and remorseless. Words are noted down, actions are watched, the very thoughts conjectured; even an expression of the countenance, a tone of the voice or whisper are reported with malicious exaggeration, and made the bases of murderous accusations. These emigrants were no exceptions to the general rule. The spies ascertained that they had discovered some secret, which it was not desirable for them to know; ascertained, too, that they intended finding out more, and, to complete the whole, presented clear and undeniable proof that two or three of the emigrants had obtained private access to a chamber, where a secret Mormon meeting was being held, and learned, then and there, of the plans and purposes of the self-styled saints.

On this discovery, another private meeting was convened, of which the emigrants, though the subjects of it, were kept in utter ignorance. It was decided that, as their offence had been clandestine, so should be its punishment, and the atrocity of that punishment was well worthy of the Inquisition of old Spain.

Shakspeare declared that, in his time, "a man might smile and smile, and be a villain," and human nature has improved very little since his days. They smiled, these Mormon saints, with murderous designs in their hearts; jested and laughed with the women, caressed the children, and managed to delay the travellers till the snows commenced falling on the mountains, and there was every appearance that the winter would soon set in. This was succeeded by the proposal that two or three of the Mormons should accompany them as guides through the most difficult part of the journey, leading them along a newly discovered route, by which the distance would be shortened nearly one half. Pleased with themselves, pleased with the Mormons, and pleased with the whole world, the unsuspecting emigrants departed. True, they had seen much in Mormonism that they did not like; they had been both shocked and astounded by the secret revelations; yet men so kind and pious and hospitable as the Mormon leaders subsequently appeared, must be good-hearted after all. Thus argued the unsuspicious emigrants, and they gladly accepted the cohort appointed them. And while deceiving them in this way, the Mormon leaders were deceiving their own people in another. The uninitiated were informed that these men were only going a day's journey into the mountains to hunt. Was ever such depravity manifested in a civilized community before?

They left the Salt Lake City, left the Mormon country, dreaming only of the bright land of gold on the borders of the Pacific, and rejoiced that they had obtained guides whose knowledge would shorten the journey to that delectable country.

Do you suppose that one of them ever reached there? Can you imagine the dreadful character of their fate? That is questionable, for the utmost horrors of imagination never equal the hideousness of reality.

The name of Sierra Nevada has been given to that huge mountain chain which forms the western rim of the Great Basin, as well as the eastern boundary of California. It is not a single mountain range, like some of those on the eastern side of the continent, with an open country lying on each side of it, but a succession of ranges and ridges, and ridges alternating with narrow glens, generally filled with torrent-like rivers and unfathomable lakes.

Bewildered among these mountains, escape is quite impossible. As well might one attempt to find his way to the open air, through the intricate chambers of the Cretan labyrinth. One mountain crossed amid all the horrors of snow and cold and fatigue, only brings you to the foot of another. Unfathomable gulfs, frozen lakes, unmeasured precipices are before and around you, and death, the most horrid of deaths, is the only relief.

Yet, with a cool circumstantiality, this Mormon elder and visitor of Mr. Ward, related all the particulars of his own villainy and the frightful sufferings of that emigrant party he had assisted to decoy. One of the wretched survivors had been discovered by a party of hunters the next spring. He lived just long enough to relate the horrible fate of his companions, and tell where their remains might be found; but the food which, administered sooner, would have preserved his life, in this last stage of famine occasioned his death. Some of these hunters were Mormons who returned to Utah, and this monster of brutality, though an elder, had gathered the information from their lips, without their knowing how deeply he was implicated in the affair.

"And they all died?" queried Mr. Ward with a slight tremulousness of voice. "Heaven knows that I had rather the weight of their death lay on your conscience than on mine."

"It was the will of the Lord," said the Mormon. "Had they not sought to betray the saints?"

Mr. Ward made no reply, and the Mormon continued:

"The guides we sent out with them assured me on their return, that we need have no further fears from them, as they were so inextricably bewildered that Satan himself would not be able to set them right; that instead of crossing they would only plunge deeper and deeper among the mountains, where cold and famine, just punishments for their persistence and curiosity, would certainly overtake them with death."

"Then they were going north instead of west?" said Mr. Ward.

"That was it; as the children of Israel wandered in the wilderness till the whole of them perished on account of their sins, so did these people. It has been revealed to me that it was according to the will of the Lord."

"It has?" said Mr. Ward, with a strange solemnity in his tone.

"It seems that after the guides left them," continued the Mormon, they entered right into the heart of the granite mountains, destitute of vegetation, and attaining a height of many thousand feet. The Rocky Mountain goat and a small animal resembling a squirrel were the only living creatures to be

18*

seen, and these were so shy that all attempts to approach within shooting distance proved in vain. The snows closed around them, and their stock of provisions daily diminished. It was impossible to make any progress amidst the ice and snow-drifts, and it was finally proposed to encamp, and remain through the winter. Fortunately as it seemed to them, they discovered a cave opening on the sheltered side of a mountain, whose icy pinnacles glittered above them at the height of 15,000 feet. Drawing their wagons up to the entrance, their goods were unloaded and most of them removed into the cavern, while the cattle were turned loose to browse on the tender twigs of the stunted bushes, and pick the scanty tufts of grass where the wind had blown the snow from the mountain sides. A party of five men went forward to explore the route, but after wandering hither and thither for nearly a week, and subsisting on the bark of trees they returned to the encampment no better off than when they left it. Again and again the same project was undertaken, but never with success. Failure followed failure. All became weary, disconsolate and despairing, while all the horrors of famine stared them in the face. One by one the cattle were killed and eaten, and occasionally the hunters would bring in some game. These resources failing, roots, the bark of trees, and even grass, afforded the means of a scanty subsistence. But the cold became insupportable; the ground was covered with tremendous snow-drifts, snow and sleet filled the air, and obscured the heavens.

The whole party were now reduced to the most distressing privation. The men looked like living skeletons. Their faces collapsed and corpse-like, with shrunken features, and eyes gleaming with the fierce, unnatural glare of famine. Some took to their beds and refused to leave them; others, whose enfeebled and emaciated limbs refused to support their weight, crawled on their hands and knees through the cold and snow to such places as the wind had left bare, and dug with their stiffened and benumbed fingers, for the roots of grass or anything else that could preserve life."

Mr. Ward had been silently walking the room. I could hear his steps backward and forward; at length he paused, probably facing his visitor.

"Why do you relate these things?" he inquired sadly.

"Because it rejoices me to think that the Lord has vanquished our enemies."

"I never was one to exult over the misfortunes of an enemy," replied my husband.

"Well, I do," said the elder. "I rejoice, I exult, I glory in them. I never experienced a sweeter sensation than in hearing him relate how husbands were reduced to the dreadful necessity of feeding on the flesh of their dead wives, and how mothers, with ravenous appetites feasted on the mangled bodies of their children. My daily prayer is that all our enemies may be reduced to the same necessities, and perish in a manner equally terrible."

Silent as death, I had listened to this dreadful narration, half doubting the possibility of such horrible wickedness, till this last horrid wish confirmed the reality. Forgetting myself, and all around me, I uttered a slight scream. In an instant the two men were beside me. I fully understood the danger of my situation, and flung myself at my husband's feet. He regarded me with a countenance of emotion and pity.

"She is doomed!" said the elder. "The sin that destroyed Eve, will be her destruction. Fatal curiosity!"

"You will leave us now," said Mr. Ward, "I wish to converse with my wife, alone, and shall be ready to discuss this very unhappy subject with you, at some other time."

The elder went away—those dreadful words still ringing in my ears: "She is doomed!"

"Do you know, Maria," said Mr. Ward, "that this foolish curiosity has endangered your life?"

"I know; yet, curiosity is not my guiltiness, but knowledge. I retired to this room without a thought of listening to your conversation. I felt no curiosity about it, and if I heard, the fault was quite as much in the speaker as in me."

It is useless to repeat the scene that followed, though it was not one of anger, reproof, or recrimination. Tears fell from other eyes than mine; anguish and agony rent another, and a manly heart. I implored him to permit me to escape from the country.

"The thing is impossible, Maria. How would you go?"

"With Harmer's party."

He shook his head. "And were you out of this country, Maria, you would not be safe. Mormonism has its emissaries in every State of the Union, who, at the bidding of the church, would discover your hiding-place, with unerring certainty; and then"——

"I should be left to their tender mercies, which are cruel," I said, interrupting him.

"Even so, and here, you have a friend."

I felt—I knew it; but, alas! that friend was a Mormon. Yet, I had all confidence in his love and truth. One question remained: would his influence avail, to preserve me from death or punishment, in the councils of the church?

CHAPTER XLVIII.

UNCERTAINTY.

DAYS passed away, during which I suffered all the agony of suspense and uncertainty. A secret meeting had been held to deliberate on my offence, but the result was neither known to me nor my husband. He had been refused admittance to the council, and the decisions of these meetings were only manifested by subsequent events. Of course, I was in a continual tremor of horror and anxiety. I trembled at the slightest noise, and fled at the approach of my nearest friends. Had I been aware of the nature, time, or place of punishment, it would have been more tolerable ; I might have prepared for it, and fortified my mind against it. I was even denied the consolation of the sympathy and advice of my friends, as Mr. Ward insisted that the only means of mitigating my punishment, would be to keep the whole affair a profound secret ; and the truth of this seemed apparent.

Meanwhile, notwithstanding my own danger, I was deeply concerned for the future fate of the California adventurers. Their preparations to remove were progressing with great rapidity, B——m and the elders giving all the assistance and advice in their power ; prescribing the route to be taken, and expatiating on the prospect of wealth and happiness that attended settlers in the Land of Gold.

Yet, their would-be victims were not wholly deceived. Mrs.

Bradish well understood their unscrupulous character. Emily had learned more of their private affairs than she felt at liberty to reveal. Harmer conceived that the danger of escaping could not be greater than to remain, and trusted, perhaps, too much in his skill to outwit his enemies; for, notwithstanding their seeming kindness, he well knew that the bitterest, blackest hate lived within their hearts. And they departed, one beautiful morning in early spring-time. The whole company numbering nearly a dozen of those who dared to dissent from the Mormon policy. I bade them farewell with a choking heart and eyes swimming in tears.

"Look out for the Indians," I said to Mrs. Bradish.

"Never fear; Anna Bradish will have both eyes open."

"Then you are aware of the dangers?"

She nodded significantly, and said, "but no greater there than here."

I said no more, for the eyes of Mr. Ward were upon me, with an expression that I well understood.

"Did they ever reach California?" you inquire.

Not one of them. They were attacked on the fourth night of their journey, and every soul of them slain. Mr. Ward told me this, and when I wept and reproached him for consenting to such crimes, he coolly answered that he could do nothing to prevent it; that so long as the majority were in favor of such doings, the minority must either keep silent, or share the same fate.

A day or two after this, Mr. Ward informed me that business connected with the church required his absence for a few days. The words in themselves were simple enough, but the anxiety of his manner, and an indefinable expression of his countenance, excited in my mind the most horrible suspicion. I would have fallen at his feet and implored him to tell me whether or not his absence was consistent with my safety, but, immediately on informing me of his design, he left the house, without a solitary embrace, or word of farewell. Apprehensive of something dreadful, and laboring under the most intolerable suspense, the thought of escaping flashed into my mind. It was not a new idea, but, hitherto, I had dismissed it as something impossible to be accomplished. This moment, however, the burning desire for liberty, coupled with the greatest repugnance to remain any longer among the Mormons, and a certain presentiment that fearful punishment awaited me, completely absorbed all the feelings and emotions of my being, and, for the time, I failed to realize that other dangers existed, or to deliberate on the best course to be pursued. Impatiently waiting the hour of nightfall, I made a few slight preparations, such as habiting myself in a suit of male attire, which had formerly belonged to Mrs. Bradish, and staining my face so as to resemble an Indian; and then, the moment that it became sufficiently dark to prevent observation, I cautiously let myself out by the back door of our house, scaled the garden fence, and descended into the valley, through which lay the Indian trail.

At first, I felt buoyant and exulting, as I walked briskly onward, through the dark shadows of the forest; but, when the sense of weariness began to overtake me, and the loud, long howl of the wolf mingled ominously with the panther's scream, and the solemn wail of the night-bird, I began to realize the full dangers of my situation, and to reflect on the temerity of leaving the habitations of men, to wander alone, and perhaps perish, in the almost interminable wilderness. In this extremity, I commended myself to God, as an ever-present Refuge in time of trouble, and took courage from the knowledge of His overruling Providence. Full of these comforting thoughts, I sat down to rest at the foot of a tree. I no longer felt afraid. The words of the patriarch were in my mouth, and their influence animated my inmost soul: " The Lord God of Israel is thy Refuge, and underneath thee is the Everlasting Arm." During these gracious meditations, I was overpowered by a deep but pleasant slumber, and awoke the next morning to find the sun shining, and the birds singing, while my spirits were refreshed, and my strength invigorated. Making a slight breakfast on some biscuit which I had brought with me, I journeyed on, and soon perceived a horse feeding on the borders of a small stream. He was bridled and saddled, and a dark stain on the accoutrements was evidently blood. He beheld, and approached me, with all the familiarity of an old friend, though, judging from his appearance of neglect, several days had elapsed since he had known the care and protection of a master. The bridle-rein was broken, and the saddle-girth displaced, probably occasioned by his lying down. I spoke to him gently, replaced the saddle, and leading him to a fallen tree, mounted without opposition. He was a fine, noble animal, with high spirits, and bore me rapidly along. It would be impossible for me to recount the emotions of gratitude and devout thankfulness that I experienced while reflecting on this timely interposition of Providence in my behalf. The steed had probably belonged to some soldier or emigrant, who had been slain by the Indians or the Mormons. I could now accomplish my journey with great facility, alternately riding and walking during the day, and resting beneath some temporary shelter at night.

At length, on the fourth day of my journey, while resting at noon beneath the shade of a tree, at the foot of a hill, I heard a rustling in the thicket, near me, and the next moment a deer, wounded to death by an arrow then sticking in his breast, flew past, but stumbled and fell, apparently dead, a few rods ahead. Immediately after, came an Indian, in all the glory of paint and feathers. Perceiving me, he gave a characteristic grunt, and paused, as if uncertain whether to advance or retire. I rose, and, approaching him, held out my hand, which he took, after some hesitation. He could speak English, and a conversation ensued, which resulted in his inviting me to his cabin. I gladly accepted his hospitality, and the deer being dressed, we started for his home. But imagine my surprise and pleasure, to find on my arrival there, an old acquaintance in its occupant.

"Ethleen!" I exclaimed in astonishment.

She started at the voice, and surveyed me with a strange mixture of curiosity and surprise. Thinking it best to throw myself on her generosity, I revealed to her, at once, all the circumstances of my escape from the Mormons, and had the satisfaction to ascertain that I had awakened in her bosom a sympathy and interest that would result to my advantage. I abode with them several days, and then the Indian volunteered to guide me to the civilized settlements. Under his protection, I accomplished the journey with comparative safety, though nearly three months elapsed from the time of my departure from Mormondom, before I reached the bosom of my friends.

Safe with them, I was too happy, for a long time, to think of writing a book; but, hearing much said about Mormonism, and the designs of its leaders, I felt a desire to present a picture of my experience to the world, that all might know the enormities of the Mormon system, and the crimes and impostures of its leading members, whose baleful influence is paramount in beautiful Utah. If any are thereby warned, my labor will not have been in vain.

THE END.

www.ingramcontent.com/pod-product-compliance
Lightning Source LLC
Chambersburg PA
CBHW020738020526
44115CB00030B/222